cultural frontiers of the peace corps

cultural frontiers of the peace corps

Lambros Comitas • L. Gray Cowan • Vernon R. Dorjahn

Paul L. Doughty • Louis Dupree • William H. Friedland

Charles F. Gallagher • Alan E. Guskin • George M. Guthrie

Dwight B. Heath • Frank J. Mahony • Gerald S. Maryanov

Margaret Mead • David Scott Palmer • David L. Szanton

edited by *Robert B. Textor*

foreword by *Margaret Mead*

THE M.I.T. PRESS

Massachusetts Institute of Technology
Cambridge, Massachusetts, and London, England

All royalties from this book will be contributed to an ad hoc committee of returned Volunteers working in Peace Corps/Washington, for use in any Peace Corps-connected activity they deem appropriate.

DEDICATION

NANCY BOYD, *Philippines*

JUDITH ANNE CORLEY, *Cameroon*

DAVID CROZIER, *Colombia*

JOY DARLING, *Bolivia*

FREDERICK DETJEN, *Colombia*

JAMES DRISCOLL, *Togo*

JAMES J. HUGHES, *Ecuador*

DONALD HUMPHREY, *Chile*

FRANCIS L. KIRKING, *Iran*

STANLEY E. KOWALCZYK, *Nigeria*

BRUCE McKEEN, *Nepal*

ROGER McMANUS, *Philippines*

PHILIP MAGGARD, *Philippines*

DAVID MULHOLLAND, *Philippines*

CYNTHIA MYERS, *India*

JOHN S. PARROT, *Kenya*

LAWRENCE RADLEY, *Colombia*

JOSEPH RUPLEY, *Venezuela*

GARETH SIMMONS, *Dominican Republic*

DALE SWENSON, *Brazil*

JOHANNES C. von FOERSTER, *Nigeria*

ROBERT ZECH, *Dominican Republic*

Foreword

THIS is a responsible book written for the Volunteers and staff members of the Peace Corps, past, present and future, for the universities that have been, and will be, concerned with training programs, and for those other agencies, governmental and voluntary, that are compared with, and that compare themselves with, the Peace Corps. Certainly its largest audience will be the many kinds of Americans to whom the idea of people-to-people contact on a world scale has deep significance. But its most diversified audience will be found in the host countries where, under extremely varied circumstances, the attempt is being made to translate a hope into a living reality. The aim of writing so that what is said will be exact, meaningful, and acceptable to everyone, everywhere, is one that anthropologists have tried to fulfill only in the last twenty-five years. The necessary skills are exceedingly difficult to acquire, and as yet we do not wholly understand them. But in this book, the editor and the authors have made a mighty effort in the direction of the purposeful inclusion of the whole potential audience in order that, in the end, each reader will appreciate the achievements and wish to correct the defects in the still developing program of the Peace Corps.

The enterprise as it emerges from these accounts is extraordinarily American in its strengths and in its weaknesses. With considered frankness, the editor and authors outline a program that was initiated by a single act of imagination, that came into existence almost overnight, in a rush and on a shoestring budget, and that started operations with an organizational framework built on the routine skills of those available within government combined with the skills of promising people who had no experience in the tasks they were set and the skills of experts who were tolerated because they were willing to act as if they had no past experience to draw on. As a group those who initiated the program were characterized by high intelligence, goodwill, an almost infinite capacity to improvise, an enthusiastic willingness to learn by doing, and a readiness to correct errors that perhaps need not have occurred. The youthfulness of the Volunteers capitalized uniquely on the American tendency to speak with the loud, sure voices of children whose parents are exhorted to listen—voices that can be tolerated more easily when the speakers really are young. This way of speaking, in which ardor blends with tough-minded realism, has provided a magnificent alternative to the scolding, setting-the-world-to-rights voice of the schoolmarm, which we sometimes adopt abroad.

The program has a very contemporary ring. For the version of American culture that has been developed by the Volunteers out of President Kennedy's original directive carries some of the most significant values of the generation that was coming to maturity in the early 1960's. As one reads, one recognizes clearly this generation's desire for commitment, their distrust of traditional politics and diplomacy, their ardent individualism, their great impatience with the career-bound precepts of formal education in the 1950's, their fretting at the incongruity between their greater understanding of the nuclear age and their deferred opportunities to be heard and, not least, their insistent belief in activism.

The accounts of Peace Corps activities in this book indicate how the program, as it develops, can engage Americans at different stages in their adult lives. It provides a place where the very young, who have not yet found themselves and have no specialized skills, can contribute fresh enthusiasm and activity. But it also provides a place where, early in their career, professionals can find an area of wider and more immediate usefulness than young teachers, nurses, architects, engineers, and others are likely to find at home as well as a place where older, retired professionals can make their long experience continue to count. Perhaps later stages of the evolving program will do more to maximize the relationships of these three groups among the Volunteers and to build on the combination in relationships to those with whom they work in the host countries.

The analyses presented here suggest that the greatest strain, conflict, and responsibility center on the country Representative and his staff. For the Representative must mediate not only between Peace Corps/Washington and the Volunteers but also between the different groups within the program and the host country. In addition, he must deal percipiently and protectively with the problems of individual Volunteers. And, in the final analysis, his multiple responsibilities make him the natural scapegoat for every group. The position of country Representative would seem to be the one in which the system and the men selected by the system may be overstrained and overdependent on the experience, the cultural sophistication, and the psychological toughness of individuals for whose selection no adequate mechanism exists. Precisely for this reason it is important to exercise the greatest care and forethought in the selection of Representatives, especially those who go to areas where they have had no previous experience, and to give adequate support to Representatives as they attempt to answer questions and solve problems that are new to anyone's experience.

This book, edited by an anthropologist and written by social scientists with various disciplinary backgrounds, is organized within a cross-cultural frame of reference. Understandably, the writers emphasize the need for more social science in the training of Volunteers, in program building, in staff selection, and in the development of relations with the governmental hierarchies in host countries. A point is also made of the extent to which Volunteers have taken the cultural anthropologist as a model or have acquired the viewpoint of the cultural anthropologist or, perhaps more accurately, the applied anthropologist. Speaking as an anthropologist who has been concerned with the development of the theory and practice of applied anthropology since its beginning efforts just before World War II, I am not certain that what the Peace Corps, as such, needs is more social science, except at the high level of abstraction exemplified by this book. It is true, of course, that any bureaucracy benefits from the systematic analysis of its strengths and weaknesses. (Suggestions about the relationship between training and program in the Peace Corps belong here.) Any organization benefits from ongoing analysis of its experience. (The systematic accumulation of data on the Peace Corps and its analysis fit in here.) Future social scientists will greatly benefit from their experience as members of the Peace Corps. And social science will also benefit from the eventual recognition by some Volunteers that they wish to work in other fields, to which they will take an invaluable transcultural experience.

Essentially, however, the Peace Corps is not an exercise in applied social science in the usual sense—as technical assistance missions should be, though often they are not. The Peace Corps is in fact an ethical enterprise, a way for an excessively fortunate country to share its optimism and generosity with parts of the world that, at a moment in time, are in need of what the Volunteers can best offer. Important as technical skills are, essential as job satisfaction is if the Volunteers are to make a solid contribution, these skills and the organization that makes job satisfaction possible are only vehicles for an activity that is important because it involves whole-hearted devotion. In this enterprise, social science skills—like the technical skills of pedagogy, engineering, nursing, architecture, agronomy, and so on—have a special part to play. But their impact is greatest when they are incorporated into the mental equipment of intelligent, educated men and women. It is in the diffusion of ideas over which battles no longer need to be fought that social science provides the basis for an activity as complex, as all-involving, and as inevitably politically significant as the Peace Corps. The strength of the Peace Corps lies in the way in which exceptional men and women, Volunteers and staff, have combined with many unexceptional and often quite unsuitable participants at every level to make a success of a magnificent new conception.

It is repeatedly asserted in these pages that the greatest benefit will accrue not to the countries to which the Volunteers go but to America to which they will return. In an even broader sense, the Peace Corps program can and certainly does constitute a response to an interdependent world. Surely each country that develops a corps of able, concerned individuals who have a vivid experience of the problems of some other part of the developing world is contributing to the safer existence of all peoples. Members of other societies who come to understand the particular virtues that Americans at their best can bring to the world are strengthened in their ability to call upon those virtues. And the inevitable tendency of those with generous minds to criticize the shortcomings of their own society, such a prominent feature of those who live in democracies, is tempered by cross-cultural contact into a willingness to use the skills and virtues that are their own constructively and with a deepened sense of responsibility.

MARGARET MEAD

Aghios Nikolaos, Crete
July 1965

Preface

AN EXPERIMENT IN ACTIVISM

ONE June evening in 1961 I returned to my apartment in Cambridge, Massachusetts, to find a note on my desk: "Phone [Charlie Smithers]* at Peace Corps headquarters in Washington." It was already 10 P.M., but I telephoned right away, and was surprised to find Smithers still in his office at that hour. Smithers said he had heard about me from several people, and that he wanted me to come down for "a few days" to help him plan the training program for the Peace Corps' first Thailand contingent, which would be one of the new organization's first dozen or so overseas enterprises.

Smithers' invitation could not have come at a less opportune time. I had just moved from Yale to Harvard, settled in, and begun writing a long-postponed book on Thai religion. The last thing in the world that I wanted was to be disturbed from this placid writing routine. On the other hand, I was excited by the idea of the Peace Corps, and eager to help if I could. I did not hesitate long. Like literally thousands of other Americans, I "dropped everything" to do what I could to help the new organization. The following morning found me on the first plane from Boston to Washington. "A few days" finally turned out to be seven months. It soon developed that the Training Division also wanted help in planning the training for Malaya One and other Far East contingents. The Office of Program Development and Operations wanted consultation on program planning for the Far East. And the Talent Search Panel wanted help in their search for talented Americans to serve as "Representatives," or program directors, in a variety of host countries around the world.

* This is a pseudonym. The first use of each pseudonym in this book will appear in square brackets.

xi

It was a hectic seven months. Everybody worked back-breaking hours. Professionally, it was a liability. Some of my fellow cultural anthropologists chided me for taking leave from my university post to go to work for a "naive" organization like the Peace Corps. What they meant was that many of the Corps' Washington officials were *anthropologically* naive. I was quick to point out, however, that these staffers were anything but naive in other respects. Indeed, they were by and large a worldly-wise group, highly intelligent, administratively experienced, and politically—in the manner of the New Frontier—"tough." At the same time, most of them were dedicated, liberal, and altruistic. My own background put me in a small minority. I was the only cultural anthropologist in headquarters, and one of the relatively few staffers who had had sustained "people-to-people" experience in the developing world of a type that was soon to become the lot of the Peace Corps Volunteer (page 9). On the other hand, I was largely lacking in the kind of sophistication in matters of government bureaucracy possessed by many of my new colleagues. All of this made communication a challenge that was at once both fascinating and frustrating. Considering the headlong pace at which all of us were working, it seems amazing in retrospect that we communicated as well as we did.

AN EXPERIMENT IN CULTURAL PREPARATION

The greatest moment in my Peace Corps service came in October 1961, when I went to Ann Arbor to lecture to the Thailand One contingent of Volunteer trainees at the University of Michigan. I had been a member of the original Selection Committee for Thailand One, and knew the names and backgrounds of these forty-odd individuals practically by heart. What I did not realize until I met them, however, was what fine and appropriately motivated people most of them were. The language and area training program which Professor William J. Gedney and I had designed for them was one that, despite many flaws, seemed to be "taking." The trainees were learning the Thai language with gusto. The questions they asked about Thai religion, about community development, about the Thai cultural value system and concepts of "progress," and about how to function effectively in Thailand—were in the great majority of cases intelligent, sensitive, and above all, *relevant*. The trainees at Ann Arbor were clearly a subculture apart, and a subculture in which I felt immediately at ease. These young Americans were ample reward, ten times over, for all the *Sturm und Drang* of

Washington—and I urged my anthropological colleagues to judge the Peace Corps not by reports on its Washington staff personnel but by direct observation of the Volunteers. And now, four years later, it would seem that virtually all cultural anthropologists in this country, and virtually all other social scientists, are essentially "sold" on the Peace Corps Volunteers.

All this while, there were growing indications that various higher level policymakers in headquarters were becoming more and more "sold" on an intensive cultural approach to training. This is illustrated by the history of Thailand One. After carefully "checking out" a rather long list of universities that could conceivably be considered qualified, I concluded that, among those available, the University of Michigan was the most appropriate institution to train the Thailand contingent. It was then necessary to persuade the relevant training officer, who contacted Michigan and secured its agreement. It was also necessary to convince Peace Corps/Washington's policymakers that we needed thirteen weeks of training, despite the fact that they had never previously approved a training program lasting longer than eight weeks, and were reluctant to spend the extra money. We built about 210 "contact hours" of Thai language instruction into the training schedule. Today, a twelve-week training period, with even more emphasis on language, is common enough. In those early days, however, such a change in training policy constituted a minor revolution. Peace Corps/Washington indicated acceptance of the intensive language-and-culture approach on page 13 of its *First Annual Report to Congress,* which singled out Thailand One in this fashion:

> Training officers asked themselves, for example, what university or college would be best suited for training Volunteers for Thailand?
>
> The ideal university for this project would need facilities for training teachers of English as a second language, technical and trade-industrial school instructors, university instructors in scientific and professional fields, as well as entomologists and laboratory technicians; would have to be able to teach the difficult Thai language, provide an atmosphere conducive to the study of Thai culture, and have a strong American studies department.
>
> Such an ideal place was located: The University of Michigan at Ann Arbor. This University has had long and close ties with Asia dating back more than a century. Its campus includes the Center for Southern Asia Studies as well as the English Language Institute, the pioneer center for study and instruction in the teaching of English as a foreign language. Approximately 40 Thai citizens live in Ann Arbor— the great majority of them students at the University—with whom the

trainees were able to talk and to exchange ideas about each other's culture.

By all indications, the Peace Corps Volunteers have written an entirely new chapter in the history of American relations with Thailand. Thais who gathered at the Bangkok airport to greet the members of Thailand One were reportedly stunned and overjoyed by what they saw—and heard. The Volunteers got off the plane and proceeded to speak *Thai*—halting Thai, perhaps, but nonetheless recognizable and usable. Before long, according to one report, the PCVs had actually created for themselves a new perceptual category in the minds of many Thai people. This category was not "Peace Corps Volunteer," but "the new kind of American who can speak Thai." For previously, most Thai people had not *expected* Americans in their midst to speak their language (except perhaps missionary Americans). All of this sent my thoughts flying back to 1957, when I worked for four months as an anthropological consultant to the Agency for International Development (AID) mission in Thailand. AID had hired me at the end of a five-year period of research in that country, during which I had spent much of my time living and working in villages, had taken orders from Thai bosses, and had developed fluency in the language. My AID co-workers were highly cooperative. Every one of them was well qualified and well motivated. It was significant, though, that despite the fact that many of them showed a sincere interest in the Thai language and culture, none of them could carry on his daily work in Thai. Nor, with rare or partial exceptions, could anyone else among the 852 Americans listed as working for the U.S. government in Thailand that year speak the local language. Now, just eight years later, the Peace Corps has given us some hundreds of Volunteer "alumni," most of whom are more or less capable of functioning effectively in the Thai language and culture. Most of these Americans are young, with their careers still ahead of them. They represent—or soon will, after further university training—a wide variety of useful technical skills and professional specialties. In a few short years, then, the Peace Corps has made it possible for the United States, for the first time in history, to choose technicians, teachers, advisers, and diplomats for service in Thailand who possess *both* the necessary professional expertise *and* the necessary linguistic and cultural proficiency. The implications of this are truly revolutionary.

Since leaving the Peace Corps/Washington staff in early 1962, my admiration for that organization, and especially its Volunteers, has steadily grown. Peace Corps/Washington has slowly but steadily improved, in my opinion, both in the caliber of its personnel and in the wisdom of its policy decisions. I have maintained close contact with the Volunteer trainees simply by never refusing an invitation to serve as visiting lecturer at a training program. (At this writing I have helped to train some 1600 Volunteer trainees in 22 training programs.) Since 1964, I have often shared the podium with returned Volunteers, many of them my former trainees. It is a deeply rewarding experience to see the more able and articulate of these young returnees lead a discussion group or conduct a role-playing training session. Their humility, sensitivity, cultural point of view, and general awareness of what is relevant—all are truly impressive. They are, to coin a term, "transcultural men"—a much-needed addition to our country's resources for international representation, communication, consultation, and administration. Invariably, I return from these two- and three-day stands as visiting lecturer with renewed enthusiasm for this great social experiment, and for the people who are making it succeed.

THE SCOPE OF THIS BOOK

As part of my interest in this new social movement, I have tried to obtain and read every serious book written about the Peace Corps. A number of such books have appeared, most of which are listed in the bibliography following Chapter 1 (page 13). Some of these books are highly competent, and may be consulted with profit. Almost invariably, however, they tend to deal primarily with the *domestic* side of the Peace Corps: with sketches of Sargent Shriver's personality; with the chronicle of political maneuvering that brought the Corps into existence; with descriptions of language training at some Stateside university, or rock climbing and survival swimming at the Puerto Rico jungle camp; with Peace Corps/Washington's various policies; with how to become a Volunteer, and so forth. This is well and good, but it must be strongly emphasized that the heart of the Peace Corps operation is *not* in Washington, or Puerto Rico, or Ann Arbor, Albuquerque, or Altoona—but *overseas*, in forty-odd host countries around the world. Yet when these books attempt to describe and analyze a program overseas, they lose much of their value—for it usually turns out that the author has never been to the host country before, or at any rate knows less about the host country and culture than do the Volunteers whose performance he is describing and, presumably, evaluating. The present book is designed to supplement the existing array of books by bringing to the reader a series of analyses of overseas programs in selected host countries, with each analysis written by an authority on that particular country.

Another valuable source of information is the stories that appear in the monthly house organ, the *Peace Corps Volunteer*—especially those stories that have been written by the Volunteers themselves. Most of these stories are fresh, personal, and informative. They are, however, usually quite journalistic in nature. Moreover, in not a few cases, especially in the earlier days, these stories seem to have been designed to "sell" rather than to analyze the Corps' overseas operations. The present book should be regarded as supplementation to these stories in the sense that our chapters are written in nonjournalistic fashion, from a perhaps more detached point of view, by trained social scientists and historians.

The precise manner in which the present book is designed to supplement existing publications is best made explicit by listing the several ways in which our book tends to differ from its predecessors.

1. Since we focus on what has happened overseas, our coverage of the domestic side of the Peace Corps is strictly limited to that which is necessary to an understanding of the Corps' overseas activities and problems.

2. Our book focuses on thirteen selected host countries. In order to secure expert coverage of these thirteen countries, fourteen authors* were selected on the basis of recognized expertise on a particular host country. These authors were culled from an original list perhaps three times as long. Each author was, moreover, an expert on that country *before* the Peace Corps entered the country, so that he knew more about the country, presumably, than did the PCVs whose performance he was observing.†

3. In order to ensure that our chapters would be written with a sympathetic understanding of Peace Corps purposes and problems, only authors who had worked for or with the Corps in some mean-

* In the cases of the Philippines and Peru, there are two authors per country; in the case of Tunisia and Morocco, one author deals with two countries; otherwise, there is one author for one country.

† This criterion had to be waived in order to secure authors who were returned Volunteers. Szanton and Guskin had not been to the Philippines and Thailand, respectively, before serving as Volunteers there. Palmer had developed expertise on Latin America generally, and had resided in Chile, before serving as a PCV in Peru.

ingful manner were selected. Every contributor has served in at least one of the following capacities, and often in more than one: Volunteer, Volunteer Leader, program consultant, training consultant, visiting lecturer in a training program, Area Studies Coordinator for a training program, Director of a training program, assessment officer, member of a selection committee, overseas field evaluator, or member of an overseas Representative staff. Such close association with Peace Corps Volunteers and Volunteer trainees has led, in every case, to what is obviously a feeling of deep identification and respect. Although various of our authors express criticism of particular Peace Corps policies, I think most readers will agree that at a deeper level all of them are decidedly "pro-Peace Corps."

4. Each contributor is a social scientist or historian, trained at the graduate level.

5. Each contributor has had an opportunity—usually a rather long one—to observe the Volunteers in action in the host country.

6. Every country chapter has been carefully checked by at least one returned Volunteer from that country, and often by two, three, or more. In addition, three returned Volunteers and some former members of the Washington staff have checked the entire manuscript. Where possible, a country chapter has been checked by an especially qualified citizen of that country. In the great majority of cases, the suggestions of these critic-readers have been incorporated.

7. Our book attempts a completely *independent* treatment of the Peace Corps. We have made no attempt to obtain the approval or authorization of Peace Corps/Washington. Unlike most books on the Peace Corps, ours bears no introduction by Sargent Shriver or any other governmental figure. In selecting contributors, care was taken to avoid anybody who at the time was regularly employed by the Peace Corps, even though this meant foregoing some very good potential chapters. Our authors were asked to treat the Corps' operations overseas "without fear or favor," in as fair, balanced, objective, and professional a manner as possible.

8. Although each contributor was free to select his own topic, nonetheless a unifying theme emerges quite naturally. Each author has, in effect, chosen to deal with what might be called a "cultural frontier" separating the Volunteer's American culture from that of the people in the host country—and with the communication and cooperation that pass, or should pass, back and forth across

that frontier. As far as I know, this pronounced cultural emphasis is unique among books so far published on the Peace Corps.

Although we hope this book will prove of some value to social scientists, we have deliberately styled it for a larger audience. We hope that some policymakers in Washington, both inside and outside of the Peace Corps headquarters, will find our product of some use. Our book is also intended for the concerned layman, and, of course, for the Peace Corps Volunteers themselves—past, present, and potential. Those Volunteers who read the book during training might wish to evaluate various of its findings on the basis of subsequent field experience.

The attention of reviewers, social scientists, and other professional readers is invited to Appendix 1, "Professional and Editorial Considerations," page 345.

ACKNOWLEDGMENTS

For whatever merit this book might possess, I am indebted to many persons. First and foremost, I am grateful to the authors of the fourteen country chapters, who gave unstinting and patient cooperation throughout. Also, I am indebted to Dr. Margaret Mead for contributing the foreword.

For their assistance in scrutinizing the entire manuscript, I owe a great debt of gratitude to Paul and Mary Slawson, who have had Peace Corps experience in Pakistan and Washington; and to Ronald and Betty Herring, returned Volunteers from the Philippines. These four people spent untold hours in this endeavor, often disagreeing, invariably coming up with constructive suggestions.

For their critical reading of substantial parts of the manuscript, thanks are due to Professor Arthur S. Banks, Dr. Lambros Comitas, Dr. Dwight B. Heath, Mr. Frank J. Mahony, Dr. Margaret Mead, Dr. Rhoda Metraux, Mr. Maurice A. Sterns, and Dr. Hans N. Weiler.

The assistance of the following returned Peace Corps Volunteers in checking particular country chapters is gratefully acknowledged: Robert F. Arnove, Randall and Nancy Blair, Fred and Naomi Bonney, Albert G. Bradford, David Fleishhacker, Michael J. Hacker, Daniel Klingenberg, Kyoko Kodama, Thoyd O. Latham, Jr., Mr. and Mrs. LeRoy M. Law, Blanche E. Lonski, Francis Lum, John and Jeanette Lynch, Philip Michael, Denis F. Mullen, Thomas Newman, Ann Rae Richard, Richard C. Rudberg,

Clarence W. Sever, John J. Shearer, Louise Stapleton, Timothy R. Storrs, Nancy Turner, and Willard D. Weiss.

Others whose editorial suggestions are appreciated include two returned Volunteers, Miss Joan Aragone and Miss Carolyn Wood, and also Dr. Stephen O. Awokoya, Mr. David B. Baradas, Dean Miguel Casas Armengol, Dr. Ruth Sutherlin Finney, Mr. James C. Frits, Dr. Frank Lynch, Mr. Pinyo Sathorn, Mrs. Lora Simms, and Mr. Richard L. Warren.

For their assistance in preparing the manuscript, thanks are due to Mrs. Marian Alexander, Mrs. Patricia Case, Mrs. Marian McRae, Mrs. Marjorie Peterson, and Mrs. Irene Wilkin.

During the final stages of preparing manuscript, the publisher requested and received from Peace Corps/Washington a large number of photographs of Volunteers overseas, for which we express our thanks. Every photograph appearing in this book has been selected from among those thus received.

Administrative and clerical expenses entailed in preparing the manuscript were defrayed by a grant from the Wenner-Gren Foundation for Anthropological Research, and by a grant from the Stanford School of Education Publications Fund, using money from the Procter & Gamble Fund. Both these sources of support are gratefully acknowledged.

R. B. T.

Stanford University
Stanford, California
November 22, 1965

Contents

1

Introduction

Robert B. Textor

THE POLITICAL GAMBLE

JOHN Fitzgerald Kennedy began his administration with prodigious energy and drive. The vigor and drama of his New Frontier were everywhere evident, but nowhere more so than in the Maiatico Building, just across Lafayette Park from the White House. Here, under the equally energetic leadership of Mr. Kennedy's brother-in-law, Sargent Shriver, the new Peace Corps/Washington organization was assembled almost overnight. The "temporary" Peace Corps owed its life to an Executive Order signed by the President on March 1, 1961, and its sustenance to funds provided by him under discretionary authority. The impatient young President, eager to "move America forward" in his own style and manner, was unwilling to wait for Congressional action. In the spirit of "Let us begin . . . ," he took the action on his own. The Peace Corps was to be the New Frontier's most original, most visible bequest to history—and perhaps also its noblest.

The first, foremost, and overwhelming concern of the officials of Peace Corps/Washington in the spring and summer of 1961 was simple political survival. Soon, they knew, they must face Congress. Congress must pass a law creating a permanent Peace Corps. Congress must appropriate funds—enough funds to give the new organization a chance to prove itself. Whereas the end-goals of the Peace Corps concerned effective performance by Volunteers in a thousand transcultural situations overseas, the means toward those goals were purely and inescapably domestic—and political. Unless Congress were conquered, there would simply be no Peace Corps,

1

and no opportunity to function effectively in transcultural situations. It was not in the jungles of Ghana or Guatemala that the major initial battle for survival had to be won—but right at home in the jungles of Washington.

To win the approval of Congress, Shriver would have to overcome enormous inertia, skepticism, and disguised isolationism—both on Capitol Hill and among opinion leaders generally. Many political leaders of both parties were publicly or privately expressing opposition. Former President Eisenhower and former Vice-President Nixon openly derided the entire idea. Phrases like "Kennedy Kiddie Korps" were widely heard. The effect of all this opposition was, of course, to raise the stakes of the "political gamble." A collapse of the far-out Peace Corps experiment would have been a severe setback for the new President, who many people thought was too young for the job anyway. Success, on the other hand, would enhance his image as an energetic and creative innovator, as just the kind of leader needed after several years of another style of Presidential leadership.

This general skepticism was also shared widely among members of what might be called the "Overseas Establishment"—the State Department Foreign Service Officers, Agency for International Development (AID) personnel, foundation officials, missionaries, and other such specialists. For implicit in the whole concept of the Peace Corps was the upsetting notion that somehow the Volunteers —mere amateurs, for the most part—were expected to do a *better* job of "overseasmanship" than they themselves had been doing. Such an implication was perceived as an insult, a threat, or both. Thus ignored or spurned by many members of the Overseas Establishment, Sargent Shriver decided to go ahead anyway, using whatever personnel were available and seemed adequate to the demands of the job. And availability, it should be added, was not a serious problem, with the droves of young men—many with political debts to collect—who converged on Washington to share in the adventure and advancement so clearly promised by the New Frontier.

Those early Peace Corps days were heady, exciting days indeed, as indicated in the preface. There was an electricity in the air, an enthusiasm stirred by the young President, an expectation that perhaps he and his administration *could* indeed "do it better." Inquiries and applications from potential Volunteers flooded into Peace Corps headquarters from all over the country. Many Americans—especially the youth—were restless for a change, eager to see whether our affairs overseas could be handled better than as described in *The Ugly American,* and personally willing to involve themselves in the task of "moving America forward." The Peace Corps idea of service was obviously tapping a deep-felt need in many people, a need for active, more or less altruistic involvement in the development process overseas, a need for personal involvement with people of other cultures—as well as a need, of course, for adventure and for various kinds of personal growth and gain.

Sargent Shriver surprised many observers by the quality of his leadership and the shrewdness of his political judgment. He and his new organization projected an image that virtually epitomized that of the New Frontier: bright, realistic, liberal, tough, and task-oriented—as well as attractive, young, and athletic. To handle his Congressional relations, Shriver appointed 27-year-old Bill D. Moyers, a protégé of Vice-President Lyndon B. Johnson, whose power and prestige remained high on Capitol Hill despite the fact that he no longer belonged to the Congress. Shriver and Moyers, reinforced by a number of other brilliant young politicians on the Peace Corps/Washington staff, assaulted Capitol Hill as vigorously, perhaps, as it had ever been assaulted. Shriver also hired a number of able journalists away from various newspapers, thereby securing not only the professional skills of these men but also the benefit of their professional contacts. The resulting publicity barrage was enormous and, by and large, skillful and successful. Shriver was outflanking Congress by appealing directly to the people. A whole Peace Corps "mystique" was being created—one that had direct, fresh, personal appeal to millions of Americans.

The basic Shriver strategy was to present Congress with a *fait accompli.* If he could somehow have large numbers of Volunteers overseas and at work *before* Congress decided whether or not to make the Peace Corps permanent, his chances for survival would be measurably improved. And he succeeded. As the result of herculean efforts on the part of a ceaselessly hard-working staff, the tasks of recruitment, training, and selection were accomplished at speeds that most people would have considered impossible. By the time Congress was ready to vote, some two hundred Volunteers were already in the field in four host countries: Ghana, Colombia, St. Lucia, and Tanganyika. The Nigeria, Chile, and Philippines contingents were finishing training and nearly ready to leave. Congress now had the choice of whether to vote for or against an accomplished fact—and sizable majorities decided not to vote against these young Americans working overseas under conditions often involving personal sacrifice. On September 22, 1961, the Peace Corps

Act became law. Shriver now had thirty million dollars of Congressional appropriation with which to work, and a twelve-month lease on life.)

Shriver's emphasis on haste and size has continued unabated. Seldom before in American history, in the absence of major war or depression, has a government agency moved and grown with such verve, enthusiasm, and speed. The bare statistics only begin to reveal the manner in which this organization—really a kind of social movement—has been reaching out into the lives of Americans. In the fall of 1965, four years after Congress passed the Peace Corps Act, there were about 12,000 Volunteers working in 46 countries throughout the developing world. Projections called for more than 15,000 Volunteers or trainees by the fall of 1966. Meanwhile, beginning with a trickle in 1963, the number of ex-Volunteers returning to the United States has been swelling rapidly. On the Corps' fourth anniversary there were almost 4,000 of them; sometime in 1966 their numbers will begin to exceed the number of PCVs then in active service. By 1970, if projections are realized, there will be 50,000 returned Volunteers. By 1980, they will be 200,000 strong.

As these figures suggest, the bold political gamble of John Kennedy and Sargent Shriver has been a success—a much more resounding success, perhaps, than even they had originally allowed themselves to hope for. Congress and the American people have "bought" the Peace Corps. So well institutionalized has the Corps become that even the rashest of politicians would now be wary of attacking it overtly. Although political skirmishes can doubtless be expected in the future, it seems clear that the major political battle has now been won.

THE OVERSEAS CULTURAL GAMBLE

Besides gambling on whether they could make the Peace Corps survive in American domestic politics, President Kennedy and Mr. Shriver were also taking another chance of no mean proportions, which this book will refer to as their "overseas cultural gamble." They were gambling that the Peace Corps organization could recruit, select, train, program, supervise, and counsel massive numbers of Volunteers to participate in a complex variety of programs in a large number of alien cultures[1] around the world. They were gambling that this new organization could produce Volunteers who would, with a reasonable degree of effectiveness and without too many debacles visible from Washington, accomplish the three objectives outlined in the Peace Corps Act.* These are

1. To help peoples of the various host countries in "meeting their needs for trained manpower." Presumably, what Congress had in mind was that PCVs would be cast in their work roles in such a way as to contribute to the self-expanding *development* of these host countries, so that eventually outside assistance would no longer be necessary. The Peace Corps was thus expected to succeed in such difficult and complex tasks where other agencies of our "Overseas Establishment" had often met with indifferent success or even outright failure.

2. To help "promote a better understanding of the American people on the part of the peoples served." This objective was often informally expressed as "projecting an improved American image overseas." The Volunteers were expected to succeed where numerous other official Americans, as caricatured in *The Ugly American*, had failed.

3. To help promote "a better understanding of other peoples on the part of the American people." The Volunteers were expected somehow to gain what this book calls cultural sensitivity and to achieve cultural and linguistic proficiency—where other official Americans had frequently been unsuccessful.

Clearly, the accomplishment of these objectives would be no easy task. Indeed, it is conceivable that if some of the early senior staff members of Peace Corps/Washington had adequately realized the difficulty of their task, they might well have shrunk from it. If this is so, then their lack of awareness was a fortunate accident indeed, for it helped bring the Peace Corps into being.

It is not difficult to divine some of the reasons why the Peace Corps was so close to John Kennedy's heart. For example, it is reported that years before he became President, he was already lamenting the fact that too few of our official representatives overseas could speak the local language and make sense out of the local culture. Even as a young Congressman on fact-finding tours abroad, Mr. Kennedy was said to have sometimes bypassed official Americans in the host country, instead seeking out local people and nonofficial Americans who, he thought, would be more knowledgeable. As a Presidential candidate, Mr. Kennedy pledged that he would appoint

* Public Law 87-293, Eighty-seventh Congress, September 22, 1961, Section 2.

ambassadors who could speak the language of the host country. Translated into the terms used in this book, what Mr. Kennedy decried was that most Americans serving officially in the developing areas were building up "overseas" experience, perhaps, but not "transcultural"[1] experience. They were too often living luxuriously in protected American enclaves, speaking English to each other, and eating imported American food. Their contacts with people of the host country—and especially those of its humbler strata—were often minimal. The Peace Corps, clearly, was intended to set matters right by affording large numbers of Volunteers the opportunity to gain a meaningful transcultural experience. The essential components of this Volunteer experience are analyzed later (page 9).

THE "CULTURE" AND "SUBCULTURES" OF THE PEACE CORPS

The Peace Corps has from the beginning been faced with another range of problems that are also, in a broad sense of the term, "cultural."[1] One may begin the analysis of these problems by observing that the entirety of the Corps' membership—including salaried staff plus Volunteers—possess a special "culture" all their own. Although they all are thoroughgoing Americans, they are at the same time different from most other Americans. They have selected from our total American repertory of values and standards a limited number to which they give heightened emphasis. By way of example, they are, by and large, dedicated to social service, and to crossing national and linguistic boundaries in quest of opportunities to serve meaningfully. Members of the Peace Corps—staff and Volunteers alike—are actionists. They crave a direct, personal involvement in developmental activities in the economically less fortunate nations. This direct involvement, they believe, should be as "nonbureaucratic" as possible. The ideal they seek is "people-to-people" contact with the ordinary citizens—not just the elite—of the countries in the developing world.

Other books on the Peace Corps have already so thoroughly explored what this book calls the common Peace Corps "culture" that no further detail is required here. What the other publications have *not* adequately pointed up, however, is the wide internal variation *within* the total Peace Corps organization. For if the total Peace Corps can properly be regarded as having its own "culture," then it is equally valid to speak of three "subcultures"[1] within that culture: the Peace Corps/Washington staff subculture, the Volunteer subculture, and—occupying a position intermediate between the two—the overseas Representative staff subculture. Almost any sensitive observer, if given two weeks in Washington headquarters and two weeks at an overseas post, would agree that the separateness of these three is something that is real and demonstrable. These subcultures possess genuinely different systems of values and standards. They have differing "standards for deciding what is, standards for deciding what can be, standards for deciding how one feels about it, standards for deciding what to do about it, and standards for deciding how to go about doing it" (Goodenough 1961, 522). A given individual, regardless of his *personal* values and standards, must adjust to the prevailing standards of the subculture in which he works, or he is likely to be ineffective, frustrated, and dissatisfied.

To a considerable extent the differences among these three subcultures can be explained in terms of three factors: (1) differences in the nature of the fundamental task that members of each respective subculture are expected to perform; (2) differences in the previous experiences of the members of each subculture; and (3) differences in the aspirations that these three sets of members have brought with them into Peace Corps service. Each of these three factors will be examined briefly.

As already indicated, the fundamental tasks of the Washington subculture have always been to secure domestic political acceptance of the Peace Corps; to perform domestic administrative tasks efficiently; and to ensure the development of wise overseas programs and then "backstop" them effectively. The organization of Peace Corps/Washington clearly reflects these tasks. (For details, see Appendix 2, page 347.) An official's promotion and indeed his very survival in headquarters depend on his meeting the Washington subculture's standards of performance in one or more of these areas. Standards for evaluating domestic political and administrative performance generally cause little difficulty, because feedback from Congressmen, or from government auditors and the like, is readily available. Standards for evaluating overseas program performance, however, are a different matter. How, for example, is Washington to know whether a particular program is working out well in Somalia? As Mahony shows (page 132), it was possible for a program in Somalia to be quite inappropriate, and quite inappropriately administered, and yet top-level Washington officials did not know about it. In other instances, Washington might possess adequate information but evaluate this information in accordance with standards at variance with the standards of the Volunteers in the host country, of the Representative stationed there, or of the people of that country.

(The fundamental task of the Volunteer in the field is to participate in, and to promote, clear communication and effective cooperation across the "frontier" that separates his culture from that of the local people.) In a certain sense, the evaluative standards of the Volunteer subculture approximate those of the host culture[1] (or of some subculture within it, such as its "modern" subculture). No communication, after all, is effective unless it is understood, and no cooperation is effective unless it is bilateral. The typical Volunteer regards the Washington staff, and the Representative staff, as means toward this end of intercultural[1] communication and cooperation. He evaluates the performance of the staff in terms of how well they facilitate this communication and cooperation while otherwise getting in the way as little as possible.

The fundamental task of the Representative is to serve as a communications and operations bridge between Washington and the Volunteers, and also between the host country's government and the Peace Corps.) Partly because there are so many different host countries, cultures, and governments, the "subculture" of the Representatives is a relatively amorphous one. Suffice it to say that insofar as a particular "Rep" understands and appreciates the host country's culture and the Volunteer subculture—and this varies widely from "Rep" to "Rep"—he will tend to judge Washington's performance and his own performance by the standards of the Volunteer subculture. This often leads him into a serious dilemma because Washington's standards for evaluating his performance are sometimes quite different from those used by the Volunteers. Added to this is the complicating fact that the subculture of a particular group of Volunteers will change through time, as they become more knowledgeable about the host country.

In terms of occupational experience, the principal difference lies between the members of the Washington and Representative staffs on the one hand, and the Volunteers on the other. Staff members are generally older and better established in American society. Many of them have distinguished themselves in their professions, and enjoyed highly responsible positions at relatively high income. The Volunteers, by contrast, are usually young, with a median age in the lower twenties. Most have yet to become well established in a career. For many, the transcultural Volunteer experience is their first major adult job experience.

While members of all three subcultures would seem to have entered Peace Corps service with somewhat more altruistic motives than are found generally in American society, it also seems generally true that the Washington staffers are more career-oriented than the overseas Representatives, and that the Representatives are in turn more career-oriented than the Volunteers. To date, it also seems that career rewards actually gained have followed the same order. A number of Washington staffers have moved on to positions of considerably higher responsibility. In terms of immediate financial rewards, too, there are important differences. The Washington officials and the members of the "Rep" teams earn attractive salaries. The PCVs, by contrast, receive no salaries. Instead, they are paid living allowances geared to the cost of living of the host country, plus seventy-five dollars per month as a readjustment allowance to be drawn upon completion of service.

The important differences in standards among these three subcultures will become clearer in the country chapters that follow, as will the important kinds of problems that result from these differences. In the final chapter, I will attempt to summarize these problems, and to suggest ways in which some of them can be solved or reduced in seriousness. For the time being, it need only be added that despite all these differences, there is one important unifying principle, namely that all three subcultures are intensely "Volunteer-oriented." All three share the value standard that the most important thing one can do in one's job is to facilitate the success of the Volunteers in the field. The seriousness with which this ethic is taken—thanks to the leadership of Sargent Shriver, Deputy Director Warren W. Wiggins, and many others—has contributed materially to the over-all success of the organization.

THE VOLUNTEER ROLE AND THE OVERSEAS CULTURAL GAMBLE

A brief analysis of the principal components of the Volunteer role sheds light on the important differences that separate the Volunteer subculture on the one hand, from both the Representative staff subculture and the Washington staff subculture on the other. The experiences that the Volunteer role entails can be simply summarized: he lives at a relatively low socioeconomic level; he carries out a middle-level job assignment; and his performance is expected to be of a high level of cultural and linguistic proficiency.

Low-Level Economic Experience

The purpose of living at a low economic level is not, of course, to perform some kind of penance for past sins of luxurious living. The purpose is simply to place oneself on approximately the same level as that of many or most citizens of the host country, so that economic barriers do not get in the way of friendship, rapport, understanding, and cultural empathy. In most but not all cases, this appropriate socioeconomic level will represent a lowering of the standards to which the American is accustomed. In even more cases, this level will be substantially lower than that enjoyed by the typical U.S. government official or businessman stationed in the same host country.

Middle-Level Job Experience

The Volunteer works in a developing country at a so-called "middle" level. He is a "doer"—not an adviser, consultant, or administrator. He typically takes orders from a supervisor of the host country, and must submit to the discipline, the constraints, and, not infrequently, to the "totally unreasonable" frustrations that often characterize work in a tradition-oriented or sluggishly functioning organizational structure. By being forced to function within the organizational structure of another culture, the American is forced to learn a good deal about how that structure and culture work.

High-Level Cultural and Linguistic Proficiency

The role of the Volunteer, as defined by the Volunteer subculture, places great emphasis on becoming attuned to the host country's culture. It calls for empathy with the local people, for the ability to "feel with" their value system. It requires that the PCV develop the ability to function effectively on and off the job. Linguistic proficiency is, of course, simply a special aspect of cultural proficiency, since language is an aspect of culture. The vital importance of linguistic competence is recognized in the Peace Corps Act itself, which sets a new precedent in American legislative history by actually *requiring* that no Volunteer be sent overseas unless he "possesses such reasonable proficiency as his assignment requires in speaking the language of the country or area to which he is assigned" (footnote, page 20).

THE FUNDAMENTAL PROBLEM

In the opinion of many observers, the fundamental problem of the Peace Corps to date is that most of the persons selected to serve in senior headquarters positions have lacked a previous Volunteer-type experience. While many of them have had "overseas" experience, few have had deep transcultural experience. The same is true for many senior members of the Representative staffs overseas. Observers find it anomalous that many officials charged with the tasks of programing and supervising the PCVs' transcultural activities are themselves lacking in any previous experience of a comparable nature. Many of the Corps' most serious problems are thought to stem from this simple fact.

To offer a thoroughgoing explanation as to why there are so many senior staff officials who lack this kind of background would be a complex undertaking requiring more information than is available. One partial explanation does, however, seem to lie in the apparent tendency to employ persons who may be useful in affecting the outcome of the political gamble or in attaining other political objectives. Such persons, it would seem, are often ill-equipped to deal with the cultural gamble.

It is possible to point disparagingly at the relative scarcity of previous Volunteer-type experience on the part of the senior staff and render a negative value judgment. Some Volunteers and returned Volunteers do just this. A more moderate position would be to point to evidence indicating that a number of these senior staff members have been reasonably well aware of their own inadequacies in this respect. At the same time, not a few of them have been quite determined to produce a new type of "transcultural" American who would be relatively free of these very inadequacies. The degree to which they have succeeded in accomplishing this end, and others akin to it, will be examined in the fourteen country chapters that follow.

NOTE

1 The terms "culture" and "subculture" have been chosen in order to maintain a terminology consistent with the general spirit of this book. However, I am not overly concerned with the problem of terminology. Other terms, such as "group atmosphere," "ethos," or "system," might serve just as conveniently. At any rate, it should be pointed out that many anthropologists prefer to use the term "culture" only where there is inter-generational transmission; that is, where much of the content of a culture is transmitted by the parents and others of their generation, to the children. Obviously, this is not the case with the total Peace Corps "culture," nor with its staff or Volunteer "subcultures." As Heath points out (page 279) the closest analog to intergenerational transmission that occurs within the Peace Corps occurs between those who have spent considerable time

in the host country and those who have just arrived: between Bolivia One and Bolivia Two, for example. "Intergenerational" transmission now frequently occurs also in the form of returned Volunteers serving as teachers and discussion leaders at training sites; two returnees from early Bolivia programs served very effectively in such a capacity during the training of Bolivia Thirteen, for example.

When this book deals with ways of life found in various host countries, the term "culture" will often be used in the sense that implies true intergenerational transmission. In Somalia, for example, much of the important content of Somali culture is learned by Somali children from the parental generation. I will not here attempt to define such usage of the term "culture" more precisely, for various of our authors might wish to define the term in somewhat varying ways. In general, I think the term's essential meaning will be clear from context. For a discussion of the innumerable definitions of "culture," see Kroeber and Kluckhohn (1952).

Other terms appearing in this book are "transcultural," "intercultural," and "acculturated." These three terms also usually have to do with "culture" in the sense that implies intergenerational transmission. When the term "transcultural" is used, it refers to the experience of an individual—often a Peace Corps Volunteer—who crosses the "frontier" between his own and a host culture. The term often implies that the individual has learned to function more or less effectively in the host culture—whether or not he "internalizes" many of its values. Szanton explores this process in the case of the Volunteers in the Philippines (page 54). "Intercultural," by contrast, refers to projects or programs involving two organizations or groups—for example, AID and the Ministry of Agriculture in Somalia—where both organizations are cooperating in an attempt to produce some change in the culture of the host country. An individual working in an intercultural project can, of course, derive a transcultural experience from it—as indeed one of our authors, Frank J. Mahony, did while working with AID in Somalia. In this book, it happens to be the case that the term "acculturated" normally means "acculturated to Western standards." That is, the term refers to persons who, through contact, have adopted and more or less internalized certain features of some Western culture. The concept and phenomenon of "acculturation" are, however, much more general than this; for extended discussion, see Barnett, Broom, Siegel, Vogt, and Watson (1954).

The "culture" and "subcultures" of the Peace Corps are a different matter. In writing about these subjects in Chapters 1 and 16, and in editing references to them in the other chapters, my usage has conformed to that of Goodenough (1961, 521–528). Specifically, I use Goodenough's "Culture 2." I distinguish four examples of what Goodenough calls a "public" culture: (1) the total Peace Corps culture; (2) the Peace Corps/Washington subculture; (3) the overseas Representatives' subculture; and (4) the Volunteer subculture. Given the newness of the Peace Corps, one might wish to regard these as "incipient" or "emerging" cultures and subcultures. The composition of these four is as follows:

1. The members of the total Peace Corps culture consist of all staff, whether in Washington or overseas, plus all Volunteers. This culture is the least clearly formed of the four. A new member would confront the greatest variety of other members' "operating cultures"—to continue Goodenough's terminology.

2. The members of the Peace Corps/Washington subculture consist of all staff working at the Washington headquarters.

3. The members of the overseas Representatives' subculture consist of all Representatives, Deputy Representatives, and Associate Representatives stationed overseas, plus other salaried Peace Corps personnel working with them.

4. The members of the Volunteer subculture consist of the Volunteers only. This subculture is the most clearly formed of the three subcultures, and is generally more similar to the overseas Representatives' subculture than to the Peace Corps/Washington subculture. It might also be convenient, for some purposes of analysis, to speak of a separate subculture for the Volunteers serving in each of the forty-odd host countries, and even of a separate subculture for each contingent within each country.

Volunteer trainees can be regarded as incipient members of the Volunteer subculture. It is remarkable to see how quickly the trainees learn how to become members of the Volunteer subculture, and how similar, in their basic standards, the trainees are from one training project to another. This is another way of saying that a new member of a training group confronts only a limited variety of other members' "operating cultures"—or, in other words, that considerable consensus exists from the beginning.

BIBLIOGRAPHY

ADAMS, VELMA
  1964   *The Peace Corps in Action.* Chicago: Follett.
BARNETT, H. G., AND LEONARD BROOM, BERNARD J. SIEGEL, EVON Z. VOGT, AND JAMES B. WATSON
  1954   "Acculturation: An Exploratory Formulation." *American Anthropologist,* Vol. 56, pp. 973–1002.
BURDICK, EUGENE, AND WILLIAM J. LEDERER
  1958   *The Ugly American.* New York: Norton.
GOODENOUGH, WARD H.
  1961   "Comments on Cultural Evolution." *Daedalus,* Vol. 90, pp. 521–528.
  1963   *Cooperation in Change.* New York: Russell Sage Foundation.
HOOPES, ROY
  1961   *The Complete Peace Corps Guide.* New York: Dial Press.
"HOUSE HEARINGS" (U.S. House of Representatives)
  1965   *Hearings Before the Committee on Foreign Affairs, House of*

Representatives, Eighty-Ninth Congress, First Session, on H.R. 9026, A Bill to Amend Further the Peace Corps Act. June 2, 3, and 8. Washington, D. C.: Government Printing Office.

KROEBER, A. L., AND CLYDE KLUCKHOHN

1952   *Culture: A Critical Review of Concepts and Definitions.* Cambridge, Mass.: Papers of the Peabody Museum of American Archaeology and Ethnology, Harvard University, Vol. 47, No. 1. On page 181, these two anthropologists conclude that most social scientists at that time would formulate the central idea of the concept of culture approximately as follows: "Culture consists of patterns, explicit and implicit, of and for behavior acquired and transmitted by symbols, constituting the distinctive achievement of human groups, including their embodiments in artifacts; the essential core of culture consists of traditional (i.e., historically derived and selected) ideas and especially their attached values; culture systems may, on the one hand, be considered as products of action, on the other, as conditioning elements of further action."

LISTON, ROBERT A.

1964   *Sargent Shriver: A Candid Portrait.* New York: Farrar, Straus.

LUCE, IRIS

1964   *Letters from the Peace Corps.* Washington, D. C.: Robert B. Luce.

MADOW, PAULINE

1964   *The Peace Corps.* New York: H. H. Wilson.

PEACE CORPS/WASHINGTON

Annual Reports.

Peace Corps Volunteer. Monthly publication for Volunteers, former Volunteers, and other interested persons. One excellent way to assess changes in Peace Corps/Washington attitudes and policies is to read a selection of issues of this journal from 1961 to the present.

"SENATE HEARINGS" (U.S. Senate)

1965   *Hearing Before the Committee on Foreign Relations, United States Senate, Eighty-Ninth Congress, First Session, on S. 1368, A Bill to Amend Further the Peace Corps Act, as Amended.* April 26, 1965. Washington, D. C.: Government Printing Office.

SHRIVER, SARGENT

1964   *Point of the Lance.* New York: Harper & Row. An edited selection of speeches and writings by Sargent Shriver.

SULLIVAN, GEORGE

1964   *The Story of the Peace Corps.* New York: Fleet Publishing Corporation.

WINGENBACH, CHARLES E.

1963   *Guide to the Peace Corps.* New York: McGraw-Hill.

2

Cultural Preparation for the Philippines

GEORGE M. GUTHRIE *is Professor of Psychology at Pennsylvania State University, where he was in charge of Area Studies and of assessment in each of the training programs for Philippines One through Four. Since then, he has lectured at Philippines training programs elsewhere, and on two occasions has visited the Volunteers in the field. Dr. Guthrie was a Fulbright Research Scholar in the Philippines in 1959–1960, and he has maintained an active interest in that country since then. He is thus one of the relatively few American psychologists who have worked and specialized in a non-Western cultural area. Professor Guthrie is a Diplomate in Clinical Psychology of the American Board of Examiners in Professional Psychology. One of his principal research interests is the psychological problems of adjusting to another culture. He is author of numerous psychological articles in various journals, of* The Filipino Child and Philippine Society, *Manila: Philippine Normal College Press, 1961, and of* Child Rearing and Personality Development in the Philippines, *University Park, Pa.: Pennsylvania State University Press, forthcoming.*

THE HISTORICAL SETTING

THE Philippines was one of the first countries to which Peace Corps Volunteers were sent. Since the fall of 1961, many hundreds of PCVs have gone to work among the thirty million citizens of that island republic. Most have served in elementary and secondary schools as "educational aides" in the fields of English and science.

In a sense America's "cultural preparation" for its Peace Corps program in the Philippines began at the turn of this century, just after the United States defeated the Spanish forces there, and then proceeded to stamp out Filipino efforts to achieve their own independence. In the years that ensued, American administrators, soldiers, and teachers learned enough about Philippine ways so that, with relatively little use of brute force, they were able to cause or catalyze a tremendous number of changes in the local sociocultural fabric. Vast developments were effected in the fields of health and education. The apparatus of local representative government emerged. And the first steps toward industrialization took place. As colonialists go, we were a relative success. Our only major venture into formal colonialism ended on July 4, 1946, leaving behind a legacy of goodwill that is still clearly apparent twenty years later.

The Peace Corps' involvement with Philippine schools also had a unique precedent. In August 1901, a military transport, the U.S.S. *Thomas,* arrived in Manila carrying several hundred American teachers who had volunteered to come to the aid of the new American administration by establishing elementary schools in the rural Philippines. Since the new group had no official name, they soon became known as the "Thomasites." Sixty years and two months later, a jet airplane arrived in Manila, carrying 128 Peace Corpsmen who had volunteered to serve as "educational aides" in a program designed to improve the quality of instruction in elementary and secondary schools in the rural Philippines. "Philippine Peace Corps One" had arrived. Pronouncing words as they are spelled, Filipinos were soon calling them the "Peace Corpse," and, even more ominously, the "First Botch."

Although the Thomasites had left behind a record of courage and accomplishment, Peace Corps officials in Manila set about deliberately to discourage comparisons between the two groups. These officials quite properly rejected many of the motives of the Thomasites as being too redolent of the era of the "White Man's Burden." And yet, at a deeper psychological level, many of the motivations of members of both groups were almost certainly similar: a desire to help, a quest for new experience, a longing to do something significant.

The Thomasites epitomized America's relationship with the Philippines during the colonial period, and indeed many vestiges of that relationship persist to this day. There is an ambivalence about this relationship that makes it perhaps unique in the history of colonialism. Because Americans never fully accepted the role of conqueror, and because the Filipinos kept alive an independent spirit, the course of events between the two peoples has always seemed to operate on several levels. Americans, aware of their own emergence from colonialism, rejected the idea that one people could be considered superior and hence entitled to rule another people. At the same time, American colonial administrators revealed in their actions an ethnocentrism common among colonialists everywhere.

Philippine institutions, they felt, were indeed inferior and in need of replacement—by *American*-style institutions, of course. In their turn, the Filipinos, who had been given little responsibility for government or education by the Spaniards, did come to see the schools and representative assemblies established by the Americans as beneficial to them.

Thus, the first half of this century saw America busily attempting to remold the Philippines after its own image. The only trouble was that the Filipino "clay" proved incapable of unlimited modeling. There are many reasons why this was so. For example, the individual Filipino, in common with his counterparts in innumerable traditional societies the world over, feels such a deep obligation to members of his immediate and extended family that relationship by blood or marriage is more important to him than friendship based on congeniality. The (bilateral extended) family becomes the prototype of most relationships, so that the Filipino feels most comfortable when he can keep formality and objectivity to a minimum and carry on his relationships, business or pleasure, in an informal personalized way. There is an enormous emphasis on good feeling between persons who know one another, with the result that other goals, such as clarity of communication, direct reality testing, and achievement of concrete technological objectives, take a lower place. The fact that they *do* take a lower place constitutes an important reason why the American colonial administration was unable to remold the Philippine system precisely as it wished. And it was clear from the very inception of the Peace Corps' Philippine program that unless such cultural features as the foregoing were known to, and appreciated by, the organization's administrators and Volunteers in that country, the result could be at best ineffectiveness and at worst actual harm.

Two generations of American presence in the Philippines have, of course, produced a sizable group of Americans who, in some sense or other, understand the Philippines. Certainly there are more American experts or semiexperts on the Philippines than there are on Afghanistan, Nigeria, or Bolivia. Nonetheless, the number of real experts is lower than one might expect. A partial explanation for this is the fact that in the Philippines (as in other countries in the developing world) American diplomatic, military, and business personnel generally live in sheltered residential and cultural enclaves. Their contacts with Filipinos tend to be made on the servant level or on the level of official transactions. Personal contact *as equals* is limited. Few of these Americans come into contact with ordinary

Filipinos in situations where true acquaintanceship and understanding can develop. And few of them ever master a Philippine language or develop a sure sense for local values. Most of them learn little more about the local culture than they need to learn in order to do their jobs, and this is often strikingly little.

While American understanding of Philippine ways is thus somewhat limited, the typical Philippine attitude toward American ways is characterized by overacceptance accompanied by intense inferiority feelings. Many Filipinos idealize America, and feel that things American are the best in the world. American goods, techniques, and ideas are often accepted uncritically. Many Filipinos seem only too willing to be our "little brown brothers," as the early Governor-General William Howard Taft so patronizingly dubbed them. In their desperate attempts to be like Americans, many Filipinos imitate the things that come most easily: American slang, clothing, popular music, comic books, and the like.

This, then, was the situation in early 1961, at the founding of the Peace Corps. On the one hand, there was a paucity of Americans possessing a thorough understanding of the relevant aspects of Philippine life. On the other hand, there was a tendency among Filipinos to accept anything American as good. It was not, all in all, a reassuring situation. Added to this were five additional distress signals: first, the program would be administered in the field by five Peace Corps Representatives, not one of whom had had significant previous field experience in, or area knowledge of, the Philippines. Second, the program had been put together in enormous haste, with limited opportunity for the concerned Philippine officials to learn the precise nature of the Peace Corps and even less opportunity for the responsible American officials to learn anything about the Philippines. Third, the Volunteers were to be sent out not as teachers—of which the Philippines already had a greater supply than could be employed—but as "educational aides," an unprecedented and unstructured role whose responsibilities were known clearly to no one. Fourth, the Volunteers would be widely dispersed throughout a number of islands, making support and administration especially difficult. And finally, Pennsylvania State University, which had been designated as the training institution, was given all of two weeks to plan a training program from scratch. Clearly, if the Philippine program was going to succeed, it would be necessary to invoke once again something like the gallant "Spirit of Bataan" that characterized Filipino-American relations during World War II!

THE TRAINEES AND THEIR MOTIVATION

During 1961–1962 we at Pennsylvania State University trained the first four groups of Peace Corps trainees destined for the Philippines. There were roughly 150 trainees in the first group, and 60 in each of the others. All but about a half dozen were recent college graduates. From these four groups, 278 eventually reached Manila as Volunteers. Numbers of this magnitude presented an extraordinary opportunity to examine training and evaluation policies and techniques, and from the beginning we made research an integral part of our program. Careful records were kept. Trainees were given a number of psychological tests and questionnaires. Plans were made to collect data on their subsequent performance as Volunteers in the Philippines, in order to assess the validity of our selection and training procedures and to provide data on the basis of which improvements might be made with subsequent groups. A report of some of this research has been made (Guthrie and McKendry 1964).

Our tests revealed a surprising homogeneity of interest patterns among the trainees (Guthrie and McKendry 1963). Eighty per cent of both the men and women evidenced interests which closely resemble those typical of social workers. A slightly higher percentage of the men had interests closely resembling those of public administrators. Among the women there was virtually no similarity to the interests typical of English or science teachers, and only 10 per cent of them had interests resembling those of elementary school teachers—facts that did not augur well for future teaching performance. The men had high interests in people-related occupations but little interest in science or business. All this is startling, because *none* of our men had selected social work or public administration as a major in undergraduate school, and only a handful of the women had done social work.

In their individual ways many Volunteers freely acknowledged joining the Peace Corps because they wanted to do something significant and because they had not found a satisfying career at home. This points to an interesting aspect of American culture. While we honor and encourage the motives of the scientist or businessman, the salesman or artist, we accord low status to social service motivations, particularly in men. Young Americans are often encouraged to conceal and deny their urges to help people. They are strongly supported in aspirations to become scientists, engineers, or businessmen, but given little opportunity to develop, and modify through learning, life goals which happen to coincide with those of public service or social concern. The Peace Corps can thus be viewed as an organization which provides an acceptable and legitimate means for the expression of social concern, since such concern somehow becomes acceptable once it leaves our shores and is directed toward members of *other* cultures—cultures doubtless perceived by many Americans as inherently inferior to our own.

THE TRAINING PROGRAM

The early Peace Corps days were marked by an almost indescribable haste and confusion. Most of the key officials in Washington's Training Division were lacking in intimate non-Western field experience. They were learning their jobs as they went. To get the job done quickly, they had no choice but to give wide scope to the universities that contracted to do the training, and then hope for the best. We at Pennsylvania State University were thus not only permitted, but also encouraged, to improvise and innovate.

As we proceeded frantically to put a program together, we rediscovered the fact that Americans really knew little about systematic cultural preparation for service in an exotic country. True, individual Americans could be found who had been very effective in their experiences in the Philippines. But we found that little of what these individuals knew, or thought they knew, about cultural preparation had ever been put systematically to the test. Thus we found that State Department precedents were not very helpful. The Pentagon replied to our inquiries by expressing the hope that they could learn from us. Other organizations' overseas programs had rarely involved full-scale formal training efforts.

Our program followed the five general rubrics set forth by the Washington headquarters, and each of these will be described.

Linguistics and Second-Language Teaching

The Peace Corps Act takes a forthright and indeed revolutionary position on the matter of linguistic preparation. It provides that "no person shall be assigned to duty as a volunteer under this Act in any foreign country or area unless at the time of such assignment he possesses such reasonable proficiency as his assignment requires in speaking the language of the country or area to which he is assigned."*

Penn State was, of course, eager to do all it could to provide train-

* Peace Corps Act, Public Law 87-293, Sept. 22, 1961, Section 24.

ing that would meet the standard prescribed by this law, and the trainees were, if anything, even more eager to receive such training. In the case of the first three Philippine groups, however, the standards of the law would have been virtually impossible to meet because program planners in Washington and Manila had for some inscrutable reason arranged to assign each of these groups over broad areas in which several different languages or dialects were spoken. There was no way of knowing in advance to which language or dialect area a particular Volunteer was going to be sent. Since the teaching of each of these languages requires special technical expertise, special instructors who speak the language natively, and special training materials, the cost of adequate language training would have been prohibitive, even if the necessary arrangements could have been made on such short notice. (Later, the policy was changed, and particular groups of Volunteers were all trained for, and sent to, a single ethnolinguistic area. Still later, in 1965, the policy was again changed, and all trainees were trained in Tagalog, a language which many of them would seldom use once they arrived at their posts in non-Tagalog-speaking areas.)

Faced with these insurmountable problems, Penn State did the best it could by offering the trainees an intensive course in basic linguistics, hoping that a knowledge of such fundamentals would help the Volunteer later to learn the local dialect on his own. (Once they arrived in the Philippines, many of these Volunteers received very brief in-country training in such languages as Tagalog, Cebuano, and Waray.) Penn State's emphasis on Linguistics, coupled with Second-Language Teaching, was also intended to equip the Volunteer with skills and sensitivities that would facilitate effective English teaching in the field. Subsequent experience showed that many Volunteers learned one or more dialects quite well. It would seem highly desirable that research be carried out to assess the relative efficacy of linguistics versus immediate dialect training (and various combinations of the two) as preparation for mastery of a language in the field.

The Teaching of Science

Here, the content of training was similar to that received by American college students majoring in elementary education. Emphasis was placed on improvisation, and on fitting the mode of presentation to the Philippine cultural setting and to locally available teaching materials.

American Institutions

This element was intended to remind the trainee of his own tradition, and equip him to discuss it more intelligently with Filipinos. In retrospect, it is clear that this component involved considerable waste of time because it was inadequately integrated into the Philippine Studies component. For example, it does little good for the Volunteer in the field to know about the historical roots of our political philosophy, if his discussions of America with people in Philippine barrios center primarily around American mores as exemplified in our movies, around America's rather uneven policy toward the Philippines, which still remains ambiguous to Filipinos, and so forth.

Health and Physical Conditioning

Our instructions from Washington called for forty hours of health instruction, and these were conscientiously carried out. Clearly, headquarters was mindful of congressional and public relations in fixing this rigid requirement. For if a Volunteer fell ill in the Philippines —and indeed one of them did die of hepatitis—the Peace Corps could at least feel that they had taken all reasonable precautions. My personal feeling, however, is that most of the health instruction should have waited until the Volunteers arrived in the Philippines for in-country training. Once in the Philippines, doctors and other instructors would be available who were intimately familiar with the peculiarities of the local situation and with the diseases typically contracted there by Westerners. Moreover, demonstrations and reminders would have been readily available.

Washington policy also required that we place considerable emphasis on physical conditioning. This we did, and the results were useful, although it is doubtful that the benefits survived the final home leave prior to departure for Manila.

The "Outward-Bound" Approach

Half of the men in our second group came to us from Puerto Rico, where they had undergone the much publicized "outward-bound" training at the Peace Corps' jungle camp. As might have been expected, this group performed much better in physical tests than did the other half of the men, who had come to Penn State directly from their homes. However, when stamina tests were readministered at the end of the training period, no differences were revealed between the two groups. The modest physical training which was part of our program had brought the second group up to the level of those who had been through the thirty-day Puerto Rico transfiguration.

The "outward-bound" emphasis of the Puerto Rico program featured rock climbing, survival swimming, overnight compass hikes, and other ordeals purportedly designed to extend the individual's awareness of his personal capabilities. However, I know of no evidence, published or otherwise, psychological or otherwise, which would indicate that this type of training extends the individual's awareness of *other* people, and of *their* sensibilities, problems, and capabilities. There is no evidence to indicate that this type of training enhances the individual's ability to adjust to a strange culture, or to empathize with a person whose value systems are at great variance with his own.

Fragmentary evidence from our experience in training the Philippines Three group suggests that the jungle camp experience tends to produce in the trainee an inappropriate sense of confidence. Such confidence, verging on arrogance, is exactly the opposite of the humility which, in my opinion, should be the hallmark of the good PCV. Since there has apparently been no systematic research to see whether Puerto Rico products achieve a significantly better or worse cultural adjustment, however, my opinion must remain simply an opinion. In any case, it would seem that this opinion is shared by General Carlos Romulo, who addressed our first group of trainees. This eminent Filipino, who understands America well, cautioned his listeners that the greatest hazards they faced lay in the social and interpersonal domain and not in the rigors of the physical environment. It would appear that rock climbing and endurance swimming are at best irrelevant to the trying demands of Peace Corps service and at worst productive of a sense of confidence inappropriate to the trainees' lack of understanding of the difficulties ahead.*

Philippine Studies

This component was based on the principle that the two main duties of a Volunteer are to *learn* and to *serve*. Learning, we em-

* As this book was going to press in August 1965, I learned that the "outward-bound" emphasis at the camp in Puerto Rico had been reduced considerably, and that new policies call for fewer trainees to be exposed to such physical trials. Nonetheless, this section has been allowed to stand as Professor Guthrie wrote it, not only because it is of historical interest but also because, at very high levels within Peace Corps/Washington, belief in the validity of the "outward-bound" approach is far from dead.—Ed.

phasized, must normally precede serving. We strove to inculcate more than a mere hollow respect for Filipino values; we wanted the Volunteers to understand and appreciate these values. Only as the Volunteer was able to see the world approximately as the Filipino saw it, would he be able to contribute in a truly effective, efficient manner. Goodwill was necessary, but of itself not sufficient. And the same was true of service motivation, of unselfishness, and of initiative. The trainees were thus offered instruction both on the content of Philippine culture, and on methods by which they could continue, on their own, to increase their understanding of the local culture while serving day by day in the field.

To supplement the content of Philippine culture presented by Penn State faculty, we invited to our campus a wide variety of recognized experts on the Philippines, to offer one, two, or more days of lectures and discussions. These included cultural anthropologists, sociologists, geographers, political scientists, economists, and others. These same lecturers dealt with problems of learning on the job. Emphasis was placed on sensitivity and empathy, and above all, on *patience*. One lecturer enjoined the trainees to "keep your mouths shut and your eyes and ears open for at least the first few months." Trainees were also encouraged to select some phase of Philippine life—perhaps music, agriculture, law, or religion—to be investigated during leisure hours as a personal project. This, we felt, would give clear evidence to the Filipinos of the Volunteer's interest in Philippine ways, provide an outlet for leisure energy, and sustain the Volunteer in adverse moments.

In the selection of material for this phase of training we were influenced greatly by the difficulties manifested by many Americans who have been sent to the Philippines. The unfailing hospitality and deference of the Filipinos, coupled with the facts that many of them can express themselves in English and show understanding of some Western values, often lead the American to feel at ease and to assume that he can function much as he would in the United States. What the American fails to realize, however, is that this cultural similarity is usually quite superficial. For in spite of long Spanish and American rule, the Filipinos have preserved much of their own culture. This is exemplified by the fact that, although English has been used exclusively in the schools for half a century, the language of home and family life remains Philippine. The result of this superficial cultural similarity is that most Americans experience a sense of confusion, perplexity, and annoyance. Faulty communication both ways begins to accumulate, and the American is frustrated in his efforts to make money, administer technical aid, gain converts, or whatever. This frustration often leads to symptoms of "culture shock." When such frustration is delayed, and endures over a longer period, a more appropriate term might be "culture fatigue" (Guthrie 1963).

It was clear from the outset that Volunteers could not escape culture shock or culture fatigue by living in a guarded compound. We at Penn State sought to prepare them to understand as much as possible of the frame of reference of the Filipino and to teach them methods of increasing this understanding from day to day while in the field. The parallels between learning to cope with a new language and learning to cope with the totality of a new culture are quite apparent. Our strategy therefore was to teach as much as possible of Philippine interpersonal patterns, value systems, family structure, social organization and areas of special sensitivity. This was augmented when possible with material on Philippine poetry, music, crafts, and dances. Our approach was based on the premise that the more the Volunteer knew about the society, the more effectively and happily he could function in it.

As will become clear in the next chapter, this emphasis on learning and serving was not entirely successful. It is no easy task to communicate what one considers to be relative truth and wisdom to an activist, egalitarian group of trainees, aching for field experience and the adventure of immediate personal involvement.

INTO THE FIELD

The field situation will be described in detail by Szanton in the next chapter. My comments will be confined to certain salient problems where the evidence is overwhelmingly clear even to someone whose opportunities for direct observation have been limited.*

* I spent two weeks in the Philippines in June 1963, as Groups One and Two were finishing their tours. I was serving as a representative of Study Fellowships for International Development, a program supported by the Ford Foundation. My purpose was to interview Volunteers (and others who had done similar work overseas) who desired financial support for advanced professional training that might lead to further work in technical assistance to developing nations. My interviews afforded an opportunity to explore particular Volunteers' field experiences in considerable depth. Counting both formal interviews and informal conversations, I had the opportunity to talk at length with as many as one quarter of the PCVs from each of the four groups trained at Penn State. This interviewing trip also took me to Thailand, Malaysia, India, and Pakistan. I was thus enabled to gain some comparative perspective.

In addition to field interviewing, my information about field conditions in

The staff to direct the Peace Corps effort in the Philippines was selected about the time our training program began in the summer of 1961. It consisted of two political scientists, a sociologist, a high school teacher who had worked in an industrial personnel program, and a graduate student in Chinese and Far Eastern history. All five men were intelligent, socially skilled, and altruistic. All had achieved success in their own culture. None, however, knew much about the Philippines. Only one had ever been there before, and he had gone as a serviceman, which is not normally a very effective way to learn about an alien culture. Nor had any of the five ever had significant experience in any other non-Western milieu. In short, they were about as innocent of knowledge of the Philippines as the Volunteers whom they had been hired to guide and lead. Yet no arrangement was made for them to learn about the Philippines with Volunteers or through other means. The inclusion of one person on the staff with some depth of understanding of Philippine society could have reduced some of the numerous difficulties that plagued both the in-country training and the subsequent placement of the Volunteers.*

The first group of 128 Corpsmen arrived in Manila in no mood for further preparation. After a stressful training period in which too many visitors from Peace Corps/Washington talked about selection, they had been sent on home leave from Penn State without being told whether they had been accepted or not. Security clearances were not complete for everyone, so all had to wait for two weeks for a telegram telling them whether or not to proceed to the west coast. Arriving in the Philippines, they were given a somewhat prolonged in-country training under conditions that suffered from a staff shortage and staff unfamiliarity with things Philippine. Frustration mounted as eager young Volunteers complained that they had now been in the Peace Corps for four months without yet "doing anything."

Then Group One moved off to field assignments. Again misunderstanding took over. The Representative staff were too few in

---

the Philippines comes from extensive correspondence with about a dozen volunteers in the field, and lengthy discussions with several dozen ex-Volunteers after their return to the United States.—G.M.G.

* While serving on the Peace Corps/Washington staff in 1961, I prepared for the Talent Search a long list of names of Americans with depth experience in the Philippines. Five of these were invited to Washington for interviews. All five indicated a willingness to drop all other activities immediately—at great personal inconvenience—and go to the Philippines for at least a few months to help get the program started. None was selected.—Ed.

number, too harassed by recurring administrative crises, and too in-experienced in Philippine ways to be able to help Volunteers de-velop realistic goals and then to choose methods of pursuing those goals that had much chance of success. The schools were not pre-pared for the Volunteers. Local teachers did not know how to use them. Too often, no one had the time or experience to bring Volun-teers and teachers together and work out patterns of cooperation that would be understood and accepted by all concerned. Left to their own devices, many Volunteers persevered and achieved a satis-fying role in the schools. A few found only a limited area of service.

The Problem of the Ambiguous Role

The problem of "the role" was a central one from the very begin-ning. One could agree that it was a good thing to teach English and basic science to Filipino children. One could also agree that the Volunteer role had to be structured in such a way as not to usurp, or seem to usurp, jobs from Filipino teachers in an already over-crowded teachers' employment market. But it is difficult to agree that it was therefore necessary that the role of "educational aide" remain virtually without definition. And yet this was the situation that con-fronted the first Representative when he reached Manila in August 1961. In the early negotiations between the Peace Corps and the Philippine Bureau of Public Schools there was somewhere, some-how, a gap in communication that never was bridged. The Volun-teer was, in effect, told to define his own role. This would be a difficult enough problem even in his own familiar cultural setting—say, in an elementary school in Iowa—and all the more so because only a minority of the Volunteers had ever taught school before. But it was a vastly more difficult problem in an alien cultural setting where the Volunteer knew neither the local situation, psychological sensibilities, nor cultural cues. With few precedents or models, and with only a limited understanding of elementary schools, particu-larly Philippine elementary schools, many Volunteers felt frustrated and ineffective. They longed to be asked to do something which would make them feel worthwhile. The Philippine schools did not have a defined position for them, nor did the Philippine com-munity. For this reason, although the needs were great, the oppor-tunities were limited. The inherent ambiguity of living in an alien society was compounded by this peculiar and unnecessary difficulty of working out a role that was meaningful to both the Volunteer and the Filipino school teachers.

Four observations should be made at this point. First, anyone who knows Filipinos realizes that they will be most reluctant to tell a stranger, particularly an American, what to do. Second, just having a prestigious stranger in the community is enough; there is little need to put him to work. It is more important that he be happy than busy. Third, it is not customary for Filipinos to spell out programs in explicit detail. They prefer a certain vagueness which leaves room for improvisation and shift if stresses reach the point of discomfort. Finally, PCVs in other countries seem to have experienced the least difficulties in adjustment where they have filled well-defined roles in society, such as that of teacher in a residential school established by a former colonial power. The Philippines program was probably one of the most hazardous in that it set about to establish a new, and accordingly unfamiliar, job role in an ongoing system of public schools. Because this role often produced the very opposite of job satisfaction, it tended to push the PCV out of the school and into the community in quest of emotionally rewarding tasks. Here, outside the school, some Volunteers found satisfaction and some did not. Regardless of level of satisfaction, however, it seems clear that the PCVs' degree of emotional involvement with the community has been greater in the Philippines than in many other countries. Certainly, as Cowan points out (page 160), it has been greater than in many ex-colonial countries of Africa where the Volunteer teachers at boarding schools often live restricted lives in expatriate enclaves secluded from the general community of Africans.

The "Gung-Ho" Syndrome

The problem of "the role" thus encouraged many PCVs to be somewhat more "gung ho" in their attempts to bring about community change than would probably otherwise have been the case. Another factor pushing them in this direction was the Representative staff, some of whom were at least as "gung ho" as the more activist Volunteers. Lacking previous transcultural experience themselves, these administrators tended to encourage quick and deep plunges into community affairs, instead of a more patient, gradual approach. The staff tended to be activist, egalitarian, and impatient —at just the time when they should have been counseling their charges to apply the brakes to such impulses.

More than one Representative repeatedly urged the Volunteers to "be perfectly frank" in discussions with Filipinos. What they failed to realize is the Filipinos just don't behave this way. While the "little white lie" and the act of tact are important to good interpersonal relationships in American culture, they are utterly vital in Philippine culture. Philippine social interaction is, to an impressive degree, based on what the Volunteers later came to call "SIR," or "smooth interpersonal relationships." Under such conditions, "Just be perfectly frank," however pleasing it might have been to the American individual, was a devastating bit of advice. It flew directly in the face of what is well known to virtually all social scientists who have ever studied the Philippines seriously. Among the leading American scholars of Philippine culture, for example, is Dr. Frank Lynch, S.J., who comments on "SIR" as follows: "For the American newly arrived in the Philippines, the most striking quality manifested by Filipinos is their pleasantness, and among Filipinos getting their first full taste of American ways, a recurrent complaint is that Americans are often 'brutally frank.' These reactions are traceable to a clear intercultural difference, for smoothness of interpersonal relations (or SIR), while valued in both societies, is considered relatively more important by Filipinos than by Americans." (Lynch 1962, 107).

The Volunteer was also under pressure from another source: Washington. The headquarters staff were intelligent, dedicated, hard-driving men who had their own notions of what a Volunteer should be and do. These notions were derived partly from American cultural experience, and partly from AID experience overseas. Although most of these officials had virtually no understanding of Philippine needs or traditions, they emphasized action, impact, and results that they could see, touch, and quantify. Very few could truly appreciate the tedium, the frustration, and the built-in limitations of the Volunteer's field situation. Their contacts with the Volunteers usually consisted of whirlwind trips to overseas operations, often to countries where they had never been before. These ten-countries-in-twenty-days affairs were more a tribute to the efficiency of travel agents than a contribution to the staff man's knowledge of the local situation. Several staffers came to Penn State to address our trainees after such trips and discovered that they could tell all they had learned, and answer all the questions they evoked, in a remarkably short period of time—as little as twenty minutes. (The trainees quickly perceived how little of value these speakers were able to contribute, and often made their feelings quite visible.) With such a lack of contact with overseas reality, it is no wonder that the Washington officials developed wild pictures of the ideal Volunteer: a sort of combination of Paul Bunyan, Astor, and Schweitzer all in one package.

In this same spirit a newsletter, *The Volunteer*, was published in

Washington and sent to every Volunteer overseas. This magazine was designed to help PCVs feel some sense of community with their colleagues in other countries. Each issue dealt in depth with one country program, singling out and magnifying significant accomplishments of particular Volunteers. This had the unintended effect of making many of the more modest and insightful Corpsmen in the Philippines feel inferior and even guilty. In one area they dubbed the publication, "Superman," and made up stories of fantastic accomplishments that outdid those they read about.

Groups Two, Three, and Four were each one third as large as the first contingent. Administratively, this was a blessing for all concerned. While formal liaison between the field operation and the training site at Penn State was largely lacking, some feedback was received, and in this way it was possible to avoid repeating some of our early mistakes. In-country training likewise benefited, particularly because new Volunteers were assigned to live with old Volunteers for periods of a week or two. As more Philippine officials and more Volunteers came to participate in discussions and decisions, there was an improvement in the placement and utilization of the Volunteers, and indeed, in the entire operation.

THE NATURE OF THE "HELPING RELATIONSHIP"

The evidence indicates that many of our Volunteers adopted a kind of "helping relationship" vis-à-vis members of the local Philippine community in which they resided. As a psychologist, I am struck with the parallels between this relationship and that which grows up between the psychotherapist and patient in our own culture. Both types of helping relationship can easily become extremely complex and deeply disturbing to the emotional poise of both helper and helped. To help another person, one must become involved with him in order to grasp something of his own view of his predicament. One must show deep interest and establish enough empathy so that the person being helped can feel that he is understood.

As the patient struggles with his problems, he may come to resent, envy, or doubt the therapist, who may in turn become impatient, angry, or discouraged in reaction to the patient's lack of progress and apparent unwillingness or inability to use the help that has been offered. In addition, the psychotherapist brings his own hopes, fears, misgivings, and frustrations to the therapeutic situation. There is a continuing danger that he will seek to satisfy his own needs through the actions of his patient, that he will try to make the patient over in his own image.

There are at least five conditions that must be present for effective treatment to take place. The therapist must have a deep understanding of his own motives; he must have a considerable understanding of the strengths and weaknesses of his patient and a belief that the patient has the capacity to improve; he needs to have other sources of satisfaction and emotional security in addition to those which he draws from his work with his patient; he must be aware of the dangers of becoming too deeply involved in the patient's problems; and he must have someone to whom he can turn and discuss his involvement and his possible errors in treatment technique. The difficulties of helping relationships and possible techniques by which these difficulties can be reduced are very much the same in any kind of serving, helping activity.

The opportunity to help is one of the strongest appeals of the Peace Corps, and properly so. At the same time, it is one of the greatest perils. Indeed, the Volunteer's helping relationship is in some ways *more* difficult than the psychotherapist's. The latter usually enjoys the advantage that his patient has come to him and *requested* help. By contrast, the Peace Corps Volunteer is dealing with school teachers who usually have *not* asked for his help; the asking was done for them by officials often far removed from or even unknown to them. Indeed, many Philippine school teachers do *not* feel that they need help. And when they do feel a need, this need is not always the one that the Volunteer wants to fill or is equipped to fill. If the Volunteer moves into his community with preconceived notions that his help is wanted, and with preconceived notions as to specifically what kind of help is wanted and needed, he usually meets trouble. As he attempts to get people to change in ways that he has predetermined as being best, he meets with rebuff and disappointment. Often, he redoubles his efforts, only to meet with more discouragement. At this point begins a cumulative process that is limited only by the stamina of the helper and the patience of the villagers.

Clearly, the Volunteer, as cultural helper, has needs that are parallel to those of the psychotherapeutic helper. The Volunteer must understand his own motives. He needs to have a deep understanding of the social processes of the people with whom he is working and a sympathetic belief in them. He cannot risk his whole feeling of personal worth on the success or failure of his helping activities. He needs to have a number of sources of satisfaction so that his feelings of worth are not tied solely to his immediate project. And above all, he needs to be able to discuss himself and his work with a person—ideally, one of his Representatives—deeply experienced with Volunteers, teachers, villagers, and the cultural milieu of the Philippines. As with the one-to-one helping relationship, a failure on any one of these five requirements endangers the entire relationship.

CONCLUSIONS

Training, both formal and informal, should continue throughout a Volunteer's entire period of service. The Peace Corps should place increased emphasis on providing opportunities for the Volunteer to continue learning on his own while in the field. This emphasis should include continued self-study of the language by daily drill, in-service seminars on the local culture as it relates to the Volunteer, and independent reading about the host country.

Sending staff abroad who are unfamiliar with the culture of their area of assignment is, in my judgment, unwise. The staff turnover in the Philippines has been relatively much higher than that of Volunteers, and their effectiveness has been reduced because they have had too little time or opportunity to understand Filipinos. For the same reason they have not been able to develop as useful suggestions for training programs as should have been the case.

The urge to make an observable contribution is understandable. But in the last analysis, the Volunteer's greatest accomplishment is to make himself unnecessary. More thought should be directed to the problem of resolving what appears to be a conflict of interests between the Volunteer's desire to do something and the local nationals' needs to build their own society.

Assessment of the Volunteers' collective impact on Philippine education, and on local communities, is a complex matter. Peace Corps/ Washington is currently underwriting an elaborate and fascinating research project on this subject by two anthropologists and a large staff, and hopefully the results will be available before too long (Lynch and Maretzki). Be that as it may, it is already clear that the Peace Corps experience has had a profound effect on many Volunteers, changing both their view of the world and their view of themselves. Approximately one half who have returned have sought further education. This is a direct product of their experience, since few had considered graduate school before they joined. Their changes of goals have often been in the direction of social service and teaching. The same urges to achieve an immediate social impact that characterized their Peace Corps experience influence their professional plans on their return. They do not enjoy discipline-oriented

American university programs, but rather look for interdisciplinary, problem-oriented approaches. In a broader sense, many of the day-to-day concerns of their peers seem trivial. The problems of peace and human dignity are more insistent. They feel something of the same impatience toward American shortcomings that they felt toward the country in which they served. The experience has done more to raise nagging questions than it has to provide satisfying answers. The Philippine barrio can assimilate the Volunteer's contribution without too much disruption of its ancient tranquility, but the Volunteer has taken from the barrio an experience that has destroyed much of his complacency and will not permit him to go on as before.

BIBLIOGRAPHY

CARROLL, JOHN J.
 1965 *The Filipino Marketing Entrepeneur: Agent and Product of Change.* Ithaca, N.Y.: Cornell University Press.
ESPIRITU, SOCCORO C., and CHESTER L. HUNT
 1964 *Social Foundations of Community Development: Readings on the Philippines.* Manila: R. M. Garcia.
GOLAY, FRANK H.
 1960 *The Philippines: Public Policy and National Economic Development.* Ithaca, N.Y.: Cornell University Press.
GUTHRIE, GEORGE M.
 1963 "Preparing Americans for Participation in Another Culture." Paper presented to the conference on "Peace Corps and the Behavioral Sciences," Washington, D.C.: March 4-5, 1963.
GUTHRIE, GEORGE M., and MARGARET S. McKENDRY
 1963 "Interest Patterns of Peace Corps Volunteers in a Teaching Project." *Journal of Educational Psychology.* Vol. 54, pp. 261-267.
 1964 "Predicting Performance in a New Culture." Paper presented at the annual meeting of the American Psychological Association, Los Angeles.
HOLLNSTEINER, MARY R.
 1961 *The Dynamics of Power in a Philippine Municipality.* Abstract Series No. 7, Community Development Research Council, University of the Philippines, Quezon City.
HUKE, ROBERT E.
 1963 *Shadows on the Land: An Economic Geography of the Philippines.* Manila: Bookmark.
HUNT, CHESTER L., et al.
 1963 *Sociology in the Philippine Setting.* Quezon City, Philippines: Phoenix.
LYNCH, FRANK, S.J.
 1964 "Lowland Philippine Values: Social Acceptance," in Frank Lynch, ed., *Four Readings on Philippine Values.* Institute of

Philippine Culture Papers, No. 2. Quezon City, Philippines: Ateneo de Manila Press.

LYNCH, FRANK, and THOMAS W. MARETZKI
Book now in preparation on the impact of Volunteers in Philippines One through Nine. Further information can be obtained from Dr. Frank Lynch, Institute of Philippine Culture, Ateneo de Manila (P.O. Box 154, Manila) or from Dr. Thomas W. Maretzki, Department of Anthropology, University of Hawaii (Honolulu, Hawaii 96882).

3

Cultural Confrontation in the Philippines

DAVID L. SZANTON *received his bachelor's degree* cum
laude *from Harvard College in 1960, with a major in anthropology. After a
year in Italy studying sculpture, he became a Peace Corps Volunteer in
the Philippines Two contingent. He spent nine months as a Volunteer
"educational aide" in a rural Philippine elementary school, after which he
was made a Volunteer Leader, with responsibility for a large number of
Volunteers spread over the Western Visayan islands. Upon completion of
his tour with the Peace Corps he received a Study Fellowship in International Development, which permitted him to earn a master's degree in
Social Science at the University of Chicago. He is presently continuing his
studies at Chicago for the doctorate in anthropology, financed by a National Defense Education Act fellowship. Mr. Szanton contemplates future
work in action programs involving social and economic development in
Southeast Asia. His publications include "Art in Sulu: A Survey," in*
Philippine Studies, *Vol. 2, No. 3 (1963), a report based on considerable
island-hopping fieldwork in the Sulu Archipelago.*

As a member of Philippines Two, I attended training at Pennsylvania State University from October to December 1961.
The description and analysis in this chapter apply primarily to
members of my own group, secondarily to members of the Philippines One group, and only passingly to subsequent contingents. My
statements are based on my experiences as a Volunteer educational
aide in a small rural school on the island of Panay, and later as a
Volunteer Leader acting as a communication and support link for
eighty-five Volunteers scattered about the Western Visayan islands.
This chapter was prepared in first draft quite independently of the
Guthrie chapter. The fact that the two of us have reached conclusions that are closely consistent will, I hope, be of some reassurance
to the reader.

As Guthrie has pointed out, the Penn State staff was aware of the
misunderstandings and conflicts that had often undone Americans
in the Philippines and accordingly designed their training program

so as to avoid repetition of these mistakes. The Volunteers were therefore encouraged to search for Philippine meanings, and to regard their overseas service as a *learning* experience. Their role model was to be not the traditional American missionary or government official but the applied cultural anthropologist, who is typically concerned with *understanding* the local culture before he attempts to help the local people change that culture. Such understanding, we were told, was normally attained only in conjunction with the development of an *appreciation* for certain features or aspects of the local culture. Accordingly, in lecture after lecture—both from Penn State staff members and outside experts— the trainees were urged to develop a "window" on the culture by making a sort of hobby out of the study of a selected aspect of the local Philippine tradition, such as music, marketing, child raising, rice cultivation, or some similar subject of interest.

REACTIONS TO TRAINING

Despite Penn State's earnest efforts, it must be reported as a simple historical fact that most of the trainees in Philippines Two were profoundly dissatisfied with the training program. Activist in concern, intent on "doing something significant," the Volunteers were repelled by Penn State's constant emphasis on "learning while serving." Instead of a green light and concentration on specific, concrete job techniques, the Penn State faculty flashed a yellow caution light, warning the trainees of the culturally lodged obstacles and frustrations they would encounter.

Most Volunteers in Philippines Two seemed committed to a kind of primitive egalitarianism which in effect insisted that since all men should properly be regarded as equal, therefore all men should properly be regarded as the same. The trainees were likewise committed to the Philippines as a country; their advance stereotypes of the Philippines were almost invariably favorable. All things Philippine were to be admired and respected, and Filipinos were regarded as being only superficially different from Americans. Thus when social scientists lectured to the trainees and presented analyses of values and motives in Philippine behavior that they did not recognize in their own behavior, the trainees rejected these lectures as implausible or irrelevant, and the lecturers as cold, callous, and unfeeling.

Unfortunately, the few Filipino members of the training staff were not as helpful as one might suppose. It is true that they did manage to convey to the trainees certain characteristically Philippine behavior patterns. This was achieved largely through their general manner and bearing, rather than by means of systematic, objective group discussions. A major problem was that most of them were from somewhat Westernized urban backgrounds and were hence often unaware of, or psychologically resistant to, behavior characteristics of the *rural* areas where the Volunteers were to be assigned. One particularly charming Filipina—with whom the male trainees almost invariably sympathized—by her pained expressions and subsequent private comments, protested many lecturers' observations about life in the less acculturated Philippine barrios. These observations concerned such practices as breast feeding in public, young Philippine men showing friendship by walking hand in hand, or the fact that some Philippine families have sometimes been known to pursue political ambitions behind the veil of a seemingly social invitation. Our own later experience in the rural Philippines eventually convinced us that these observations were indeed accurate—but most of us simply could not accept them during training.

In many respects, the Volunteers' negative experiences during training presaged similar negative experiences during the first year or so in the field. Their activism, their impatience, and their primitive egalitarianism died hard, even under field conditions. Not having adequately adjusted their expectations and aspirations during training, they found that their early experiences in the field directly conflicted with their preconceived attitudes and assumptions. Rather than accept this new information and experience, learn from it, and alter accordingly their accustomed patterns of thought and judgment, many PCVs deperately rejected it, remaining essentially culture-blind for months after arrival in the Philippines, much to their own detriment.

THE PHILIPPINE SCHOOL AND COMMUNITY

Philippine hospitality more than lived up to its advance notices. People in the communities to which we were assigned all but overwhelmed us with welcoming parties and dinners—often leaving us longing for a little peace and privacy. Although there were some supply and administrative problems, our first weeks were generally filled with excitement, goodwill, and novel experiences.

Getting Ourselves Off the Pedestal

It was immediately evident that there were serious differences between the Volunteers' and the Filipinos' conceptions of who we were and what we were to do. Part of the problem lay in the fact that our role of "educational aide" was poorly defined, as Guthrie has already pointed out (page 27). But even if we had had a better defined role, the Filipinos would still have tended to perceive and treat us like other Americans previously resident in the rural areas: missionaries, administrators, teachers, and supervisors. Almost inevitably, the high status accorded these individuals was transferred to us, sight unseen. This is readily understandable since we were, after all, teachers of some sort and might be presumed to be experts—and therefore, in effect, supervisors. To be sure, the Peace Corps Representative staff and Philippine educational officials had attempted to counteract this notion by holding orientation sessions, whenever possible, at each school to which a PCV was to be stationed. They explained that the Volunteers were merely teachers' assistants, who would try to live and work as regular members of the community. But this the Filipinos found almost impossible to believe: Americans, they knew, were accustomed to an easy and luxurious style of living. "What is your mission?" and "Why do you want to live with us?" they asked. "In order to work in the schools" seemed an inadequate and implausible motive. More than a few local people, at least at first, suspected that the Volunteers' real task was to report on local Communist activities, or perhaps to prepare the country for purchase and eventual (American) statehood!

An American, a "personal representative" of President Kennedy at that, living happily without electricity or running water, in a bamboo house with a nipa thatch roof, was extremely difficult to imagine—and the selection of local housing often brought the issue to a head. The Peace Corps staff were seeking simple accommodations comparable to those of the local Filipino teachers, but the local authorities would feel obliged to offer one of the largest and most modern buildings in the entire community! Housing negotiations were usually entered upon with goodwill and positive concern for the other party, but both sides often emerged somewhat shaken and dismayed. They were working with different sets of expectations and tended to talk past each other, although eventually appropriate housing was usually somehow found.

Thus, despite the school orientation meetings and housing negotiations, we found ourselves perched uncomfortably on high status pedestals. While we did not realize it, and perhaps many Filipinos were not consciously aware of it, these pedestals did serve certain social functions. They placed us in the usual American-in-the-Philippines status position, one which the Filipinos found familiar and manageable. The pedestal also kept us visible, and therefore perhaps somewhat less of a threat. Finally, it kept us apart from the daily events of the community, some of which the local people perhaps thought best kept to themselves. And anyway, most local people could hardly believe that the PCVs would want to share in such mundane, humdrum matters. Needless to add, the Volunteers' egalitarian values were seriously challenged by all of this "pedestal" treatment. Like the PCVs in Peru later described by Doughty (page 227), they immediately started searching for ways of climbing down from that position and establishing themselves as "mere" human beings.

The Volunteer's Role in the School

In taking up their positions as "educational aides," the Volunteers accepted the necessity of simply sitting in on classes, as observers, for a while. The actual length of this observation period ranged from one week to several months, during which time the PCV would sit in the back of the classroom—doubtless in some cases inadvertently succeeding in unnerving the Filipino teacher. For some of the PCVs, the observation period quickly bore fruit, in the form of elaborately scheduled plans for their in-school activities. Others made suggestions for in-service training programs in which they would attempt to upgrade the teaching methods of their Philippine colleagues—suggestions that all too often proved irrelevant to the teachers' real concern. Other PCVs reacted with confusion and despair, as they began to realize the immense and inherent difficulty of altering established teaching patterns. Throughout this travail, the Volunteers received little help or practical guidance from members of the Representative staff. Though most of the staff were trained social scientists, they unfortunately lacked both experience in the Philippines and in elementary education. The most concrete advice they could offer was, "Be creative."

Thus isolated and left to their own devices, the Volunteers responded by a wide variety of stratagems, which ranged all the way from trial-and-error groping (based on their own dimly recalled elementary education) to genuine creativity. Not many of these initial attempts produced the hoped-for results, however, due to a lack both of technical skill and of consistency in application. Some PCVs demonstrated new teaching techniques in regular classes or in special sessions for groups of teachers. Others did "team teaching," sharing a class with a regular teacher. Still others built simple demonstration equipment for science lessons, or assisted with lesson plans for unfamiliar units. Sometimes the PCV would teach a whole unit while Filipino teachers observed; or sometimes he would encourage or organize the Filipino teachers to demonstrate their best lessons to their colleagues. In order to relate science classes to daily life, Volunteers took the children to airports, ice factories, beaches, and rice fields. Specially talented Volunteers occasionally taught classes outside their regular fields of science and English, most often in music, art, or physical education. Volunteers developed library programs, curriculum guides, and in-service training programs; they wrote and directed children's plays; they coached exceptional or retarded students during recesses and after classes. Few Volunteers held exclusively to one approach. Most worked with several, at different times and with different Filipino teachers.

What lasting, constructive results did all this activity produce? It is of course too early to say, and even if it were not, a great amount of careful research will first be necessary before anyone can state with confidence what the Volunteers' impact on the rural Philippine elementary schools has been. One thing, however, is certain: the immediate impact was smaller than most PCVs and staff members had at first hoped or expected. The culture of the Philippines, or the subculture of its school system, could hardly be expected to change in any regular and permanent way as a result of scattered innovative projects on the part of a relatively small group of Volunteers, most of whom lacked training or experience in teaching. On the other hand, it is unquestionably true that the educational experience and intellectual horizons of some thousands of Filipino students and teachers were somewhat broadened by the temporary presence of a Volunteer in their midst.

Ironically, a PCV's professional inadequacies as a teacher, although they led to personal frustration, did at least help to produce one result that the PCV himself avidly sought: it helped to get him off his high pedestal. More precisely, we may speak of two pedestals, the social and the professional. Throughout his term in the Philippines, the typical PCV remained on a high social pedestal because of the mere fact that he was an American. He was also put on a high professional pedestal, *at first*. However, our Philippine teacher colleagues soon discovered that most of the PCVs practiced unfamiliar (and often fruitless) brands of pedagogy. The Volunteers' frequent and awkward attempts at introducing more "progressive" teaching techniques made little sense to the many older teachers whose training and experience had led them to rely heavily on rote memorization techniques. As a result these Volunteers were usually viewed as amateurish by the Filipinos, and the process of professional "de-pedestalization" began. This process was normally so subtle that I suspect few Volunteers were aware of it at the time. Filipino teachers remained polite at all times, rarely offered criticisms or suggestions to the Volunteer, for fear of shaming or embarrassing him, and thus preserved "smooth interpersonal relations" (pages 28 and 43). And yet, behind his back private gossip circulated. Generally speaking, prestige in Philippine educational circles is accorded to those teachers who are recognized as being superior at the art of teaching. And, since the Philippines is a former colonial dependency of the United States, it is not surprising that the criteria of excellence used are not too dissimilar to those found in the United States. By these criteria probably only a minority of the Volunteers in the first and second groups were judged by their Philippine colleagues to be effective teachers. A privately circulated survey revealed that Volunteers in Philippines Three were also, by and large, not considered by the Filipinos to be very effective in the classroom—with, of course, outstanding exceptions.

Community Involvement

In some cases spurred by discussions of local problems, in others by considerable frustration in the classroom, many PCVs sought to make contributions and gain gratification outside the school, in various sorts of "community development" projects. Here, their "de-pedestalization" in a professional sense was no particular handicap, and the fact that they remained high in general social prestige was a definite asset. An added asset was the interested, friendly, outgoing personal manner of most Volunteers. This style of interpersonal approach is greatly valued in Philippine culture—and doubly so when it comes from a relatively high-status Westerner who doesn't really "need" to go out of his way to be friendly—but does so anyway.

The Volunteers' participation in community activities can be classified into three categories or approaches. The first, and mildest, merely involved lending his or her prestige to some local organization, perhaps giving a brief speech or, better yet, singing a song at a community development or 4-H gathering. The second approach called for actual participation in an ongoing local program, such as aiding in a privy-building campaign or in the establishment of a community center. The third, and most questionable, approach was to unilaterally initiate a project that the PCV presumed to be useful to the community—such as a lending library, a demonstration garden, a pig or poultry farm, or an adult education class. Any of the three might yield success, but the third approach was generally least satisfactory because most PCVs necessarily had limited understanding of local problems, obstacles, and felt needs. At least one Volunteer established a relatively large poultry farm—but few of his Filipino neighbors seemed interested, and none followed his example. Others grew rice by the very best techniques—only to discover that the rent plus the cost of seed, fertilizers, insecticides, and pesticides equaled or surpassed the value of the crop! Few Filipinos followed these examples either. On the whole the first and second approaches were more appreciated, for they indicated the volunteer's willingness and concern to work together *with* his neighbors. In such cases, although "successes" might be small, they were at least relevant to the interests of the people. Moreover, the Filipinos seemed far more pleased when a Volunteer joined *them* in *their* projects, rather than relentlessly striking off on his own.

PROBLEMS OF CULTURAL CONFRONTATION

Differences in Values

Before a Volunteer can make a useful contribution to either the local school or the local community, he or she must be able to bridge the vast cultural gap that separates middle-class America from the rural Philippines. Bridging such a gap, it is important to realize, is *both* an intellectual *and* an emotional process. Unless a PCV is emotionally willing to discover important differences between his own culture and that of the Filipinos, he is unlikely to discover these differences on an intellectual level, or if he does discover them intellectually, he is unlikely to understand them fully and accurately. Confronting the cultural gap, I would argue, requires emotional readinesss as a *prerequisite* to accurate intellectual perceiving or cognizing of cultural differences. For in transcultural situations like these one's attitudes precondition one's perceptions and cognitions to a marked degree.

By the end of the training period at Penn State, most of the Volunteers were to some extent intellectually aware that the two cultures would prove different. They were also intellectually prepared to confront some of the more superficial differences between the two. They were not, however, intellectually prepared for the deep and pervasive differences between their culture and their hosts', in large part because they had not been emotionally willing to acccpt much of what their lecturers had had to say.

Upon arrival in the Philippines, however, the cultural confrontation could no longer be avoided. Suddenly, the enormous reality of Philippine-American cultural differences pressed in on the Volunteer from all sides. The sheer weight of this experience forced even the most recalcitrant, activist, egalitarian PCV to recognize at a deep emotional level that vast differences did indeed separate him from the Filipinos. But for most PCVs this early emotional awareness was gross and crude; and certainly did not immediately lead to *acceptance*, to the development of an ability to "live with" these cultural differences. In fact, it seems that it is only *after* one develops an attitude of acceptance that he has achieved the basis on which to build a reasonably accurate cognitive awareness of just *what* the relevant cultural differences are and how they pattern together. I should add, incidentally, that "acceptance," as I use the term, does not necessarily imply "agreement"; an American can learn to live with certain Philippine values without necessarily approving of them. He can simply regard them as different, but also valid and proper, ways of going about the business of living.

Examples of Philippine-American value differences which many Volunteers had difficulty learning to live with are readily at hand. The following seven points were all thoroughly covered in training lectures at Penn State, yet emotionally resisted by the majority of the trainees:

1. The PCV who is "perfectly frank" with a Filipino, who expresses criticism openly, does so at considerable risk. In the Philippines such behavior can lead to painful embarrassment, loss of face, and shame—indeed to a sudden and severe denial of the social support needed to maintain the individual's psychological equilibrium. The forthrightly frank American is likely to evoke a reaction of hostility, or even possibly violence.

2. A related fact is that the Filipinos place great stress on "Smooth Interpersonal Relations," or "SIR." They handle potential disagreements by ignoring them, by pretending that they do not exist, or by designating intermediaries to conduct negotiations between the parties involved. American directness and "sincerity" are hence quite out of place.

3. Filipinos develop long-lasting mutual assistance alliances based on reciprocal obligations, which often override personal consequences, and often "get in the way" of accomplishing specific technological or managerial tasks. Americans, by contrast, tend toward more short-range, impersonal, contractual, functionally specific relationships.

4. Open striving for power and prestige is socially acceptable (and expected) for individuals and families in the Philippines. Middle-class Americans tend to mask or deny their power drives.

5. The Philippine kinship system gives greater prominence to relatives whom Americans consider distant. A Filipino's efforts and savings are hence likely to be "drained off" to the benefit of these "distant" relatives, rather than devoted to economic and technological investments.

6. Deference to persons of higher status, including elderly people, is a much more pronounced feature of life in the Philippines than it is in egalitarian America.

7. On all socioeconomic levels, hospitality is extended to visitors far more elaborately and continuously than on comparable levels in America.

These seven generalizations are well known to virtually every social scientist who has studied lowland Christian Philippine society. If the PCVs of Philippines Two had been able to accept emotionally such points as these when presented by lecturers during training, their early adjustment in the field would have been much easier. This, however, was generally not the case. Indeed, as the Volunteers in the field painfully sought means of comprehending the unfamiliar Philippine behavior patterns that surrounded them, it was some of those who had most adamantly resisted the training lectures who now most bitterly condemned Penn State for not having more adequately prepared them!

Albert G. Bradford, by general consensus one of the most culturally sensitive members of the Philippines Two group, summarized the problem of value differences in a letter written to me after he had been in the Philippines two years (Bradford 1963):

> Do you remember when we first came here to N—, and went into the schools? I remember how quickly I discovered that people didn't understand me. The simplest things to me seemed not all familiar to them. I tried to explain, but the further I got into an explanation, the sillier I looked; suddenly I felt undermined; the most basic premises, values and understandings were of no help to me with the people here when I first faced them, for these understandings and ways of doing and seeing things just didn't *exist* even. There was a big gap.
>
> This gap is a crucial thing. What choices do I have when I see that the most basic things I act on and am comforted by are not understood in the least by someone else I am working or living with? When that queasy feeling of groping and groping uselessly, desperately for a bridge, some tie, something which will make us less separate, will make us feel

recognized by the other, begins to make me tremble and feel utterly sealed away from the other, what do I do?

Since Penn State did not provide language instruction to members of the first four Philippines contingents, Volunteers' early attempts to bridge the cultural gap necessarily involved exclusive reliance on English as the medium of communication. After forty-odd years of American tutelage, English had become by far the most widely spoken Western language in the Philippines and had assumed something of the function of a lingua franca throughout the archipelago. However, as one might expect, the "Filipino English" spoken by the majority of educationally less privileged Filipinos was a far cry from American English. The difficulty was not just that Filipino English was different in matters of pronunciation, syntax, and grammar. More importantly, it was also different at the semantic level, for Filipino English assigns to common English words and expressions new meanings derived from local linguistic and cultural usages. Linguistic and communications problems thus mirrored the broader problems of intercultural communication that plagued the PCVs' dealings with the Filipinos from dawn till dark. For example, a Volunteer might offer an English-speaking Filipino a soft drink. The latter would *decline* initially by saying "Thank you" in a tone which to the American implied acceptance. The Volunteer would then open the bottle and pour the drink for the Filipino. This time the Filipino would again refuse, saying, "No, No," possibly adding some vague excuse. If the Volunteer then took his guest at his word and drank the drink himself or set it aside muttering unkind words under his breath, he would again have misunderstood the situation. His guest probably really did want the drink. But the guest, sensitive to the need to maintain smooth interpersonal relations at all times and the need to be unobtrusive before a status superior, felt it to be impolite to accept an offer before it had been made several times. This type of encounter, leaving the Filipino embarrassed and the Volunteer frustrated and annoyed, might occur dozens of times before the Volunteer finally caught on.

The cultural confrontation also caused great frustration for the Volunteer in the classroom. One of his purposes was to try to improve his Philippine colleagues' teaching techniques. To do so, he often made suggestions as to how better to design a science experiment or how better to conduct English pattern drills. Much more often than not, he was chagrined to see that despite his best efforts the teacher simply did not alter her traditional approach to the subject. She might discuss and examine with him a particular, discrete practice, but seemed incapable of relating suggested innovations to the *general* body of ideas and values in which it was embedded. A better way of stating the problem is that in the PCV's perception the particular practice was enmeshed in a certain general body of ideas and values, but this was not necessarily so in the perception of the Philippine schoolteacher. Indeed, I would say that the degree to which a PCV learned to communicate to his Filipino co-teachers, clearly and understandably, the relationship between a particular practice and a general body of values and ideas could be taken as a fairly valid measure of the headway he had made in learning Philippine culture. Only when the PCV began to understand the integration and patterning of the seemingly strange customs and practices that he observed all around him could he begin to find ways of making his own ideas meaningful and sensible to his hosts. Only by learning the patterning of their ideas and values could he begin to communicate his own.

Unstructured Roles

As Guthrie has already suggested (page 27), the fact that the role of "educational aide" was an unprecedented, unstructured one made for real problems in the field. There was no yardstick to use as a measure of one's performance. There was no model to follow. Skills, circumstances, and relationships with Philippine teachers were so varied that even the most spectacular "successes" of neighboring Volunteers did not too often serve as useful models. Philippine teachers offered few guidelines and usually encouraged the PCVs to "do whatever you would like." Filipino supervisors were rarely seen; most were too busy, or else somewhat hesitant about personally directing the Americans. To make things worse, most of the PCVs were impatient for tangible results, for the "significant" contribution, and rapidly shifted from one approach to another, often before the first had been given an adequate trial. Discouraged by the vagueness and immensity of their assigned task of "improving English and science instruction," many came to doubt seriously their ability to contribute anything meaningful to the Philippine school system.

One PCV complained: "I have used up all my tricks and I no longer know what to do." Another felt as though he was "beating his head against a sponge-rubber wall." Some Volunteers concluded that the Peace Corps did not belong in the Philippines at all. A few actually resigned. Many proposed shifting to a more structured job, and several succeeded in getting temporarily reassigned to high school teaching jobs.

The problem of "the role" was summarized by a psychologist, Dr. Nicholas Hobbs, then of the Peace Corps/Washington staff, after visiting the Philippines (Hobbs 1962):

> The Volunteer in the Philippines has an extremely difficult role. It is very easy for an individual to fail, or to feel that he is failing when the outlines of his job are so tenuous, when there are no established standards for accomplishment. It is also possible for a person to be tremendously effective if he has the resources to be so. It is a situation in which the job does not carry the individual; rather, in the Philippines, every Volunteer, every day is faced with the task of deciding how that can be made a significant one. I suspect that we have no program that makes as great a demand on individual initiative, autonomy and self-appraisal as does the Philippines program.

PSYCHOLOGICAL REACTIONS

The cultural confrontation was an all-day, seven-day-a-week affair. Aside from a rare trip to the near-anonymity of Westernized Manila, it could not be avoided. Visits to other Volunteers or brief vacations to other parts of the country might help, but Philippine culture was always present and to be contended with, always making demands on the intellectual and emotional resources of the PCVs. With so many of their expectations shattered and so many of their values defied, the Volunteers spent much of their first year in the field directing their attention—often hostile attention—toward the three objects available for blaming: toward the Peace Corps for getting them into all of this; toward Philippine culture itself for presenting so many problems; and finally, inward toward themselves, for being inadequate to the situation.

Anti-Peace Corps Feelings

The Volunteers' simplest reaction to their frustration was to make bitterly hostile remarks against the Peace Corps staff. Feeling impotent in the midst of so many "obvious" economic, public health, and social welfare problems, Volunteers felt wasted by seemingly blind members of the Peace Corps/Washington staff, who had negotiated for Philippine acceptance of the "educational aide" project. (From the earliest days of the training program, feelings toward Peace Corps/Washington had been mixed because of rapidly changing policies and procedures, and because the members of the Washington staff who frequently visited Penn State seemed remarkably vague and ill-informed about the Philippines.) The same hostility was frequently directed toward members of the Representative staff, who, although not responsible for the original programing, nonetheless at least at first knew less about the Philippines, less about barrio schools, and less about village and small town life than did the Volunteers themselves. In the midst of the PCV's painful predicaments, he did not find it especially comforting to be reassured by a Representative staff member that he was in an "experimental" or "pioneering" group paving the way for others, or that in the "long run" many of his difficulties would gradually resolve themselves. To anticipate a phrase from the chapter by Maryanov that follows, not until they had been in the country for about a year did Philippines Two Volunteers have access to a single staff member who was qualified, by training and experience, to serve as an "intercultural mediator." Some of the anti-Peace Corps feeling did, then, have a basis in fact.

The Representative staff, largely composed of men with academic backgrounds, was unaccustomed to running a governmental bureaucratic operation, and in a foreign culture at that. It should therefore not be surprising that certain logistical and procedural problems were not always handled with the utmost efficiency and elegance at first. Mistakes were made and sometimes Volunteers suffered from them. However, frustrated Volunteers frequently magnified small errors on the part of the staff out of all proportion, making the staff a scapegoat for problems whose true origins lay elsewhere. One can almost say that, especially for a new Peace Corps program, an unwritten aspect of the Representative's role is that he must serve as a scapegoat for frustrated Volunteers!

Culture Fatigue

A second major complex of reactions, as Guthrie has already suggested, can be summed up by the term, "culture fatigue" (Guthrie 1963). This term refers to a phenomenon different from the "culture shock" experienced by many Americans immediately after they enter a new culture (Oberg 1955; Foster 1962; Lundstedt 1963). For most members of Philippines Two, "culture shock" was far less of a problem than "culture fatigue," which appears much more gradually. Culture fatigue is the physical and emotional exhaustion that almost invariably results from the infinite series of minute adjustments required for long-term survival in an alien culture. Living and working overseas generally requires that one must suspend his automatic evaluations and judgments; that he must supply new interpretations to seemingly familiar behavior; and that he must demand of himself constant alterations in the style and content of his activity. Whether this process is conscious or unconscious, successful or unsuccessful, it consumes an enormous amount of energy, leaving the individual decidedly *fatigued*. For Volunteers who learned of it, the term "culture fatigue" immediately struck home.

One interesting thing about the fatigue of many of the PCVs is that it so closely resembled the fatigue observed by Guthrie in the behavior of American business and governmental personnel in Manila. Interpersonal behavior of a traditional Philippine nature tended to be viewed in a negative light. Strong Philippine family ties came to be seen as "clannishness," personal sensitivity as "sulkiness," concern for reciprocity as "scheming," deference to age and status as "obsequiousness," ignoring disagreements and avoiding unpleasant subjects as "dishonesty," and lavish hospitality as "wastefulness" (Guthrie 1963).

One factor conducive to the development of culture fatigue was the Filipinos' apparent cultural similarity to Americans, derived from four decades of American domination, followed by some years in which American cultural influence has been stronger than that of any other outside nation. This similarity, however, is in fact quite superficial. I find it helpful to conceptualize Philippine culture as being something like an onion with various layers. The outer layer is American in cultural coloration, especially in large urban areas such as Manila. Underneath this layer is a Spanish Catholic layer, acquired during more than three hundred years of Spanish domination. The core of the onion, however, is distinctively Malaysian and non-Western. The PCV, especially when newly arrived, has difficulty determining where one layer ends and the next begins. Noting the surface similarity to his own culture, he is *doubly* disappointed when he finds that Philippine responses to his ideas and actions are not what he would expect in an American situation. He is thus doubly susceptible to the malady of culture fatigue. Had he been working instead in un-Westernized portions of rural Thailand, for example, his problem would be less serious because he would *expect* different, and even exotic, responses. In his chapter on Jamaica, Comitas explores this phenomenon of superficial cultural similarity in greater detail (page 213).

Culture fatigue was further abetted as the PCVs came to know more about the particular elements of American culture to which their Philippine opposite numbers seemed most attracted. Since the

Volunteers were bent upon producing "development," they naturally hoped, and expected, that their Filipino co-workers would share a similar ethic. While such Filipinos did indeed exist, they seemed altogether too difficult to find amidst the blare of transistor radios, rock 'n roll "twist" music, Elvis Presley movies, comic books, and other similar imported elements of American culture that enjoyed popularity among the Philippine students at the in-country training centers. The PCVs disparaged this tendency to import the most banal elements from American culture, and took to calling the result the Philippine "Coca-Cola Culture."

Another factor contributing to culture fatigue was what the PCVs quickly dubbed the Filipinos' "colonial mentality." The Volunteers felt that the Filipinos lacked self-respect and were cursed by a pervading sense of inferiority vis-à-vis Americans and their technology, efficiency, wealth, and luxury. To the Volunteers, it seemed that their hosts had seen—and believed—too many Hollywood movies, that they were too quick to downgrade their own country, and too ready to mock the foibles of their fellow countrymen. The Filipinos avoided raising embarrassing questions about race relations in America, or even about the touchy issue of American military bases in their country. In their never-ceasing efforts to be polite, smooth, and hospitable, the Filipinos actually succeeded in angering their American guests by florid praise of the "great sacrifices" the PCVs were making by working in the rural areas!

The Americans also reacted against the Filipinos for the latter's apparent unwillingness to accept responsibility or to keep what appeared to be promises. In the classroom, if the PCV appeared inexperienced, if his approach and motivation seemed outlandish, if his recommendations for change seemed irrelevant or implausible—still, his Filipino colleagues (seeking to avoid embarrassing him) would nod approval. And of course no action would ever be taken on his recommendations. Similarly, Volunteers discussed with town officials the local needs for health clinics, reading rooms, or extra classrooms —and usually went away with the feeling that "finally something is going to get done." But far more often than not, nothing happened. Usually, Filipinos simply failed to act or appear at a designated time, and if questioned, directed the blame onto an elaborate series of unforeseen circumstances. The Volunteers reacted. Not only were the Filipinos erratic, inefficient, and unreliable, but they were patronizing as well! In fact, of course, they were simply practicing smooth interpersonal relations. Any Filipino bystander—or even a sensitive American who had been in the country for some time—would have recognized that the Volunteer was not really receiving a positive response. As one PCV later commented, "It took us a long time to realize that 'yes' meant 'maybe,' and that 'maybe' meant 'no.' "

It is probable that all of the Volunteers experienced some culture fatigue. Perhaps this is an inevitable part of the process by which a Volunteer discovers, emotionally, that Philippine culture is indeed and in fact very different from his own. Some PCVs overcame their culture fatigue much faster than others. A few never seemed to recover at all.

Some members of Philippines Two openly expressed their negative, fatigued feelings to Filipinos, perhaps as the result of advice received from some of their Representatives that they ought to "act naturally—be yourself." Others were more tactful and judicious. Still others had few negative feelings to express. All in all, it seems likely that many Filipinos must have suffered considerably at the hands of Volunteers. Fortunately, however, most of them understood that the PCVs were in the throes of an "adjustment problem," and were therefore patient. Another factor that sometimes protected the feelings of the Filipinos was the simple fact that they, lacking familiarity with American cultural and linguistic cues, frequently missed the full import of the Americans' comments, especially when expressed as sarcasm.

Introspection

The third main reaction to the stressful cultural confrontation took the form of introspection. The intimate juxtaposition of two cultures has probably promoted introspection in man for countless ages past. In any case, the continuous separation from the familiar enforced by life in a rural Philippine community undoubtedly caused even the least introspective PCV to search his soul more avidly than before.

One important area of introspection was the egalitarianism of the Volunteers. Certainly they rejected the paternalistic and patronizing attitudes of their grandparents' generation toward their "little brown brothers." And yet they could not deny their own tired anti-Filipino reactions—reactions that inescapably implied a sense of superiority to their hosts. This quandary often produced powerful feelings of guilt for not living up to one's own professed ideals—one hated oneself for hating the Filipinos—and this in turn forced many Volunteers to reconsider the meaning and reality of their egalitarianism. After some while in the field, many PCVs did finally begin to accept emotionally the idea—and its extraordinary implications—that a people could be equally human, could be equally entitled to consideration, while at the same time they were significantly *different* in their values and behavior. Difference, in short, no longer implied inferiority. Differences, indeed, were to be respected. And to respect cultural differences meant first to understand them, which required one to take one's time, to empathize, to comprehend. Surely this was the opposite of the activism and impatience with which many Volunteers were imbued when they first arrived. Such typically American attitudes now began to appear as dysfunctional, or at the very least inappropriate in the Philippine setting, and possibly in need of serious re-evaluation.

Introspection also centered on a related problem, that of job goals and the PCVs' difficulties in reaching them. The Volunteers shared with the American public and with the Peace Corps staff a highly idealized image of "The Peace Corps Volunteer." Not only this, but they were urged by the Peace Corps/Philippines staff—none of whom had ever lived in a Philippine barrio or taught in a barrio school—to initiate a "revolution in Philippine education," and to "release the latent creativity of the Philippine child." While pondering these lofty goals, they were simultaneously confronted with the hard reality that it was going to be a major accomplishment merely to achieve some kind of basic, meaningful verbal communication with the local teachers and children! Instead of great accomplishments, they had small successes and large problems. The gap between what they felt they ought to achieve and what they were actually achieving was so great as to produce, in many cases, considerable anxiety and guilt. Under such stress, Volunteers introspectively searched back through their experiences asking themselves whether perhaps they had used the wrong approach to the problem. Some while later, perhaps after many months in the field, some Volunteers began to feel that perhaps it was "the problem" itself that needed redefinition, that perhaps the original goals as articulated by Peace Corps/Washington and Peace Corps/Philippines had been unrealistic.

A third area of introspective concern was that of the PCV's self-conception, identity, and personal integrity. The typical Volunteer cherished directness, sincerity, efficiency, and quality. Yet all these values were challenged by the foreign culture in which he worked, to the point where pursuit of them could be counterproductive. Realizing this, the Volunteer was likely to pose for himself some searching questions, such as, "If all I do is play a part, adjusting my behavior to my hosts', then what will I be contributing to the community?" and "Should I be, and can I be, actor enough to be false to what I value as right and good?" And ultimately, dormant identity problems were likely to reappear in the form of the question, "Can I not be myself?"—which inexorably led to the unnerving, "Who am I?"

These three reactions—anti-Peace Corps, anti-Filipino, and introspective self-analysis—might be experienced by a particular Volunteer consecutively or simultaneously. The Volunteer might discuss his reactions openly or repress them as much as possible. Some PCVs doubtless avoided some of the reactions, although I doubt if any of them avoided all three. As a rough guess, I would say that some Volunteers overcame all three reactions—at least in their stressful forms—within perhaps six months; for the majority, the period would be perhaps ten to twelve months. And finally, there were a few who still suffered from one or more of these reactions even at the end of their service in the Philippines.

PATTERNS OF CULTURAL ADJUSTMENT

This section on cultural adjustment should be prefaced by the statement that some Volunteers never adjusted. Some resigned and went home. Others, too proud to quit, spent their entire tours in the Philippines "at war" with the local culture. The great majority, however, made some sort of peace, worked out some kind of adjustment, usually after about a year in the field. Adjustment seemed generally to follow two modes, though there was, of course, the occasional PCV who worked out a *modus vivendi* quite unique to himself. The two modes were (1) withdrawal from the culture and (2) accepting the culture in the sense of learning to live with it. If we conceive of extreme withdrawal and extreme acceptance as ends of a continuum, then it would be theoretically possible to place the great majority of Volunteers somewhere between the extremes. Few if any Volunteers could properly be classified as "pure" cases of either withdrawal or acceptance. Those whom I would readily classify as being essentially acceptant doubtless would occasionally indulge in withdrawal behavior, and the converse would also be true. Nonetheless, my rough impressionistic conclusion is that, as time passed, most Volunteers moved discernibly toward one or the other pole of the continuum, while relatively few remained close to the midpoint.

Withdrawal

A minority of the Volunteers in Philippines One and Two "solved" the problem of cultural adjustment by deciding, in effect, not to fight the local culture, but not to confront it either. Confrontation, and acceptance, were simply too difficult, too trying, to be worth all the effort. The alternative was to withdraw. In a sense, they did what many American businessmen, government officials, and military personnel stationed in the Philippines do: they created their own little American cultural enclave and spent most of their time there. For them, "Little America" normally consisted of their domicile in the town or barrio. It was, of course, far less grandiose than the officers' quarters at Clark Air Force Base or the night clubs looking out on Manila Bay. And yet, the function served was the same: to re-create a bit of "home," and to erect protective barriers against the inhospitable, uninviting culture on the outside. These PCVs fulfilled their daily technical commitment to the schools, and then retreated to "Little America" to read, write letters home, take correspondence courses from the United States, plan their trip home, or perhaps to muse about life in the Philippines. At every opportunity they escaped to American-style companionship in a large city, preferably Manila. Probably only a few of these with-drawers were guilty of slacking on the job; the majority quite faith-fully met the minimum formal requirements of twenty hours a week in the school. Seldom, however, did they do much more than the minimum. Essentially, they were serving their time, counting the days until it would all be over.

Acceptance

Toward the other end of the continuum were the majority of the Volunteers, those whose adjustment largely took the form of accept-ing the local culture in the sense of becoming emotionally capable of living with it relatively comfortably and developing a positive appreciation for some of its elements. The onset of an acceptant attitude sometimes occurred quite rapidly. Often the PCV would suddenly decide that he wanted to move away from the house he shared with one, two, or three other Volunteers into a Philippine home where he would be the only foreigner. While previously he was largely lacking in knowledge of the local language, he now developed a real appreciation of its importance to an understanding of the total culture and set about to learn it as best he could on his own, or in special in-service language training institutes estab-lished by the Peace Corps organization at his behest.

As they learned more about their hosts, most Volunteers began to realize that Filipinos were less interested in them as technical ex-perts in a certain area of education (which few of them really were, anyway!)—than as human beings involved in a web of social rela-tionships. Some tried to recall the lectures at Penn State and began to appreciate, at a deeper level, the notion repeated constantly during training that Filipinos are "person oriented," while Americans tend to be "goal oriented." They began to compare and contrast Philippine culture and American culture as two distinct, but equally valid, frameworks for a meaningful existence. "Being" and "Doing" became two quick labels for the Philippine Way and the American Way, and long philosophical arguments raged as to which one was ultimately preferable.

The old stereotypes of the "Coca-Cola Culture" and the "Colonial Mentality" lost their significance and currency. Volunteers became more aware that many educated Filipinos were just as upset by the Coca-Cola Culture as they themselves were, whereas other Filipinos, especially in the barrios, were largely unaffected by it. As for the colonial mentality, the PCVs now saw it as only one part of a complex Philippine world view which also includes elements of Philippine culture that the Filipinos consider to be superior to comparable elements in American culture. (Subsequent travel en route back to the United States further confirmed the fact, for many PCVs, that the Coca-Cola Culture and the colonial mentality have their counterparts in most countries of the developing world, and are not at all peculiar to the Philippines.)

It should be added that many Filipinos, especially those more Westernized, were quite willing to shed nationalistic pride and criticize analytically their own culture for what they considered to be its shortcomings. However, these feelings would not be expressed to a Volunteer until the Filipino liked, trusted, and respected him— until a real rapport had been established. And such rapport was unlikely to develop until the Filipino came to believe that, in general, the PCV looked acceptantly upon most of the basic Philippine cultural values.

The acceptant Volunteer did not, of course, "become" a Filipino. Nor did he or she "go native." The accepter did not lose himself in the Philippines; far from it, he tended more fully to *find* himself, to become more explicitly aware of himself as an individual and as a member of American culture. His curiosity had now been piqued and his compassion stirred, as he tried to understand his hosts in *their* own terms. For several of the more acceptant Volunteers, this discovery of a whole new perspective on humanity and on themselves, seemed to be an almost "religious" experience—not in the sense of conversion but in the sense of a reordering, clarification, and deepening of their ultimate values as a result of a new awareness of another people's very different value system.

The more acceptant Volunteers came more and more to see the essential wisdom of the training program's basic emphasis on the two interrelated goals of *learning* and *serving*—first on learning as a means of serving more effectively; and second on serving as a means of placing oneself in an appropriate social role where deep transcultural learning can readily take place. Learning about Philippine culture through serving members of it had now become an all-absorbing challenge. The PCV's relationships with Philippine teachers and students, while continuing to be a worthwhile end in itself, had now also taken on significance as a means to the end of understanding the school and its place in the community. Although a desire to help improve the traditional form and content of Philippine education remained the Volunteer's ultimate goal, the immediate concern of the more acceptant Volunteer was to discover the meaning of education in a rural Philippine community and the direction his hosts wanted it to take. Instead of simply demonstrating *his* way of doing things, the acceptant Volunteer tried to re-examine the basic problems involved and make his actions relevant to Philippine concerns. The Volunteer was shifting his goal from "activism" to "communication." Having originally come to work his effect *upon* the Philippines, he had learned the necessity of working *with* Filipinos by means of a two-way transcultural dialogue.

As a crude impressionistic estimate, I would say that well over half of the Philippines One and Two Volunteers were rapidly approaching an acceptant adjustment by the end of their tour in the Philippines. About 10 per cent of them extended for another six months to two years. Many others sadly complained that at termination they had just begun to understand the country and their work!

Intermarriage

It could be hypothesized that one index of the rate of acceptant adjustment is the rate of intermarriage between Volunteers and citizens of the host country. While I do not have precise statistics, it does seem that this rate is significantly higher in the Philippines than generally in the forty-odd host countries where Volunteers are now serving. While many Volunteers married other Volunteers, approximately an equal number of them married Filipinos or Filipinas. Moreover, of those who married locally, about as many female Volunteers married Filipinos (tending to stay in the country) as male Volunteers married Filipinas (tending to bring their brides back to the States). And one is impressed by the rather high percentage of these intermarriages that give every evidence of being at least reasonably happy. It should be added, however, that among the female PCVs were some who were perhaps unaccustomed and unprepared for the sudden and lavish attentions they received from local Philippine men. Among this group were a few girls whose unhappy marriages to Filipinos quickly broke up.

A slight digression might be justified at this point in order to speculate briefly on some of the reasons for the high rate of inter-marriage. One obvious factor is that, in comparison with other Peace Corps host countries, the Philippines has a relatively high proportion of persons who are university-educated and hence at least somewhat Westernized: the sort of people who are likely to have a good deal in common with the Volunteers. Two other related factors are the idealized view of American life that is prevalent in the Philippines and the generally high esteem with which Americans are still regarded there. From the point of view of most Filipino families it is a social and possibly economic asset to have an American in their ranks.

It has also been suggested that decisions to marry are somewhat more likely to be made under circumstances where the alternative of promiscuous behavior is largely lacking. Such in fact was the situation in the Philippines. We were teachers, and in that country, as generally, teachers are expected to be moral exemplars in their community, and to remain nonpromiscuous. Furthermore, most of the communities where we worked were small; individual behavior was highly visible; and gossip was rife. Finally, and perhaps most important, most of the Volunteers desired to project a positive "Peace Corps image," that of a new kind of American, dedicated, sympathetic, and helpful—and less than normally subject to promiscuous inclinations. It may be that these restrictions on promiscuity were conducive to the high cross-cultural marriage rate. I am, however, skeptical of this argument, for it was my impression that those Volunteers who married into Philippine families tended to fit the "acceptant" category described above, and were rarely the individuals from whom one would expect a great deal of promiscuous behavior even under more "normal" circumstances.

If I can generalize, I would say that by and large the PCVs endured their celibacy or semicelibacy relatively well, or at any rate were discreet enough so that the image was fairly effectively preserved. In fact, many Filipinos obliquely compared us male Volunteers to Catholic priests, and occasionally, some of our male friends would jokingly ask why more of our men did not "leave a souvenir behind." By and large, as far as sexual behavior is concerned, it seems clear that the PCVs were perceived as different from most other Americans they had known or known about.

THE IMPROVEMENT OF PROFESSIONAL PERFORMANCE

As time went on, there was encouraging improvement in the professional assignments and performances of the Volunteers. In late 1963 the formal role of "educational aide" was changed to that of "co-teacher." In theory at least, the Volunteer would now cooperate fully with his Philippine co-teacher, and there would be co-planning, co-teaching, and co-evaluating of classes. (Informally, many PCVs had already evolved a co-teacher role for themselves.) While the crucial factor determining success of this new arrangement remained, as before, the quality of the interpersonal relationship between co-teachers, it does seem that the results of the co-teacher system have been gratifying.

Encouraging progress has also been made in improving teaching techniques. Largely at the urging of the Volunteers themselves, a number of in-service training institutes have been held. These have brought together Volunteers, their co-teachers, and their Philippine supervisors. A wide variety of classroom problems have been discussed in an open and professional atmosphere. Techniques for coping with these problems have been demonstrated and practiced. Most Filipinos and Americans who have had a chance to observe the PCVs in the classroom both before and after their in-service training attest to the effectiveness of this approach. Most Volunteers would seem to agree, and also to feel, that in-service training is considerably more valuable than any pedagogical training that could be offered by a stateside Peace Corps training program. It seems clear that the principal reason for the success of the in-service approach is that it reaches the Volunteer at a time when he is particularly receptive, that is, *after* he has been in the field for several months, after he has found out *for himself* what his problems of communication and pedagogy are, and, in some cases, after he has begun to develop an acceptant attitude toward Philippine culture.

CONCLUSIONS

The fact that some of the PCVs "adjusted" by withdrawal to a protected American enclave is hardly surprising. Withdrawal is a very human phenomenon. Parallels can be found throughout the world and throughout history. In withdrawing, these Volunteers were behaving like Americans in the Philippines have traditionally behaved. What *is* surprising, however, is the fact that the with-drawers were clearly outnumbered by the acceptant Volunteers, those who learned to accept their new cultural environment (though not necessarily to approve of it without qualification) sufficiently so that they could begin to function within its framework. And inci-dentally, there is no reason to assume that the early psychological reactions—anti-Peace Corps, cultural fatigue, and introspection—were any the less traumatic for the accepters than for the with-drawers.

Guthrie (page 30) has already mentioned the Volunteer's role in the Philippines as a form of Rogerian "helping relationship" (Rogers 1961, especially pages 39–61). Rogers has marshaled a great deal of evidence attesting to the effectiveness of such relationships well outside the confines of the psychological clinic. The usual trans-cultural technical assistance situation would almost seem to *require* such a relationship before any meaningful work could begin. Given their differences in cultural background, it is almost inevitable that the host and the foreign change agent will have very different ex-pectations about each other, different definitions of the situation, and different approaches to the "common" problem they face. Un-less the expert goes a long way toward *accepting* the host's under-standing of that problem, it is difficult to see how he can be of use in solving it.

In time, the recipient of the help might come to understand the helper's view of the problem, but having been requested to deal with the host's difficulties, the foreign expert cannot make this a prerequisite to his presence or assistance. It might not be until rela-tively late in the relationship that there is any "learning" on the part of the person being helped. Indeed, when both at last recognize the other's viewpoint, a great deal of the line between "helper" and "helped" is erased. At that point their relationship becomes one of "mutual participation," in Szasz and Hollender's terms (1956), and the problems they are facing become part of a process unfolding from joint interaction and experience.

The Volunteers of Philippines Two arrived firmly determined that they were going to "help" the Philippines. They had a firm grip on reality—*their* reality, consisting of a self-image, certain ex-pectations concerning their hosts and their work, and a set of goals to be achieved. Then they were plunged into Philippine communi-ties, relatively isolated in the midst of a seemingly all-engulfing Philippine culture. Under such circumstances, it was their *own* reality—and not that of their Filipino hosts—which was brought into question; and it was their hosts who were before long helping the Volunteers to discover new and much larger "realities." It was the Volunteers and not the Filipinos who had to start changing, first. And it was only later, when the Volunteers understood their hosts well enough to begin to communicate (and often unconsciously) in Philippine terms, that the Filipinos might begin to learn from their guests, to change, to add new understandings to their "realities." In effect, the Filipinos, Philippine culture, and the whole Peace Corps experience were tyrannizing the Volunteers, forcing them to learn before they would allow the Americans to begin adding to the experience of the Filipinos. Herein lies the reason why Volunteers who have completed their service so often comment that they learned far more than they taught, that the experience produced far greater change in *them*, than they were able to produce among the Filipinos.

Reflecting on my experience as a Volunteer, and also later as a Volunteer Leader observing Volunteers in action, I would certainly concur with the ideas advanced by Guthrie regarding the Rogers model. As an impression, I would certainly judge that the acceptant Volunteers were more effective in the classroom, and in the community, than were the withdrawing PCVs. This, however, is simply an impression. There is need for much more research on the whole question of cultural adjustment and effectiveness in a foreign culture. Let it be said for now that the Peace Corps experiment in the Philippines, like all good experiments, has answered a few questions, but raised many more.

BIBLIOGRAPHY

NOTE: See also the bibliography for the Guthrie chapter, page 33.
BRADFORD, ALBERT G.
    1963   Personal communication. Quoted with permission.
CLEVELAND, HARLAN, AND OTHERS
    1957   *The Art of Overseasmanship*. Syracuse, N.Y.: Syracuse University Press.
    1960   *The Overseas Americans*. New York: McGraw-Hill Book Co.
FOSTER, GEORGE M.
    1962   *Traditional Cultures and the Impact of Technological Change*. New York: Harper & Row, Publishers.
HOBBS, NICHOLAS
    1962   Mimeographed report to Peace Corps/Washington. July 1962. Quoted with permission.
GUTHRIE, GEORGE M.
    1963   "Preparing Americans for participation in Another Culture." Paper presented at the Peace Corps-National Institute of Men-

tal Health conference on "Peace Corps and the Behavioral Sciences." April 1963.

LUNDSTEDT, SVEN

1963a "Human Factors in Cross-Cultural Adjustment." *Journal of Social Issues,* Vol. 19, No. 3 (July 1963).

1963b "An Introduction to Some Evolving Problems in Cross-Cultural Research." *Journal of Social Issues.* Vol. 19. No. 3 (July 1963).

OBERG, KALVERO

1955 *Consultation in the Brazilian-United States Cooperative Health Program.* Discussed in Foster, as previously cited.

ROGERS, CARL R.

1961 *On Becoming a Person.* Boston, Mass.: Houghton Mifflin Co.

SANDERS, IRVING T., Editor

1958 *Community Development and National Change.* Cambridge, Mass., Center for International Studies, Massachusetts Institute of Technology. Seventh Annual Report. This is an excellent general treatment of the practical and theoretical issues concerning community development in various cultures.

1959 *Interprofessional Training Goals for Technical Assistance Personnel Abroad.* Ithaca, N.Y.: Cornell University Press.

SPICER, EDWARD H.

1952 *Human Problems in Technological Change.* New York: Russell Sage Foundation.

SZASZ, THOMAS S., and MARC H. HOLLENDER

1956 "The Basic Models of the Doctor-Patient Relationship." *Archives of Internal Medicine,* Vol. 59, pages 585-592.

THURBER, CLARENCE E.

1961 *The Problem of Training Americans for Service Abroad in U.S. Government Technical Assistance Programs.* Unpublished doctoral dissertation, Stanford University.

4

The Representative Staff as
Intercultural Mediators in Malaya

GERALD S. MARYANOV *is Assistant Professor of Political Science at the University of Iowa, having previously held teaching positions at Indiana University and the University of Illinois. In 1961–1962, he took leave for a year to serve as Associate Peace Corps Representative in Malaya, and played an important role in the establishment of the program in that country. In 1965–1966 he again took leave, this time to serve as Visiting (Fulbright) Professor of Political Science at the University of Malaya, Kuala Lumpur. Dr. Maryanov's interests in the Indonesia-Malaysia area stem from the early 1950's, when for two years he served with the Ford Foundation-Indonesian English Language Project at various places in Indonesia; during this period he acquired a fluent command of Indonesian/Malay. Professor Maryanov has lectured to Malaya Peace Corps training groups, and in 1963 served as Director of Area Studies for the training of Indonesia One at the University of Iowa. His various monographs, articles, and reviews deal primarily with the political problems of Southeast Asian countries, seen in broad sociocultural perspective.*

As the editor has already pointed out, there are two very distinct subcultures within the total Peace Corps organization, that of the Washington staff and that of the Volunteers. These two subcultures are separated by a gap—in attitudes, in values, and in understanding—which is often quite broad. One of the purposes of the Representative staff in a particular host country is to attempt to mediate between these two subcultures. In many ways the Representative staff is well equipped to do this, for it shares some attributes with officials in the Washington headquarters and some attributes with the PCVs in the field. Like the officials in Washington, the "Reps" enjoy regular salaries and the exercise of very considerable administrative power. Like the Volunteers in the field, the "Reps" experience contact with the local social realities that should be, and sometimes is, close and perceptive.

In a second and more obvious sense, too, the "Reps" in Malaya were intercultural mediators. It was our task to serve as a bridge of communications between the general culture of the United States as reflected by both the Washington staff and the PCVs; and Malaya—which, as will soon become clear, is a many-cultured land.

In this chapter, I will cover the activities of Malaya One and Two during the period of August 1961 to August 1962 when I served as Associate Representative in that country. I will concentrate on the early problems of establishing an organization, communicating to Malayans what the Peace Corps was and was not, and negotiating job assignments for the PCVs. My remarks are limited to peninsular Malaya, as distinct from the new Federation of Malaysia which was established in 1963 and included within its borders peninsular Malaya, the territories of Sarawak and Sabah on the island of Borneo, and, until August 1965, the island of Singapore. I must emphasize that my opinions are solely my own and are not intended in any way to represent the opinions of the two other members of the Malaya staff, the Representative and Deputy Representative. Nevertheless, my two former colleagues are part of this report, for they contributed profoundly to my education during the period of our association, and I am grateful to them.

THE MALAYAN SETTING

Peninsular Malaya, roughly equivalent in area to the State of New York, supported a population of approximately seven million in 1960. (The merger into the Federation of Malaysia more than doubled the territory and increased the population to ten million.) Malaya forms the tip, the last five hundred miles, of an elongated arm of land stretching southward from the mainland of Asia to the island world of Indonesia. Communication patterns in Malaya have tended to run along the coasts and up the short rivers, rather than across the mountainous green-jungled central spine of the peninsula.

This division into east and west is significant in Malayan thinking and in the facts of Malayan life. Population has clustered along the coasts—and to a far greater extent along the west coast than the east. Most of the economic development of twentieth-century Malaya has been concentrated on the west coast, where are found the production centers for Malaya's two great export products, rubber and tin. Most of the great cities of Malaya—Kuala Lumpur, Ipoh, Malacca, Georgetown—lie along this west coast, as do the major north-south roads and railroad. And it was to the west coast that most immigrants came—Chinese to work the tin mines, Indians to tap the rubber trees, British to establish political dominance.

This east-west division is secondary to an even more important characteristic of Malayan society: ethnic division into three major groups—Malays, Chinese, and Indians. Plural societies are not uncommon in the contemporary world, but Malaya's problem is unusual because of the relatively equal size of the two larger groups. In 1960, roughly 50 per cent of the population were of Malay or other ethnolinguistically similar identity; 37 per cent were Chinese; and 11 per cent were Indian. Among the urbanized population, it was largely on the less developed east coast that the Malays predominated over the non-Malays.

Politically, Malaya is ruled by an alliance of parties representing the three major ethnic groups: The United Malay National Organization, The Malayan Chinese Association, and the Malayan Indian Congress. The alliance is officially dedicated to solving the interethnic "communal" problem. In practice, at a formal level, much progress has indeed been made in inhibiting interethnic animosity and encouraging national integration. But there is widespread awareness that the communal problem still persists, perhaps just below the surface, as a dangerous and potentially explosive issue.

One factor contributing to Malayan ability to suppress the communal problem is the relatively widespread prosperity that the country has been enjoying. It seems likely that as long as economic benefits can be distributed fairly widely, there will be no major or violent upset of the current *modus vivendi*.

Malaya's prosperity is based on the production and export of rubber and tin. Both products, however, face uncertain futures: rubber because of increased competition from synthetics; tin because of dwindling reserves. In order to prepare for the future, Malaya has undertaken national development programs that are generally considered to be among the most promising and successful in all of Asia.

These two basic domestic problems—national unity and economic development—have faced Malaya ever since independence was gained from Britain in 1957. But there is consolation in the fact that Malaya has confronted her problems with a combination of assets not often found in newly independent countries: effective national leadership, a relatively efficient national bureaucracy, a fairly good supply of highly trained technicians, and good relations with the former colonial power—which has meant, among other things, no sudden break in public or business administrative practices.

Malaya has received outside technical assistance, mainly in the form of technicians supplied through the Colombo Plan, and to a lesser degree through United Nations agencies. To these should be added the sizable number of expatriate British officials remaining in their posts after independence. While the government realized that it needed, initially, to retain numerous British officials to help run its affairs, it has also been heedful of great pressure to "Malayanize" the civil service by replacing British officials with Malayans. While many Malayans believe that Malayanization cannot come too quickly, a number of outside observers believe it has proceeded too rapidly for the good of the country. While Malayans have received technical training at home and in Commonwealth countries such as Australia, the supply of trained manpower has remained seriously short of the need. This was the situation into which the Peace Corps stepped in 1961, in an effort to provide needed "middle-level manpower" to schools, hospitals, and other organizations. And it seems clear that one reason why the PCVs were welcome in Malaya was that they were temporary personnel, hardly likely to develop vested interests in retaining particular jobs against Malayan competition.

We can summarize the Malaya in which the Peace Corps found itself in 1961 by stating that in many ways the host country was typical of the world's so-called "emerging nations." The per capita income was low by world standards (though not by Asian standards). The rural-urban gap was marked by a traditional-modern dichotomy. Most of the population was concentrated in villages. Most of the people derived their living from some form of primary production. Most of the territory was inaccessible to modern transportation. Public health measures were more or less restricted to urban or urbanized centers. National independence was recent. National unity was an issue. And development plans had been promulgated and were being carried out.

THE PEACE CORPS IN MALAYA

Little information is available about the early negotiations for a Peace Corps contingent in Malaya. The first big event occurred in May 1961, when Sargent Shriver and a few assistants stopped off in Kuala Lumpur on their widely heralded trip around the world, designed to explain the Peace Corps to various governments and to ascertain whether Volunteers would be welcome. The Shriver group's visit was brief. Considerable confusion must have reigned, for apparently the Shriver group was not familiar with Malaya, and Malayan officials knew little about this improbable new American organization and its altruistic purposes. In any case, the Shriver group met with an apparently enthusiastic response, and left two of its members behind to carry on additional negotiations for a few days longer.

The early summer months were characterized by confusion both in Kuala Lumpur and in Washington, where an understaffed, over-worked headquarters organization was fitfully beginning to take shape. During the summer an official request from the government of Malaya was received—a necessary formality because officially the Peace Corps establishes programs only in countries that request them. Creakingly but rapidly, the Washington headquarters then proceeded with necessary steps. Volunteers had to be recruited. Selection machinery had to be established. A training site had to be arranged, and a training program organized. And, the Representative staff had to be selected, appointed, and dispatched to Malaya to lay the groundwork for the coming of the Volunteers.

The Malaya One group, thirty-six strong, finally arrived in Kuala Lumpur on January 12, 1962. Twelve were connected with the Ministry of Education or were to do some kind of teaching; twenty were in public health; and four were in the catchall category of rural development.[1]

When Malaya Two arrived on June 1, 1962, it added thirteen secondary school teachers and two technical college instructors to the education program; ten nurses and two laboratory technicians to the health program; and one engineer, two animal husbandrymen, and one veterinarian to the catchall third category. Thus, by August 1962, the end of the period covered in this chapter, there were sixty-seven Peace Corps Volunteers in Malaya, the two largest components of which were twenty secondary school teachers and twenty-five nurses.

TASKS AND GOALS OF THE VOLUNTEERS

The primary task of the Volunteers, of course, was to do their formal jobs—the teachers to teach, the nurses to nurse, and so forth. But obviously, working in a strange new environment under the aegis of a boldly experimental organization, the typical PCV set for himself many tasks and goals that would never appear in a formal job description. The challenge was not just a matter of learning work procedures and routines, or fitting unobtrusively into his or her work organization—which, incidentally, was usually quite well structured. Beyond this, the PCV also had to relate himself to his total community, both in the narrow sense of his community of working colleagues and also in the broader sense of the total community where he resided. While resisting the temptation to become a pseudo-Malayan, the Volunteer had to learn to be a good American guest—not only vis-à-vis those Malayans who came to know him directly but also in the perception, often vague, of innumerable people who were merely passively aware of his presence. And finally, the Volunteer had to maintain that intangible something, a style, which in Malaya was called the "Peace Corps image."

There was one additional "task" which some Peace Corps/Washington officials apparently expected from the Volunteer—and indeed, many Volunteers arrived in Malaya thinking it part of their obligation. According to this view, the PCV was to stimulate or instigate change, both technical and social, by teaching a "better" way of doing things, and by "transmitting" their skills to the people with whom they worked. In my opinion, this "task" was entirely inappropriate to the role of the PCV—or at least, to the PCV working in Southeast Asia. Peace Corps Volunteers are sent abroad to work *with* people in the host country, not *on* them. This distinction constitutes an important innovation, one which has helped to make the Peace Corps distinct from other overseas assistance programs. Were a Volunteer in Malaya to presume or profess superior wisdom, his behavior would be resented by most Malayans (unless, of course, his job specifically called for teaching). Such behavior would effectively stand in the way of meaningful personal relationships. By deliberately setting out to transmit his skills, when that was not what his colleagues expected, or by trying to teach those who were not formal students, the Volunteer would, in my opinion, actually inhibit the possibility of his colleague learning from his example. Here then is an apparent paradox: the most effective way to transmit skills is to refrain from deliberately trying to do so; the effective way to *prevent* the transmission of skills is to set out deliberately to transmit them. What the Volunteer must do is simply to be there, and do his job. If his colleagues are to "learn new skills," it will be because they set out to do so, on their own terms, in their own way, and in their own time.

THE REPRESENTATIVE STAFF

Quite correctly, the role of the Peace Corps Representative staff has received relatively little attention in the general publicity and reporting on Peace Corps activities. The main emphasis, and properly so, has been on the work of the Volunteers, which, after all, provides the "payoff" for the Peace Corps experiment. But the over-

Rapport

Communication

Cooperation

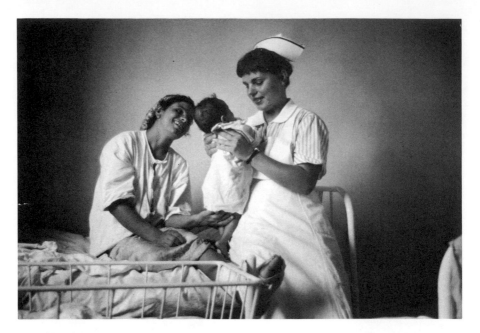

Aspiration

Expression

Response

Release

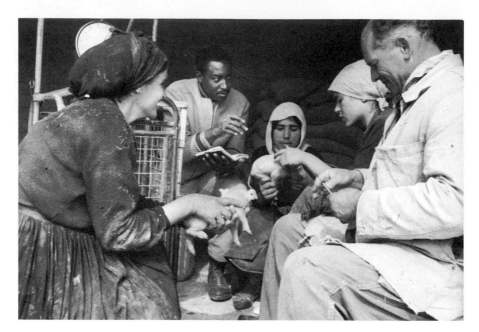

Production

Consumption

Maintenance

Repair

Transaction

Challenge

Prevention

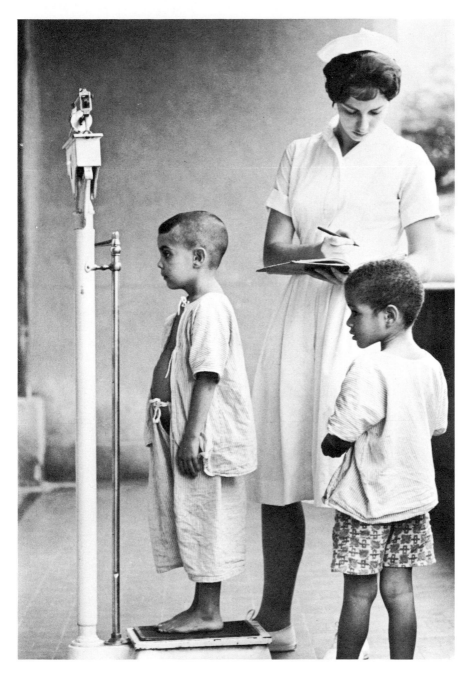

Cure

Elicitation

Participation

Initiative

Interlude

Respite

Relief

Acceptance

Aloneness

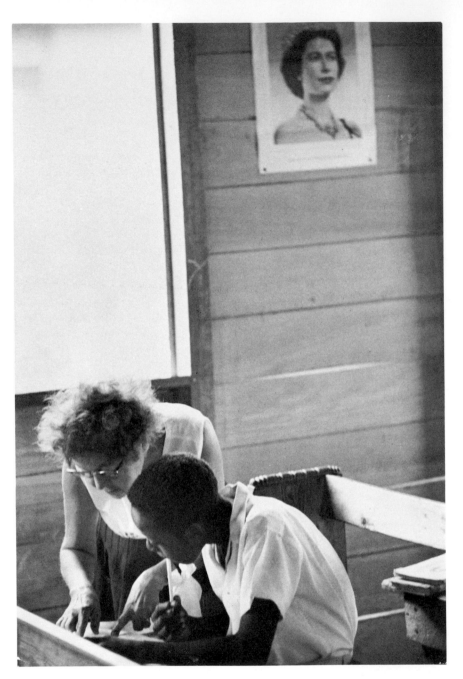

Patience

seas staff is nonetheless an important part of the story, important to the extent that it influences the life and role of the Volunteer; his job assignment and effectiveness; his living conditions, allowances, and rules of conduct; the growth of his transcultural understanding and personal maturity; and indeed the whole matter of his morale, satisfaction, and fulfillment. The staff is responsible for over-all supervision of the Peace Corps presence in the host country, under directives established by Washington headquarters and subject to the general authority of the American ambassador in that country.

The regular Peace Corps staff in Malaya consisted of three people: the Representative, the Deputy Representative, and the Associate Representative. While there was no strict division of tasks, there was a difference in emphasis making for three distinct roles. The Representative was in over-all charge of the program. He carried out most negotiations at the ministry level, and was the public spokesman for the program. The Deputy Representative established and controlled the management and logistics of the program. The Associate Representative was the field contact man, both with the Volunteers and with the local officials.[2]

Again, it should be emphasized that these divisions were not absolute, so that all three had a feel for the problems and participated in the decisions affecting the whole program, both in the office and in the field. The atmosphere was one of hectic activity, yet casual informality—an atmosphere that has seemed to characterize Peace Corps operations the world around.

Of the three regular staff members, two had had extensive experience in Southeast Asia, both academic and practical.* The third demonstrated a humility and a willingness and capacity to learn that was remarkable. He brought to Malaya a prototype of the best Peace Corps spirit. Personal familiarity with Malaya on the part of the Peace Corps Representative and the aura of goodwill carried by the Deputy Representative were undoubtedly major contributions to the genuinely warm relationships enjoyed with Malayan officials.

Given the backgrounds and training of its three members, the staff

* One, Dr. J. Norman Parmer, had lived and done research in Malaya for more than two years. The other, Dr. Maryanov, had lived, taught, and done research in culturally similar parts of Indonesia, and enjoyed a fluent command of Malay. Of the nine Representatives sent to Southeast Asia by the end of 1961, only these two could be described as culturally qualified. As far as is known, two of the remaining seven had been to the area before as servicemen or tourists, while the other five had not been to the area at all. Moreover, as far as can be learned, none of these remaining seven had had substantial transcultural or Volunteer-type experience in any other part of the developing world.—Ed.

had available a thorough knowledge of Malayan history and culture; a good command of the language; experience in practical work in an Asian environment; experience in working with Asian officials; and a knowledge of how to adjust to Asian ways of life. It also had familiarity with concepts of cultural adaptation and change, and personal experience with manifestations of Asian nationalism. Through familiarity with problems of overseas programs, the staff had a concrete awareness of possible goals for a Peace Corps-type approach. And, the staff had a healthy dose of the Peace Corps spirit. What was lacking was experience in governmental administration.

The Staff as Mediators

The precise task of the Representative staff could not have been predicted in advance, for in 1961 the office was a new one. The few directives issued by Washington were general enough to be variously interpreted. The details could only be worked out in practice, and it is likely that, in the beginning, the practices were as diverse as the individuals who held the posts. The very casualness of the procedures, the emphasis on "playing it by ear," lent strength to the image of a new force, a nonbureaucratic spirit of creative imagination that the Peace Corps claimed as its hallmark.

But there was one task for the overseas staff that might well have been anticipated and prepared for: the task of accommodating disparate views on the nature of the Peace Corps and the nature of the needs of the "developing areas" that the Peace Corps is supposed to help satisfy. For the views held on this subject by Peace Corps/ Washington officials and Americans in general were disparate indeed, from the views held by the officials and people of Malaya.

Serving as communications bridge between Malaya and the Washington administrative subculture was not always easy. Few if any of the administrators in Washington were familiar with Malayan conditions. Different Washington officials had different ideas about what the Peace Corps' philosophy ought to be, about what its program ought to be. Many of the top officials of the Division of Program Development and Operations, to whom we reported directly, were on loan from AID (Agency for International Development) and possessed views fairly typical of that organization. Some revealed a tendency to lump all of the "developing areas" into a single category, and thus to be insensitive to the fact that Malaya, while economically not well developed by Western standards, had one of the most sophisticated intellectual elites and government administrations to be found anywhere in the "underdeveloped" world. Many of our opposite numbers in Washington were insensitive to Malayan feelings while at the same time revealing unrealistic, overenthusiastic notions as to how fast economic and cultural change could occur. Many of them tended—often automatically and usually subconsciously—to assume that Malayan problems had simple answers— *American* answers. Despite these attitudinal obstacles to mutual understanding, it was always vitally important that we in Malaya find ways of maintaining effective communication with Washington. For it was Washington that made the decisions as to program content and, equally important, as to the degree of freedom to be allowed the Peace Corps Representative in his attempts to make the local program harmonize with the peculiar social, political, and cultural conditions of the host country.

Communicating with Malayan officials also posed problems. A basic problem was the understandable existence among some Malayan officials of a hypersensitivity in dealing with representatives of a great power like the United States. Lurking behind many Malayan reactions was the inchoate and unspoken suspicion that cooperation with the Americans meant over-Americanization. A relevant fact is that Malayan officials had had far fewer dealings with American officials than was true of other Southeast Asian countries; the United States, for example, has never had an AID mission in Malaya. Another important fact was that, especially in the early days, many Malayan officials developed opinions about the Volunteers without ever having seen any of them in action; it was thus doubly necessary for the staff to maintain communication with the bureaucracy at levels far removed from operations, yet close to policy decision making.

Complicating the entire picture was the fact that administration and technology in Malaya bear a heavy British imprint. As will become increasingly clear in subsequent chapters on Somalia, Tanganyika, Nigeria, Sierra Leone, Tunisia, and Morocco, the fact of recent colonial dependence adds complexities to a Peace Corps operation. And this is especially true where, as in Malaya, many administrative posts—including some very high ones—were still held by expatriate officials from the former colonial power. Thus, Peace Corps teachers in Malaya had to adapt, not so much to Malayan standards and expectations as to *British* ones. Peace Corps nurses, for example, were initially suspect because few of them were qualified in midwifery—an art that is a standard part of the British or Malayan nurse's preparation.

If there was one principle that governed the Peace Corps staff's relations with Malayan officials, it was that we were there to serve the Malayan government's needs and that only the Malayan government could properly specify what these needs were. The staff would ask questions. The staff would sometimes initiate suggestions. And the staff would interpret and transmit messages to and from Washington. But the final decisions were Malayan.

It is one thing to state the foregoing principle—it has been stated many times before. It is quite another thing to put this principle into practice. Involved is the whole question of interpersonal relations between Americans and Asians, including such details as the style and tone in which conversations are held. The staff, headed by a scholar whose works on Malaya were widely respected in that country, was able to establish a warm and cordial relationship that pervaded almost all conversations with Malayan officialdom and eased the process of decision making on Peace Corps matters.

But, a relationship is a two-way affair. If the decisions were to be made by Malayans, they had the problem of communicating with the Peace Corps staff, that strange group of American officials with their strange new program. Fortunately for us, we were dealing with officials most of whom had known and worked with Westerners, that is, British administrators and technicians. Their experience prepared them, to a considerable degree, to deal effectively with us, and, later, with the PCVs. Malayan administrative efficiency was to be found even at the local level, that of school principal, hospital administrator, and the like. It is therefore not too surprising, yet at the same time worthy of proper emphasis, that a large part of the credit for the success in creating a cooperative atmosphere was due to the sensibility and goodwill of the Malayans. This is not just empty, formal praise or courtesy. The cooperative atmosphere was genuine, and it characterized the entire Peace Corps program at all levels.

The Question of Volunteer Qualifications

The first job of the staff—in addition to setting up an office—was to establish working relationships with the various Malayan agencies requesting Peace Corps services and to obtain a clarification of the nature of the jobs to be filled and the qualifications necessary for each job. This phase was far more subtle and important than outward appearances would indicate, for it was here that the various strands of the staff's "intercultural mediator" role came together. The nature of the Peace Corps resource had to be explained repeatedly to Malayans at all levels, and the nature and basis for the

Malayan requests had to be translated and transmitted to Washington.

Malayan officials were generally deeply and quite accurately familiar with their personnel needs, which were usually reflected in their requests for Peace Corps personnel. The Ministry of Education was constantly reminded of shortages of teachers, as reports to that effect kept piling up from school headmasters and Chief Education Officers in the various states. The Ministry of Health well knew that just about every hospital in the country needed nurses, and that far too few were coming out of the few existing training courses. Development planning in agriculture was being seriously held up for lack of trained soil survey specialists. And so on.

When we first arrived in Kuala Lumpur, one problem that confronted us was that Peace Corps skills had been "oversold." The original Shriver group had apparently left the impression with some Malayan officials that here was an exuberant offer of fully trained personnel at no extra cost to the Malayan government. Thus, for example, the expectation developed among some officials in the Ministry of Education that they were going to get trained, experienced teachers. In the actual event, however, all the Peace Corps could usually offer was recent college graduates without previous teaching experience. The staff thus had its hands full of problems in which it was necessary to mediate between the supply and the demand for qualifications.

A related set of problems grew out of the fact that Malayan expectations and standards of appropriate on-the-job behavior often differed considerably from our own. Malayan expectations in the realm of education, for example, call for considerable formality on the teacher's part. Typical American casualness, informality, and egalitarianism could be grossly out of place in a Malayan classroom. Again, the staff was called upon to serve as intercultural mediator.

Staff Work at the Local Level

Well before Malaya One was due to arrive, the staff took to the road on an exhaustive mission of communicating to Malayan officials at all levels, and to anyone else in the local community who showed an interest, just what the Peace Corps was and was not. Trips were made throughout the country, to every state and to all the important administrative centers. As a matter of courtesy, the staff paid a call on the Chief Minister of each state (the top political official) and on the State Secretary (the top administrative official), in order to explain the Peace Corps and its purposes, answer questions, and prepare the official for the possibility that the government of Malaya might assign PCVs in his area. Wherever possible, the staff communicated in similar fashion with such officials as the Chief Education Officer, the Chief Medical and Health Officer, the State Engineer, the State Development Officer, and so forth. In some cases, this was the first specific information the local officials had received about the Peace Corps.

It must be emphasized that the staff *never* "promised" Volunteers to a local administrator. Such promises were not ours to make. New requests for Volunteers, we pointed out, would have to be channeled through the appropriate authorities in Kuala Lumpur. Rather than to promise, our purpose was to explain. Rather than to assume a power role ourselves, our purpose was to engender the feeling that it was up to the Malayans themselves to decide how best to use the new Peace Corps resource.

Besides visiting state-level officials, we also dropped in on as many secondary schools and hospitals as possible, as well as other locations where there was some possibility that a Volunteer would be assigned. In talking with headmasters of schools, medical officers and matrons at hospitals, and similar officials, we once again explained the Peace Corps and its purposes. We gave assurances that any Volunteers posted to their organization were to be at *their* service and under *their* control, and were not intended to disrupt the normal routine and procedures of their organization. Nor, above all, were the PCVs to be allowed to displace Malayans, nor stand in the way of Malayans' advancement. We made it clear that we stood ready to be of service if any difficulties arose which were too sensitive to be communicated through normal bureaucratic channels. In such ways we tried to make the Peace Corps a genuinely mutual endeavor, and to avoid the sort of situation that sometimes occurred in other countries, where a Volunteer arrived unheralded and unannounced—an experience that can be unnerving for the local administrator and demoralizing for all concerned.

The Question of Job Locations

The staff also assisted and advised the Malayan officials in decisions on job assignments. Here again, Malayan and American outlooks had to be accommodated within the range of available alternatives.

From the Malayan side, deference had to be paid to an important political fact of life, namely that Malaya was organized as a federation of eleven states. And all eleven of them were competing for attention in the country's general development programs. A new resource such as the Peace Corps had to be distributed fairly among them. Malayan officials, still uncertain as to the quality of the new resource, had to be judicious in distributing it. They were aware of personnel needs in a variety of locations, ranging from comfortable, modern Kuala Lumpur to the smallest of towns, and even to isolated jungle stations. Their image of the Westerner was that he loved comfort and had difficulty adapting to the lack of "amenities" in the "ulu," or back country. Why not, then, assign the PCVs to urban posts, to well-structured jobs where little initiative was required in adapting? Why not, indeed, since in most cases the need for trained manpower in the cities was great—in some cases as great as it was in the back country, or perhaps even more so!

But Malayan officials were not the only ones whose images were inaccurate or unrealistic. The general American image of "aid to under-developed areas" tends to emphasize "roughing it" in the most "underdeveloped" or "backward" villages deep in the rural hinterland of the host country. In point of fact, however, development planners in the "newly emerging" countries are more and more coming to conclude that many types of technical aid can be best absorbed and put to use in urban or quasi-urban settings, where people's attitudes are more receptive to change, and where the necessary social and technological organization and equipment are available. While not themselves neglecting the needs of villagers, leaders in such developing countries as Malaya must deal with hard social and cultural factors, as well as just the technical ones. They may well have a point when they say, as they sometimes do, that the blind application of technical skills in traditional villages—no matter how well intentioned—may at best be useless and wasteful, and at worst, harmful. At any rate, ministry officials in Malaya proceeded with caution in determining the job assignments of the PCVs.

An added problem on the American side was the fact that our own image of the nature of the Peace Corps was characterized by ambiguity, confusion, and disagreement. Again, we deal here with a matter that is far more subtle and complex than appears at first glance. In the Peace Corps/Washington organization itself there was no clear-cut definition of that image but rather a multiplicity of often conflicting views, depending on the person's background and training in intercultural relations, foreign languages, technical assistance, international politics, and "overseasmanship." Fortunately, however, there was one point on which Peace Corps/Washington, the Malaya Representative staff, and the Volunteers were all agreed, and that was the hope that the PCVs would gain a meaningful transcultural experience by living among the people at levels set by the society itself.

The staff in Malaya started from the premise that to show that Americans did not need luxury was only one part of the Peace Corps image—and a part that could be damaging if it was effected by "demanding" that the Americans pick and choose their own situations, and "insisting" that the Americans have the final word. A more important part of the Peace Corps image, we thought, was to demonstrate that the Americans could do whatever was required of them regardless of hardships, if such was their lot. Potential hardship, in other words, should never be a criterion for rejecting an assignment; but neither should it be an absolute condition for determining an assignment.

To sum up, the staff's position in discussions with Malayan officials was that if an alternative were available between the capital city and other places, it would be desirable to avoid the capital city. If the choice were between the west coast and the east coast, the less developed east coast would be more attractive. If there were a choice between a highly structured work role and a less structured one, the latter would be chosen because it afforded more scope for adjustment and creativity.* Needless to add, whatever the job assignment, it must always involve a service considered useful by *Malayans,* and not just by the Peace Corps.

On the basis of all these considerations, and in an atmosphere of cordiality and cooperation, the decisions were made as to assignments. For some of the Volunteers, no choices were available. The two business school teachers, for example, had no place to go but to the Rural and Industrial Development Authority Training Center in Petaling Jaya, a suburb of Kuala Lumpur.

The assignments of the secondary school teachers had to follow priorities established by the Ministry of Education; certain schools had first call on the supply of teachers. Otherwise, dispersion was the rule. Thus, of the twenty teachers in the first two groups, twelve went to west-coast locations and eight to the east coast. By August 1962,

* Note that Dr. Maryanov is referring to actual, *established* roles in Malayan society and governmental structure. This is to be contrasted with the situation in the Philippines, where the job role of "educational aide" was *new,* unprecedented, and created especially for the PCVs—a fact that led to serious role problems. See page 27.—Ed.

Peace Corps teachers were at eighteen different schools in fifteen different cities in ten of the eleven states.

Several decisions had to be made concerning the nurses. The Malayan medical system included general hospitals in most of the state capitals, district hospitals in several other cities and towns, and a growing number of rural health centers in smaller towns, servicing neighboring rural areas. Nurses were needed at all levels. Here the staff was called upon to mediate between the American system of nursing and the British system. Important differences had to be taken into account. Friedland will more fully explore these differences in the British and American nursing traditions, in his chapter on Tanganyika (page 148).

The initial thinking of ministry officials called for concentrating the nurses at well-developed, highly structured facilities, such as in Kuala Lumpur.* This, they thought, would ease the task of cultural and job adaptation. We assured them that adaptation would not be that difficult, and after lengthy negotiation a compromise was reached. The nurses would initially be assigned to district hospitals and less well staffed general hospitals, from which they might later be transferred, once they had become familiar with the Malayan scene. So it was that the first group of fifteen nurses went to eight different hospitals in eight different states. Several of the girls, however, felt that their work was still too routine. At their request, and after further negotiation, they were transferred to rural health work. By August 1962, when there were twenty-five Volunteer nurses in Malaya, eight were doing rural work, and altogether the girls were serving at twelve locations in eight states. And it seemed generally true that those in the rural clinics, where the job role was less structured and where they could serve as "generalists," were the happiest.

Partly because of patient and detailed preparations, and partly because of the spirit of cooperation at all levels, the job assignments in Malaya proved to be remarkably stable. For Malaya One and Two, fewer than 10 per cent of the initial assignments had to be altered, and rarely because of maladjustment or lack of adaptability on the part of the Volunteers.†

* See the Friedland chapter, page 143. The *reasons* why the host government preferred concentrated assignments for the PCV nurses were, however, quite different in the Tanganyikan case.—Ed.

† By contrast, in the Pakistan One group, approximately two thirds of the Volunteers reportedly had to be reassigned.—Ed.

The Question of the Volunteer Level of Living

A widely proclaimed policy of the Peace Corps, and one which has succeeded in differentiating it from other overseas programs, is the insistence on relatively frugal living standards for the PCVs. Volunteers were not to have cars, but could have bicycles. Motorized transport of any kind could be provided only if essential to the working situation. And so forth. Washington also ruled that there could be no differences in the living allowances paid to Volunteers in a given country. As a means of minimizing envy and the crippling effect it can have on morale, all PCVs in Malaya were to be paid the same amount, unless specific authorization to do otherwise was requested, and justified to Washington's satisfaction.

Determination of the exact amount of the PCVs' allowance in a particular country was left to the Representative in that country. In making this determination, we were told by Washington that the PCVs should receive enough money to permit them to live as much like the people of the host country as possible. When faced with the reality that the people of a country like Malaya live in various ways according to their means, which are not always negligible, Washington officials were prone to rephrase the principle so as to have the PCVs live in the same manner as their Malayan co-workers. But we in Malaya were still left with the problem of *which* co-workers to use as models. Should it be the relatively well paid engineers? Or the relatively poorly paid nurses?

In wrestling with this quandary, the staff in Malaya reasoned that the amount of the allowance should be in accordance with the overall Peace Corps image. We believed that rigid adherence to the style of life of a co-worker was not a goal in itself but at best a possible means to achieve a goal. The actual goal was twofold: to become as much a part of the community as possible rather than becoming part of a Western enclave and to demonstrate by personal conduct and example that monetary rewards are not the only source of satisfaction for Americans, that Americans can find personal rewards in work accomplished and in service to a principle.

On this basis, the staff in Malaya worked out a formula tied to the cost of living in Malaya as encountered by Volunteers in the more expensive areas (meaning, of course, the capital city). The allowances provided for food purchases in Malayan markets, emphasizing Malayan foods (rather than imports), personal necessities, and modest entertainment. No arrangement under such circumstances could be completely satisfactory to all Volunteers, and one drawback to this arrangement was that some of the more highly skilled Volunteers in the cities—engineers, for instance—actually could not afford the social amenities that their Malayan engineer colleagues took for granted, with the result that off-the-job contact was made difficult.

The question of housing for the Volunteers was approached in much the same way, with one additional factor involved. While the Peace Corps undertook to provide everything necessary for the life of the Volunteer in the host country, thus including housing, it was hoped that the PCV might be provided with government housing if such housing was normally provided for Malayans in similar situations. In requesting this, the staff made it clear that in no case should a Volunteer displace a Malayan from housing, nor stand in the way of housing becoming available to a Malayan in his normal turn. On this basis, most of the Volunteers were provided with government housing. The nurses were housed in nurses' hostels attached to the hospital. Thus they shared dining facilities, and in some cases, rooms, with their Malayan co-workers. At many of the schools, teachers' quarters were available. In these cases, the Volunteers usually shared a house with several Malayan teachers. For those Volunteers for whom government housing was not available, the staff rented quarters, usually with the assistance of local officials.

Liaison with the Training University

The process of clarifying the details of the program in Malaya, and establishing specific job locations, extended over a period of several months during the latter part of 1961. While these discussions were proceeding in Malaya, Peace Corps headquarters was establishing a training program (located at Northern Illinois University, De Kalb, Illinois), compiling a list of potential Volunteers for Malaya, extending the invitations, and so forth. The training program actually started in October 1961, and lasted for eight weeks.

This is not the place to discuss the organization of a Peace Corps training program, but one problem of training deserves mention here, for it involved the task of the staff in the field. In order to prepare the Volunteer most efficiently for living and working under Peace Corps conditions, it would seem desirable to have not only general cultural conditions presented to the trainees, but also as much information as possible about the general Peace Corps program in the host country, plus up-to-date information about specific conditions in specific places and for specific jobs. In other words, it would seem necessary to have a continuous flow of up-to-date information from the field to the training program.

In the other direction, the staff needed the fullest possible information, as soon as it was available, on the Volunteers, their skills, interests, strengths, shortcomings, and so forth. The staff, after all, was assisting in making decisions that would affect the entire experience of the Volunteer in Malaya, yet it was doing so with no knowledge of the persons involved. And the Malayan officials, of course, were quite interested in learning of the qualifications of their future workers.

Peace Corps/Washington, to my knowledge, had no built-in mechanism to assure such a flow of information in both directions, and, indeed, may well not have considered it a problem. But the Malaya program was fortunate—to the point of being almost unique —in finding an "accidental" solution to this problem. The man who became the Peace Corps Representative in Malaya came from the university at which the training was given, and, in fact, helped establish the first training program. Thus, on the basis of personal contact, outside the regular organization, communication between the field and the training site was good.*

THE VOLUNTEERS IN THE FIELD

When the Malaya One group arrived in Kuala Lumpur, it would have been difficult to say who was more nervous about the event, the

* All subsequent contingents of trainees bound for peninsular Malaya (as distinct from other portions of the Federation of Malaysia) have also been trained at Northern Illinois University. As far as I know, this makes Northern Illinois virtually unique in the sense that training for successive contingents of PCVs for all other host countries or territories has, practically without exception, shifted at least once between universities (or other training institutions). For example, training for Thailand has so far been carried out in at least five universities, and training for the Philippines in at least six. When this happens, it is virtually inevitable that many of the same mistakes will be repeated, for the administrators of the training program at the new university, though almost invariably eager and hardworking, usually are unfamiliar with conditions in the host country and usually learn relatively little about the host country or about training methods from the university that trained the previous contingent. In other words, there is usually a lack both of expertise and of feedback. As one who has been a guest lecturer at every Peace Corps training program sponsored by Northern Illinois, I have been struck by the degree to which feedback, continuity, and accumulating experience have resulted in the steady improvement of the quality of training, and in the systematic elimination of approaches that are ineffective, or inappropriate to Malayan needs. An added factor contributing to Northern Illinois' effectiveness in training for Southeast Asian countries is that in some cases the director of the training program has been an expert on the host country. Ed.

"Rep" staff or the Volunteers. On arrival, the PCVs were taken to the University of Malaya for a four-week in-country training program. University officials, such as the head of the residential college (dormitory) that housed the PCVs, and the Registrar of the university who made most of the arrangements, could not have been more hospitable. And the same could be said of Malayans, from the Prime Minister on down, who entertained the Volunteers almost too generously.

The Volunteers, who had been trained intensively at De Kalb for eight weeks, were impatient to begin the actual Peace Corps experience of a specific job. Four weeks of additional training turned out to be painfully too long. (In-country training was reduced to ten days for the second group.)

One characteristic of the Malaya One Volunteers was an intense ingroup solidarity. Having shared an experience of unusual intensity in the training program, and now entering the unknown and threatening atmosphere of a transcultural situation, most of the PCVs relied heavily on their group for strength and reassurance. To them, the staff, being of the Peace Corps but not of the group, was to be looked on with suspicion and treated warily. For the first time, we on the staff realized vividly what a distance can exist between the staff subculture and the Volunteer subculture.

This artificially intense ingroup solidarity was a transitory phenomenon, which largely dissolved once the Volunteers separated to assume their individual assignments. Indeed, it was fascinating to watch the growth of self-reliance on the part of the individual Volunteer as he started on the job and came to realize that he, individually, by his own effort and personality, could and did adjust, adapt, and perform. When the Volunteers came together for a meeting some months later, they were a collection of responsible individuals rather than an artificially interdependent group.

Generally speaking, the Volunteers fitted in well. Almost all of them, in my opinion, rendered some kind of useful service to Malaya. A few were given dramatic "image" assignments in a leprosarium, or among the aboriginal hill people, or on a remote and relatively untouched off-shore island. Most, however, drew assignments of a fairly humdrum nature. Perhaps greatest credit should go to those few who, despite the best efforts of all concerned, were misassigned, whose jobs turned out to be more or less illusory, whose talents were not fully utilized. Lacking the satisfaction of work accomplished, these PCVs were still responsible for maintaining the standards of Peace Corps conduct. They could not complain too bitterly, nor criticize too openly, nor storm into their superior's office and demand American notions of efficiency. They had to bear their frustration cheerfully, while waiting for adjustments to be made—if possible at all—through the channels of staff negotiation with ministry officials. Had these Volunteers not conducted themselves with a great deal of restraint and responsibility, the difficulties they might have created would have damaged, if not destroyed, the reputation for service being painstakingly built up by the entire Peace Corps effort in Malaya.

One measure of the success of Malaya One is seen in the enthusiastic reception accorded Malaya Two less than six months later. By this time the Peace Corps had attained a sufficient reputation that the Volunteers were received in audience by the Yang di-Pertuan Agong, the Paramount Ruler, or King, of Malaya. And the initiative in arranging this audience had come from His Majesty.

Once the Volunteer started to work, the job of the staff took on additional dimensions of responsibility for the care of the Volunteers. Minimally, the new tasks included arranging for living allowances to reach the Volunteers, and checking on their health (the job of the Peace Corps physician). More broadly, the task was one of maintaining communication with the Volunteers, giving support and alleviating difficulties wherever necessary—and possible.

By and large, the staff took the position that the success of the Peace Corps would be made or lost on the basis of the sense of *individual* responsibility of each Volunteer. Thus the PCVs should be given logistical, administrative, and psychological support where needed—but not to the point where their own independent initiative and responsibility would be impaired. The staff was thus at pains to avoid intruding on the Volunteer's relationship with his job and his new community.

Communication across the subcultural gap between a well-paid staff, which theoretically and officially possessed great power over the Volunteers, and the Volunteers working in humble positions in the field was inherently far from a simple matter. It would have been easy for the staff to slip over into an authoritarian role and to insist on their own interpretations of the entire Peace Corps presence in Malaya. And occasionally that did occur, less justifiedly in some cases than in others. On the whole, however, I think it is fair to say that relations between the staff and the Volunteers were excellent.

The staff engaged in continuous dialogue with the Volunteers on the development of the Peace Corps experience, individual and collective, in Malaya. These discussions resulted in a clearer perception and appreciation of the experience on the part of the Volunteer, and thus eased the process of adjustment through making it possible for the Volunteer to gain a more realistic comprehension of the intricacies of the transcultural situation.

To the extent that this more realistic comprehension was achieved, the Malaya program suffered little from the demoralization and frustration that evidently plagued some other Peace Corps programs. The main factor in overcoming frustration was certainly the high sense of individual responsibility that each Volunteer manifested. Each, it seemed, made the personal decision to cope with whatever arose, and then lived up to the decision. But the continuing dialogue with the staff—in a way an extension of training—by clarifying what it was the Volunteer was coping with, also helped. What this dialogue accomplished was to modify the image the Volunteers held of themselves, of the Peace Corps, of their role in Malaya, of Malaya itself, and of their expectations—and thus their sense of accomplishment. The Volunteers were helped in developing a clearer comprehension of the situations they found themselves in, such as those where there was too little to do, or those where one had to accept "inefficiency" gracefully. They developed a deeper appreciation of the justification for the code of personal conduct, not only for the purpose of "making friends," but as a concrete manifestation of an attitude toward work and service. And they learned to tolerate some of the seemingly illogical demands put upon them.

Volunteers learned that they could not indiscriminately and vocally go about trying to train "counterparts," nor insist on trying to teach Malayans "better ways of doing things," without creating more barriers to communication than they could break down. They learned that their greatest contribution was being there, with dignity and humility, doing their jobs with their obvious sense of responsibility. Thus, if "better" ways were to be learned, it would be from personal example rather than from directed effort, and this, while slow, constituted the best hope of success. And, the Volunteers learned that their own greatest satisfaction would come from two years of rich and rewarding work and experience in living among people of another culture.

Obviously, these things were not *taught* by the staff; they were learned from the personal insights of the Volunteers themselves. What the staff did was to open the way to such insights by discussing with the PCVs alternative explanations of what was happening to them.

In part, the difficulties faced by the Volunteers were inevitable in the transcultural situation. But in part, problems were built into this situation by the sometimes blind enthusiasm of Peace Corps official-dom in Washington. Although they knew less about Malaya than did the Volunteers, these officials were making decisions and establishing rules influencing what the Volunteer should try to accomplish and how the Volunteer should view his situation. If a touch of messianic zeal infiltrated the Peace Corps, it was mostly to be found in the Washington subculture, rather than among the PCVs. For the PCVs, at least in Malaya, were best characterized as "responsible," rather than "dedicated"—and the difference was obvious. The picture of glamorous hardship in village and jungle, of enthusiastic welcome to selfless Americans, of eagerness of "backward people" to move toward "modernity" and "better" ways—all this crept into the expectations and images with which the Volunteers were filled, *until* they got to work. Then they discovered that that picture was inaccurate, and that they simply had to make their own, the real, adjustment.

FINAL REMARKS

The Peace Corps program in Malaya has been, I think, a success. It has succeeded not because of Peace Corps/Washington but largely in spite of it. Credit must go to the individual Volunteers, and to the large number of Malayans who greeted the new idea with sympathy (as a concrete example of the American dream, in action rather than in promises) and who treated the Americans with respect, friendship, and understanding.

So far the Peace Corps has been fortunate in the quality of its Volunteers. They generally have made the necessary adjustments without too much friction, or too much harm to themselves or others. Future success depends on a more realistic appraisal of the possible and desirable goals for effort, and of the intricacies of effective transcultural work. Or else it depends on continued good fortune.

NOTES

[1] Seven of the twelve teachers were assigned to secondary schools to teach science subjects and mathematics. All were placed in schools using English as the medium of instruction. Of the other five, one was assigned to the Technical College in Kuala Lumpur, an institution that was being built up to become a professional engineering school. Two were sent to a special school established to teach business and secretarial skills. This

school, run by the Rural and Industrial Development Authority (RIDA), was exclusively for ethnically Malay youth. One PCV was assigned to the Ministry of Labor to teach in an Apprenticeship Training scheme to prepare workers in technical skills. And finally, one engineer was assigned to the Architects Division of the Ministry of Education.

Of the twenty Volunteers for public health, fifteen were nurses, assigned to hospitals. Four were laboratory technologists intended for hospital laboratory work. And one was given the title of medical assistant and assigned to help the physician attached to the Aborigine Department, for the purpose of caring for the health of the 45,000 people who live in the jungles of Malaya and are classified as aboriginal.

The remaining four Volunteers included two surveyors assigned to the Ministry of Public Works for road construction projects, one agronomist assigned to the soil survey being undertaken by the Ministry of Agriculture, and one radio technician, assigned to the technical department of Radio Malaya.

2 Two other staff positions should be mentioned: the Peace Corps physician and the secretary. The primary concern of the physician was the health of the Volunteers. He visited them in the field periodically, and was on call for any emergency. Actually, these responsibilities did not occupy his full-time efforts, and he was assigned to part-time duties in a Malayan hospital, thus contributing to the total Peace Corps effort in Malaya. The contribution of the secretary is not as easily described, but was as significant as that of any other member of the staff. Though not a Volunteer, she still had responsibility for helping to maintain the Peace Corps image in terms of personal conduct and level of living. As part of the Peace Corps presence, she was responsible for staff-Volunteer relationships, and she had as much of an obligation to learn about Malaya as any Volunteer. She had also to cope with a hectic office, which was her primary responsibility. Staff and Volunteers alike were unanimous in praise of her contribution, which was a significant factor in maintaining the total Peace Corps spirit in Malaya.

BIBLIOGRAPHY

GULLICK, J. M.
    1963 *Malaya*. London: Ernest Benn, Ltd. A good introductory survey.
MARYANOV, GERALD S.
    1965 "American Political Science and Southeast Asian Political Development." *United Asia*. Vol. 17, No. 4 (July, August). A preliminary formulation of some of the theoretical questions underlying American overseas efforts. Some of the points raised here are reflected in my comments on the Peace Corps.
MASON, FREDERIC
    1959 *The Schools of Malaya*. Background to Malaya Series, No. 3. Singapore: Eastern Universities Press. A short account of educa-

86 GERALD S. MARYANOV

tion in Malaya, now unfortunately largely out of date due to rapid developments in the educational field.

OOI JIN-BEE
1963 *Land, People and Economy in Malaya.* London: Longmans Green and Co. A detailed geography.

PARMER, J. NORMAN
1964 "Malaysia," in George McT. Kahin, ed., *Governments and Politics of Southeast Asia.* Second edition. Ithaca, N.Y.: Cornell University Press. An excellent survey of the political system, written by the first Peace Corps Representative in Malaya.

SILCOCK, T. H., Editor
1961 *Readings in Malayan Economics.* Singapore: Eastern Universities Press. A collection of technical papers offering detailed analyses of the subject.

SILCOCK, T. H., and E. K. FISK, Editors
1963 *The Political Economy of Independent Malaya.* Singapore: Eastern Universities Press. More general than the preceding item, and offering good chapters on society and government.

WANG GUNG-WU, Editor
1964 *Malaysia: A survey.* New York: Frederick A. Praeger. A comprehensive survey of Malaysia including geography, history, literature, society, economy, and government; by an impressive list of experts mostly connected with the University of Malaya.

WINSTEDT, RICHARD
1961 *The Malays: A Cultural History.* London: Routledge and Kegan Paul, Ltd. A survey of the development of traditional Malay culture as it comes down to the present. The most comprehensive single work on the subject, by one of the leading British scholars of Malaya.
1962 *Malaya and Its History.* London: Hutchinson University Library. A short popular history.

5

Tradition and Change in a
Thai University

ALAN E. GUSKIN[1] *received his bachelor's degree in psychology, with honors, from Brooklyn College in 1958, and a master's in the same discipline from the University of Michigan in 1959. During the following two years, he was a doctoral candidate in social psychology at the University of Michigan, where he hopes soon to return to complete his studies. During the presidential campaign of 1960, Mr. Guskin was a leader of a student group that pressed for the establishment of a Peace Corps, and which is generally credited with causing candidate John F. Kennedy to make his now-historic Peace Corps speech at the San Francisco Cow Palace on November 2, 1960. During the summer of 1961, Mr. Guskin and his wife, Judith, worked in the Division of Selection of Peace Corps/Washington, and returned to Ann Arbor that fall as members of the Thailand One training group. As Volunteers, the Guskins served as instructors at a university in Bangkok. Upon returning from Thailand, Mr. Guskin joined the President's Task Force on the War Against Poverty and later became the first Director of the Division of Volunteer Evaluation and Placement, VISTA, Office of Economic Opportunity. At present he is Director of the Florida State Migrant (farm worker) Program sponsored by the Community Service Foundation under a grant from the Office of Economic Opportunity. Mr. Guskin's publications include two monographs listed in the bibliography to this chapter.*

How can a university help solve the manifold problems of a developing nation? How can a Volunteer teacher in such a university find a role that is meaningful, constructive, and satisfying? What problems does he confront along the way? I will attempt to come to grips with these questions as they apply to [Krungthep University], a pseudonym for a large university in Bangkok, Thailand. I base this chapter on observations gathered by my wife and me during two and a half exciting years, 1962–1964, as teachers at Krungthep and as members of Thailand One. The chapter is also based on the results of two social surveys carried out with Thai colleagues and students. The first of these deals with students' attitudes (Guskin 1964a); the second with problems of university instructors (Guskin 1964b).

This chapter focuses on Krungthep University's *problems*, especially those that arise from efforts by Thailand's leaders to change the nation from a traditional to a modern one. I hope that Thai readers will constantly bear in mind that I am well aware of Krungthep's many fine and laudable points, and equally aware of the numerous and difficult problems faced by universities in my own country.

THE UNIVERSITY

Thailand is a country of almost thirty million people, some 80 per cent of whom are farmers, many of them living at or near the level of poverty. All activity—whether governmental, commercial, educational, cultural, or otherwise—is centered in the country's only metropolitan area, the capital city of Bangkok. It is in this great metropolis of about two million people that Krungthep University is located. Until the summer of 1964 no university existed outside the limits of this city and there were only two universities within it.[2]

Krungthep University has an enrollment of over 6,000 and a staff of 565, of whom 118 were, as of a recent date, studying abroad—mostly in the United States. At the present time, Krungthep is the only university in the country which prepares students in both the arts and the sciences, as well as in a number of professional areas. A graduate of Krungthep is practically assured of a decent job in government administration, teaching, or some other profession. A Krungthep diploma unlocks the door to membership in the country's elite. The work of Volunteer instructors at Krungthep will therefore have an effect throughout the kingdom for many years to come.

Krungthep is divided into seven faculties or colleges, which, for the most part, are administratively independent units, each having its own dean, registrar, and schedule of classes and final examinations. On the whole, students spend most of their time taking classes in their own faculty, where the emphasis is professional and job oriented. Many students in the various faculties become teachers after graduation.

The university is a government agency and all staff members are government civil servants. At the present time, Krungthep is governed by three separate bodies, each of which almost always has overlapping responsibilities with at least one of the others. Below these three bodies is a Council of Deans, which sets the specific policies of the university, and three Deputy Rectors, who administer these policies. The Chairman of the Council of Deans is Rector of the University; he is also an army general, a Deputy Prime Minister, and Minister of Interior.

The real power within Krungthep lies with the deans, who are actually in control of everyday activities in their respective faculties. Their responsibility and power are total and unquestioned by the staff of the university and by other deans. Promotions are often decided single-handedly by the dean. Many instructors feel that the usual criteria for deciding upon promotions are personal favor and connections.[3] Instructors generally do not agree with such promotion policies but almost never overtly voice objections for fear of losing their own promotions. In general, the instructors as a group perceive themselves as not having any important responsibility for the administrative affairs of their faculty.

The Role of the Thai University Instructor

There are two basic, pervasive Thai culture patterns that place sharp limits around the ability of the instructors to express their feelings about the conditions under which they work, or to promote constructive changes in these conditions. These are that:

1. Overt displays of hostility or conflict should be avoided at all costs; interpersonal relationships should be smooth, comfortable, and easygoing.*

2. Subordinates must always show respect and obedience to their superiors.

An awareness of the importance of obedience to one's superiors is crucial to understanding the situation that faces the young, modern-oriented instructor at Krungthep. The process of socializing new instructors is especially illustrative of the way in which this submissiveness is reinforced. Because Krungthep has only recently begun a very modest graduate division, it has had to depend for qualified instructors on individuals who have received their under-graduate training at Krungthep and their graduate training abroad. The recruitment problem is complicated, however, by the fact that qualified young graduates of Krungthep are usually not able to

* The parallel with "smooth interpersonal relations" as a basic culture pattern in the Philippines (page 29) is immediately evident.—Ed.

secure scholarships to study abroad immediately after obtaining their baccalaureates. A further complication is that in the Thai occupational structure an individual who is hired by a particular organization is expected, and expects, to spend the remainder of his life in that organization. As a result of these two factors, the university usually finds itself hiring its own recent graduates as instructors in order to avoid permanently losing gifted prospective instructors to other organizations. Thus many a young person is hired as an instructor in the same department in which, a few weeks before, he was a student. His new colleagues are his former teachers. Since in the Thai tradition a student owes his teacher lifelong deference and loyalty, the new instructor treats his new colleagues with the same deference as before, and is careful *never* to contradict them, regardless of how old-fashioned and maladaptive their ideas might be.

At least in some of the faculties at Krungthep, the new instructor is rarely assigned to academic duties. Instead, he is given a variety of minor clerical tasks to perform. To the Western eye these tasks often seem to be of doubtful utility—until one learns to view them as a form of ritual obeisance whose latent function is to help maintain the existing hierarchy of status and respect relationships. After two or three years the instructor is usually sent overseas at the request of his chairman or dean. For this preferment he must, of course, remain forever grateful, loyal, and deferent.

When the young instructor returns from his graduate studies abroad he is often filled with enthusiasm. He is full of impatient eagerness to introduce modernizing changes which he feels are necessary both for his university and his country. (In this respect he is not too different from many PCVs newly arrived in Thailand.) But soon the returnee finds that this is not to be. His superiors have other ideas. They have a heavy stake in the status quo. Often they know less about their discipline than does the new returnee, and hence feel a threat to their academic positions, their professional reputations, and their self-respect. It is difficult to have professional discussions with old-fashioned Thai superiors because any professional disagreement will be perceived by them in *personal* rather than professional terms. The *content* of the discussion is less important to them than the maintenance of a pecking order of personalities and a hierarchy of respect relationships. Quickly it becomes more and more poignantly clear to the returnee that the same old deference and respect patterns are expected of him now, as before. Despite his new master's degree, or even doctorate, he is still perceived and treated as young and "immature," still a former student, albeit a bit more prestigious.

The typical returned instructor is thus caught in a painful dilemma. His choice is between status advancement and professional innovation. After so many years of study, it is no wonder that a young person brought up in this status-rigid culture should yearn for the prestige and respect that can ordinarily come only through the attainment of high formal rank. And yet he wants to introduce modernizing change, to move his country forward along lines that, to him, are so obviously appropriate and necessary. But to introduce change is often to "fight city hall," with the end result that *both* the attempted innovation and the promotion of the young instructor will be impeded. On the other hand, giving in is easy and often brings tremendous rewards and preferment. For the Thai status system is a highly rewarding one—once one has achieved a reasonably high position in it. Status is often achieved by hard work and a combination of professional performance and appropriate deference behavior. However—and this is a crucial point—once one has "arrived" at a high status position there is no real need for him to continue to excel in a professional sense. Once he has arrived, his status becomes *ascribed* to him, and his achievements are no longer important. Hence, if one keeps quiet he gets promoted; if one gets promoted he has a greater chance for future promotions; and once one achieves high status it is extremely difficult to lose it. How easy it is, then, for the young instructor to reason—or rationalize— that in the future he will be in a position to do what he wants if only he keeps quiet at the present time!

However, keeping quiet is not an easy psychological experience for the instructor returning to Krungthep's various faculties after study abroad. Frustrations must be smothered. Hostilities must remain unexpressed. Smooth interpersonal relations must at all times be preserved. One's superiors must not sense one's frustrations —which indeed they usually do not. One's superiors must be constantly placated and gratified by the performance of a variety of obeisant clerical services, many of which are really unnecessary. To make this obeisant role at all palatable, many young returned instructors resort to the psychological mechanism of separating the job from the self, and of deriving their personal satisfactions away from the university rather than in the performance of their truly professional duties. They drift further and further away from their classrooms, their students, and their research.

But this traditional pattern of silent, deep frustration is beginning to change, as more and more young instructors return to Krungthep from graduate study in the West. These returnees are beginning to get together and share their common frustrations. They provide some psychological and political support for each other. They are beginning to express their frustrations to their superiors. However, it is important to point out that these ideas for change are still met with some ambivalence, not only by the superiors, as would be expected, but also by the young returnees themselves.

The typical Krungthep instructor remains in his position despite frustration, discouragement, and some alienation. Some have no other choice; no other government agency or private firm has need of their services and skills. Others could find new employment, but remain at Krungthep for reasons of financial security and hoped-for advancement to higher rank and prestige.

The Thai Instructor-Student Relationship

The frustrations stemming from the young instructor's relations with his superiors are to some extent relieved by his relations with those below him, namely, his students. In many ways, the young instructor is, or becomes, just as insensitive to his students as his superiors are to him. In our study of instructors and their problems (Guskin 1964b), a large percentage of the instructors expressed the opinion that students at Krungthep are not responsible enough to be in the university, and did not feel that their students were enjoyable to talk with or to become personally involved with. These survey results, plus my personal observations, suggest that despite their training in the West these young returnees are staying well within the traditional teacher-student relationship: the teacher is the transmitter of knowledge and deserves every possible deference and respect; the student is immature, passive, and ignorant—an empty vessel into which proper knowledge must be poured. In short, the instructors tend to perceive their students as not yet having received responsibility, and hence as not worthy of receiving it.

It would be unfair, however, to imply that the instructors completely lack respect for their students. On the contrary, most instructors seem to believe that the students are the best in the country, and this belief carries with it a measure of respect. Nonetheless, many instructors condescend to their students to a remarkable degree. And one could hypothesize that those instructors who are more condescending are the very ones who are finding their *own* positions in the status hierarchy less emotionally rewarding. In one faculty especially, this condescension reaches extreme proportions. For example, one day an instructor, who was advisor to a group of upperclassmen, called a meeting of students. He accused them of being disrespectful to their instructors. He made clear that thereafter whenever they passed a teacher in the hallway they were to stop and give the "wai" salute.* He admonished the students not to move until the teacher passed them. Next followed a lecture on grooming for boys and girls and a lecture on proper dress. Another instructor in the same faculty at a different time lectured the students on cleanliness, on the fact that they ate in dirty restaurants and didn't know how to take care of themselves. At yet another time the graduate and undergraduate students were told that they did not look like students because they did not carry enough books. After each of these lectures the students were furious—but they never expressed their feelings in any form to their instructors.

Condescension also occurs in other forms. Student organizations are discouraged. Student debates normally deal with frivolous, "safe" subjects. The student union is housed in an old and impossibly small building.

For their part, the students outwardly accept their subservience and immaturity—because it is culturally expected of them. They maintain a "face" to the world that pleases others and makes others feel that the expectations of them as students are accurate. Yet they are unhappy and frustrated. As seen in *Changing Values of Thai College Students* (Guskin 1964a), they desire to take part in the future development of their country; they desire to be stimulated by their instructors; they desire to participate in the learning process; they want their instructors to be concerned with them. They know in a sense that they must accept responsibility for the future of Thailand by becoming responsible teachers and civil servants. And yet, when talking about their own maturity, they are confused; they lack faith in themselves. They know that they do not study enough, that they often do not act responsibly in their own very limited student government, and that their discussions are often about trivial matters. They seem afraid to act, to discuss, to become involved. Often they blame their instructors or the authorities; at other times they blame themselves.

* The Thai "wai" salute is one in which the palms of one's hands are touching as in the Western praying position and the fingertips are placed under the chin. The junior salutes first, and then the senior returns the salute. There are subtle gradations of position that communicate how seriously the junior takes the senior's status position, and vice versa.—A. E. G.

It seems clear that part of the reason for condescending to the students is a fear—unspoken and doubtless often unconscious—of what would happen if the students were to group together and frankly voice their demands. Authorities and instructors seem to fear that such a development would upset their hierarchy, undermine their own statuses, and bring about chaos. Doubtless they are right if we assume that all these events would occur suddenly. But a gradual relaxation of anachronistic rigidities in status behavior would, in my opinion, cause few serious upsets. Moreover, such a relaxation is absolutely necessary if Thailand is to continue her march toward modernization. For modernization requires that individuals be able to discuss technical and professional problems and work out solutions on the basis of the professional *issues* involved, rather than on the basis of who has the superior status. Given the modernization ends that the leaders of Thailand themselves have determined, therefore, it follows that relaxation of status rigidities is a necessary means toward those ends at many places in the social structure, and certainly at Krungthep University.

Lack of Social Service Orientation

The notion of social services or extension services to help solve social problems as well as to educate the general public is not a part of Krungthep University's program. Moreover, when students take educational field trips to the hinterland, these are likely to have more of the atmosphere of a picnic than a serious educational experience. Individual instructors are often asked to give lectures to different types of groups—almost always a short seminar or in-service training program of a few days to a week run by the government, which teachers or other government officials are expected to attend. Instructors are also sometimes called upon for consultation, and a few of them are asked to help with research projects. Krungthep University, however, even though it is itself part of the government and is located in a rapidly expanding urban community, does not attempt to coordinate these individual endeavors, nor does it seek out special functions that it could perform.

The instructors' lack of social involvement is passed along to the students. Courses are taught primarily by sheer resort to textbooks. Course content is seldom related to Thailand's pressing social, demographic, and developmental problems. Students almost never become involved in social service activities. Indeed, almost all of them leave the university without having been led to think in meaningful and concrete terms about the problems facing their country and what could be done to solve them.

It is no wonder, then, that students rarely go into community development type work after graduation, and that those who do usually do so only with the hope of soon getting higher government positions in Bangkok. This latter fact has led to general disappointment with the role that university graduates have played in these vital programs. It also is no wonder that many students desire to remain in the capital or in the larger urban centers, where promotion comes more easily, where part-time outside employment opportunities are numerous, and where medical services, entertainment, and other amenities are available.

Identification with the West

This lack of involvement on the part of the instructors and their students serves to reinforce the ever-growing cultural gap that separates the university from the masses of people. A majority of the instructors were born and reared in Bangkok, or else in upcountry families culturally oriented to Bangkok rather than to the local countryside. Almost all were educated at the baccalaureate level in this capital city, and more than half have received a master's degree abroad—usually in the United States. As a result their knowledge of the rural areas of the country, where more than 80 per cent of the people live, is decidedly limited. Indeed, one "unintended consequence" of increased education of young Thais abroad is that a further wedge is being driven between the elite and the masses.

Increased overseas education has also led to a greater emphasis on course content dealing with the United States and Europe, to the detriment of adequate coverage of the problems of Thailand or other, comparable, Asian countries. The instructors themselves place a higher value on "things" American than they place on things from Japan, India, or Malaysia. The students naturally form a similar identification.

An important reason for the general lack of involvement of the educated Thais with other Asian countries is the historical fact of Thailand's continuous independence throughout the entire period of European colonization in Asia. While many newly independent Asian countries are striving for their own identity as well as an identity as Asians, Thailand has felt little need for this. As a result, the educated Thais have continued their identification with Europe and the United States and have not attempted to reach out for a new identity as Asians. Possibly the recently formed Association of Southeast Asian countries (ASA) among Thailand, Malaysia, and the Philippines—though weak and unstable because of present political problems—will begin to have some effect on the educated Thais' identity with their neighbors.

Limited Research Activities

Research activities of Krungthep instructors in our study are extremely limited: less than 20 per cent have written any type of research report, textbook, or paper (mimeographed or printed) related to their general academic area and only about 10 per cent did so within the last three years. The reasons for this are numerous: promotion almost never takes into account research activities; to write a report is a commitment on paper to ideas that may not be in agreement with those of a superior; all activities of the instructor must be approved by his superior who may not feel that the research interests of the instructor are important; facilities available for publication are extremely limited; only small amounts of research money are available; there is a lack of stimulation from colleagues, most of whom are not interested in research; good library facilities with up-to-date journals from overseas are lacking; there are few professional forums of like-minded people who desire to listen to reports on each other's work; there are few, if any, graduate assistants to help the instructor carry out research projects; the instructor's time is taken up with long hours of teaching, committee assignments, clerical tasks; and so on. No doubt if more emphasis were placed on doing research and if their colleagues were interested in research, many more instructors would be producing research. While it is important and exciting to note that about 50 per cent of the research reported has been accomplished within the last three years, the need is so enormous that this represents only a small proportion of what should and could be done.

THE ROLE OF THE VOLUNTEER

Thailand One arrived in the host country in January 1962. In this contingent were forty-five PCVs of whom ten were assigned to Krungthep University as instructors in a variety of fields.

We soon learned that the Volunteer instructor's role was to be sharply different from that of his Thai colleague in a variety of ways. While the Thai instructor is involved in a lifetime job, the PCV is in Thailand for only about two years. The Thai instructor will be bypassed for promotion if he argues with his superior; the PCV will at most be simply disregarded. The Thai instructor occupies a low rung on an institutional ladder. The Volunteer is in many ways considered special, invited to high-level social gatherings, and at times permitted to bypass the hierarchical structure if he wishes to speak directly with high-level authorities. This special status affords him an opportunity to fulfill functions that are needed and that his Thai colleagues may have difficulty performing.

The PCV is challenged by his opportunities, but also feels ambivalent about his position. He is egalitarian and does not want to be given special treatment. This section will discuss how a number of Volunteers have played their role.

The Volunteer-Student Relationship

The typical PCV at Krungthep went out of his way to form close relationships with his or her students. The PCV emphasized discussion in the classroom, and otherwise attempted to create an atmosphere in which the students could participate in the learning process. He confronted his students with questions about Thailand, problems of Thai national development, and the students' future role in this development.

In general, the students responded favorably to this approach. They seemed to exhibit enhanced self-respect when asked about their own future role in Thailand's development. They seemed to appreciate the opportunity to discuss questions openly. Many of them approached the Volunteer instructor outside the classroom, plying him with questions about the United States and a myriad of other subjects. Some students sought the PCV's counsel about personal problems.

In all, I think the Volunteer-student relationship was a healthy one. It was healthy for the students because it hastened their maturity somewhat and encouraged them to look for new approaches to Thailand's problems, approaches in which *they* could participate. The extended dialogues between Volunteer and student helped each to question his own beliefs and values in an atmosphere where introspection and change could take place.

The Volunteer's Identification with Asia

At Krungthep, the Volunteers were dismayed to discover what a high value was placed on "things" American and European. They had come to Thailand to learn about Thailand and Asia—not the West! Ironically, one of the PCVs' greatest accomplishments at

Krungthep—as elsewhere in Thailand—might prove to be simply the de-emphasizing of "things" Western. The typical Volunteer instructor introduced course content designed to focus attention on Thailand as an Asian country, and upon other, comparable Asian countries. By studying what other Asian countries have borrowed from the West, and what they have refused to borrow, Thailand's future leaders will be in a better position to guide the borrowing process in years to come.

Social Service Orientation

The general absence of social service orientation among the instructors and students at Krungthep was quickly evident to the typical Volunteer instructor, who naturally moved to fill this gap. One of them, for example, attempted to involve a branch of the university in the support of a village primary school by bringing the school's teachers to Krungthep for special in-service training; by taking some students from the university into the school and its surrounding village community to do research on villagers' problems; by providing the schoolchildren with needed clothing, vitamins, milk, and books; and by providing the school with audiovisual aids. All of these gifts to the children were given by local groups or by local offices of international organizations. There have been other similar attempts. These activities and concerns of the Volunteers sometimes stimulate their students to think more about the less fortunate members of their society who reside in the urban slums and in the poor rural areas.

Stimulation of Research

The PCVs at Krungthep have had some impact in stimulating social research by their Thai colleagues and students. Most of this research has been of an applied nature, geared to Thailand's problems of modernization. The usual pattern has been for the PCV to collaborate with a research-oriented Thai instructor, using students as research assistants and interviewers. Two of the greatest problems have been simply to encourage the students to believe that their own ideas are important and to train them in thinking independently and creatively.

New Curriculum Offerings

Volunteers in Thailand One stimulated and aided various departments of the university to develop new courses or curricula. They helped establish the first graduate program in educational psychology, a new curriculum for the Department of City and Town Planning, and a new program in physical education.

Support for Younger Thai Colleagues

As we have seen, young Thai instructors returning from their studies abroad are usually frustrated, both personally and professionally. Friendship with a PCV often helps to reduce this personal frustration. The PCV provides the returnees with an American friend who is similar to the people with whom they have spent their last few years, yet who is now living in their own country and facing a very similar work situation. Their professional frustrations can also sometimes be reduced by collaboration with a PCV on joint research and teaching projects or by informal discussions of professional topics which will keep alive their desires to help Thailand and keep their professional skills from becoming rusty. The PCV can, in short, informally help bring about a healthy readaptation by the Thai returnee to his own country.

PROBLEMS OF THE UNIVERSITY VOLUNTEER

The problems and frustrations of the PCV at Krungthep are numerous; they stem both from violations of his preconceived notions of his role and from difficulties in the objective cultural situation in which he finds himself. Below are presented four major problem areas.

"Rural Image" Versus Acculturated Reality

Before joining the Peace Corps, the image that the potential PCV develops of his role overseas—through Peace Corps publicity and folklore—is that he will work in rural areas, in isolated, unacculturated places. He pictures himself teaching children through an exotic language, roughing it on a community development project, or introducing new agricultural techniques to people still adhering to a comparatively "pure" tradition much different from the American. A metropolis like Bangkok does not, to him, represent the "real" Thailand or the "real" Thai people. And Krungthep University, run by a faculty who are in many ways highly acculturated to Western norms and values, hardly presents the monolithic cultural challenge anticipated by the Volunteer. As a result, it is probably generally true that PCVs assigned to the metropolis have been less happy than those assigned upcountry.

This rural image was reinforced during training. Much of the better available published information on Thailand deals primarily with rural areas.[4] Most lecturers to the Thailand One group at the University of Michigan tended to deal primarily with the rural, unacculturated Thai people. Much of this emphasis was appropriate enough since most of the group were destined to work in small upcountry towns and cities where the general level of acculturation and Westernization is much lower than that found at Krungthep University.

Peace Corp trainees at the training site usually quickly form into a tight in-group and develop their own little subculture of understandings and values. Thailand One at the University of Michigan was no exception. The members were intensely interested in Thailand, in Thai culture, language, and cuisine—indeed, in everything Thai. The commitment was almost total. We were dedicated to proving that Americans can live at the level of their Thai co-workers—which was pictured as being a humble level indeed. We were committing two years of our lives to service in a country that was *different* from our own—and it was these differences that we learned about and built into our expectations.

After such preparation, assignment to a large urban university can come as a shock. In the case of my wife and myself, for example, our expectation was that we would teach in the upcountry city of Chiengmai. Only at the last minute was our assignment unexpectedly changed to Krungthep—much to our disappointment.

When we arrived at Krungthep University, we were eager to demonstrate our willingness and ability to deal with the Thais on Thai terms—and to us this meant *traditional* Thai terms. Little did we realize, however, that many of our acculturated Thai colleagues were just as eager to deal with us on Western ("farang") terms. Some of our Westernized Thai colleagues and other urban acquaintances felt a persistent need to be recognized by Westerners as professionally competent and personally acceptable. At the same time, our Thai colleagues were flattered and reassured when we showed an interest in their own traditional forms of behavior and an ability to adhere to these forms, and often they encouraged our efforts in this direction. A good part of our first year at Krungthep was therefore characterized by confusion as we struggled to learn when to behave in the Thai mode and when in the Western. Often, we would behave in the Thai mode, only to perceive that our Thai acquaintance wanted to deal on Western terms—or vice versa. At such moments, the simplicity of the "rural image" seemed particularly inviting. Our difficulties were graphically illustrated in a picture on the front page

of an English-language newspaper in Thailand: a Volunteer, recently arrived from the United States, was giving the traditional
Thai "wai" salute to a welcoming Thai official, who in turn was
extending his hand in anticipation of a Western handshake.

But the problem was much more than simply one of how to
behave under given circumstances. It also presented difficulties of
identification. We all went to Thailand hoping to make good and
lasting Thai friends. We found this to be relatively easy where a
Thai was either quite traditional and unacculturated, or where he
was highly Westernized and spoke idiomatic English. In either case,
we found his behavior "easy to take," and found it relatively easy to
establish a friendship or relaxed acquaintanceship. The difficulty,
however, was that many of our Thai colleagues at Krungthep were
of neither pure type, but rather an uneasy, ambiguous mix of
traditional and Western values and behavioral tendencies. To over-
simplify a little, they were "neither Thai nor Westerner." To gain
the meaningful and enduring friendship of such a person, on terms
that are rewarding for both parties, requires no little amount of
patience and effort on both sides.

Avoiding an Inflated Ego

The typical American Volunteer is automatically perceived by
all Thais as a "farang," or Westerner. And the Thais automatically
ascribe high status to the "farang," unless he is obviously a serious
reprobate of some kind. There are three principal explanations for
this phenomenon: the fact that the Thais identify overwhelmingly
with the West; the fact that they have never been colonized and
hence have no reason to hate Westerners on that score; and the fact
that most Westerners have indeed held relatively important positions in the Thai social and governmental hierarchy, as teachers, as
advisors, as administrators, and as businessmen or missionaries. Many
Thais would thus consider it almost unnatural, for example, were
they to see a Westerner in Thailand working with his hands. For
all these reasons, colleagues and students at Krungthep were soon
deferring to the PCVs to a degree that was unexpected, undesired,
and, at times, downright embarrassing.

Being placed on a pedestal is anathema to the PCV for a number
of reasons. First, the Volunteer is by ideology an egalitarian. Second,
he wants a "people-to-people" experience and resents any status
differences which come between him and the people. Third, he is
usually modest in a quite genuine sense; he does not regard himself
as very important and hence resists "V.I.P." treatment. Fourth is

the fact that the PCV is directly supervised by a Thai boss. In this respect he is unlike most AID (Agency for International Development) advisors, American businessmen, or State Department personnel, all of whom normally report to an American supervisor.

Thai status behavior is, nonetheless, sufficiently tempting and subtle that it is easy for even a determined PCV to fall its victim. In a thousand different ways, the colleagues and students of the PCV instructor can flatter and praise. Generations of cultural emphasis upon status deference and smooth interpersonal relations come to bear upon the Thai-Volunteer relationship. What many Thais really want, however, is to be recognized as equals, or at least as somebody special, by the Volunteer whom they place on this high pedestal.

The Volunteer must cope with a status system in the process of slow egalitarian change, about which most Thais at Krungthep feel considerable ambivalence. The rules of the game are ambiguous, and the cues are often subtle and unspoken. The PCV must learn quickly that spoken agreement often does not mean real agreement, that flattery is often *pro forma*, and that almost all of his colleagues and students do not want him to *act* important, whether or not they feel that he really is important.

It is probably fair to say that most Thailand One PCVs at Krungthep did eventually learn to cope with the pitfalls of the status system, and did learn to avoid an inflated ego. They learned to work with their Thai supervisor, even where that person might have been technically less competent than they were. They generally avoided drifting into an "advisor" status. In one instance where such a drift did occur, the effectiveness of an otherwise very competent PCV was curtailed. Eventually the department concerned quietly disassociated the Volunteer from itself. As a result, when work originally requested by the authorities was finished, it was not looked upon as having been produced by a member of their own staff, and such work will probably not prove as effective in the long run as it might have been.

"Rocking the Boat"

It is probably generally true in the underdeveloped world that the introduction of new, modern teaching techniques will often "rock the boat" of status relationships within a university or school. Certainly this was the case at Krungthep. The authorities and senior faculty at Krungthep were unenviably caught between the forces of the status quo, which affords them much enjoyable prestige and privilege, and the forces of change and development, which they often see as socially desirable, or at any rate inevitable. While many of Krungthep's senior faculty members are deliberately introducing change and others are not resisting it, they understandably want to make sure that this change does not threaten their own status positions too strongly or too soon. Consciously or otherwise, they often introduce or permit change in such a way that the consequences will not become threatening until at least such time as they are ready to retire.

In such a situation, the PCV has a certain advantage. He has the technical competence to introduce change, especially American-style change, which nowadays in Thailand is particularly valued. But at the same time he is temporary and does not occupy a position on the status ladder. He thus does not directly threaten the status position of the senior Thai faculty member. So far, so good. However, the threat commences when the PCV begins to associate with his junior Thai colleague just back from study in the West. For this junior colleague *is* a threat, at least potentially, to the senior faculty member. And the threat becomes compounded when the PCV begins treating his students in unorthodox democratic ways that cannot help but lead to student expectations that their Thai teachers ought to treat them that way too, or at least more nearly that way. Thus, there is initially little threat when the PCV introduces improved methods for the teaching of English as a second language, new audio-visual aids, or new research equipment. But then the boat starts to rock as the Volunteer begins collaborating with newly returned Thai colleagues on action-oriented research projects. And it rocks some more when the PCV innocently starts teaching English with materials whose cultural content deals with Thailand and Asia rather than Britain and America, for now it becomes difficult for Thai colleagues to continue teaching the same course using an American textbook. And when the Volunteer sits on the grass talking with a small informal group of students about himself, the United States, current events, and so on—in Thai as well as in English—he is indeed threatening the traditional teacher-student relationship. At some level of consciousness, the senior Thai administrators accurately perceive that the more the PCV proceeds to lead his students to think critically and freely, the more he is threatening the rigidities of Thailand's traditional academic status system. Thus, it requires considerable ingenuity and intellectual and professional competence for the PCV to perform his role without unduly antagonizing his superiors.

Qualifications and Placement

The problem of qualifications is an important one. In Thailand One, underqualified PCVs had difficulty gaining the respect and confidence of their Thai colleagues and had considerable difficulty relating effectively to them—especially when, as sometimes happened, the supply of qualified Thais was quite adequate. Their Thai supervisors were placed in the unhappy position of finding ways to keep these Volunteers occupied. And the PCVs themselves were unhappy because they were unable to do a satisfying job of teaching.

At Krungthep, and perhaps at most universities in the economically less developed areas, the problem is to avoid both underqualification and overqualification. Generally speaking, the qualifications that seemed most appropriate were at least a master's degree with perhaps some work accomplished toward the doctorate. In most cases, however, a doctorate would represent overqualification. Holders of doctor's degrees are still uncommon enough at Krungthep so that it would be an anomaly for such a person—even in PCV status—to hold a "middle-level manpower" position. And, at least in certain faculties, the temptation would be too great—both on the part of the Thais and of the PCV—to use the latter's services in a supervisory or high-level advisory capacity.

CONCLUSIONS

This paper might lead one to feel that Thailand is a difficult place to live. This is not so. The Thai people almost always smile, they are almost always courteous and good natured, and they are the most magnificent hosts one could hope to find anywhere. Discussions and gatherings invariably end up in a great deal of fun. In fact, having fun is considered one of the most important things an individual can experience, for this is a culture still basically oriented toward "being," rather than toward "doing." It is, as most tourists describe it, a land of happy-go-lucky people.

But this is only one aspect of Thai life. The Volunteer sees a different, deeper picture. And the Volunteer at Krungthep sees the mold of the old and the portent of the new perhaps more vividly than those assigned upcountry, where change is slower. He sees the mask of the happy-go-lucky, peaceful Thai person, and is glad that he does. But he also sees beneath this mask. There he sees all sorts of forces pushing or pulling in the direction of social, cultural, and political change. Aspirations toward modernism clash with reactions of those who cling to cherished status. Achievement vies ever more strongly with ascription as the basis for social status and economic reward. Problems of urbanization intrude ever more pressingly, and refuse to be ignored. And lurking just over the horizon is the most complicating factor of all, the demographic explosion: for while there are only thirty million people in Thailand today, there will be fifty million fifteen years from now!

To cope with the pressures and counterpressures of work at a place like Krungthep is not easy. It requires careful preparation of a special sort. It requires special training to prepare the PCV for the ambiguities he will confront in an acculturated milieu. It requires preparation to achieve effectiveness both in the professional and in the personal sense—and the requirements of these two kinds of success are mutually antithetical to a degree. And of course it requires a sense of humor, for the Thais love humor and fun—and it is fun to be in Thailand.

NOTES

1 I would like to thank Arthur and Ann Feraru, Samuel Guskin, and my wife, Judith, for making many valuable suggestions in an earlier draft of this paper.

2 Officially Thailand lists five universities in Bangkok. However, one of these is a medical school complex (including a hospital, dental school, and so on), another an agricultural college that is being converted into a university, and another a Fine Arts School that eventually will be part of one of the two universities existing at present. In June 1964, a third university was opened in North Thailand, at Chiengmai.

3 All references to the attitudes of instructors represent the results of a questionnaire study as supported, and at times extended, by my own observations.

4 This is partly due to the fact that most of the research on Thailand has been done by anthropologists whose major concern is the rural area. Peace Corps literature also emphasizes jobs in the rural areas.

BIBLIOGRAPHY

BLANCHARD, WENDELL, et al.
    1958   *Thailand: Its People, Its Society, Its Culture.* New Haven, Conn.: Human Relations Area Files Press.
GUSKIN, ALAN E.
    1964a *Changing Values of Thai College Students: A Research Report.* Bangkok: Faculty of Education, Chulalongkorn University. (With the assistance of Tussanee Sookthawee.)
    1964b *A Study of Chulalongkorn University Instructors.* Mimeographed.

HERMAN, S. N., and E. O. SCHILD
    1961   "The Stranger Group in a Cross-Cultural Situation." *Sociometry,* Vol. 24, pp. 164-177.
KAUFMAN, HOWARD KEVA
    1960   *Bangkhuad: A Community Study.* New York: J. J. Augustin.
MOSEL, JAMES N.
    1959   "Thai Administrative Behavior," in William J. Siffin, ed., *Toward the Comparative Study of Public Administration.* Bloomington, Ind.: Indiana University Press.
PASLOV, EUGENE
    1964   "Is It 'Peace Corps' in the City?" *Peace Corps Volunteer,* Vol. 2, No. 4. (July).
SKINNER, G. WILLIAM
    1957   *Chinese Society in Thailand: An Analytical History.* Ithaca, N.Y.: Cornell University Press.
SMITH, M. B., J. FAWCETT, R. EZEKIEL, and S. ROTH
    1963   "A Factorial Study of Morale among Peace Corps Teachers in Ghana." *Journal of Social Issues,* Vol. 19. No. 3, pp. 10-32. This study found, among other things, that Volunteers assigned upcountry tended to have higher morale than those assigned to larger urban centers.
WILSON, DAVID A.
    1962   *Politics in Thailand.* Ithaca, N.Y.: Cornell University Press.

6

Moving Mountains in Afghanistan

LOUIS DUPREE[1] *received his doctorate in anthropology from Harvard, specializing in the Indo-European language areas of the Middle East and Central Asia, especially Afghanistan and Iran. He is a Research Associate of the American Museum of Natural History, under whose sponsorship he has made two field trips to Afghanistan. Dr. Dupree has held teaching positions as Associate Professor of Middle Eastern Studies at the Air University and Associate Professor of Anthropology at Pennsylvania State University. Since 1959 he has been an Associate of the American Universities Field Staff, in which capacity he has spent three extended periods in Afghanistan, and has had a continuing opportunity to observe the Volunteers in action there. Besides his frequent reports for the American Universities Field Staff, Dr. Dupree has published numerous monographs, articles, and reviews dealing with Afghanistan and neighboring areas, and with the fields of anthropology, archaeology, geography, geology, and zoology.*

THE first group of nine Peace Corps Volunteers reached Afghanistan in September 1962, the result of a triumphant American bureaucratic accident and much Afghan soul-searching. If the bureaucratic system of the American government selects the right man for the right job at the right time, many outsiders (including myself) assume the appointment must have been a mistake. So it appeared when Mr. Cleo Shook came to Afghanistan to "sell" the Afghans on a program. Mr. Shook, fluent in Afghan Farsi (Persian), had served in Afghanistan as Director of the Afghan Institute of Technology from 1953 to 1956, and as an AID (Agency for International Development) official there from 1957 to 1960. The Afghans greatly respect his personality and talents.*

* Unbeknown to Dr. Dupree, Mr. Shook's assignment to Afghanistan was indeed a kind of mistake. In the summer of 1961 I worked in the Far East Programs section of Peace Corps/Washington. One day the Acting Director of that section told me that Mr. Shook would soon join his staff. I asked him

Before Mr. Shook's selling visit, many observers predicted that the Afghan government would flatly reject Peace Corps Volunteers for three very cogent reasons: (1) Soviet propaganda, which labeled the Peace Corps as a callous American attempt to spread a subversive intelligence network throughout the developing world under the banner of humanitarianism; (2) Afghan fears that acceptance of Volunteers would jeopardize their neutral image on the international scene; and (3) Afghan concern that the Soviets might offer to flood the country with Young Pioneers to counteract the Volunteers.

Cleo Shook convinced the Afghan government of the purity of the Peace Corps. The Afghans, however, were so eager to allay Soviet fears of their becoming more pro-Western, that they requested only fourteen Volunteers, of whom five were lost during training and selection, so that Afghanistan One consisted of only nine PCVs. The Soviets, for their part, have shown no interest in shipping Young Pioneers to Afghanistan, particularly after the dismal failure of their "virgin lands" experiment in Kazakhstan.

Afghanistan One was thus greeted by Afghans who viewed them with suspicious concern. The Soviet personnel in Kabul continued to consider the Peace Corps as an adjunct of the Central Intelligence Agency. The reaction of other foreigners in the capital ranged from incredulity to contempt. Some members of the American colony in Kabul coddled the "poor dears," while other Americans remained aloof and even disparaged the PCVs' initial efforts to be effective. Among these latter were a number of "experienced" AID and embassy personnel who doubted that the young, raw PCVs could avoid making mistakes. Before we examine the activities of Afghanistan One, however, let us describe the cultural matrix in which it operated.

---

why Mr. Shook was not going to be assigned to the Near East-South Asia Programs section, which included Afghanistan and Iran, whose language Mr. Shook speaks. I was told not to worry about this—for the obvious though unspoken reason that the Far East Acting Director wanted to build up his staff, and that this was more important to him than considerations of cultural competence. (It was true that Mr. Shook had also worked in the Far East area, but his principal competence was clearly and overwhelmingly in the Afghanistan-Iran area.) At that time, to the best of my recollection, there was no one in the Near East-South Asia Programs section who fluently spoke a language indigenous to that area. It was only months later that it somehow happened that Mr. Shook was freed from his Far East assignment and made his programing trip to Afghanistan.—Ed.

A LAND ONCE GREAT

Afghanistan has an estimated population of 13 million living in an area approximately the size of Texas. Two United Nations estimates indicate the relative state of modernity: even after a decade of developmental activity there is still 90 to 95 per cent illiteracy and 40 per cent infant mortality up to two years of age. In addition, about 90 per cent of the people engage in basic food production, in contrast to about 6 per cent in the United States.

Until the late 1950's, practically no roads worthy of the name existed, and Kabul, the capital, had no adequately paved streets. Almost no wheeled vehicles could be found in Afghan villages, and donkeys, camels, horses, mules, and even cattle served for transport. A notoriously incompetent telecommunications system made overall government supervision and control difficult or impossible, except in zones of easy accessibility.

An oligarchy of the Royal Family ruled (Dupree 1963*a*), and the government, although oriented toward development in the economic sense, suppressed political opposition. A continuing border problem with Pakistan effectively closed Afghanistan's economic relations with the West several times from 1947 to 1963 (Dupree 1961*a,b*). There is little socioeconomic mobility. Civil servants remain underpaid, and—in order to survive—continue to accept "baksheesh" for anticipated services. Clerks, often the products of nepotism, clutter up offices, laboriously recording data which the government seldom uses.

Given these facts, it is no wonder that superficial observers see Afghanistan as being a backward, conservative, landlocked, relatively isolated, lethargic, illiterate, priest-ridden country with little past and less future. Such a view cannot go unchallenged, however, because the area we now call Afghanistan once served as a great transmitter of peoples and ideas, and was once one of the most important commercial centers in the history of Asia.

Important archaeological finds indicate that prehistoric Afghanistan probably helped support one of the three great early riverine civilizations made possible by controlled food production: the Indus Valley. The Nile Valley and the Tigris-Euphrates produced the other two (Casal 1961; Dupree 1963*b*; Fairservis 1961).

The importance of the Afghan area continues in the historic period. Alexander the Great subdued but never completely subjugated the Afghan hill tribesmen, nevertheless leaving behind him a cultural legacy of Hellenism with its humanistic philosophy.

Buddhism came next, pushed out of India by a resurgent Brahman-
ism; it became established in Gandhara in what is now northwest
Pakistan and southern Afghanistan. The Afghan town of Bactra
served as the central transshipment point along the fabled Silk
Route which extended from Rome to Cathay. Indian caravans from
the south, Arabs and Persians from the west, Mongols and Chinese
from the east and north, all unloaded their luxury goods, reloaded
others, and returned to their respective lands. Ideas and peoples as
well as commerce poured along these routes until periodic invasions
from Central Asia, Persia, and India disrupted the trade.

Islam exploded into the area in the eighth century, gaining political control a century or two later. An Islamic culture flowered at
Ghazni, a great capital which played host to thousands of scholars,
artists, and poets.

Several processes led to the downfall of the great Muslim civilizations of Afghanistan. Invasions by Mongols and Turco-Mongols
during the thirteenth and fourteenth centuries wreaked havoc upon
the all-important irrigation systems. Fratricidal wars led to fissions
and fusions. A strong man would unite several tribal units into a
kingdom which often incorporated other kingdoms to form an
empire. At his death his male kinsmen would fight for control of
the empire or a part of it, leading to breakdown and dissolution.
And then another charismatic leader would rise. And so on.

By the time European imperialists arrived in the nineteenth
century, Afghanistan was a mere geographical expression, a loose
collection of tribal units. The czarist Russians gained control of
several central Asian khanates. The British reacted militarily to
real or imagined threats to their Indian empire. Not until 1880 did
Afghanistan begin to become a nation-state, when Abdur Rahman
became Amir of the kingdom of Kabul, and commenced to spread
his influence—if not his control—throughout the area we call
modern Afghanistan. This process of nation building still continues
(Fraser-Tytler 1953; Wilber 1962).

SOCIAL STRUCTURE AND CULTURE

Afghan society can be examined from several vantage points:
religion, politics, economics, ethnic groups. From the Peace Corps
point of view, however, all discussion focuses on one factor: literacy
versus illiteracy, or 5 per cent of the population versus the other 95.
Afghanistan is typical of many developing nations in that it possesses a literate religion but a largely illiterate people. The great
and classic tenets of Islam must filter down to illiterate tribesmen

and villagers through priests who are themselves often semiliterate or illiterate. Islam as practiced in tribes and villages thus often bears little resemblance to Islam in the high literate tradition. Sophisticated religious philosophy gives way to backcountry beliefs, to homegrown saints and witches, to amulets and magic.

An Inward-Looking Society

Tribalism and local Islamic traditions combine to produce an inward-looking society. A man born into such a society is born into a set of answers, while in outward-looking Western society a man is born into a set of questions. When a Westerner answers one question, he merely opens a Pandora's box of further questions. Answers for the illiterate Afghan generally relate to local interpretations of Islam, including "adat" (custom). (Though the "adat" often antedates the advent of Islam in Afghanistan, many people believe it to be Islamic in origin.) The basic concept is fatalism: Allah has made the mouth, He will also provide the bread. Folklore and folksongs tend to reinforce group beliefs and discourage individual dissidence. A potentially disruptive question is asked only if the answer is known. "Why didn't it rain this year?" "Allah willed it." "But why?" "Someone has broken the laws of Islam."

In such a tightly knit, inward-oriented society, a man's economic and political roles, his social status, and even his mate have largely been determined before his birth. Marriage customs reinforce ingroup solidarity, the preferred mate being father's brother's daughter.

An inward-looking orientation functions in two major ways. It reinforces ingroup cohesion in order to reduce local tensions and increase survival potential, both economically and politically. It also insulates the group against outsiders. An integrated village seldom submits its full allotted quota of rent, taxes, or conscripts to the national government. Resistance to change increases in intensity as one leaves zones of easy accessibility along the main roads.

The literate 5 per cent of the population generally look outward, but *away from* the village-tribal matrix and toward the technological goodies (consumer products) of the West. Except for a notable few—fortunately including most of the current power elite—Afghan literates form vested interest groups, mainly the royal family, religious leaders, landlords, businessmen. At times these groups unite in a common front against particular reforms, but more often they remain divided and hostile in their mutual competition for the souls, bodies, and pocketbooks of the Afghans. Within these groups schisms exist. Within the royal family, for example, are many who actively support the new reforms begun in March 1963 (Dupree 1963a). King Mohammad Zahir is the prime mover behind the new modernization attempts that culminated in September 1964, when the Loya Jirgah (Great Assembly of Notables, including the National Assembly, intellectuals, and tribal and religious leaders) approved a new liberalized constitution.

The relationships between the literate class and the village-nomad milieu have seldom been cordial, however. Few educated young men want to work in the provinces, and the villagers themselves prefer to keep government representatives outside their inward-oriented lives. Several abortive attempts have been made to improve the lot of the villagers, who view all such activities with suspicion. The general pattern has been one of *extraction*, a one-way flow of material and people *away* from the village, with nothing coming back in return.

Islam

A power-vested interest group, the conservative religious leaders, support this system of extraction. They are against reform. They insist that the people must resist reforms as anti-Islamic. These religious leaders oppose land reform, since they are large landholders. They reject secular education because, until recently, they controlled education. They object to political reforms because this would mean a diminution of their political power.

Superficial observers often malign Islam, and call it a conservative, backward, antiprogressive faith. The reverse is true: Islam, in essence, can be most progressive, if interpreted in the light of modern social thought. Islam must be considered at two levels to clarify this statement: the eternal precepts of Islam found in the divinely inspired Koran, and the action component, the religious leaders who codify and interpret Islam. As holders of political and economic power, as arbiters of the daily lives of the people, most religious leaders tend to interpret Islam conservatively. There are, however, some younger, Western-educated members of old religious families who have begun to view Islam in a modern way, as a beacon to progress, rather than as a blanket to keep the people in medieval darkness. The resulting clash of generations and wills resounds throughout Afghanistan and the rest of the Muslim world.

Modernization and Its Requirements

It was in such a milieu that the Volunteers of Afghanistan One found themselves. And they have helped to introduce change into this milieu without appearing to interfere. Naturally, however, everything they did constituted interference of one form or another. In a developing society such as Afghanistan, with its relatively unchanging patterns, outside impetus is necessary in order to introduce cultural changes and—more importantly—to perpetuate them.

The Peace Corps has contributed to what appear to be the ultimate American aspirations for Afghanistan. It seems fairly clear that the American government would like to see Afghanistan politically stable, economically viable (or as viable as possible given the resources of the country), and moving progressively toward a form of representative government consistent with Afghanistan's past and present patterns. A primary ingredient for the creation of a democratic system is a literate middle class. Given its own resources and its inward-looking society which resists change, Afghanistan cannot accomplish these goals alone. American and Soviet aid have helped Afghanistan develop stability and an economic infrastructure capable of expanding the benefits (and trials) of a modern state to the village-nomad camp level. But the human factor still dominates. In a society with 5 per cent literates, how many can be teachers? The government needs most of the educated individuals to handle the daily business of a growing development bureaucracy and to serve as physicians, engineers, diplomats, soldiers.

The solution, simple to articulate, is difficult to activate. The key word is *involvement*. The villager must get involved with the government in his development, and the unilateral process of extraction must end. If mutually beneficial interaction takes place, a literate middle class will be created—but in how many generations? The road stretches long and unpaved.

AFGHANISTAN ONE: THE PENETRATION

What could a few American youths do in such a situation, which demanded subtlety of understanding and the harsh necessity of undermining cultural patterns so that the blow would fall the lightest on the most? When President Kennedy first announced the Peace Corps concept, my wife succinctly described its potential, "It will either be the greatest thing that America has done in this century or become the twentieth-century children's crusade." She was right, for by its very nature the Peace Corps involves constant face-to-face contact with Afghans, the most important way to action in this society. Failure would be a face-to-face failure, which no amount of money could cover up, as it can technical mistakes in road building, dam construction, and the like.

The first nine Volunteers arrived in September 1962: six women (three English teachers, three nurses) and three men (two English teachers, one mechanic). They would have preferred to work in villages rather than in Kabul, the capital city of about 250,000, which possessed, however, few of the amenities of a Western city of equivalent size. The PCVs settled in modest Afghan houses over the objection of the Afghan government, which thought they should live in a manner commensurate with their American background— in other words, like American technicians working for AID. The Peace Corps furnished the Volunteers with bicycles, still the primary Volunteer transport in Afghanistan.

The PCVs quickly realized why they could not work in villages: few Afghan officials work anywhere near villages; Kabul needed all their talents badly; they were on trial. If Afghanistan One succeeded in impressing the Afghans, the door would open wider for future Peace Corps groups.

Some predicted the Afghan teachers and nurses would object to the Volunteers and consider them threats to their positions, but little friction developed and friendships grew as Afghans accepted this strange new breed of American. Although the Afghanistan One Volunteers had been well briefed as to the lack of physical amenities, some were nonetheless shocked when they first confronted the country's monumental needs in the schools, hospitals, and workshops. On the whole, however, they began to adjust rapidly and well.*

The mechanic Volunteer, a skilled and energetic man, moved into the Zendabanon automotive workshop which services private and government vehicles, including 300 Soviet and American buses. Using local materials, he helped devise procedures to make the workshop function more effectively, although for years AID had poured money and technical aid into the project without notable success. The secret ingredient supplied by this PCV was personal, daily, face-to-face contact with Afghan mechanics and other personnel at Zendabanon, plus the utilization of anything at hand to solve problems—no waiting around for superior American parts to arrive. When he terminated in June 1964, his Afghan superiors had

---

* Perhaps contributing to their adjustment were the facts that they were only nine in number; that they were all stationed in the relatively compact area of Kabul and environs; and that they were supervised by a Representative who possessed a deep familiarity with the local language and culture. Afghanistan One stands in striking contrast with the 128-member Philippines One contingent, who were scattered over several islands and language areas, and supervised by Representatives new to the country.—Ed.

not requested a replacement; hence several of his instituted changes now sadly fade away. His case again demonstrates the necessity for sustained outside impetus in order to catalyze, achieve, and *perpetuate* change at the workaday level. It also demonstrates the simple fact that such change cannot be perpetuated unless reasonably strong cooperation is received from key local officials.

The teachers confronted several built-in problems that plague the Afghan educational system, including the most important, a shortage of qualified teachers. Certain religious leaders objected to the Volunteer teachers, just as they object to all foreign teachers, claiming the foreigners will teach anti-Islamic (Christian or Communist) tenets. For generations Afghan students have learned by rote, a technique that is easy for the teacher but hardly capable of developing in the student the type of quantitative and reasoning skills required for participation in a modern society. The clash of differing cultural values was even more visible in the matter of cheating, a time-honored tradition in Afghan schools, and one that fits nicely into the cultural pattern. In Afghanistan, classmates have fierce ingroup loyalties, just as nomads have fierce tribal loyalties. If any member of a class fails an examination or does badly in recitations, the entire group feels the disgrace. So the students cooperate in classroom work and on examinations through ingenious sets of signals that often escape even Afghan teachers. If an Afghan boy or girl fails an exam and if he or she has influential parents, subtle pressure or not-so-subtle threats and bribes descend on the poor teacher. Few Afghan students fail.

The three nurses moved into a nightmare of sanitation—and a paradise, therefore, for the dedicated medical worker. Dealing as they do with matters of life and death, the nurses probably came closer than other Volunteers to an awareness of the importance of Afghan fatalism. They saw people die of neglect while the family of the victim shrugged their collective shoulders and blamed it all on the will of Allah. Few in the hospitals genuinely understood the germ theory, or if they did, could relate their theoretical knowledge to the practical problem at hand. Western-trained doctors seemed to accept the unsanitary status quo, a fact which further shocked the Volunteer nurses as they waged their constant battles for more sanitary conditions. Then there were the illiterate cleaning men and women to contend with, not to mention the patients themselves, or their relatives who often camped in the hospital with their sick loved one, hoping for miracles but accepting death, either being the will of God. After a while the nurses discovered that much can be done within the existing patterns. They tackled the sweepers and moppers and the patients and their relatives, explaining what must be done to keep the sick from getting sicker. With continued substantial aid from MEDICO, a succession of such Volunteer nurses working persistently over the next decade or so will gradually improve urban hospital conditions and even see their influence penetrate further, into the provinces and villages.

The nurses (as did most female Volunteers working with Afghan males) met resistance from Afghan doctors and male nurses, as would be expected in a male-oriented society. This problem still exists in a diminished degree.

Afghanistan One Volunteers proved to be excellent social as well as professional beings. Several participated in productions of the Kabul Amateur Dramatic Society and often provided impromptu entertainment for the Kabul community, both Afghan and foreign. The folk song syndrome sweeping the United States penetrates Peace Corps Volunteer groups as well, and all three groups in Afghanistan have had their share of guitar twangers and hootenanny singers.

Five of the six girls in Afghanistan One were single, and eligible Afghan and foreign males squired them everywhere. No unpleasant incidents occurred, but occasional touch-and-go situations did arise. One nurse terminated early to marry a West German. A female teacher extended until October 1965, in order to marry a member of Afghanistan Three. The other seven terminated on schedule in June 1964.

The success of Afghanistan One can be measured with several yardsticks. Probably the most important would be Afghan reactions. In private, Afghans were before long expressing admiration for the accomplishments of the nine PCVs, as indeed also were most foreigners—often grudgingly. The Afghan government, however, made no official statements until the spring of 1963, when the Peace Corps Representative in Kabul asked if they would like additional Volunteers. The Ministry of Planning politely received his request, sent it to the various ministries for their requirements, and returned the list to the Representative. He glanced at the requests, stunned. He had hoped the Afghans would ask for at least another seven or eight. Instead, the various ministries put in bids totaling between seventy and eighty! While part of this new enthusiasm is perhaps ascribable to a change in the Afghan government in March, there is little doubt that the primary reason was that the Volunteers had gained the confidence of Afghanistan's leaders. The Representative realized that seventy or eighty would be too big a jump in personnel, but he pleaded with Washington for as many as he could get. The Afghan government's confidence was further revealed by the assignment of seventeen Volunteer teachers, including several women, to provincial teaching jobs. This represented a significant break with past policy, which had sternly discouraged Americans from living and working in smaller outlying towns.

AFGHANISTAN TWO: THE BREAKTHROUGH

The arrival of Afghanistan Two signalized the emergence of the Peace Corps as a conspicuous part of the Afghan development scene. The contingent included nine women and seventeen men. Three terminated early: an elderly couple for medical reasons and a young man "to return to college." Of the twenty-three remaining, seventeen taught in secondary, vocational or high schools, and two at Kabul University (one teaching English, the other physical education). The four printers worked at the Ministry of Education printing press, which was sponsored by the Asia Foundation, until Franklin Press (Tehran) took over. They then transferred to either the Ministry of Press and Information or to the Ministry of Finance Press.

The Volunteers in Afghanistan Two maintained the high work standards established by One. They continued and broadened the PCVs' involvement in extracurricular activities. Two Volunteers worked in a quartet organized by one of them, giving Kabul a sustained earful of good jazz.

Physical Education and Modernization

Knowledgeable Afghans have long recognized the importance of physical coordination in a mechanized society. Afghan children usually grow up without mechanical toys and without organized sports. One Afghan official asked me to bring back mechanical toys and children's construction sets from the United States for his children. "You must grow up with machines to really understand them," he said. He also realized that the coordination necessary to operate large machine complexes develops in early childhood, especially from the type of physical training taught by the Volunteer physical education teacher. (The Peace Corps did not originate the physical education program, however, for the Asia Foundation has sponsored such specialists in Afghanistan since the 1950's.)

Physical coordination is, after all, a product of cultural conditioning. The body or any part of it reacts in an eye-to-mind-tomuscle sequence. Watching Afghan villagers or tribesmen cross the streets of Kabul illustrates this. The villager's peripheral vision tells him something is moving toward him. His cultural conditioning leads him to expect a camel, or at the fastest, a horse. In Kabul, unfortunately, it will more likely be an automobile. The villager will take an extra step or two actually looking at the car, because he has not reacted fast enough. Many accidents occur this way. In addition, Afghan drivers often have difficulty in judging time-motion ratios while driving automobiles.

Another reason for encouraging organized athletics at Kabul University is political. The physical plant for the university, built with American funds by a German company and completed in 1964, brought the student body together in one place for the first time. Previously, the various faculties were scattered all over the city. Now that the students live and study together, extracurricular activities will increase. The university administration hopes to encourage organized athletics as a way to drain off some of the excess student energy now being generated. Kabul University has yet to have a real student riot, but when it occurs, the students will probably feel they have come of age. And the first time a demonstration is held in front of a foreign embassy (probably the American), student maturity (in the Asian sense) will have arrived.

Lack of Afghan Cooperation

Several Afghanistan Two Volunteers complained of overwork. The Afghans recognize their abilities, and want to get maximum performance out of an institution that costs them a minimum. The Afghan government agreed, in theory, to pay the Volunteers a living allotment equal to that paid to Afghans working in similar slots. In practice, some Volunteers have received no money because of interministry squabbles about fiscal responsibility.

Another common gripe concerns the role of the Volunteer as teacher. Often, a PCV performs his or her job for the entire tour, and the Afghans working with the Volunteer sit back and do nothing, or else simply go through the motions. This naturally frustrates the Volunteer, who wants to leave with the knowledge that somebody will continue to perform the job. He hopes this person will be an Afghan, but such is seldom the case. Indeed, sometimes there is neither an Afghan nor a PCV replacement. A related complaint is that it sometimes seems as though PCVs are sent to provincial posts only to permit certain Afghan teachers to be transferred from the provinces to Kabul, which is considered by the Afghans to be a much more desirable post.

AFGHANISTAN THREE: THE PEACE CORPS BECOMES AN INSTITUTION

By the time the Afghans submitted their requests for Afghanistan Three, everyone in Kabul (even the Soviets, who still believe most Volunteers are CIA agents) accepted the Peace Corps as a going and continuing concern. The more than one hundred job requests for Three included secretaries, bank clerks, and telephone operators, as well as more teachers. Peace Corps/Washington assigned almost forty bodies to Three, to be trained at the Experiment in International Living in Putney, Vermont. The Experiment obtained five excellent language instructors among Afghan students studying in the United States, led by Mohammad Ehsan Entezar, Assistant Professor of Linguistics, Kabul University (Entezar and Burns 1964).

The assassination of President Kennedy jarred the world during Afghanistan Three's training period. I was in the United States at the time, and the staff at Putney had asked me to come up for several days of lectures and informal discussions with the trainees. I was to arrive the day after the assassination, so I telephoned and asked what to do. Officials at Putney said, "Come on up. Shriver has said for all training to continue. The President would have wanted it that way." So I flew up.

The trainees held a brief, simple service on the day the nation buried Kennedy. The Afghan language instructors bought a wreath and placed it around a portrait of the late president, and at the end of the service asked if they could say something. One of them read a moving poetic tribute in Persian. Then, the training continued.

Afghanistan Three arrived in Kabul in January 1964, during one of the worst winters on record. Most of the group functioned smoothly from the start. The accountants, however, could find no one in the Ministry of Public Works who could adequately use their talents, so the Afghan government agreed to their transfer to the Ministry of Justice. Here they studied the administrative situation and made several recommendations, which hopefully will eventually be implemented. Now the accountants work in the Ministry of Finance and continue to seek out ways to break administrative logjams.

For several years various organizations have tried to help the

Afghans devise more effective administrative procedures. These assisting agencies include the United Nations, AID, Robert Nathan Associates (Washington, D. C.), Public Administration Services (Chicago, Illinois), International Monetary Fund, Asia Foundation, and Soviet advisors. The five secretaries, three accountants, and one statistician of Afghanistan Three have been successfully introducing several elements of the new systems devised by the Public Administration Services assistance team. Unfortunately, however, Afghanistan Four and Five do not include accountants, so that in their case the all-important continuity of effort will be lost.

The Afghan government asked for over two hundred Volunteers for both Afghanistan Four and Five. Afghanistan Four included teachers, nurses, irrigation construction aides, mechanics, and secretaries. Afghanistan Five, scheduled to arrive in the spring of 1965, would bring the total number of PCVs in Afghanistan at that time to about 150. Afghanistan Six was due to arrive in September of 1965, bringing about forty-five Volunteers in the fields of teaching, accounting, office administration, and laboratory technology.

EFFECTIVENESS DESPITE FRUSTRATIONS

As one Volunteer put it, "In a place like Afghanistan, it is difficult not to contribute something constructive." The country lacks so much, that almost anything is a contribution. Yet it would be a mistake to assume that the PCVs in Afghanistan are "do-gooder" automatons. On the contrary, they fall ill with "Kabul tummy." They occasionally feel the acute lack of modern amenities. They miss mail from home and they miss home. They bemoan Afghan—and American—bureaucratic inefficiency. They fall in love and get married (as three couples have done, and three others plan to do), or simply fall in love. The Afghan cultural environment appears less strange the longer they remain, and often, because of this, PCVs become less tolerant of Afghan shortcomings, developing what Guthrie has earlier called "culture fatigue" (page 48). Many PCVs readily admit that a training program, however good, cannot knock out cultural bias. Those engaged in medical work never quite become accustomed to the lack of sanitary conditions. Teachers often feel they fight a losing battle against the rote system and cheating. Those involved in office work grow depressed at the amount of paper work necessary to obtain even a few pencils or a ream of paper. Female telephone operators would like to teach their skills to Afghan women but often must be content simply to operate switchboards under the suspicious gaze of Afghan male operators. Accountants and statisticians sometimes believe no progress in their fields will be possible for a hundred years.

Relations with AID personnel engender problems in two senses. First is the fact that some Volunteers doubtless sometimes envy the refrigerators and plush living standards of AID and other official American employees. More important, though, is the fact that the typical AID official enjoys high enough status so that he can often get things done in the labyrinths of Afghan bureaucracy. Several PCVs feel that their key accomplishments would never have been made unless an AID official had gone to bat for them with high Afghan officials. While most Volunteers would be strongly opposed to integrating the Peace Corps into the AID mission, they are in favor of coordinating efforts without rivalry whenever this would serve the interests of all concerned.

However understandable these frustrations, some Volunteers fail to realize the significance of their contributions. Since decisions are made at the upper levels of government, this is where AID and other foreign development officials usually operate. Often, they succeed in stimulating and implementing policy decisions at that level. Unless, however, there are appropriate new attitudes and techniques at the middle and lower levels, these new policies are unlikely to reach fruition. Thus simply by working with Afghans at the middle and lower levels, the PCVs make an impact—though it is often invisible, and this naturally disturbs the Volunteers. But in years to come, the rising middle-class officials will remember and talk about the accomplishments of the PCVs with whom they worked. Consistency and continuity are the two best ways of encouraging changes at the middle and lower levels of government, and it is here that the Volunteers serve best.

CONCLUSIONS

No nation lasts forever, and great empires leave behind great ruins. Men, not gods, create nations. Regional and national greatness varies in time and space. While Englishmen were still painting their bodies blue, the Middle East supported high civilizations. The bulk of the foods upon which we base our Western civilization came from the Middle East, including Afghanistan. One common factor (others exist) that makes nations great is waste potential. During those periods when Afghanistan flourished, it had large food surpluses and great numbers of poets.

The United States today has the greatest waste potential in history, but it does not follow that these human, technical, and natural

resources should be wasted. Exploited, yes; wasted, no. The social-
ization of the young in the United States often lasts twenty-five or
more years before the individual becomes a contributing member
of his society. The Peace Corps taps the formative two years of many
of our potentially most productive citizens, and prepares them for
the world to be—in contrast to the world that is (or never was),
which many wish to continue.

The 1950's on university campuses was a decade of apathy.
Threats of nuclear destruction, the inequities of the draft, myths
and legends about the Korean War, McCarthyism, payola, graft in
high and low places, and Charles Van Doren's quiz fiasco, all contributed to student apathy.

A new élan came to Washington with the election of John F.
Kennedy, and with it the birth of the Peace Corps. In my travels
and lectures for the American Universities Field Staff at universities
from Harvard to Hawaii, from Carleton College to Kansas and
Tulane, I find the 1960's developing into a decade of commitment.
No longer do students and faculty feel the inevitability of nuclear
destruction, of graft and corruption. Change can be made a reality,
change in the United States and in the rest of the world. The
Peace Corps serves not only to prepare the Volunteers to contribute
overseas but to reintroduce them to their own basic American
values.

In the past, American assistance programs usually consisted of
money (grants and loans) and technical assistance—without any
guarantees of continuity. Under such conditions, the result can be
a dam, a road, or a university left empty and functionless on the
landscape of a developing country—a magnificent ruin. Tractors
and buses with no provisions for spare parts or maintenance often
sit idle and useless for months. The Peace Corps Volunteers,
especially in Afghanistan, try to fill these longitudinal needs, to
continue the processes begun. They try to do this gently, within
the cultural pattern, and not with a heavy, alien, self-righteous
hand. This patient day-to-day, face-to-face contact with their Afghan
supervisors, assistants, and acquaintances will help to introduce and
perpetuate the ideas which stimulate permanent technological
change. It will also, incidentally, have some effect in the general
direction of creating a literate, responsible, outward-looking middle
class which some day might form the bulwark of a representative
government.

The street runs in two directions. The Volunteers will broaden
their vistas. They will make constructive adjustments. And these

adjustments, as they should be in American society, will be individual—the sum total of the pre-Peace Corps past of the Volunteer, his training, and the impact of the foreign country on the Volunteer. The total of all the individual impacts will probably create a group of Americans with a pragmatic outlook toward the outside world. They have seen the need. They have tackled it. They realize that solutions to development problems are not simple, just as answers to the question of "Why aid countries like Afghanistan" are not simple.

A memorable event symbolized the success of the Peace Corps in Afghanistan. On August 19, 1964, King Mohammad Zahir gave an unprecedented afternoon tea party for the American Peace Corps Volunteers. All the diplomatic eyebrows in Kabul shot up, because no other development group had received such recognition from the King. In his remarks to the Volunteers, His Majesty said, "I do not wish to make light of the American Ambassador [John Milton Steeves, who was present], but I do wish to say that you Peace Corps Volunteers are the true American ambassadors in Afghanistan."

John Fitzgerald Kennedy would be proud of his legacy in Afghanistan.

NOTES

[1] I wish to thank the following for their cooperation in collecting data for this paper: Robert Steiner, Peace Corps Director in Afghanistan; Robert McClusky, Deputy Director; Mrs. Roberta Auburn, Peace Corps secretary, Kabul; and the Peace Corps Volunteers of Afghanistan One, Two, and Three.

Most of the material in this chapter appeared originally in "The Peace Corps in Afghanistan," an AUFS Report published by American Universities Field Staff, Inc. (Copyright 1964).

BIBLIOGRAPHY

CASAL, JEAN-MARIE
    1961   *Fouilles de Mundigak*. Paris: Mémoires de la Délégation Arch-
            éologique Française en Afghanistan, Vol. 17.
DUPREE, LOUIS
    1961a   "The Durand Line of 1893: A Case Study in Artificial Bounda-
            ries and Culture Areas," in T. Cuyler Young, ed., *Current
            Problems in Afghanistan*. Princeton, N.J.: The Princeton Uni-
            versity Conference, pp. 77-94.
    1961b   " 'Pushtunistan': The Problem and Its Larger Implications."
            Part I: "The Complex Interrelationships of Regional Disputes."
            Part II: "The Effects of the Afghan-Pakistan Border Closure."
            Part III: "The Big Gamble Continues." New York. *American*

Universities Field Staff Reports, Vol. 5, Nos. 2, 3, and 4, respectively.

1963a "Tribalism, Regionalism, and National Oligarchy: Afghanistan," in American Universities Field Staff under the editorship of K. H. Silvert, *Expectant Peoples: Nationalism and Development*. New York: Random House, pp. 41-76.

1963b *Deh Morasi Ghundai: A Chalcolithic Site in South-Central Afghanistan*. New York: Anthropological Papers of the American Museum of Natural History, Vol. 50, Part 2.

1964a "Tribal Traditions and Modern Nationhood: Afghanistan," in *Asia: A Selection of Papers Delivered Before the Asia Society*. New York: The Asia Society, Vol. 1, pp. 1-12.

1964b "Prehistoric Archaeological Surveys and Excavations in Afghanistan: 1959-60, 1961-63." *Science*, Vol. 146, No. 3644, pp. 638-640.

ENTEZAR, M., and D. BURNES

1964   *Farsi Reference Manual: Basic Course*. Putney, Vt., Peace Corps and The Experiment in International Living.

FAIRSERVIS, WALTER

1961   *Archaeological Studies in the Seistan Basin of Southwestern Afghanistan and Eastern Iran*. New York: Anthropological Papers of the American Museum of Natural History, Vol. 48, Part 1.

FRASER-TYTLER, WILLIAM K.

1953   *Afghanistan: A Study of Political Development in Central and Southern Asia*. New York: St. Martin's Press. Second Edition.

WILBER, DONALD

1962   *Afghanistan*. New Haven, Conn.: Human Relations Area Files Press. Second Edition.

7

Success in Somalia

FRANK J. MAHONY[1] *received his master's degree in anthropology from the University of Chicago in 1950, and spent the next ten years with the U.S. Trust Territory of the Pacific Islands, applying anthropology to the problems of island administration. From 1960 to 1964 he served as an applied anthropologist with AID in the Somali Republic. During this period, he developed the ability to carry out field research in both the Somali and Italian languages, and has now had more research experience in Somalia than any other American scholar. Mr. Mahony first met the Somalia One Volunteers during a brief lecture visit to their training program at New York University. He then returned to Somalia and, since his job called for frequent travel, he had the unique opportunity of becoming well acquainted with most of the Volunteers and observing them in some detail in their actual working situations. Subsequently, Mr. Mahony directed and taught the Area Studies portion of the Somalia Two training program at Eastern Michigan University during the summer of 1964. In the fall of 1964, he resumed long-delayed studies for the doctorate in anthropology, at Stanford University.*

ABOUT one year after the Peace Corps was organized someone asked Sargent Shriver which of all the countries in the world was proving the most troublesome for the Peace Corps to work in. Without a moment's hesitation Shriver named the Somali Republic. Though he could not possibly have known it when he spoke—the worst was yet to come.

The vicissitudes faced by Volunteers in the Somali Republic had few if any parallels elsewhere. At times these difficulties combined with a muddled administrative situation to produce utter confusion and dismay. This took a heavy toll of Volunteers. Out of the original fifty trainees, forty-five were selected to go to Somalia. At the end of not quite two years, however, only twenty-seven were left—an unprecedented dropout rate of 40 per cent. These twenty-seven included a number of hardy survivors and a few who were psycho-

125

logically no longer capable of accomplishing very much. Finally, even these remaining Volunteers had to be prematurely evacuated from the country.

Yet, in spite of all its troubles, the Peace Corps effort in the Somali Republic must be pronounced a huge success. In this brief report I will try to cover the salient features of the Volunteers' experience and attempt to describe the kind and degree of their success.

BACKGROUND

In areas of the Somali Republic where the soil is fertile and the rainfall adequate, particularly along the Scebelli and Giuba Rivers in the south, an agricultural system of small but growing importance is practiced by people living in permanent settlements. In the rest of the country, however, pastoral nomads still herd small flocks of sheep, goats, camels, and cattle over dry countryside in search of green pasture and fresh water.[2]

Since the advent of Europeans, permanent settlements have grown up in nomadic areas and now serve as centers where people can come to sell surplus livestock, buy trade goods, and sip tea in local restaurants. The larger of these towns are seats of government and are often sites of elementary and intermediate schools, and in a few cases, high schools. Many of the Volunteers in Somalia One were assigned to intermediate and high schools in towns such as these.

The Somali people are almost all devout adherents of the Muslim faith. They speak an extraordinarily complex language rich in vocabulary, idiom, and proverbial expression. Somali poetry, which depends more on alliteration and chanting rhythms than rhyme, is often an artistic embodiment of the highest aspirations and most profoundly felt sentiments of the Somali people.[3]

Though semiarid, the country is more aptly termed savannah than desert. During the rainy season, when grass springs up and acacia trees turn green, the countryside can present a truly beautiful aspect. Nevertheless the potential for agricultural expansion is severely limited and in the absence, so far at least, of substantial mineral discoveries, the economic outlook is darkly discouraging. Indeed, prospects for economic development are among the bleakest in all Africa. The Republic's young nationalist leaders, however, are undaunted in their efforts to develop their new nation. They rely heavily upon foreign aid, and by steering a neutral course have managed to obtain one of the highest per capita aid levels of any African nation.[4]

Cultural Unity

To a degree unusual in Africa, the four and a half million people of Somalia are united by a common language, a common heritage, a similar culture, and a social system that relates each and every Somali to every other Somali. In spite of this deeply felt unity, however, colonial interest in the Horn of Africa helped to divide the people into five separate regions, symbolized today in the five points of the star on the flag of the Somali Republic. These five areas were French, British, and Italian Somaliland, and parts of Ethiopia and Kenya. In 1960 British and Italian Somaliland gained their independence and united to form the Somali Republic.

This still left large numbers of Somalis in other areas outside the Republic. Somalis have always resented this seemingly arbitrary division of their land and people, and have written into the Republic's constitution a provision to seek the union of all Somalis by every peaceful means.[5]

American Involvement and Image

Somali people everywhere feel that United States policy has played an important role in supporting the distasteful divisions existing among them. Since World War II, for example, the United States has been supplying and equipping the Ethiopian Army with everything from jeeps to jet planes. At the same time the United States has been allowed to maintain an important military communications center near Asmara, Ethiopia. Since Ethiopia controls territory where many Somalis live, she is regarded by Somalis as an enemy. "And," says a former Somali Prime Minister, "the friend of our enemy is also our enemy."

Not long ago the United States acted to counter this impression by offering Somalia its own military aid program. The United States, along with a few other Western nations, offered to equip a 10,000-man Somali Army. News of this offer was no sooner out than the Soviet Union stepped into the picture with an offer to equip a 20,000-man army. The Somali Government quite naturally accepted the Russian proposal instead.

Since 1954 the United States has also had a program of economic and technical aid in the country, and it has made a few notable achievements. Nevertheless Somalis in various stations of life have acquired the over-all impression that the aid program has been spending money but not accomplishing very much.[6]

The Russian aid program on the other hand, though criticized for getting off to a slow start and for the suspicious and unfriendly attitude of many of the Russian technicians, is now bringing some highly visible projects to completion. These include a radio station, a printing press, a milk factory, a meat factory, a fish cannery, several state farms, and so forth. Although some of these projects may not work out very well, the over-all program is beginning to have a favorable impact on Somali public opinion.

Another factor that embarrasses the United States in its relations with Somalia is the race problem. Racial difficulties in the United States are given wide publicity in Africa, and Somalis are often puzzled or angered by what they hear. Somali students who come to study in the United States, though Hamites rather than Negroes, are sometimes discriminated against because of their jet black skin. They thus add bitter personal experiences to the general fund of knowledge of American race relations.

By the same token, relations between Americans and Somalis in Somalia itself have left a good deal to be desired. Americans working in that country prior to 1962 seem often to have perceived themselves as kind, generous people. Somalis, by contrast, often perceived these same Americans as thoughtless or indifferent to all except the highest officials or most important people in Somalia. Quite naturally, Somalis tended to compare Americans with the two other Western groups whom they knew best: their former colonial rulers, the Italians and the British. The Somalis tended to see the Italians as thoroughgoing colonialists, but also as kinder and more considerate than the Americans. Locally resident Italians are perceived as humanistic and gregarious—willing to associate in friendly fashion with the Somalis—though on Italian cultural terms, to be sure. The British were perceived as colder and more aloof. And yet in many cases they were admired for their dogged determination to learn the Somali language, to travel by camel back into the backwoods to learn about tribal conditions there, and the like. By contrast, the Americans tended to be perceived as possessing the ethnocentrism of the Italians without their gregariousness, and the aloofness of the British without their interest in Somali language and culture. In all, then, the pre-Peace Corps perception of the United States and of American character was not a highly favorable one.

EVERYTHING WENT WRONG

It is difficult to think of a single thing that could have gone wrong with the Peace Corps program, that did not. From beginning to end, the Somalia One experience assumes the proportions of a case study in how *not* to conduct a Peace Corps operation.

Inadequate Training

Fifty Peace Corps trainees entered the training program at New York University in the spring of 1962. All were earmarked for teaching jobs in Somalia. Unfortunately, the training program did not provide the kind of intensive background on the culture of the host country that is so vital to each individual's understanding and eventual adaptation. While the Peace Corps attempted to obtain properly qualified teachers, it nonetheless confronted the stubborn fact that experts on Somalia are scarce. As a consequence, few of those involved in the training program had had any previous experience in the country. And of those who did, most were familiar only with the former Italian Somaliland—despite the fact that the great majority of the PCVs were to be assigned to schools in former British Somaliland, an area that differs administratively and to some extent culturally from the former Italian area.

As a consequence, Volunteers were not informed of a number of significant factors. They were not told, for example, that under the influence of Egyptian propaganda Somalis were likely to voice anti-Semitic notions and attitudes. As a result some Volunteers were later surprised and deeply hurt. One personable Jewish couple, for instance, became very friendly with a Somali official and entertained him often at dinner. One evening after dinner the official innocently remarked that while Somalis could get along with anyone, the only people they really hated were the Jews. Although the wife later broke down in tears, the couple contained their reactions so well at the time that the incident passed unnoticed. But the spiritual wound never healed completely.

The training program also failed to inform the PCVs that some Somalis tend to look down on Negroes. This also left certain Negro Volunteers unprepared to make the necessary adjustment, and led to the same kind of painful surprise.

Despite these and other shortcomings, the forty-five Volunteers who arrived in the Somali Republic were convinced of the importance and dignity of their coming role as teachers. Although uncertain of their technical qualifications, they felt themselves possessed of sufficient good judgment and maturity to be able to adapt to their new situation as responsible adults.

Inappropriate Leadership

The PCVs were unfortunate, however, in one of the Representatives whom Washington had sent out to lead them, a man totally

lacking in previous transcultural experience—in Somalia or anywhere. This official, doubtless with good intentions, tried to live up
to the absolute letter of Peace Corps regulations, but in doing so,
his very inflexibility and lack of human sensitivity succeeded instead
in violating the underlying spirit of the Peace Corps idea. He
promptly proceeded to threaten the PCVs' sense of maturity and
responsibility. Instead of relying to some extent on the Volunteers'
own judgment, he treated them like children. He laid down a long
series of strict rules and regulations regarding conduct. The PCVs
were told not to join the local expatriate club, not to operate motor
vehicles or obtain driving licenses, not to obtain firearms or hunting
licenses or to go hunting, not to drink alcohol or chew "qat" leaves
(nonintoxicating but having benzedrinelike effects) with Somalis,
and so forth.

These rules had no sooner been laid down than some of the
Volunteers began to test their force and validity by violating each
and every one of them. They joined the expatriate club, obtained
licenses, drove, hunted, drank, and chewed. The Representative
ignored these direct challenges to his authority, pretended everything was the way it ought to be, and continued to send long and
glowing progress reports back to Peace Corps headquarters in
Washington.

As a result some Volunteers fell into the habit of resisting any
authority and disregarding and disobeying any rule or regulation—
even those concerning their own health and safety. This later had
consequences of its own.

Logistical Failures

Housing for those few Volunteers working in the South was a
problem. Although the agreement with the Somali government
stated that housing was to be provided, a number of Volunteers
were unable to find space. Peace Corps officials took this as a sign
that the government was indifferent, and unwilling to support Peace
Corps activities. What they failed to realize was that the Volunteers
were not being treated differently from anyone else. In the early days
of independence, expatriate and Somali civil servants were attempting to integrate the inherited British and Italian administrative systems and inefficiency was at a peak. Somalis employed by their own
government often went for months, or even years, before they got on
the payroll. In this situation it was unrealistic to expect the Somali
government to handle Peace Corps matters with great efficiency.

Job Frustration

In meeting their teaching responsibilities in the classroom, many Volunteers at first tried to establish rapport with their students by being "regular guys." Somali students quickly sensed the Volunteers' insecurity and lack of experience, took advantage of their goodwill, and tested them to the limits. Classroom discipline soon became a major problem, in a few cases breaking down completely. Many Volunteers responded by administering corporal punishment—or calling on school officials to do so.

Volunteers were plagued by other frustrations as well. Schools lacked books and supplies. Even basic necessities, such as pencils and paper, were often completely lacking. At times the available books would be locked up in the school library by the principal, who would then disappear into the capital city hundreds of miles away, to remain for weeks or months at a time. Nor did it help matters when teaching aids, promised by Peace Corps/Washington, would sometimes fail to materialize.

When Volunteers tried to eliminate poor, noisy, or rebellious students, local politics often put them right back into the classroom. Students banded together, told the PCVs what and how to teach, and occasionally refused en masse to take examinations. And not infrequently when certain rules or teachers displeased them, the students would walk out of school on strike. All of these strikes were eventually settled, by varying combinations of concessions, punishments, and threats. In each case, however, the strikes entailed one or two or more weeks of aimless confusion which served further to reduce Volunteer morale.

Loneliness and Boredom

Perhaps the most serious problem of all was simply that there was not enough adventure or diversion. To their surprise, Volunteers discovered that being a teacher was in many respects a tedious, tiring, and humdrum round of activities, almost completely devoid of romance or adventure. Life was a treadmill existence: prepare lessons, go to school, teach classes, go home; prepare lessons, go to school, teach classes, go home; day after day after dismal day. And in the remote outposts there was hardly a diversion to lighten the load: no bar or restaurant, no dance hall, no girls to date, not even the lowest grade movie to help while away a dull weekend.

Psychological Isolation

The daily tedium, the loneliness and isolation of distant posts, might have been bearable if somebody had seemed to appreciate their efforts. But this was not the case. Their Somali teacher colleagues and other Somali officials seemed apathetic to say the least. Their own students were defiant and seemed highly unappreciative. The Volunteers felt that all was useless and pointless, that they were accomplishing little or nothing of any value. Their self-esteem was deeply wounded. They had started out as enthusiastic idealists, and now their morale was slipping ever lower.

They needed somebody to talk to, somebody who could give them psychological and logistic support, somebody who could help them make sense out of the local culture. But there was nobody. Clearly, their Representative was not such a person. And Washington was too far away.

Washington did, however, send a man to Somalia to do an evaluation study. The report he submitted to his superiors accurately reflected the poor state of Volunteer morale and the need for immediate corrective action. But the report departed so drastically from the glowing reports Washington had been receiving from the Peace Corps Representative in Somalia, that it was deemed unbelievable. As a result no corrective action was taken at that time.

Political Rioting

As if all the foregoing were not trying enough, the capricious political situation in Somalia added further fuel to the fires of frustration. In March of 1963, the British were getting ready to grant independence to Kenya. After first implying the possibility of some sort of compromise, the United Kingdom abruptly announced that the so-called Northern Frontier District—where 200,000 Somalis live—would become a part of the independent republic of Kenya. A wave of indignation swept over the people of the Somali Republic. Anti-Western riots erupted all over the country. Thus began a series of violent public demonstrations that brought about severe property damage, bloodshed, and death.

As a result of the British decision, the Somali government broke off diplomatic relations with the United Kingdom. To make up for the consequent loss in revenue, the government revamped the tax structure, revising it upward. Quite inadvertently, however, and more as a result of the inefficiency noted earlier, the tax structure was revised in a manner that clearly discriminated against the northern, formerly British sections of the country. A new wave of anger consequently swept the north. Townspeople organized themselves and elected committees. They closed down the shops, opened black markets, halted truck transport, and, in Hargeisa at least, brought legal commerce to a virtual standstill. The government was able to restore order only after reducing taxes and making a strong public demonstration of force, as the result of which several persons were killed, over a dozen wounded, and hundreds clapped into jail.

This political unrest affected the PCVs in a variety of ways—all of them frustrating. They often had to be restricted in their activities or confined to quarters under police guard for their own protection. And such vital commodities as coffee, tea, sugar, or flour were obtainable, if at all, only by resort to the black market.

DROPOUTS

Conditions in Somalia were so discouraging that a high rate of dropouts was virtually inevitable. While it seems true that better selection and training would have kept the rate of attrition lower, in the given circumstances the rate would still have been relatively high. In fact, the actual dropout rate was, as far as I know, the highest of any Peace Corps project up to that time.

The first dropout occurred within a month after arrival. Several others quickly followed. Some PCVs left for health reasons, ostensible or real. Others left for reasons of a relative's health back home. A few left "because they wanted to," but, not wanting to pay their own way, they provoked their Representative into sending them home. And some of the married women were sent home when they became pregnant.[7]

Finally, a substantial number of Volunteers were sent home for disciplinary reasons. During the disturbances in Hargeisa, for example, the local Peace Corps staff suggested that the PCVs gather in a central location for their own safety. Feeling safer where they were among their own students, several Volunteers refused. Later, when explicitly ordered to assemble, they complied reluctantly and with vociferous objections, accompanied by deliberate defiance of curfew regulations. As a consequence, they were sent home. When friends and sympathizers of this group protested, they too were sent home.

When these Volunteers reached Washington, almost all of them were promptly sent right back—most to the Somali Republic, a few to other African countries. For with large numbers of Volunteers coming through Washington and telling their stories, headquarters became aware that the Volunteers were not altogether to blame and that administrative changes were urgently required. A new Representative was therefore dispatched to the country to try to hold the project together for the rest of its tenure.

WARFARE AND EVACUATION

The new Representative barely had time to get acquainted when, in August 1963, Somalis living just across the border in the Ogadeen area of Ethiopia, rose up in armed revolt. A Somali resistance movement was formed and armed bands started an active guerrilla campaign against units of Emperor Haile Selassie's military police forces. When the Ethiopians struck back, Somali refugees began pouring across the border into the Somali Republic. And once again the people of Somalia took to the streets—this time to protest against United States military assistance to Ethiopia and against alleged Ethiopian atrocities.

Tensions between Ethiopia and Somalia continued to increase until, in February 1964, military units of the two countries clashed and open war broke out all along the border. Despite a truce arranged by the Organization for African Unity and meetings between representatives of the two governments, violence continued to flare.

As a security measure and prelude to evacuation should it prove necessary, Volunteers in the Northern Regions were brought together in Hargeisa, former capital of British Somaliland and the site of a small international airport. Not long afterwards, Ethiopian aircraft, possibly mistaking the Desert Locust Control Center at Hargeisa for a military camp, bombed and strafed it. Unfortunately, American-made planes and weapons were used. This led to wild rumors of American complicity, rumors that might have so inflamed local opinion against the PCVs as to have led to open violence. Thus the Volunteers were in danger from both the Ethiopian and Somali sides. The Somali police informed the Peace Corps Representative that, despite elaborate precautions, they could no longer guarantee the safety of the Volunteers. The decision was therefore taken to evacuate all Volunteers, not only from the areas immediately affected but from all Somalia. (By this time, most of the PCVs were within three weeks of finishing their term, anyway.) Before the Volunteers knew it, they had been airlifted to Aden—so suddenly, in fact, that they were forced to leave many of their personal effects in scattered disarray behind them, thus adding a poignant final touch to what had been a difficult and trying experience.

IN SPITE OF IT ALL, SUCCESS

In the meantime the Somali people had been making a quiet evaluation of the Peace Corps, and it was highly favorable. For the most part the Volunteers themselves were unaware of just how highly they were regarded. Somalis were not telling *them*—they were telling each other! And in the Somali Republic, which possesses a degree of linguistic, social, and cultural unity greater than that found in almost any other African nation, ideas can spread far and fast by word of mouth. An unforgettable comment made by the then Governor of Hargeisa to a group of people in his office was typical. In an American cultural context his statement sounds almost banal—a Peace Corps publicity agent's handout. In Somali cultural terms, however, the Governor was not being at all banal, for the Somalis are a forthright people little given to flattery. Moreover, the Governor was speaking in words that to him were foreign and consequently far from trite; "The Peace Corps," he declared, "is winning the hearts of our people."

In a country where so many with so much had tried in vain to make a favorable impression, how was it that a mere handful of Peace Corps Volunteers was winning the hearts of the Somali people?

Most Somalis inevitably contrasted the Peace Corps Volunteers with the only other large group of expatriate teachers in the Republic—the Egyptians. Though they share Islam in common, Somalis tend to regard Egyptians very much as they regard Westerners. To them, Egyptians appear just as ethnocentric and prejudiced as do many Westerners. More than one Somali traveler in Egypt has been confronted with the phrase—"And whose slave are you, black man?"

Egyptian teachers have also sometimes given Somali education officials a difficult time. One complained, for example, that he could not teach at a given hour because he had to be home to have tea with his wife. Others would not accept the housing provided—it was not nice enough, or it was too small, or it had ants. Another refused to walk a quarter mile to school, insisting that daily transportation be provided. Almost all complained about what they identified as ignorance and indifference on the part of students and school officials alike. Many declared that once they returned home they would "never leave Cairo again."

In the classroom the Egyptians talked more often about Nasser, said Somalis, than about the subject matter at hand. When class was over they rushed back to their homes and clubs, seldom mixing with the local people. And Somalis—sharp traders all—scorned the occasional manipulation of religion as, for example, "Why do you charge me fifty cents, for these limes—after all we're both Muslims aren't we?"

The Peace Corps Volunteers were a study in contrast. They made the best of the housing provided, and in many cases improved on it with local materials and with their own labor. They walked to school rather than rode. And they stuck to subject matter in their classes, eschewing propaganda. When class was over, they accompanied their students to the school gardens and worked with them side by side. They took on extra duties such as building a science laboratory, writing a textbook, or constructing a windmill.

Above all they did not try to set themselves apart. They entered Somali communities and mingled with the people as equals, not superiors. They sipped tea in local restaurants and talked and laughed with whomever was there. They did their own shopping in local stores and bazaars and made a joy of it by using the few Somali words at their command. And amid all the individual failures—those who gave up and went home, and the few who found something to criticize in everything Somalis did—the impression of the Peace Corps Volunteer as a decent, friendly, affable human being was the one that lasted.

The Director of Education for the Northern Regions said once that he thought all foreigners were too "delicate" to live the way Somalis lived—but that was before he became acquainted with Peace Corps Volunteers. The foreigners he had known never walked anywhere when they could ride. They seldom did their own manual work, especially since Somalis could be hired so cheaply to do it for them. And they rarely mixed socially with Somalis just for the genuine pleasure of it. But this Director of Education discovered to his surprise that Peace Corps Volunteers did all of these things and did them, to quote his own words, "just like Somalis."

Although Volunteers filled a real need for teachers in the Somali Republic, they won respect and admiration not for what they did but for the way they went about it. They got to know the people and the people got to know them. And the real and lasting significance of their achievement lies in the simple fact that for the first time in the history of United States relations with the Somali Republic, Somalis began to regard Americans as a genuinely friendly, likeable people.

The Somali reaction to the PCVs was becoming increasingly evident during the second year of Somalia One. It was for this reason that many supporters of the Peace Corps in Somalia urged the formation of a Somalia Two contingent. In view of all the difficulties encountered by Somalia One, however, it was no wonder that there were those who argued against a second contingent. In the end, the decision was taken to form Somalia Two.[8]

RETURN TO SOMALIA

The Somalia Two group was larger and better trained.[9] Training took place at Eastern Michigan University, which also had a contract with AID to provide the initial teacher-training staff for the Somali Republic's National Teacher Education Center, built by the United States.

The Somalia Two Volunteers received a warmer welcome than did Somalia One. National elections resulting in a change in government had brought about a more efficient administration, which was strongly influenced by the favorable response of the Somali people to the Peace Corps. The aimlessness that characterized the early stages of Somalia One now no longer prevailed. Instead the new Somali administration, assisted by Peace Corps Representatives possessing previous transcultural experience, put the Volunteers right to work.

"We have been here a little over six weeks and all are well settled and working full schedules," wrote one Somalia Two Volunteer. "I would say that the Peace Corps situation in Somalia is pretty good. Everyone has been friendly and seems glad that we are here."[10] This favorable reaction may be contrasted with a report from the Peace Corps Secretary to the Somali Project, who had had an opportunity to observe both the Somali One and Somali Two groups in action. She wrote: "The Ministry of Education was just absolutely, unbelievably and wonderfully magnificent," and acted with "fantastic speed and efficiency" in getting Volunteers to their posts.[11]

In the light of these reports it is clear that these and future Peace Corps Volunteers will add a fine and worthy record to the achievement of the first group. What little the first group was able to accomplish, it accomplished in the face of really stupendous odds. But as a result of the individual efforts of this small group of Americans, the Somali people began to change their whole concept of the United States and of the character of the American people.

NOTES

[1] I would like to express my thanks to all the many Somalis who patiently helped me toward an understanding of their culture, especially Mohammed Farah Jama (Musa Shina). My thanks, too, to each of the

Peace Corps Volunteers for so enriching my life. For their courage and wisdom in trying to apply anthropology in their administrations, Willard C. Muller and Alfred M. Hurt, former AID Directors, Sal Tedesco, former Peace Corps Representative, and Horace G. Torbert, current Ambassador to the Somali Republic and one of the finest ambassadors anywhere, deserve the highest praise.

[2] See especially I. M. Lewis (1961) for a masterful account of nomadic life with emphasis on political relations. Mahony's (1961) report illuminates certain essential features of pastoral life. Somewhat lighter travel books helpful in attaining an understanding of Somalis are Burton (1894) and Laurence (1964).

[3] Cf. Andrzejewski and Lewis (1964).

[4] Though his work is now dated and deals mostly with the Italian south, Karp (1960) helps explain the Somali economy.

[5] See Drysdale (1964) for an excellent account of recent history in the Horn of Africa from a Somali point of view. Touval (1963) is also helpful.

[6] The evaluation that United States economic aid is getting a cold reception from Somalis is no exaggeration of the facts. Even AID's highly paid Somali employees are almost completely unsympathetic with its program and its policies. Sometimes, it ought to be said, unfavorable attitudes have developed despite the best efforts of particular American officials.

[7] In this connection an interesting and unusual statistic emerging from the Somalia One Project is the fact that seven of the Volunteer women (out of a total of nine) married seven of the Volunteer men. In other words a total of fourteen out of forty-five Volunteers got married—and in every case to another Volunteer. This was partly a function, I believe, of the extent to which the Volunteers felt insecure, anxious, and isolated from almost everyone but themselves.

[8] Special credit should go to Sal Tedesco, then Peace Corps Representative in Somalia, for the courageous stand he took in favor of continuing the Somalia program. A majority of the Volunteers were also in favor of continuing the project. Mr. and Mrs. William Levine, who had been Volunteers but were later appointed to the Peace Corps/Washington Staff, were able to promote this point of view effectively.

[9] Two Volunteers who returned from the Somali Republic, Thom Ris and Janet Shoemaker, helped make the training program more successful.

[10] Personal communication from Volunteer Stephen Wilson.

[11] Personal communication from Miss Betsy Campbell.

BIBLIOGRAPHY

ANDRZEJEWSKI, B. W., and I. M. LEWIS
    1964 *Somali Poetry*. Oxford, Eng.: The Clarendon Press.
BURTON, RICHARD
    1894 *First Footsteps in East Africa*. London: Memorial Edition.
DRYSDALE, JOHN
    1964 *The Somali Dispute*. London: Pall Mall Press.

KARP, M.
   1960   *The Economics of Trusteeship in Somalia.* New York: New
          York University Press.
LAURENCE, M.
   1964   *Prophet's Camel Bell.* London. Also published as *New Wind in
          a Dry Land.* New York: Alfred Knopf.
LEWIS, I. M.
   1961   *A Pastoral Democracy.* London: Oxford University Press.
MAHONY, FRANK J.
   1961   "Evaluation of a Pilot Project in Range Management Near
          Afmadu." *Community Development Review,* Vol. 6, No. 1.
TOUVAL, S.
   1963   *Somali Nationalism.* Cambridge, Mass.: Harvard University
          Press.

8

Nurses in Tanganyika

WILLIAM H. FRIEDLAND, *a sociologist, is Associate Profes-sor of Industrial and Labor Relations at Cornell University. During 1958–1961 he held a Ford Foundation Foreign Area Training Fellowship, six months of which were spent at the University of London's School of Oriental and African Studies. This was followed by fourteen months of field research in Tanganyika, devoted primarily to an analysis of the ways in which Africans adopt and adapt modern forms of administrative and social structure, particularly labor unions. Dr. Friedland has lectured to every Peace Corps training program for Tanganyika (Tanzania), and was Director of Area Studies for Tanganyika Two, with which the present chapter deals. In mid-1963 he carried out three intensive weeks of field work in Tanganyika, during which he was able to see almost all members of Tanganyika Two in action. Professor Friedland has written numerous articles on sociological theory and on labor in the developing areas. Be-sides those publications listed in the bibliography to this chapter, he is author of* Unions and Industrial Relations in the Underdeveloped Areas, *Ithaca, N.Y.: New York State School of Industrial and Labor Relations, 1963.*

THIS chapter will examine the experiences of Tanganyika Two in order to glean lessons that might be of general value. Like many other chapters in this book, it will pay particular attention to the negative aspects of the program: to the strains, the problems, and the failures. For if there are lessons to be learned from the endeavor of Tanganyika Two, they can best be learned by discussing the program's shortcomings.

However, let it be emphasized at the outset that, measured by most standards, Tanganyika Two was a success. In spite of serious problems of morale, the group made an important contribution to Tanganyika's health services. Perhaps the most convincing evidence of success is that, as this chapter was being written, Tanganyika Three was in the process of being trained. Included in its ranks was

141

a contingent of nurses who were scheduled to follow up the work of Tanganyika Two.

BACKGROUND

Origins of the Program

Little information is publicly available on the formulation of Tanganyika's original request for Peace Corps Volunteers, but by the spring of 1961 negotiations had been completed and recruitment was under way in the United States. By late summer, Tanganyika One— an all-male contingent of surveyors and geologists—was in the host country. In December, Tanganyika achieved its independence from Britain. (The present United Republic of Tanzania resulted from the union of Tanganyika and Zanzibar in April, 1964.)

The Tanganyika Two project traces its origins to the preindependence period when Mr. Derek Bryceson, then Minister for Health and Labour, recognized that independence would create serious strains on the country's health services. He foresaw the departure of many highly trained European personnel. And he was well aware of the heavy political pressure for "Africanization" of the country's administrative and social services—despite the critical shortage of trained Africans to look after the needs of ten million Tanganyikans in such fields as medicine, nursing, and public health. Mr. Bryceson therefore welcomed the prospect of using a contingent of Peace Corps nurses to help stabilize the situation in Tanganyika's hospitals.

Characteristics of the Tanganyika Two Group

In July 1962, the twenty-eight trainees of Tanganyika Two assembled for training at Syracuse University. One elderly woman quickly left the program by mutual consent. The remaining twenty-seven—twenty-five nurses and two laboratory technicians—were unusually homogeneous for a Peace Corps group. All were female. All were well trained. All the nurses were either registered or had completed training and examinations.

It was also a young group. Seventeen of the twenty-seven were under twenty-four years old, and only four were over thirty. Thus, the bulk of the group either came directly from nursing school or else had had only a few years of nursing experience. The marriageability of the group augured dangerously for the future and, as we shall see, helped to produce a high rate of attrition in the field.

The unusual homogeneity and small size of the group had important consequences for Tanganyika Two. The similarity of background and education meant that the training program could move at an even pace. Like most Peace Corps groups, the trainees were highly motivated. However, since all of them had been (or could have been) occupying useful positions in American hospitals, none was confronted with the problem that bedevils many PCVs, that of "what to do with myself after college." Since the group was so small, everybody got to know everybody else well, and close personal relations were established with the staff.

Training

The training program for Tanganyika Two differed from most Peace Corps training programs in that it took place at a university that possessed rich resources for the teaching of area studies. Syracuse University has an ongoing East African Studies program with a considerable number of East African students and with many American students involved in East African studies. It was therefore possible to staff the area studies program largely from local resources. This obviated the problem of building team spirit or involvement among the area staff. The staff thus devoted far more attention to the training program than has been the case in any other program of which I have knowledge. Contacts between the area staff and the students were not limited to formal classroom work and occasional formally ordained informal contact. Interaction was continuous all day long, and indeed, well into the night on many occasions. The continuous presence of deeply involved students from East Africa helped to create an atmosphere where interest in the Swahili language and in African nationalism ran high. The singing of the Tanganyikan national anthem was not only a formal feature of each day of area training, but was greeted with enthusiasm. Even more significant were the drumming sessions, dances, and songs that were imparted through dozens of informal and genuinely spontaneous sessions. As will be seen, however, this high commitment of the training staff had both positive and negative consequences.

The training period lasted from July 2 to August 25, with area studies concentrated in the final month. All twenty-seven trainees survived final selection, despite some doubts about several of them. After a brief home leave, the group reassembled in New York and flew to Tanganyika for two months of full-time Swahili studies. In November they took up actual work in hospitals.

An Overview of the Record in Tanganyika

The initial assignments of the Volunteers concentrated them at three hospitals in important population centers of Tanganyika: sixteen at Dar es Salaam, eight at Tanga and three at Moshi. The concentration of so many PCVs in Dar es Salaam is somewhat understandable because that city's Princess Margaret (now Muhimbili) Hospital is the country's largest hospital and its major training establishment. On the other hand, most of the girls were not expected to be involved in training activities initially except in some peripheral sense. Moreover, there were ample indications of serious personnel shortages in many of the hospitals of Tanganyika. Nonetheless, concentration in the three centers was maintained until *late 1963* when, after many bitter complaints, some of the girls were reassigned from Dar es Salaam to two other towns. There is reason to believe that the initial concentration of the PCVs took place because some highly placed British civil servants in the health service were concerned about the introduction of a possible "infection" of ideas by the American nurses, and sought to minimize this infection by concentrating and isolating them.

Between November 1962 and January 1964, attrition reduced the size of Tanganyika Two from twenty-seven to nineteen. Marriage accounted for half of this unusually high 30 per cent rate of attrition; sickness and "other" reasons each claimed two girls. "Fall-out" began almost as soon as the girls took up their assignments in the hospitals. It continued at an almost steady rate until January 1964, when the situation stabilized.

The marriage rate of this nubile Tanganyika Two group was augmented by the fact that Tanganyika One, consisting entirely of men, was already one year old when Tanganyika Two arrived in the field. The girls were literally met at the airport by panting, eager young American men—just as had been prophesied by Peace Corps Director Sargent Shriver in his speech inaugurating the training program.

There are some reasons to believe that the rate of marriage might have been slightly lower had the girls encountered less frustration in working within the social structure of Tanganyika's hospital system. Indeed, as Mahony has pointed out in the case of Somalia (page 133), attrition of whatever type would perhaps have been lower if there had been better integration, involvement, and utilization of the Volunteers.

Further contributing to the high dropout rate may have been the encapsulated atmosphere in which each of the three groups was originally placed. Volunteers were housed together in single housing units and assigned their own mess area which was rapidly converted into a "Little America." When I visited the groups midway through their tour, the prevailing atmosphere was almost entirely American with a few Tanganyikan overtones—rather than vice versa. This was hardly conducive to high morale, since in the training program much emphasis had been placed on the need for integration with Tanganyikan society.

PROBLEMS OF THE TRAINING PROGRAM

As Director of Area Studies and lecturer in the training program at Syracuse University, I tend to look back upon it with nostalgia. Indeed, my honest opinion is that the training was, on the whole, extremely successful. However, the program had two major deficiencies which are highly instructive: (1) it fostered certain illusions about the work the nurses would be performing, about Tanganyikans, and about Africa; and (2) it left untouched certain important aspects of behavior which happened to fall into an interstitial zone between "area studies" and "technical studies."

The Fostering of Illusions

While a major effort in the area training program was devoted to a realistic presentation of the nature of Tanganyikan society and culture, a number of important illusions were inadvertently imparted to the trainees about their work in Tanganyika and the nature of their welcome. This was largely due to the incredibly rapid changes that had taken place between the time those of us teaching in the area program had last been in Tanganyika and the time the nurses arrived in the country. Independence had come on December 9, 1961, and in the period just before and after that date the spirit of Tanganyikan nationalism had grown by leaps and bounds. The Tanganyikans had become definitely—though mildly—xenophobic. And yet not one of the members of the area training staff had been in Tanganyika during this crucial period. We ourselves were unaware of the dimensions of this new xenophobia. Little wonder, then, that we were remiss in alerting our trainees to its full significance, and in teaching them how to cope with it.

Another element in the development of unreasonable expectations stemmed from the high commitment of the area training staff to the training program. As already indicated, the interaction between staff and trainees was far more intense than is found in most Peace Corps training situations. Because the staff, and especially its African members, had been so "open" to the trainees, they undoubtedly developed the expectation that Tanganyikan society would be equally open.

These expectations were unrealistic. Indigenous African society was to remain largely "closed" because of linguistic and cultural barriers. Also—to put it succinctly—the Westernized elite of Tanganyika had by this time become "fed up" with Westerners. By the time of independence, the number of Europeans and other outsiders descending upon the country had reached such staggering proportions that most Westernized Tanganyikans were only too happy to avoid most of these visitors, reserving their energies for only the most important ones. Thus the area staff, being out of touch with the changing realities of Tanganyika, led the trainees to develop unrealistic expectations about their welcome.

Furthermore, the area training staff tended to forget that while the political rule of the British had ended, significant decision-making powers remained in the hands of many of the expatriate British civil servants still in the country. While we correctly explained that major *policy* decisions were now being made by Tanganyikans, we failed to prepare our trainees to cope with the British expatriates who still held many important *administrative* reins.

The Neglect of Interstitial Areas of Instruction

The problem of the articulation of different components of a training program appears to me to be endemic in the Peace Corps approach to training. It must be resolved by careful, planned coordination of the various components of a program, especially area studies, American studies, world affairs and communism, and technical studies. Although over-all coordination of the Syracuse training program appeared adequate at the time, subsequent problems that emerged in the field indicated much to be desired.

Starting out with pious hopes and expectations about "working together," which were manifested primarily in ritualistic staff meetings, each segment of the training staff would proceed along its own lines and pay relatively little attention to other segments. Thus, for example, in the Tanganyika Two program (and in a number of others in which I have participated) area studies instructors would prefer that world politics instructors "stay off" the African continent. Similarly, American studies teachers were not overjoyed when area studies teachers used American examples for comparative purposes in explaining life in the host country.

In the particular case of Tanganyika Two, substantial problems developed in the field because of a failure of articulation of area training and technical training. Area studies are devoted to the preparation of the trainees for life in the host country, and concentrate, of necessity, upon the character of the society, economy, local cultures, politics, and the like. The area training staff at Syracuse left *the hospital as a social situation* completely alone because they felt it to be within the "jurisdiction" of the technical training staff. In addition, few of us knew very much about hospitals as social systems in Tanganyika. While the general character of the civil service was discussed, as was the general subject of race relations in the host country, no one on the area staff attempted to deal with concrete manifestations of these problems in the hospital.

Technical training is devoted to the preparation of the trainees for the jobs they will perform in the host country. Although there was concern with *nursing in Tanganyika,* and the coordinator of technical studies actually went to Tanganyika for a brief study of the field situation, the actual training was carried out by technical staff unacquainted with the detailed situation in the host country and unaware of Tanganyika's political, social, and economic history. They were thus unprepared to deal with social and cultural problems of Tanganyikan hospitals in other than a *technical* fashion. The trainees were not sensitized to the differences in attitudinal orientations between American and British-Tanganyikan nursing.

Thus, the existence of interstitial areas between components of the training program meant that in an extremely crucial subject— the social structure and culture of the Tanganyikan hospital—no proper orientation was given to the trainees. And the consequences were soon to be felt.

PROBLEMS IN THE HOSPITAL

Not long after arriving in Tanganyika, an incident occurred that points up important differences between the British and American styles of nursing. The Tanganyika Two nurses were to meet the matron to whom they had been assigned. The group assembled in a room for the meeting and when the matron arrived, *remained seated.* This behavior, understandable in the mores of American nursing practice, represented the apogee of bad behavior. To the British it probably indicated the "bad" training of the American nurses, their lack of respect for the matron, for the entire system of nursing in Tanganyika, and so on. Repercussions were immediately forthcoming in the form of a public dressing down. The event assuredly was communicated throughout the nursing system by informal channels.

It is, incidentally, not clear whether the Volunteers remained seated because of ignorance of the mores of British nursing or because of American obstinacy. Certainly the area studies part of the training program had not prepared them for the mores of the nursing profession in Tanganyika. At any rate, it cannot be doubted that the incident helped to crystallize the already existing hostility of many British personnel toward the Peace Corps project, strengthening their desire to maintain a prophylactic situation by concentrating the Volunteers geographically and limiting the possible spread of the American "infection" to other parts of the hospital system.

The British Colonial Heritage

Like colonial systems generally, the British colonial system has not always attracted the most capable or highly trained personnel from the home country. The most accomplished graduates of the elite universities in Britain, if attracted to the civil service, were normally recruited into the home civil service. Of those interested in work in the colonies, the best were normally recruited into the elite Indian Civil Service and Sudan Service. This does not mean to say that the Tanganyika Service was composed entirely of second-raters; on the contrary, I met considerable numbers of highly accomplished civil servants during the course of field work there. However, I also met many semicompetent, barely competent, and incompetent persons— and even a few nitwits.

The onset of independence in 1961 did not help the situation since it triggered the general departure of British personnel. While a considerable number of the best people stayed on, many also left. All too frequently, those remaining were of lesser competence, having stayed because of their inability to find decent jobs back home. The hospital system of Tanganyika was no exception to this general rule. Thus, while there were many excellent physicians, nurses, and other personnel, the average level of competence left something to be desired.

The PCVs' lack of preparation for functioning in a British colonial hospital milieu is exemplified in the difficulty they had adapting to the situation in a large pediatrics ward where the British physician made his entire tour in a period of minutes. One of the Volunteers, in frustration over the unwillingness or inability of the physician to stop and diagnose a case of typhoid in a child, engaged in a public shouting match with him. The insistence on a formal apology to the doctor as a prerequisite for the American nurse's remaining in service afterward—though her diagnosis proved to be correct—did not help to better relations between the Volunteers and their British co-workers.

Differences in Status Attitudes

Differences between British and American nursing are found not only in the technical aspects of the profession but, equally importantly, in the social aspects. Nursing is universally characterized by well-demarcated hierarchies *within* the profession, and a variety of symbols are utilized to mark off the various strata of nurses. Most of these symbols, though unintelligible to the lay public, hold great meaning and value to the nurses. There is also an exaggerated demarcation of social distance between ranks, and deferential behavior by subordinate ranks toward superiors.

Although the Tanganyika Two nurses were well accustomed to a hierarchy in carrying out the formal duties of nursing, they were quite unprepared for the strict British maintenance of social distance in off-duty and peripheral activities. Thus, it came as a shock to discover that tea breaks were marked by rigorous maintenance of social distance, with each stratum of nurses gathering in physically separate areas to take tea with peers of the same stratum from other parts of the hospital. The PCVs' background had led them to expect less formal interaction—on the basis of working in the same part of the hospital or of sharing common interests.

Differences in Service Attitudes

Still another source of strain was differing attitudes toward preparation for emergencies. It is not possible here to examine the details of these differences, but my impression is that American training emphasizes that emergencies are expected to develop regularly during the normal course of hospital work; nurses are therefore trained to be prepared for emergencies and are prepared to handle them without undue excitement. British training, on the other hand, appears to deny the existence of emergencies. That is, the work of the hospital is always crucial and, therefore, emergencies do not exist.

An illustration of the problems that can arise from these differences is found in the case of one Tanganyika Two Volunteer who had an unusual type of blood which was required for an emergency case at another hospital than that in which she was working. She was on duty at the time and requested permission from her British superior to leave. This was denied although a replacement could have been arranged. She appealed the decision to the next rank of authority but was again refused. After receiving desperate calls from the other hospital, she left her post—informing her superior that she was doing so—and went to give blood. Essentially, the attitude of the nurses in charge was that no emergency existed and that the Volunteer should continue the normal course of her duty until it was completed. The insistence that the Volunteer formally apologize to her superiors created further strain.

Contacts with Patients

On the whole, contact with Tanganyikan patients brought the Volunteers enormous satisfaction. The Volunteers found African patients and their families to be more grateful and much less demanding than the American patients they were used to. Where American patients might be screaming for sedation and demanding their "right" to attention, Tanganyikan Africans accepted any assistance with gratitude, as if it were something special. The Volunteers unanimously found the Tanganyikan patients more friendly in the hospital context, less involved with themselves, their diseases, and their pains. Accordingly, they appreciated the Tanganyikans as patients and, indeed, admired them extravagantly.

Since the bulk of the patients were working-class Africans, the language problem was a serious obstacle. Although Swahili had been a crucial part of the training program, several of the Volunteers never acquired more than minimal facility in the language. Others achieved considerable proficiency and could carry on extended conversations. The majority learned enough to handle routine problems of hospital work and engage in minimal social interaction with patients, but not enough to communicate effectively in the everyday variety of situations.

As a consequence, associations with Africans as patients were considerably limited. Although the fact that the Volunteers were girls may have been a barrier to friendly interaction, the normal cultural barriers seem to have been more important—and were intensified by the lack of common experience, since the girls were professionals dealing primarily with proletarians. Some of the girls were invited to visit African homes in the countryside and to see various traditional ceremonies. These visits were interesting and worthwhile, but could hardly be expected to produce enduring social relationships.

Collegial Relations on the Job

In the course of their work, the Volunteers came into contact with many Africans at all levels in the hospital hierarchy. The overwhelming bulk of these contacts were routine and normal—the kinds of contacts that take place in all hospitals: a nurse requests an orderly to empty a bed pan and the job gets done; transitions are made as one shift comes on duty and another goes off; and so on. Such contacts involved little strain and were understood by all participants—African and American.

To this was added a somewhat unusual, although considerably muted, dimension: the existence of a form of xenophobia on the part of many Tanganyikans. Although xenophobia refers to a "hatred of foreigners," the term "hatred" would certainly be too strong to describe the situation confronting the Volunteers. To my knowledge, no Tanganyikan ever suggested that any of the nurses ought to leave Tanganyika. However, little incidents did occur in which Tanganyikans indirectly communicated that the PCVs' presence was not regarded with unqualified joy. The Volunteers, for example, would become upset to see Tanganyikan nurses running their fingers over sterile hypodermic syringes before making injections, to remove any particles that might be adhering to the syringe. When the PCVs tried to illustrate sterile procedures used in American hospitals, it was made clear that the Tanganyikans were following their own procedure—and that this was none of the Americans' business. As one Volunteer expressed it, it was as if the Tanganyikan nurses were saying: "We may be doing wrong, and we may even know that we're doing wrong, but it's none of your business; keep out of it; a patient may die but we are going to learn from our mistakes in our own way."

Collegial Relations off the Job

This xenophobia was also reflected in the lack of social interaction between the Volunteers and their Tanganyikan colleagues off the job. Other factors also contributed to this isolation. For example, the heavy stress placed on social distance between various strata of the hospital hierarchy in Dar es Salaam was undoubtedly maintained in off-the-job context. To be sure, there were some Tanganyikan nurses in the same stratum as the Volunteers, but even here, cultural barriers and linguistic problems still had to be confronted. As a result, social contacts were mainly peripheral, or occurred at formal social occasions. *Informal* off-the-job association was rare. Thus, evidence indicates that by the middle of 1963—halfway through the program—not a single Volunteer could say that she had established a friendship of any depth with an African nurse.

PROBLEMS OUTSIDE THE HOSPITAL

In seeking to make Tanganyikan friends outside of the hospital milieu, the Volunteers confronted the same kind of mild xenophobia. The PCVs were perceived as being "mzungu," or Europeans. Prior to independence, Europeans had insisted upon social deference from Africans in all situations. Then, with independence, came a revolution in attitudes. Now Africans began stating, in effect: "This is *our* country and *you* are visitors!" Thus, while the Volunteer nurses' routine contacts with Tanganyikans outside the hospital were marked by the usual courtesy Tanganyikans extend to foreigners, xenophobia lurked just beneath the surface and emerged in unpredictable ways.

The example that best illustrates these changes can be found in the changing attitudes toward the camera of the foreign visitor in various periods. In the preindependence period before the nationalist movement developed great strength, Tanganyikans were largely indifferent to cameras. Then, as the independence, nationalism, and modernization movement gathered strength, more and more Tanganyikans began to resent the foreigner's camera, and the foreigner's tendency—real or apparent—to prefer photographing aspects of Tanganyikan life which they were trying to forget or eliminate: traditional dances and rituals, beggars in the city streets, and the like. Just prior to independence, it was a foolish visitor who took photographs of Africans without obtaining prior consent. By the middle of 1963, visitors arriving in the country were being warned in writing by the National Tourist Commission that Tanganyikans sometimes objected to being photographed and might say "Hapana" (No). Similarly, when I visited one hospital to talk to some of the Volunteers and—being aware of camera sensitivity—took photographs of the hospital buildings from a considerable distance, some patients asked one of the Volunteers who the "mzungu" was who took *their* picture! As a sad postscript, it should be reported that two of the nurses from a later Tanganyika group were summarily sent out of the country for having taken a photograph in the delivery room of the hospital where they worked.

While most social interaction with Tanganyikans outside of the work situation was normal, several incidents took place that left indelible impressions on all PCVs—including those who were not actually present at the incidents. One of the most traumatic took place when a group of Volunteers went to meet a plane on which some other Volunteers were arriving. As it happened, there was a high government official on the same plane and as he alighted the usual officials of the Tanganyika African National Union (TANU) were on hand to greet him. Also present was a local choir which broke into the national anthem. (This was during a period in which the peregrinations of various officials of the government and TANU were marked by excessive ceremonialism—so excessive that President Nyerere shortly afterward felt it necessary to issue public warnings about "pomposity.") The Volunteers had all learned the National Anthem and probably knew its words (in Swahili) better than 95 per cent of the Tanganyikan population. Unfortunately, however, two of the PCVs were leaning against a fence while the anthem was being sung. In all likelihood, being some distance off, they regarded themselves as onlookers and *not* as participants in the occasion. As soon as the anthem was completed, a policeman rushed over and proceeded to take action against the two girls for "disrespect." Although the incident was a tempest in a teapot it was channeled upward until it came to the personal attention of the Vice President, who also took a serious view of it. The matter was later dropped, but it left an indelible impact on all of the Volunteers as to the enormous sensitivity of the African population to any slight—real or supposed —originating from Europeans.

PROBLEMS WITH THE HOST GOVERNMENT

Many of the difficulties experienced by Tanganyika Two stemmed in part from conditions within the host government. For example, Mr. Bryceson, the minister who originally negotiated the project, had been shifted to another ministry before the PCVs even arrived in Tanganyika. The new Minister for Health, Mr. Maswanya, while favorable to the project, was less enthusiastic.

Even had Mr. Bryceson remained, however, this would not have guaranteed effective cooperation at the working administrative level. In Tanganyika, as doubtless quite generally in the developing countries, enthusiasm at the policy level does not necessarily mean enthusiasm at the working level. And it is important to remember that at this time the Tanganyikan civil service was undergoing substantial change and was deeply preoccupied with serious problems of internal organization and stability—while at the same time attempting to maintain the normal work of government administration. It is not surprising, therefore, that Tanganyika Two did not receive the kind of enthusiastic welcome or administrative cooperation that would be likely to lead to effective communication.

Morale Sags

When I visited the Tanganyika Two group in mid-1963, there were serious morale problems in all three of the towns where the nurses were posted—and seemingly in inverse relation to the size of the group. Thus morale was apparently lowest in Dar es Salaam, where the girls complained of underutilization in the face of crying needs for nursing services elsewhere in the country. Several of them were able to accept their situation, although with reluctance. Others developed a monumental sense of grievance. I asked each of the nurses: "If you had it to do over again, would you do it?" In every case the answer was "Yes." But when the question was reformulated as "If you had it to do over again knowing what you now know, would you do it?" the answer was uniformly "No."

The reasons for the girls' dissatisfaction in Dar es Salaam would seem to have much in common with the reasons why PCVs around the world tend to be less satisfied with assignments in larger cities. Dar es Salaam is relatively impersonal; one gets lost in the shuffle; one has difficulty finding a way to make a contribution that one can call one's own. Up-country assignments, by contrast, are usually more flexible. While an up-country post might lack social amenities and contacts, this is often overbalanced by a freer, more informal style of life, and by greater opportunities for making a contribution that is uniquely one's own. The distinction between these two types of assignment is illustrated by the case of three of the apparently happiest nurses in Dar es Salaam who, by dint of their own initiative, managed to create for themselves the spare-time role of caring for the health of children in an orphanage there.

Because the nurses in Dar es Salaam had the lowest morale and the closest contact with the country Representative, it is not surprising that they tended to feel that many of their problems stemmed from his inability to convey to the government some of their grievances, and especially their complaint about overconcentration and underutilization. Undoubtedly, this illustrates a latent function of Representatives everywhere: to serve as scapegoats. My own estimate, however, was that this Representative could have been more effective, and that adjustment of the problem of overconcentration took longer than it need have.

Morale Improves

At long last in late 1963, the oversized group in Dar es Salaam was dispersed. Some were restationed in Tabora and others in Mwanza. By this time also, some of the more dissatisfied PCVs had eliminated themselves through marriage, sickness, or on other grounds. Morale began to pick up. One girl even re-enlisted for a second two-year period. Writing in May 1964, another of them expressed these feelings in a letter:

> Time is flying by quickly now and it seems impossible that there are only three months left. I've been amazed at my own reactions now that it's almost over. Maybe I've just finally adjusted to the place but I'm almost sorry to leave. I can think of so many things I'll genuinely miss and people that I'd like to see more often. I've been getting more satisfaction from my work possibly because [the nursing sister in charge] lets me proceed on my own. I certainly can't say that professionally I've accomplished what I had hoped for but the time has not been wasted and I wouldn't exchange it for anything. The project as a whole could have stood improvements and I do so wish they'd utilize some of our suggestions for the next one. . . .

LESSONS TO BE LEARNED

In this chapter, I have concentrated on deficiencies and problems. Lest I give the wrong impression, let me again state that I believe Tanganyika Two was not a failure but a qualified success. Nonetheless, I believe that we can learn several lessons from the experience, lessons that will help to avoid repetition of mistakes. These can be summarized as follows:

1. Area training should not only impart an accurate and sympathetic understanding of the host culture but should also strive to include adequate coverage of recent and rapid social change.

2. More attention must be devoted to the interstitial areas of training, and especially to presenting technical studies, American studies, and world affairs and communism in the light of the *host* country's culture and immediate situation.

3. Good morale in the field is heavily dependent upon the Representative's close rapport with the Volunteers, his knowledge of the local culture and situation, and his effectiveness in communicating with key officials in the host government.

4. Volunteers should not be assigned in large groups as this denies them easy access to citizens of the host country and makes cultural

rapport more difficult. Since friendships with the local people and partial integration into the local community are among the PCVs' most cherished goals, overconcentration in assignment leads to low morale.

5. Finally, nothing will more surely produce low morale than ineffective utilization of the Volunteers' skills. The Tanganyika experience confirms what has been learned elsewhere, namely that the Volunteers are job-oriented, and that if they have job satisfaction, many other problems will tend to resolve themselves.

BIBLIOGRAPHY

BATES, MARGARET L.
 1962 "Tanganyika," in Gwendolen M. Carter, ed., *African One-Party States*. Ithaca, N.Y.: Cornell University Press.
BURKE, FRED G.
 1964 "Tanganyika: The Search for Ujamaa," in William H. Friedland and Carl G. Rosberg, Jr., eds., *African Socialism*. Stanford, Calif.: Stanford University Press, for the Hoover Institution on War, Revolution, and Peace.
FRIEDLAND, WILLIAM H.
    "The Evolution of Tanganyika's Political System," in Fred G. Burke and Stanley Diamond, eds., *The Transformation of East Africa: Studies in Political Anthropology*. Forthcoming.
INTERNATIONAL BANK FOR RECONSTRUCTION AND DEVELOPMENT
 1961 *The Economic Development of Tanganyika*. Baltimore, Md.: The Johns Hopkins Press.
LESLIE, J. A. K.
 1963 *A Survey of Dar es Salaam*. London: Oxford University Press.
SOUTHALL, AIDAN
 1961 *Social Change in Modern Africa*. London: Oxford University Press.

9

The Nigerian Experience and Career Reorientation

L. GRAY COWAN *is Professor of Government and Director of the Institute of African Studies at Columbia University. He has made many trips to Africa and spent in the aggregate some five years in field research and travel on that continent. From the early days of 1961, Dr. Cowan has served the Peace Corps' West Africa programs in a variety of capacities, as program consultant, training coordinator and lecturer, and overseas evaluator. His Peace Corps involvement has touched not only Nigeria, but French-speaking West African countries as well. Professor Cowan has been Secretary-Treasurer of the African Studies Association since its founding in 1958. He is a member of the Board of Trustees of the African-American Institute, the Council on Foreign Relations' Africa Study Group, the Social Science Research Council's Committee on Africa, and the Department of State's Public Advisory Committee on Africa. His publications include* Local Government in West Africa, *New York: Columbia University Press, 1958; and* Dilemmas of African Independence, *New York: Walker and Co., 1964.*

THE Federation of Nigeria, which gained its independence from Britain in 1960, is in many ways the most challenging country in Africa. On its 357,000 square miles of territory live scores of ethno-linguistic groups. Nigeria has a total population variously estimated as high as 55 million, or one fifth the entire population of the continent of Africa. Despite a somewhat creaky federal structure of four semiautonomous regions plus the federal district of Lagos, the nation's leaders have so far been able to hold Nigeria together—and without the use of strong-arm tactics now increasingly prevalent in other parts of Africa.

The Peace Corps' Nigeria program was one of the first, and has become one of the largest and most ambitious. At the end of the Corps' third year, for example, there were 508 PCVs serving in Nigeria, and another 252 in training, which represented the second largest Peace Corps investment anywhere in the world; only that in Colombia was larger. Overwhelmingly, the Peace Corps investment in Nigeria has been in the form of secondary school teachers, and these will be the subject of the present chapter.

THE EMPHASIS ON TEACHING AND PROFESSIONALISM

Those of us who planned and participated in the early training programs for Nigeria placed great emphasis on preparing the prospective Volunteer for the personal adjustments necessary to living in an African culture and community. However, as more and more PCVs entered the teaching field in Nigeria (and elsewhere in West Africa), it became increasingly clear that while cultural preparation was absolutely necessary, there was also an imperative need to place additional emphasis on specialized preparation for the actual professional job of teaching. Feedback from the field, and later from returning PCVs, left little doubt on this score. For it was evident that the Nigerians—government officials, principals, fellow teachers, students, and the general community—were judging the effectiveness of the PCVs primarily on the basis of their performance as teachers, and only very secondarily on the basis of their participation in the broader community. What mattered to them most was effectiveness in the classroom. They cared much less whether the PCV was effective in his spare hours as a community developer, club advisor, technological innovator, or the like.

We in the training programs discovered that the Volunteers must be trained not only in teaching but specifically in teaching *in a Nigerian setting*. Friedland has already made a similar point in stressing the need to train nurses to function effectively in a Tanganyikan setting (page 147). This Nigerian setting is heavily British in its structure and style. The newly independent Nigerian government inherited a British system of education more or less intact, and saw little reason to make any basic alterations. And in any case, independence is so recent that there has been no time for basic alterations, even had they been wanted.

In judging the performance of the PCVs, Nigerians naturally compared them with Nigerian teachers, and in some cases with expatriate British teachers who had remained on after independence. This led to frustration in two respects. First, many of the PCVs had never taught before, and had never received training in pedagogy—save for what little we were able to give them during a brief and hectic Peace Corps training program. And second, the

PCVs were being judged according to British standards, by people who often knew no other standard, and who certainly had no intimate familiarity with American standards, which were perceived as inferior or irrelevant. Under such circumstances, it is not surprising that comparisons of the PCVs' performance with that of their Nigerian and British colleagues did not always come out to the advantage of the Americans.

The teaching experience was not without its value conflicts, which had the effect of heightening the PCVs' frustration and perhaps of reducing their pedagogic effectiveness. For example, it is part of the Nigerian expectation in some schools—especially boys' secondary schools in the remoter areas where quite a number of PCVs served—that teachers will resort to "caning" their students as punishment for various infractions of the rules. Many of the Volunteers, however, were extremely reluctant to treat their students in this way. The students observed this reluctance and grew to respect their American teachers less—at least in the short run. A similar problem has already been reported by Mahony for Somalia (page 131).

As is clear from previous chapters, one of the most common, and strongest, urges found among Volunteers is the urge to innovate, to find a way of doing something better, to "leave behind" a new method or technique. Here again, the particular style of the Nigerian educational system caused frustrations. For in the Nigerian system—as generally in the former British empire—all secondary examinations are graded in accordance with standards set originally and ultimately in England. Nigerian principals and teachers are judged by the percentage of their students who pass the so-called "Cambridge" examinations.* The entire life chances of a Nigerian student hinge on his performance on these examinations. Under such rigid conditions, especially in more remote and less privileged secondary schools, the PCV is not likely to find much ready receptivity to his attempts to innovate—along, say, inductive or Deweyan lines.

---

* Years ago this examination's content was determined by the Cambridge University Syndicate. Then for many years the responsibility was carried by London University, although the examination continued to be referred to as the "Cambridge" examination. Recently the responsibility has shifted to the West African Examination Council, a statutory body set up by the governments of Nigeria, Ghana, Sierra Leone, and Gambia. Standards attained by West African students on this examination are accepted by the examining boards for the General Certificate of Education in the United Kingdom as equivalent to British standards.

PROFESSIONAL ROLE VERSUS COMMUNITY INVOLVEMENT

At the heart of the Peace Corps approach is the notion of the Volunteer's involvement in the life of the local community. While the typical PCV certainly wants to make a solid contribution on the job, he also looks eagerly forward to developing meaningful relationships off the job, in the broader community in which he finds himself. Some Volunteers are relatively satisfied with what might be called a "static" role in the community: one in which they get to know and appreciate the local people, and the local people get to know and appreciate them. Others, however, seem to require a more dynamic involvement, a participation in some innovative social movement, such as community development in some form.

For purposes of supplying contrast, we should also mention here the most extreme form—the limiting case—of community involvement: that in which the PCV's actual full-time job is that of community developer. About half of the PCVs in Latin America are assigned to such duties, which will be described for Peru by Doughty (page 224). Here the PCV can freely exercise his social skills and innovative abilities. Far from having to fit into an existing local organization with a tight, confining structure, the community-developer PCV often has no other choice than to help *create* a local structure from scratch.

The role of the secondary school teacher in Nigeria (and in much of West Africa) discourages almost any kind of community involvement—static *or* dynamic. A great distance often separates the PCV teacher from the local community, a distance that can be summarized under three rubrics: physical, social, and cultural.

Physical Distance

The Volunteer teacher carried a load of twenty classroom hours per week which, in the initial stages at least, allowed him little time for anything but eating, sleeping, preparing lessons, teaching, and marking examinations. This heavy routine in the usual case practically necessitated living at the school rather than in the town. Not only this, but the town was not infrequently some distance away from the school. Only in occasional cases did the Volunteers possess transportation, and even this was, by Peace Corps policy, limited in use to official trips to town for group shopping. Public transportation by "mammy lorry"—a crude jitney bus—was erratic at best even when it was available, and the better part of an evening might be consumed in getting to and from the town. Under these circumstances, contacts in town were usually limited to one day a week during the school year.

Social Distance

Under the British-molded Nigerian system of education, secondary teachers were expected to maintain social distance. Initially, these teachers were expatriates, largely British, and they tended to remain aloof—as the British generally did throughout their empire. When the expatriates were replaced by Nigerians, there was frequently little change in the system itself, partly because for the Nigerians, the very fact of their education separated them from the uneducated strata within the community. The Nigerian teacher frequently felt himself to be above the petty (as he considered them) problems of the town in which the school was located.

The Volunteer's housing was another factor that tended to increase the social distance between him and ordinary, less acculturated Nigerians. Peace Corps policy has generally encouraged the Volunteers to live as their Nigerian teacher colleagues live. This has usually meant living in the school compound—which in many areas would be practically the only available option anyway, because of housing shortages in Nigeria's crowded, burgeoning towns and cities. Housing in the compound is European in style and comes with modern conveniences and "stewards," or servants. Such a level of living has much in common with that enjoyed generally by Nigerians working in reasonably high positions in the modern sector of Nigerian society: civil servants, accountants, architects, lawyers, doctors, and the like. For the Volunteers, it had the advantage that it freed them from the menial tasks of daily living, permitting them to concentrate more effectively on their teaching duties. At the same time, however, it conflicted with the "Peace Corps image," and produced a profusion of guilt feelings.

The Volunteers' relatively high standard of living also served as a status symbol—a fact that many of the more egalitarian among them regarded as a decidedly mixed blessing. They discovered, however, that their own students *expected* them to live in this relatively exalted manner, and had quite definite ideas as to what constituted sufficiently dignified behavior for a teacher. Thus, for example, when egalitarian young Peace Corps teachers went to town by "mammy lorry" rather than by personal automobile (which of course they did not possess), it was their *students* who experienced an acute loss of face!

Cultural Distance

Cultural distance is a difficulty that bedevils the PCV almost regardless of where he is stationed in sub-Saharan Africa, as is attested to by Friedland's chapter on Tanganyika and Dorjahn's on Sierra Leone. And given the fact that Nigeria (like almost every other sub-Saharan country) is a complex mélange of ethnolinguistic groups, cultural distance is often a problem for the Nigerians themselves. It often happens, for example, that a Nigerian teacher will be assigned to a school in an area where he does not speak the local language. In such instances, his communication difficulties and cultural strangeness not infrequently make him unacceptable to the local community. Under such circumstances, neither the teacher nor the community is likely to expect, want, seek, or achieve a very warm or deep relationship with the other. When a PCV steps into such a situation, the community is likely to apply to him some of the same standards and expectations they apply to the strange Nigerian teacher who does not speak their language—although the PCV is helped by the built-in "status symbol" of his white skin. Compounding the PCV's difficulty further is the fact that he often knows no Nigerian language whatever; in other cases, he has been trained in a language not spoken in the area to which he is assigned.

Another factor that made for cultural distance was the extreme cultural conservatism of some Nigerian communities. This was especially true in the heavily Muslim Northern Region, with its relatively closed communities and kin groups, which recall the "inward-looking" society described by Dupree for Afghanistan (page 111). Because of the Muslims' extremely conservative attitudes toward the woman's role in society, female PCVs complained of great difficulty in getting to know people in the local community.

The Influence of the Expatriate Community

Exacerbating the effects of physical, social, and cultural distance was the influence of the local expatriate communities, particularly in the Northern Region. In most cities of that region the expatriate community remained, even after independence, a closed circle. The European club, with its facilities for tennis and other games, is seldom joined by Nigerians. The temptation to spend time at the club almost exclusively in the company of expatriates was always before the Volunteers. Some resisted the blandishments of European facilities and comforts and made an effort to spend as much of their free time as possible with Nigerians. Others succumbed entirely to the life of the expatriate, having in some cases neither the desire to associate with Nigerians nor the strength of character necessary to withstand the often outspoken disapproval of Africans by the expatriate community—who regarded any foreigner who sought out the company of Africans as being imbued with excessive idealism.

It should be added that not infrequently the problems of the Volunteers outside their specific job situation stemmed more from members of the expatriate community than from Nigerians. Both in ex-British and ex-French countries of West Africa, expatriates have frequently regarded the members of Peace Corps as the vanguard of American influence seeking to take over where the influence of former colonial power has begun to wane after independence. Perceiving a threat to their prestige and positions, these expatriates frequently voice criticism of the PCVs. This criticism, of course, must be expressed in terms that do not seem too transparently self-seeking. At its most convincing, it takes the form of pointing out how ill-prepared some of the PCVs are in a professional sense. Other criticism points to the Volunteers' youth and to their desire to help the African community apart from the purely formal instruction given in the classroom. The Volunteer, faced with this continuous criticism in the close contact of the day-to-day school situation and confronting resistance on the part of the African community toward his efforts at closer contact, found himself almost unconsciously absorbing the viewpoint of the colonial civil servant. By far the bulk of the Volunteers in Nigeria, however, were aware of this dilemma and made successful efforts to escape from it—sometimes at the cost of difficult personal relations with their European colleagues.

Bridging the Distance

Reflecting upon these factors of physical, social, and cultural distance, it is now perhaps easier to see why professional effectiveness on the job has become such a central concern in evaluating a PCV's over-all performance. In a very real sense for some PCVs, there just was not a great deal more to their total role in Nigeria than their teacher job role. And many local people seemed to want it that way: a teacher teaches; he doesn't penetrate further into the community.

When I visited the PCVs in the field, many of them expressed complaints that sharply pointed up their difficulties. While they were grateful to their Nigerian principals and teacher colleagues for cordial and proper professional relationships, they complained that

that was usually about as far as the relationship went. Especially in the Northern Region, many complained that even at the end of two years they had not been invited to the homes of their Nigerian colleagues, nor had they had the opportunity to meet their colleagues' families. Such complaints illustrate the wide divergence between Euroamerican customs for entertaining guests and those found in various parts of Nigeria. Unacculturated Nigerians generally are reluctant to entertain Western guests because of uncertainty as to what kind of hospitality would be acceptable—beyond eggs and oranges, which often appear to be the only African foods that white men accept and eat. In Nigeria, friends are not invited; they just come, usually in the cool of the evening. They drop in without invitation, share in their host's meals, contribute in cash or in kind when there are funerals or naming ceremonies to be celebrated, join in buying dresses for special occasions, and feast together frequently. Such are the accepted modes of showing friendship, and it normally takes a long while for a Westerner to adjust to them, if he ever does.

But fortunately the story does not end here. For despite all three types of distance separating Volunteer from community and despite the exacerbating influence of the expatriates, some few Volunteers had the initiative and good fortune to be able to play an active part in community development while at the same time carrying their full teaching load. One, for example, in the Mid-West Region, was able to enter so fully into the life of the community that he was made an honorary member of one of the traditional societies and his advice was sought by the community leaders on a number of local problems.

For the bulk of the Volunteer teachers, however, meaningful contact with Nigerian communities was possible only during vacation time. Some of the PCVs made trips to their students' home villages and visited the students and their families in their own homes. Such visits not only enhanced the PCVs' knowledge of the students' backgrounds but also created an enormous fund of goodwill—since no teacher had ever before been known to express a sincere interest in the students' own culture.

Vacation time was also "project" time. Each PCV was expected to develop a project that would be of use to Nigeria and would extend his knowledge of the local people and their culture. Much ingenuity was displayed in searching out projects that would be both useful and interesting. In northern Nigeria the services of some PCVs were utilized to assist in gathering census data. In so doing, the Volunteers not only provided valuable help to the hard-pressed local census officer but were able to see remote villages (usually on horseback) which they doubtless would not otherwise have seen. Other Volunteers carried out projects in hospitals or rural dispensaries. Still others worked on land resettlement projects. By such resourceful means, the PCVs reached out for community involvement. Given the circumstances, they did well. But clearly their community participation could not hope to equal the close and continuous community contacts of the community developer in Latin America or the elementary teacher in the Philippines.

A REORIENTATION OF ATTITUDES

The Nigerian experience produced personal growth in a number of directions. For many Volunteers, it made clear for the first time the value of the formal education they had received at the university level. Much of what had seemed useless except for satisfying formal requirements, was now vital and important in the teaching situation.

Those Volunteers for whom the experience was most meaningful were those who acquired clear insights into the problems confronting a developing society. Their concrete experiences gave them what training in the States could not: a direct, acute, visceral awareness of just how slowly culture change usually proceeds. While it is common nowadays in textbooks and training programs to discuss the rapidity of social change in Africa, the Volunteers were now keenly aware that the term "rapidity" is a purely relative one. While there is no doubt that the rate of sociocultural change in Africa has been vastly accelerated by the passing of colonialism, this rate is still considerably slower than many of the Volunteers had originally imagined—especially in the rural areas, where most Africans live.

Volunteers have also learned how to accept African viewpoints and values, in the sense that Szanton has used the term "accept" (page 54). With this acceptance has come an understanding of the forces underlying resistance to change. The more successful among the PCVs have also become quite adept at transcultural communication: they have been able to illustrate, by means of small projects of technical assistance, the value of certain modern techniques. For example, one Volunteer was able to do for a few individuals what many large-scale aid projects have been unable to accomplish. Aware of the problem of the "school-leavers" in his community— that is, of the inability of primary school graduates to secure suitable jobs—he responded to the request of a group of boys to teach them something by which they might earn a living. He set up, at his own expense, a small egg-production scheme. Using simple techniques and low-cost equipment, he was able to provide the group with the knowledge necessary to produce better-quality eggs, for which there was a ready local market. Through his efforts he was able to persuade the boys to stay in a rural area instead of joining the massive march to the urban centers where the prospect of jobs is constantly shrinking. Had it not been for his continued presence in the community over a period of more than a year, his rapport with the local people, and his understanding of their problems, the boys would not, of course, have had the confidence in him to accept his suggestions in the first place.

A REORIENTATION OF CAREERS

In spite of the relatively limited community involvement of the average Nigeria Volunteer, it is striking to observe the genuine reorientation of career goals that occurred in many instances. I have observed this reorientation in various visits to Nigeria, and especially during a trip in which I served as field interviewer for Study Fellowships in International Development. My task was to interview Peace Corps and other similar volunteer-type workers in their actual work setting, as candidates for graduate fellowships that would enable them to prepare themselves for careers in international development. As a field interviewer, I had my hands full, for a very large proportion—something like half—of the PCVs wanted to return to the universities for additional study. Relatively few of them were to remain on long in Nigeria once their Peace Corps service had ended. (One exception was a Volunteer forester whose services were in such immediate demand that at the end of his Peace Corps Service, he returned immediately to his post as a contract employee, taking with him a wife whom he had met while she was a Volunteer teacher in Nigeria.)

The Discovery of Teaching

Most of the Volunteer teachers had not taught before, nor had they regarded teaching as even a remote possibility for them within the American educational system. The low income and low prestige usually attached to secondary teaching in the United States had discouraged any interest they might have had.

Then came the Nigerian experience. Many PCVs discovered that they enjoyed teaching, that a teaching career could be personally rewarding. Not only did they enjoy helping to shape young minds, but in truth most of them probably also enjoyed the relatively high social position of the secondary teacher in Nigeria—especially the white secondary teacher. Their position had been higher by far than that of secondary teachers in the United States, and higher than most of them could have attained back home, at their young age, in any occupation. For many, it was the first truly adult role they had ever played, and to play it at such a high prestige level was a heady experience.

And so, many of the PCVs decided to shift to teaching as a career. Of these, however, a substantial number looked for their future satisfaction only to teaching overseas in the developing areas—where results would be more visible, and where they themselves would be more visible (and prestigious). These Volunteers were aware, too, that their decision involved certain pitfalls. For example, future years will inevitably see the progressive Africanization of positions in teaching and educational administration in countries like Nigeria. Nevertheless, many of the Volunteers felt that the challenges involved in the development of new educational systems in Africa were so great as to outweigh the risks of a possible foreshortening of their long-range career plans.

Akin to those Volunteers contemplating teaching careers are those who have returned to do graduate work in education, educational planning, and educational administration. These returnees were impressed by the need to adapt the educational system established by the colonial power to the needs and demands of a rapidly modernizing Nigerian society. Some, for example, have entered graduate study in the field of the Teaching of English as a Foreign Language. Their future careers might involve serving as curriculum advisors in Nigeria or in other new nations where English is the lingua franca and language of administration, science, and technology.

It should also be noted in passing that many PCVs with a continuing interest in Africa hoped to secure positions in fields other than education. Notable among these are Volunteers contemplating careers in the field of economic development, after first pursuing graduate study in economics.

A Shift to the Social Sciences

Regardless of whether they intended to become teachers, there was a marked shift during the Peace Corps experience toward an active interest in the social sciences. This was particularly noticeable among those who had gone to Nigeria to teach in some aspect of the natural sciences, having specialized in a natural science during their undergraduate days. Over 50 per cent of people in this category whom I interviewed indicated that their attention in graduate school would now turn toward the social sciences.

The reasons for this radical change in outlook were frequently not clear to the individuals themselves, and certainly were difficult to articulate. The interviews suggest that for many people in this category, the requirements of an undergraduate natural science specialization allowed little contact, even in a liberal arts curriculum, with various aspects of the social sciences. Thus the Peace Corps training brought with it the new, and interesting, experience of exposure to a variety of social sciences and social scientists.

Then came the two years in Nigeria, and with it the opportunity to witness for the first time the concrete problems faced by a developing society. Out of this experience arose an intensified social consciousness and a desire to explore these new fields of interest in an organized fashion at the graduate level. While these former natural science majors were not prepared to deny the important role that pure science could play in the development of Nigeria over the coming years, they nevertheless felt that pure science—as opposed to its practical application in the process of social change—was now of less interest to them *personally* than it had previously been.

My interviews tempt me to a very tentative hypothesis. I suspect that many of those who switched from natural to social science had in fact not been particularly fond of natural science in the first place. The Peace Corps provided an opportunity for an escape, a chance for further exploration, a moratorium before final commitment. In any case, social science will be the richer for their apostasy, for they will bring with them a training and discipline in quantification and in scientific rigor.

CONCLUSIONS

The experience of the Volunteers in Nigeria has beyond doubt been of immediate and substantial help to that country in the educational crisis which it faced at independence. But the long-range value of the Volunteers' Peace Corps experience is perhaps more important than its short-range accomplishments—from the viewpoint both of the execution of American foreign-aid policy and of understanding by Americans of the purpose of foreign aid. Among the returned Volunteers are some who have learned more about certain aspects of Nigerian life than any American previously knew. Those returnees who, usually after further graduate training, join government or other agencies concerned with the administration of foreign aid will bring to their tasks a background of experience, empathy, and understanding that has hitherto too often been sadly lacking. And the number of returnees with such career intentions is encouragingly large. The thousands of ex-Volunteers who return to their home communities will constitute a nucleus of informed citizens, to whom the problems of the developing areas will be immediate, vivid, and concrete, and who can pass on their knowledge to others in meaningful, convincing terms. The experience of Peace Corps service cannot be forgotten. Indeed, it may well be that through the Volunteers the United States has gained far more than it has given—in terms of a new understanding of the problems of peoples emerging into the modern world.

BIBLIOGRAPHY

COLEMAN, JAMES S.
   1958   *Nigeria: Background to Nationalism.* Berkeley: University of California Press.
COWAN, L. GRAY
   1964   "British and French Education in Africa: A Critical Appraisal," in Don C. Piper and Taylor Cole, eds., *Post-Primary Education and Political and Economic Development,* pp. 178-199. Durham, N.C.: Duke University Press, for Duke University Commonwealth-Studies Center.
COWAN, L. GRAY, JAMES O'CONNELL, and DAVID G. SCANLON, Editors
   1965   *Education and Nation Building in Africa.* New York: Praeger.
OTONTI, NDUKA
   1964   *Western Education and the Nigerian Cultural Background.* Ibadan, Nigeria: Oxford University Press.
POST, KENNETH W. J.
   1963   *The Nigerian Federal Election of 1959: Politics and Administration in a Developing Political System.* London: Oxford University Press, for the Nigerian Institute of Social and Economic Research.
SKLAR, RICHARD L.
   1963   *Nigerian Political Parties: Power in an Emergent African Nation.* Princeton, N.J.: Princeton University Press.
WEILER, HANS N., Editor
   1964   *Education and Politics in Nigeria.* Freiburg, Germany: Verlag Rombach.

10

Transcultural Perceptions and
Misperceptions in Sierra Leone

VERNON R. DORJAHN[1] *is Associate Professor of Anthropology and Chairman of the African Studies Committee at the University of Oregon. He has been a specialist on Africa since his undergraduate days, and wrote his Northwestern University doctoral dissertation on the demographic aspects of African polygyny. Professor Dorjahn has made two year-long field research trips to Sierra Leone under National Science Foundation sponsorship, the first dealing primarily with traditional cultures and societies in that country, and the second concentrating on the phenomena of urbanism and modernization. The materials for this chapter were gathered during his second field trip, in 1962–1963, when Dr. Dorjahn had extensive opportunities to observe the Volunteers in action. Except when he was away in Sierra Leone, he has lectured to every Peace Corps training program for that country. Professor Dorjahn's publications, besides those listed in the bibliography to this chapter, include numerous articles on Sierra Leonean societies and cultures.*

WITH the arrival of the initial group of Peace Corps Volunteers in Sierra Leone during the first week of January 1962, a new dimension was added to American assistance and the "American image" in that small West African country. Previous American aid to Sierra Leone had been minimal, totaling only about one million dollars between 1953 and 1961. In the eyes of most Sierra Leoneans, the Peace Corps Volunteer was the first visible sign of United States government interest in and assistance to their country. By late 1963 there were over two hundred Volunteers in Sierra Leone; on a per capita basis this meant that there were more Corpsmen there than in any other country in Africa. The great majority of these Volunteers were secondary school teachers. The rest were either medical personnel or rural community development workers. Most were thus to be found in the urban areas, although in one capacity or another PCVs have reached most of the readily accessible portions of the country.

Since the Volunteer teachers were in such a heavy majority, this chapter will deal primarily with them.[2] My acquaintance with the PCVs stems from having been a training lecturer to Sierra Leone One and Two, and from having observed members of both groups in action during 1962–1963. My generalizations apply primarily to teachers in the Northern Province, secondarily to teachers elsewhere in the country, and only slightly to the other Volunteers.

CULTURAL DIVERSITY AND PROBLEMS OF NATION BUILDING

Since gaining independence from Britain in 1961, the British-trained leaders of Sierra Leone have been hard at work attempting to unify and modernize the country. The fact that it is a small country—just over two million people living on roughly 28,000 square miles of land—would seem to augur well for these nation-building efforts. There are, however, many cultural barriers to be surmounted on the path toward a unified and modernized Sierra Leone. There are also certain underlying elements of cultural unity. On the basis of such unity—and with help from such organizations as the Peace Corps—Sierra Leone's leaders are struggling to find the formula for modernization.

The majority of Sierra Leoneans are African tribesmen of varying degrees of acculturation to the British model in such matters as language, law, social organization, and political practice. The minority are much more Anglicized Creoles centered in and around the capital city of Freetown. I will discuss the majority first.

The Tribal Sector

The tribal sector of Sierra Leone is, unfortunately from the standpoint of nation building, characterized by considerable cultural heterogeneity. There are twelve tribes that can be regarded as indigenous in the sense that each has at least one chiefdom where a ruler of that tribe is paramount. The languages of these twelve tribes are mutually unintelligible. Members of each tribe have strong ingroup feelings, and hold to certain cultural beliefs and practices that they regard as unique, as setting their tribe off from all the others. Intertribal suspicions and cleavages are rife—if often latent. A Temne is likely to suspect the motives of a Mende politician. A Limba teacher is too often believed incompetent by his Susu or Koranko students until he proves otherwise.

Despite the subjective differences, however, there are certain objective cultural similarities among the various tribes that augur well for modern Sierra Leone's leaders as they pursue their efforts to unify and modernize the country. All of the tribes, for example, have the same subsistence base: rice farming. All have similarities in settlement pattern and in social organization, with unilineal descent systems and chiefdom organization. The *Poro* society for men is found throughout much of the country, while the *Sande (Bundu)* society for women is nearly universal. The smaller tribes have long been influenced through political and cultural domination by the stronger Mende and Temne tribes. Most of the cultures of Sierra Leone have been shaped to some extent through long contact with immigrant Muslim Fula and Mandingo.

The Creole Sector

From 1462 when the Portuguese first sighted the "Lion Mountains" behind what is now the city of Freetown, Europeans of various nationalities have stopped, settled, lived, and died along the Sierra Leone coast.[3] In 1787 the first colonizing expedition, composed of freed Negro slaves and Europeans, landed at Kru Bay and established the first settlement. During subsequent years several major increments were added, particularly the "Nova Scotians" and the "Maroons."

In 1808 the Freetown settlement became a British crown colony. During the first half of the nineteenth century Britain made the slave trade illegal. As the colony became better established and the slave trade was outlawed by more and more nations, Freetown became the site for various courts where offenders apprehended on the high seas were tried. The slave cargoes were freed and a significant proportion of these "Liberated Africans" settled in and about the city. Before long they came to outnumber the indigenous tribal Africans in the immediate area of Freetown. Biological and cultural crossbreeding then proceeded apace—both between Africans and Europeans and among Africans from various parts of the continent. The result was the Creole population and culture. The Creoles soon became a vital force in the development of Sierra Leone and, indeed, of the whole of British West Africa and even beyond.

From time to time the boundaries of the colony area were expanded, and in 1896 a British protectorate was established over a large part of the tribal hinterland. The colony plus the protectorate thus came to constitute what is now Sierra Leone.

The "Colony-Protectorate Gap"

The Creole population has preferred to remain in the colony, rather than mixing with the tribal populations of the hinterland.

In the colony, their own Creole values have held sway, while in the protectorate life has remained tribe- and tradition-oriented. While some Creole merchants did venture into the hinterland during the nineteenth century, they limited their contacts largely to commerce and did not mix much with the local tribal population. While some tribal people moved into Freetown, they, too, had limited social contact with the Creoles. Relations among members of the two groups have not always been cordial. The Creole has typically been perceived by the upcountry tribesmen as the "son of a slave," an inferior imitation of a European, or a "black whiteman." On the other hand, the Creole has perceived the tribesman as an illiterate, uncouth barbarian worthy of exploitation but not respect. This antipathy between Creoles (including upcountry people "passing" as Creoles) and upcountry tribesmen is reflected in the still commonly heard phrase, "the colony-protectorate gap"; the phraseology is retained despite the fact that, strictly speaking, the words "colony" and "protectorate" are now obsolete.

With the advent of independence in 1961, the cultural gap between colony and protectorate suddenly assumed new and larger political significance. The constitution of independent Sierra Leone provided a broad electoral franchise, which now made it possible for the largely illiterate, tribally oriented majority to outvote the better educated, more Westernized Creole minority. Independent Sierra Leone's first prime minister, the late Sir Milton Margai, made no secret of his belief that his nation's most pressing problem in human relations was to find a way to bridge the colony-protectorate gap.

THE ROLE OF EDUCATION IN NATION BUILDING

In bridging the gap that separates tribe from tribe, and colony from protectorate, the role of education is obviously paramount. The basic framework of education in Sierra Leone is, of course, British. English is the official language of the country, and the medium of instruction in all forty of its secondary schools. Even today, a majority of the principals of Sierra Leone's secondary schools are expatriates, primarily from Britain or other English-speaking countries. It should also be noted in passing that a majority of the country's secondary schools are run by missionaries, who come primarily from English-speaking countries.

The secondary schools are crucial in promoting cultural change and national unity for the added reason that they are located in or near the growing upcountry cities and towns. Attendance at a secondary school thus entails an experience in urban living—new for many students. In Sierra Leone, as elsewhere generally, it is the urban areas that are the focal points for cultural change, for it is here that the educated, modern-thinking populace is concentrated. Most towns are ethnically diverse. They are composed of smaller households. They have a greater division of labor and a higher proportion of specialists and persons who work for cash income. In the towns a greater proportion of the training of a greater proportion of children is carried on outside the household, principally in the schools. Therefore the PCVs as teachers, and as teachers of potential teachers, become more important as models, as pacesetters, and as vectors of new ideas, values, and ways of doing things.

At first glance, the process of modernization would call for assignment of substantial numbers of Creole teachers and principals to upcountry schools in tribal areas, there to impart modern ideas and knowledge. Unfortunately, however, the Creole or significantly Creolized teacher or principal does not often wish to live and work upcountry. Some Creoles have even suggested that they ought to receive a "hardship bonus" when posted upcountry, where, as one Freetown man put it, "there are no chances to further my education, no books, no friends, and no social life." I was told of one case where a Creole principal of a Freetown secondary school threatened to resign rather than be transferred to the provinces—and his threat was so convincing that he was left where he was. Those Creoles who are posted upcountry keep largely to themselves and have few if any contacts with the local population that they can avoid. Most of them know little about local affairs, learn little while there, and care to learn even less.[4] Among the upcountry people, few would want it any other way, for the Creole is perceived as a stranger, and local affairs are none of his business.

Such was the situation in which the Peace Corps teachers found themselves. Technically, they were simply secondary school teachers. In effect, however, they were also to serve as catalysts in a process of national unification and continuing modernization for an independent Sierra Leone—along lines already more or less clearly laid down by the British. Both the cultural and the political situations were sufficiently complex so that misunderstandings could well have been expected on both sides, and some misunderstandings did develop.

SIERRA LEONEAN PERCEPTIONS OF THE VOLUNTEERS

The very presence of the Peace Corps indicates a kind of approval by the host government. The repeated requests for additional Volunteers that have come from Freetown suggest that the Sierra Leone government is, at least in a general way, satisfied with the Corps' performance. On the other hand, acceptance or even enthusiasm on the ministerial level does not necessarily indicate that Africans on the local level are always happy and satisfied. Although there have been no incidents in Sierra Leone comparable to the unfortunate "postcard" episode at Ibadan in Nigeria, criticisms of particular Americans and of the Corps in general do occur. Although these criticisms are sometimes unfair and often inaccurate, they are symptomatic of friction, resentment, and a lack of knowledge on both sides.

It should be emphasized that to some educated or marginally literate Sierra Leoneans the very presence of the Peace Corps is an affront. It is a painful contradiction to them that while Sierra Leone is now an independent nation, she is still dependent on other nations for technicians of many kinds. Such people are ready to give vent to their resentment whenever a Volunteer commits even a minor transgression. In their assessment of individual Volunteers, such people are seldom willing to extend the benefit of the doubt.

General Perceptions

In the course of research in the Northern Province of Sierra Leone, I repeatedly encountered the belief, most often among literate Africans who had little or no direct contact with the Peace Corps, that the Volunteers were actually spies from the neocolonialist United States, which coveted the wealth of Sierra Leone.[5] Some Africans thought it outrageous that their government was paying living allowances to American spies who taught school and worked in other government departments as a cover-up for their sinister activities. Sierra Leone, of course, does *not* pay the living allowances of the Corpsmen, but it is hard to convince some Sierra Leoneans of this.

The suspicions of some are also aroused by weekend get-togethers of Volunteers working in widely dispersed communities. One distrustful African observed, "I can only guess at what they are talking about, but I don't trust them." It is tempting to interpret this clubbing together of Volunteers as an indication of their failure to adjust and participate fully in local life; in some individual cases this interpretation is correct, but in most it is erroneous. The Volunteers are "strangers" and in the tribesman's own experience, one stranger always seeks out others of his kind; this is considered perfectly natural and acceptable. The stranger is always suspect; he would perhaps be even more suspect if he did *not* fulfill the role of stranger by seeking out his own, but rather meddled in the affairs of his hosts—at least initially. In Sierra Leone, cultural participation in a meaningful sense often comes slowly and always by invitation.

Most Sierra Leoneans must form their opinions of the Volunteers primarily by observing their nonprofessional leisure-time behavior and by listening to what others, particularly servants and co-workers, say about them. The Americans are often judged on the basis of whether or not they drink or "chase women," whether or not they like Africans and are generous.

The relative paucity of material goods owned by Corpsmen is, in terms of transcultural perception, a complicating factor. Thus, one unskilled laborer, watching a PCV walk down the road carrying his groceries, patted the bell on his old Raleigh bicycle and remarked in pidgin: "I be big man past him. He no get bicycle." The Corps apparently has the intention of projecting the image of the young, enthusiastic, hardworking, and generous American youth, an ideal highly valued in the United States. It is less highly valued in traditional Sierra Leone societies. Euro-American children learn that the tortoise bested the hare through diligent hard work and a never-say-die attitude, but in West Africa the tortoise prevails not through perseverance but through trickery. What, after all, is the purpose of hard work and perseverance if it does not yield even an old Raleigh bicycle or some comparable badge of higher status?

Perceptions of the Volunteers as Teachers

Fellow teachers are always in competition with one another, in some sense of the word. Where they differ markedly in cultural background, professional training, and experience, as in the present case, it is not surprising that difficulties have arisen. Interviews with African teachers in various schools yielded two basic criticisms of the Americans: (1) they are incompetent, and (2) they are over-industrious. Too many times, the Africans allege, the PCV mispronounces the names of African people and places, and in so doing, offends. Some Volunteers are characterized as "poor teachers," as having had no teaching experience and as having come to Sierra Leone to teach because they are not qualified to teach in the United States. The same individuals, however, are often criticized for working too hard and too well at their jobs: this girl tutors her students in English after hours, that man reorganized the track and field team and takes them to other schools on weekends to compete, while another one takes students out to trap insects and snakes to dissect in his biology class. The motivation underlying this criticism was perhaps best revealed by an African teacher who complained: "He [the Peace Corpsman] started this athletic [track and field] team, but when he leaves, the students and the principal will expect me to keep it up and I will not. He made my job harder, and I must work here the rest of my life."

Disagreements between teachers and school administrators are common in all cultures, since neither apparently ever fully appreciates the efforts made and difficulties faced by the other. In this instance there are very real differences in patterns of showing respect, in teaching methods, and in conceptions of classroom discipline. The well-intentioned Volunteer who seeks only the easy familiarity with superiors that is commonplace at home offends the African principal who assesses respect in terms of social distance and verbal deference. African school principals are usually too circumspect to criticize Volunteers directly, but fragmentary evidence indicates they feel that the Volunteers fail to give them due respect, laugh at them behind their backs, and, with specific exceptions, are poor teachers and poor disciplinarians.

It is evident that many Volunteers enjoy close friendships with some of their students in and outside the classroom. Often friendships originate on the athletic field, from the loan of books and newspapers, and from discussions of class materials after hours. Many of the American Corpsmen have protégés whom they help financially and whom they wish to aid in coming to the United States for higher education. In the long run, these friendships between Corpsmen and students will probably be more important than the sometimes less congenial relations with African teachers and principals.

VOLUNTEERS' FRUSTRATIONS

Most Peace Corps teachers were willing to discuss their professional problems, successes, and failures openly and candidly. Generally there is no real problem in motivating a student to study, since a secondary school education is highly prized in Sierra Leone, where it is regarded as the key that will secure wealth, respect, prestige, a wife, and a physically easy job. The problem, however, is to get the students to study *efficiently*, to generalize from a series of specific cases, and to draw inferences—rather than simply to memorize and take one text or source as the whole truth. Discipline also is a problem for some Corpsmen, probably because they are less formal and less authoritarian in the classroom than their African colleagues.

Some African teachers refuse to let students ask questions, whereas the Americans encourage discussion.[6] Discussion has on occasion led to quarrels and such displays as one student challenging another, and even challenging the teacher's knowledge. One Volunteer teacher answered a question by citing multiple effects of a particular historic event and was criticized by a student for not giving the answer, verbatim, from the text.

African teachers are criticized by Corpsmen as being (1) incompetent, (2) unfamiliar with modern teaching methods, and (3) ego-involved and hypersensitive. Thus one African teacher in a Freetown school allegedly "can't spell," and all that another "knows about history is what's in his textbook; he's never read anything else." One American teaching a second-year language class charges that in the previous year his African counterpart had covered only slightly more than half the lessons in the first-year syllabus, forcing the PCV to cover the balance—and that if his students did poorly on their examinations, the principal would blame him and the Peace Corps for being incompetent.

One Volunteer teaching in a secondary school told of an African teacher who copied a paragraph out of the text verbatim on the blackboard, had three students read it aloud in turn, and then had the class copy it in their notebooks—even though each student had his own copy of the text. Such practices, all too common in the primary schools, are rarer on the secondary level.

In discussing the presumed hypersensitivity of his African colleagues, one Corpsman stated

> When I ask so-and-so about how he teaches geometry, he gets real agitated. He thinks I'm spying on him, that I want to show him up. In fact, whenever I mention anything about lessons or students, he gets defensive and thinks I'm criticizing him. You can't get through to a guy like that.

The African teacher is as good or as bad as his training was, and the range of variation is considerable. Many recognize their deficiencies, pointing out the very limited opportunities for in-service training, and even for buying books, outside of Freetown. Few, however, would admit these deficiencies to their competitors, especially strangers who are beneath them in seniority. Indeed, there is an unfortunate attitude among some educated Sierra Leoneans that because they have a teaching certificate or other credentials they have reached the zenith, that nothing more can be required of them and that if they do something it has to be right because they are who they are. Accustomed to the accolades and abject respect of less well educated Africans, rarely questioned as to why they act or decide as they do, such people do not readily accept questions or criticism from strangers. In the long run, however, such questioning of the educational establishment, while it makes few friends at the time, may have a salutary effect in improving the educational system by prompting self-analysis.

Corpsmen also criticized the school principals and the "school administration" in general. Some complained that they were assigned heavier over-all teaching loads than their African colleagues—although I personally have direct knowledge of only one such case. Others complained that they were given introductory rather than advanced courses to teach, while their qualifications, they felt, entitled them to the latter. In evaluating such complaints, however, it must be kept in mind that a teacher's previous experience in preparing students for the British-style West African Certificate Examinations* is also an important consideration in making assignments, and that it would be an imprudent principal who counted any more heavily than he had to on an inexperienced, expatriate teacher—especially a non-Briton. A principal's success and advancement depend in part upon the ratio of students in his school who are successful in these examinations, and self-interest dictates the best use of teachers available to him.

Daily and weekly schedules are made up for both students and staff, but one PCV charged that he was the only staff member who observed his program: "If I deviate from it, I'm called on the carpet, but if an African leaves two hours early, nothing is said."

Uneven disciplining of students on the part of the principal was frequently mentioned; the same punishment was given for great or small violations, while on another occasion, two students guilty of the same offense were penalized very differently because, it was charged, one student was related to politicians and administrators and the principal feared pressure from above.

The charge of incompetence or poor administration was often made: "Our textbooks didn't arrive until the third month of school." Or, "He [the principal] gave me last year's history syllabus and I didn't learn until the fifth month that it was obsolete and had been superseded. When I asked him for the new one, he assured me the one I had was correct. We both knew he was wrong, but he would not admit it."

* See footnote, page 159.—Ed.

It should be stressed that the principals are sometimes blamed for inadequacies that are not their fault. Their clerks are slow and can do little beyond the simplest routine work without direct supervision; thus the principal has much paper work to do himself. Requests and orders for supplies take time, and to blame the principal is not always just. On the other hand, there are principals, disgruntled at being posted to the Provinces or complacent in their positions, who are less than zealous in carrying out their duties.

OPPOSITION FROM THE EXPATRIATES*

While space does not permit going into detail, it should also be mentioned in passing that the PCVs met with considerable opposition, both overt and covert, from expatriate principals and teachers. In the public secondary schools, these expatriates were mostly British. In the private schools, they were mostly American missionaries. In either instance, the PCVs were an upsetting influence. Although assigned as teachers, only a minority of them had been professionally trained as teachers. Even those who were professionally trained were not familiar with the intricacies of the British educational system. PCVs who drank alcoholic beverages were decidedly not welcome in schools run by some missions. On the other hand, to the extent that the PCV teacher *was* effective on his job, he was even more of a threat. He was a threat to the very job of his expatriate opposite number. Many of the expatriates—especially the British teachers and principals in the public system—were in the unenviable position of having "nowhere else to go." Many had transferred to Sierra Leone from some other British colony or ex-colony and were perhaps not highly qualified in a professional sense, yet were already beyond the age where further university training was feasible. They were, in short, "hanging on for dear life" to their present posts and hardly likely to welcome competition from any quarter.

The expatriates' reactions were therefore often defensive in motivation and negative in result. PCV teachers would be "boxed off" by being assigned to special and trivial duties. Rumors would be circulated as to how "professionally unqualified" the Volunteer teachers were. Such rumors made little sense, of course, when considered alongside the fact that all the PCVs had bachelor's degrees,

* Dr. Dorjahn wishes to make it clear that material in this section was provided to the editor by a returned Volunteer teacher from Sierra Leone One. Dr. Dorjahn's own data on this subject are quite limited, but do generally confirm the returnee's views.—Ed.

while the typical African secondary teacher in Sierra Leone has only a secondary education and often not even that.

PROBLEMS OF ADJUSTMENT

How well have the Volunteers adjusted to their jobs and lives in Sierra Leone? Relatively few have quit and gone home. A few have stuck it out when it might have been better for all concerned if they had resigned. A few other individuals have been transferred repeatedly, suggesting marginal adjustment or minimal performance.

The PCV's first impressions of Sierra Leone are normally highly positive. The initial "red carpet" period of adjustment in Freetown is usually a captivating one. The people and the city are new and fascinating. The PCVs are welcomed and briefed at University College in Freetown by capable, urbane, cosmopolitan Sierra Leonean officials. Few Volunteers fail to be charmed.

After they have arrived at their posts, however, disappointment and frustration sometimes set in. Initially there are formal teas, receptions, and cocktail parties, but suddenly the job begins and things seem very different: "I had all my African colleagues in for dinner as soon after my arrival as I could, but in the eight months I've been here, only one of fifteen even invited me to visit him, let alone for a meal," says one Corpsman.

Canons of hospitality differ, however, and this failure to reciprocate on a dinner invitation reflected not unfriendliness but insecurity—a feeling that to invite the American and not do things in a way that would seem proper in his eyes would put the host in a worse light than not to invite the PCV in the first place. Western food preferences also differ strikingly, and to invite a Westerner to dinner means securing expensive tinned foods, preparing and serving them in unaccustomed ways, and so on. There is always the chance that the guest will find the food too highly seasoned, the water "unsafe," or the African's table manners embarrassing. The possibilities for embarrassment are limitless. Finally, it should be borne in mind that an explicit invitation to visit and chat is not so necessary in upcountry Sierra Leone, for traditionally a "big man's" house is always open to visitors, and to visit a man at his house is to show respect for him.

On the professional level, the insecurity and tension that any new teacher faces in his first year are compounded for the Corpsman working with students who do not share his cultural background, within the framework of a British educational system and philosophy that differ significantly from his own.

Faced with professional and personal frustration, a few Volunteers reacted by withdrawal. They would band together, going impressive distances to meet with their own kind on weekends. Here they would swap experiences and reactions and withdraw from the African reality to the remembrance of a near-Utopian America. One perceptive Volunteer spoke of a trio of his fellows in this way:

> Outside of their regular teaching duties, they have almost no contact with Sierra Leoneans. They associate only with each other or else hole up in their rooms with records, the *New Yorker*, or *Esquire*, counting the days until their annual leave. They are defeating the purpose of the Peace Corps and they are unhappy.

It should immediately be emphasized, however, that many PCVs achieve a better adjustment. They establish transcultural friendships and come not only to accept but to enjoy their experiences. It is significant that the situation referred to arose in Freetown; I know of no comparable instance from the provinces, where nearly all students are boarders and where more out-of-class contact is unavoidable. In Sierra Leone, as elsewhere, it seems to be true that PCVs assigned to less acculturated localities generally seem happier.

INTERCULTURAL OBSTACLES TO ADJUSTMENT

What makes successful adjustment so difficult? In the first place, the Volunteers fail to conform to the expectations of most Sierra Leoneans, and hence the African is uncertain how to act toward them. The image of the Euro-American was formed chiefly on the basis of limited face-to-face contacts or hearsay accounts of other people's contacts with British colonial officials and missionaries of various denominations and nationalities. The colonial stereotype of the "superior Euro-American"—aloof, wealthy, better educated, and possessed of a near monopoly on technical knowledge and power—still exists in the minds of many Sierra Leoneans, and the Peace Corpsman does not fit it.

For the most part the Volunteer is aggressively friendly and does not, at least initially, maintain the degree of social distance expected. Americans generally—and the Corpsmen are not exceptions—are prone to evangelize their egalitarian values. But Sierra Leonean society is not egalitarian. Ascribed differences are regarded as natural, proper, and just. All men are *not* created equal; all men

are not treated the same way, either in terms of etiquette or litiga-
tion. The British official who accepted his superior status, even if
only as a defense mechanism, was *easier* for the African to deal
with. The PCV has few of the material goods locally accepted as
status symbols: few of them have the use of a car, or own a bicycle,
or employ many servants. Clearly, they do not hold positions of
power or authority. There is doubt in the minds of some Africans
as to whether such young people, lacking the obvious indicators of
wealth and influence, ought to be treated and respected as the
colonial official or missionary was, even if these newcomers seem to
be so sure that they know better than their predecessors.

On the other side of the coin, most Sierra Leoneans do not live
up to the preconceptions of the average Peace Corps Volunteer, an
image formed from limited contacts with African students back in
the United States and from reading books on West Africa. Sierra
Leone is not peopled solely with self-sacrificing idealists dedicated
to improving their country and requiring only the enthusiasm,
example, and "know-how" of the American Volunteers in order
to make quick dramatic progress. When a more realistic appraisal
of the situation is made and the magnitude of the task appreciated,
the mood swing of the American can be extreme. As one PCV put it:
"It's hopeless; I'm the only one here really interested in helping
Sierra Leone. The Sierra Leonean only wants to help himself."

Whether such a remark represents transitory frustration or deep
disillusionment is not always easy to tell. Nonetheless, two general
observations might be entered. First, the Sierra Leonean student
and even teacher is sometimes undernourished or in ill health, and
hence physically incapable of the degree of mental and physical
exertion sometimes expected by the PCVs. And second, it is well
to remember that there is little altruism in African cultures (and
probably less in our own than we care to recognize). In a country
like Sierra Leone, the horizons and spheres of interest of people are
relatively more restricted to family, lineage, village, and tribe.
Stated another way, one of Sierra Leone's problems is to transfer
more of the individual's loyalty from the small local groups to the
nation.[7]

A second difficulty is a lack of local understanding, and hence
often a misunderstanding, of the purpose of the Peace Corps and
why the Volunteers are in Sierra Leone. Increased and improved
communication plus the passage of time and more frequent face-to-
face contacts should greatly improve understanding. The local press

and the Government Information Service have not given much publicity, good or bad, to the Peace Corps.

A final difficulty is that many of the Americans seem to know little of Sierra Leone. The Peace Corps goes to considerable expense to provide training programs involving the best qualified lecturers available. The trainees work hard, but they must start from scratch. The root of the difficulty lies in our own educational system, where little is taught about Africa. No accelerated training session can completely fill this void.

CONCLUSIONS

It is much too early to reach firm conclusions about the impact of the PCVs on Sierra Leone. This is particularly true of the teachers discussed in this chapter, for the results brought about by teachers are always much more difficult to measure than the results of bridge builders, surveyors, or library catalogers.

As classroom teachers, the Volunteers have left a considerable quantitative impact on the long-run development of Sierra Leone. They have contributed an important percentage of the total amount of secondary school instruction offered in the entire nation in recent years. Their qualitative impact is, of course, more difficult to assess. To some degree they have been hampered by courses of study and lesson plans that leave something to be desired. The fact that many of them have not been trained as teachers is another important limiting factor.

As members of the school community outside the classroom, the Volunteers have probably registered somewhat less impact. To be sure, they have sometimes served as academic and vocational counselors. They have not usually been able, however, to serve as personal counselors. Like the expatriate and the Creole, the Volunteer teacher is a stranger, and Sierra Leoneans do not usually confide personal problems to a stranger but rather to their own kinsmen.

Both inside and outside the school, the PCV has served as exemplar and role model in a variety of ways. His or her behavior is carefully watched and not infrequently copied. What he says, and how he says it, both inside and outside the school, has a conditioning effect on the values, attitudes, and behavior patterns of the community. This is particularly important in view of the fact that the secondary schools are characteristically located in the growing cities and towns of Sierra Leone, where traditional and modern values come into conflict and where townsmen struggle to resolve these conflicts in a not too painful way. The townsman will often pick up clues from what Volunteers say and do as he weighs a decision involving, for example, whether to use surplus wealth to honor kinship obligations or to start an orange grove for personal gain.

The Peace Corps' impact on girl students is likely to prove greater than on boy students, if only because education for girls has lagged seriously behind that for boys. Employment prospects for educated women are improving and secondary school girls are questioning the correctness and justice of the traditional position of women in the light of new possibilities.[8]

Perhaps more important than the Volunteers' impact on Sierra Leone has been Sierra Leone's impact on the Volunteers. The program has enabled a sizable number of young Americans to undergo a type of experience in transcultural learning that has previously been reserved for a handful of specialists. Their firsthand involvement in the human problems of cultural change has made a lasting impression on most of them. Their perception of foreign relations and "the development of the underdeveloped nations" will henceforth be deeply influenced by this experience. Some have been stimulated to continue their formal education in a wide variety of social science disciplines with a focus on Africa and African problems. This will be good not only for them but for African Studies as well. Eventually some of them will undoubtedly contribute both to the resolution of African problems and to the development of the social sciences.

NOTES

[1] This is a considerably expanded version of my article, "The Peace Corps in Sierra Leone," published in *Challenge*, May 1964, pp. 16-19. Permission to republish is gratefully acknowledged.

[2] There are two reasons for this concentration on teachers: first, no community development projects had been undertaken in the chiefdoms where I worked; and second, it would have been impossible to conceal the identities of my friends, both Africans and Volunteers, in relation to the Peace Corps medical team's operations.

[3] For the history of Sierra Leone, see Kup 1961, and Fyfe 1962.

[4] I base this statement on Khuri 1964, and on my own inquiries in other urban centers. It must be stressed that there are exceptions, some of whom I number among my good personal friends.

[5] This belief was also held by at least some Nigerians following the arrival of the Peace Corps in that country. See the article entitled "Are Kennedy's Peace Corps Spies?" *Drum* No. 145 (May 1963), pp. 19 ff.

6 The emphasis on rote learning of the teacher's pontifications, so evident in the primary schools, is on occasion found in the secondary schools as well. The questioning student who inquires about the "whys" of something is often disciplined rather than encouraged to search further for possible answers.

7 This problem, which is common to all new nations, is discussed in Wallerstein 1961, especially in Chapter 5.

8 For example, my questionnaire data on a series of female secondary school students and a control series of village girls of the same age who had never attended a primary school, indicate that the former strongly prefer (a) to raise and train their own children, (b) to share with their husband the decision making on how to spend the income from their own labor, and (c) to avoid polygyny. The village girls prefer the traditional practices of (a) giving their children to relatives to train, (b) giving the income from their labor to their husband to do with as he alone sees fit, and (c) having a co-wife.

BIBLIOGRAPHY

BASCOM, WILLIAM R., and MELVILLE J. HERSKOVITS, Editors
    1958   *Continuity and Change in African Cultures.* Chicago, Ill.: University of Chicago Press.
DORJAHN, VERNON R.
    1960   "The Changing Political System of the Temne." *Africa,* Vol. 30, No. 2 (April) pp. 110-140.
    1962   "African Traders in Central Sierra Leone," in Paul J. Bohannon and George Dalton, eds., *Markets in Africa,* pp. 61-88. Evanston, Ill.: Northwestern University Press.
            "Women's Education in Sierra Leone." Forthcoming in a volume on education and the status of women to be published by UNESCO.
DORJAHN, VERNON R., and C. H. FYFE
    1962   "Landlord and Stranger: Change in Tenancy Relations in Sierra Leone." *Journal of African History.* Vol. 3, No. 3, pp. 391-397.
FYFE, C. H.
    1962   *A History of Sierra Leone.* Oxford, Eng.: Oxford University Press.
KHURI, F. I.
    1964   *The Influential Men and the Exercise of Influence in Magburaka, Sierra Leone.* Unpublished doctoral dissertation, Department of Anthropology, University of Oregon.
KUP, PETER
    1961   *A History of Sierra Leone, 1400–1787.* Cambridge, Eng.: Cambridge University Press.
WALLERSTEIN, IMMANUEL
    1961   *Africa, The Politics of Independence.* New York: Vintage Books.

11

Programs and Potential in

Tunisia and Morocco

CHARLES F. GALLAGHER[1] *served as a Japanese language officer during World War II and later, in a civilian capacity, as Cultural Property Officer in the occupation of Japan. Since 1951, he has been engaged in the study of Arab and Islamic society. After graduating* summa cum laude *from Harvard College, he did graduate work in Paris and North Africa under Ford and Fulbright Fellowships, specializing in North African history. In 1956 he became an Associate of the American Universities Field Staff, and since that time he has resided primarily in the Arab world, traveling extensively and sending home frequent reports analyzing current political and social developments. Mr. Gallagher has had contact with North Africa Volunteers not only through having observed them in the field but also through having helped to train some of them. He is the author of* The United States and North Africa *(Cambridge, Mass.: Harvard University Press, 1963); in addition he has contributed chapters to several books on political development as well as articles for a number of journals.*

I T ought to be said at the very beginning that the Peace Corps has been a considerable but qualified success in both Tunisia and Morocco. This alone is an item of importance, because the operations in these Maghrib countries are the only ones so far undertaken in any of the Arab states, most of whose Middle Eastern members have shown more recalcitrance about such projects than has been found anywhere else in the non-Communist world. The Peace Corps is in politics from the start in most Arab lands, and at the highest level, because of the highly charged emotional climate which surrounds initiatives by the American, or any other Western, government. The touchiest point, however, although played down, is the issue created by the reluctance or refusal of some Arab countries to allow American Jews to enter their territory, a rock on which several other bilateral agreements have threatened to founder before the

Peace Corps came into being. When the Corps first offered itself to prospective suitors in 1961, it was hard to believe that it could work successfully in any Arab country save possibly Lebanon or Tunisia. International complications in the form of pressure from other Arab countries might menace it in Lebanon, and in any event it is little needed there; it is questionable whether Lebanon should be considered a really underdeveloped country. That the Peace Corps has now made its mark in Tunisia comes as no great surprise, but that it has established itself in Morocco in the past year is a source of some encouragement. I for one am more than pleased to have begun erasing some of the doubts I held on the latter case and to give credit to both hosts and guests. The not unimportant point has been made that young Americans of all kinds and faiths can work together with North African Arabs in reciprocal goodwill. There remain the questions of what they were doing and whether they were working at what was most needed as of the time of my observation in February 1964.

THE TUNISIA PROGRAM

The Tunisia operation got under way in the summer of 1962, and by early 1964 there were just under a hundred Volunteers working in this nation of four million people. Despite a masterful selling job originally undertaken by an Embassy attaché in Tunis, vis-à-vis high Tunisian officials in public-health and public-works services, the first group was greeted with some hesitancy. In particular the nurses were looked at askance, but gradually, working in pairs in Tunis and outlying cities, they completely won over erstwhile critics, who are clamoring for as many more of them as can be obtained. Equally outstanding is the record of a score of young architects in the country. They have responded to the opportunity of being able to work and design freely immediately upon graduating from architecture schools instead of being confined as junior line-drawing draftsmen in the United States. In some cases their youth made them suspect at first, but as with the nurses, their general level of competence and enthusiasm has carried the day to the extent that the Tunisian government does not wish to renew the contracts of a group of Italian architects employed in technical assistance who were receiving salaries ten times as high. The Peace Corps architects have designed low-cost public housing (two rooms, bath, kitchen, and courtyard for $1,200) in the capital and three other towns. One of the architects was taken by President Bourguiba to help further embellish his hometown of Monastir. In keeping with the Tunisian tradition of drawing on multiple sources for help, Volunteers have cooperated with Communist-bloc technicians such as the Bulgarian engineer in charge of the Le Kef housing project; have replaced Czech mechanics who found the language barrier too formidable; and have been competing with French and Italian technicians in several fields. Besides nurses and architects, the Volunteer group was made up of mechanics, who carried out preventive maintenance on public-works equipment; physical education instructors, who worked mainly in the Bourguiba Villages for poor and orphaned children; trainers of Tunisian athletic coaches; and English teachers. The last group was used in secondary schools and in the modern language institute in Tunis. The categories more recently requested by the Tunisian government are doctors and medical technicians, more nurses, demographers, and statisticians (the lowering of statistical standards over the past decade is a semihidden but serious problem), and workers for the agricultural extension program.

THE MOROCCO PROGRAM

In this nation of twelve and a half million there were 104 Corpsmen in early 1964. There were thirty-seven English teachers, twenty-seven surveyors, fifteen irrigation specialists, twelve athletic coaches, nine art and music teachers, and four in miscellaneous fields. Having gotten a later start here than in Tunisia, and working in a more complex environment, the Moroccan operation had still not produced the visible results evident in the first country. Still, the Corps is warmly appreciated at all working levels. A high official with whom I spoke at length praised the general idea of the Corps and the specific quality of some of the men working in the Forestry Office. More than anything else he was enthusiastic about the mutual advantages of having Corpsmen living in the "bled" (back country) and the possible use of Volunteers as a catalyst for social transformation in rural areas. (In December 1964 an ex-Volunteer concurred in the opinion that the forestry program was an excellent one, but reported that it would not be continued because of professional jealousy and personality clashes among various officials in the Moroccan bureaucracy.)

The same high Moroccan official was of the opinion that the work of the Volunteer surveyors, while needed, was badly organized and misdirected. In part this stemmed from the fact that most "chefs de district" are French engineers with fixed workways and styles. Thus, up to early 1964 at least, much of the surveyors' activity was confined to elementary sightings and mappings, while under proper circumstances and with a free hand they could have been used in a program to train Moroccans for increased responsibilities.

As for the teachers of English, the Corps itself questions their immediate value. Those working in some of the better "lycées" and colleges are possibly performing a worthwhile service to a very limited number of students, some of whom may go on to use English professionally. But there are other Volunteers who are doing little more than filling in at big-city "medina" schools, which resemble blackboard jungles. At bottom, the fault lies with the Moroccan Ministry of Education, which has yet to formulate and carry out a coherent policy regarding secondary and higher instruction; lacking such a policy, it goes on with stopgap measures, offering subjects merely because teachers are available. Since the Ministry is considering phasing out English instruction in 1966 except on a specialized basis, there is reason to question the appropriateness of the Peace Corps committing its limited resources to this transient task.

Even a brief analysis of the problems of the Peace Corps in North Africa would have to separate them into those of procedure and general operations on the one hand, and the specific issues related to particular areas and cultural problems on the other.

GENERAL OPERATIONAL PROBLEMS

In general operations there is little difficulty. In neither country are extreme hardships encountered; the recent massive growth of tourism shows that many people would consider it a pleasure to be paid to "rough it" in many parts of the area. In Tunis, the Volunteer nurses who have been moved into the native quarter, rather than being housed in European-type apartments, sometimes end up with accommodations that their compatriots find romantically enviable. In both countries, climate and amenities are well above the general standard for underdeveloped countries. (Meal for meal, one eats better and cheaper in even the smaller towns than in their counterparts in, say, Ohio.) The surveyors and irrigators lead lonelier lives, but most of them expect to. And for the former at least—often ensconced in snug mountain cabins of the Forestry Service, fitted out with handsome rugs, local handicraft furniture, and abundant help —there is probably less suffering involved than in holding down a similar post in the Rockies. Personal relations between Corpsmen and the local population have been fine without exception; in Tunisia, Americans have always enjoyed a solid popularity, which could be arguably attributed to their previous absence. Moroccans have, perhaps for the wrong reasons, further taken them to their hearts since the Moroccan-Algerian border skirmishes when it was widely assumed by the ordinary Moroccan that Washington was firmly supporting Rabat.

For some of the same causes, relations between the Corps and host governments are quite good on the whole, but with differences which relate to the relative efficiency of the hosts. It is hard to get action for any project in Morocco, and dealings with several branches of various ministries tend to bog down in rivalry or apathetic handling. In the effort to place Volunteers in the United Nations-sponsored Lalla Mimouna pilot village projects, for example, it is necessary to work with representatives from Youth and Sports, Public Works, Urbanism, Interior, and the National Office for Rural Modernization. Furthermore, the direct interest shown by the head of state in Tunisia has not been noticeable in Morocco. In Tunisia, Volunteers have pretty well built an image for themselves, whereas in Morocco they have not yet—as may be essential in this personalized country —come under the patronage of a powerful figure.

Some of the difficulties may stem from the anomalous position of the Corps as an institution, and of Volunteers as individuals, within the hierarchy of the American community. In this sense the Corps has not fully, in the Moroccan instance, established its separate identity with the highest echelon of government officials in Rabat, through no fault of its own. The ambivalence of a host government is understandable to a degree. The PCVs are clearly official, and they benefit from some carefully negotiated agreements: they receive housing or monetary allowances in lieu thereof; they are exempt from local taxes (as French technical assistants, for example, are not in most cases); they are authorized to buy certain basic items at United States government expense, and so forth. Yet, to many Moroccans, they do not fit into a preconceived notion of the American official family in their country, and it is not easy to know how to treat them. (This might not be wholly a disadvantage in a society where poverty and saintliness have often been associated; Morocco is a country where for some time several hundred American beatniks in residence were shown a high esteem, from which they have now fallen, and where the chief of police in one city likened them to holy men.) However, so far as official contacts are concerned, it would seem desirable to strengthen as far as possible the direct support of the Corps from Washington, while at the same time allowing the Volunteers to flourish as freely as possible without either excessive local American control or—equally unwanted and potentially more dangerous—local official indifference. In part, the

Peace Corps is seeing a repetition of the AID problem. It runs the risk of being treated as an even shabbier relative, but given the greater motivation and quality among its personnel and some preventive warning, its future course need not be so unfortunate as that of many American economic missions abroad.

AREA AND CULTURAL PROBLEMS

However, the most serious thought should be given to those facets of the operation that are connected with the special problems of this area. The Peace Corps now works in more than two score countries of widely varying background. In many of these, as in Latin America and the Philippines, the American image is the major foreign one with which these societies have dealt in the recent past, and the Corps' activities mesh in a total, understandable framework. In others, of which Nigeria—which says it can use one thousand Volunteers—is a good example, PCVs are in effect supplementing an Anglo-Saxon tradition, which in law, language, and much of its custom has already taken root in the country. In most such cases there are, moreover, few other agencies directly competing with the Corps on a mass, official basis.

The French Cultural Superstratum

Not so in North Africa at all. Here the American presence is a hazy one, except for the semidirect contact with several thousand airmen in Morocco during the past decade. Their departure, consummated in 1963, and their replacement by Peace Corps Volunteers (as the only Americans visibly active in the country apart from diplomats) is laudable from the viewpoint of developing more wholesome contacts in a new setting. However, it does not alter the main fact that there are few parts of the underdeveloped world so saturated with one set of European-inculcated standards and techniques as this. It should be remembered that France maintains almost 24,000 teachers in the three Maghrib countries of Tunisia, Morocco, and Algeria. It also maintains more than 15,000 other employees-on-loan and technical assistants, a figure which does not include the bevies of short-term specialists who come and go incessantly between Paris and North Africa. Even the states of the French Community in black Africa do not present an analogy to this except in limited degree, and they lack a further element that has blanketed the indigenous Maghribi concept of foreign civilization: the presence of the settler en masse functioning as agriculturalist, lawyer, doctor, engineer, businessman, and the like.

The result, as is known, has been the development of a French superculture imposed on the Arab substratum to an unparalleled degree and the pervasive imposition of French norms. It is with this complex that the Corpsman is forced into competition and rivalry, both conscious and unconscious. Here he is not reinforcing the self, as in the Philippines, or supplementing it, as in Nigeria, but threatening to change and replace. Thus the Volunteer surveyors find their work suspiciously judged by French technicians as well as by Moroccans who know only French standards and alternate in their reactions between confusion, interest, and irritation. Thus, too, Volunteer teachers' qualifications are viewed in the strict French academic light of *équivalences,* and some of the teachers complain of feeling that they are somehow unnecessary but tolerated adjuncts of a closed system. The issue is not only one of competition but also of enforced emulation, for the Corps overwhelmingly uses French as its main language for working purposes and deals with local governments in it. There is little if any remedy for this at the moment, not only because the number of individuals who can function in a technical field in Arabic is countable on one hand but also because—and this is crucial—most North African officials expect to direct their transactions with the modern, secular, outside world through the Gallic prism that seems to them more suited to the technical affairs of the twentieth century than does Arabic, and they know no other than this.

There is another point at which the PCV diverges from the multitude of French *coopérateurs* who surround him in North Africa. The Volunteer is often confronted with young Frenchmen who were born in this area, or who have had military service here which has led to a good deal of expert knowledge. A large percentage of those engaged in the technical assistance programs are politically *engagé* on the left or the extreme left; they are in touch with North African students and student groups almost unanimously socialist or Marxist, and they are politically sympathetic to them and to many of the alert, younger civil servants who share these ideas, but not necessarily to the regimes in existence. The Peace Corps Volunteer, however, if it were only in pursuance of the directives given him during his training period, must remain apolitical; and he is, in fact, less integrated in the social scene and on the whole less partial in his political choices. Thus, he loses some of his effectiveness with many of the most dynamic young elements in the society. Yet, though this is inevitable in a society that is highly politicized at all urban levels and increasingly so in certain rural ones, it can also be claimed that better results will be produced in the end by strict adherence to the performance of a technical task without overtones. Whatever the outcome, this confrontation of method and attitude exists. The role of the French left has been controversial but capital in recent years in North Africa, and the new technician of *coopération* is continuing that influence and refining it to the highest degree. In a situation that hovers between reform and revolution, those who are not actively working for one or the other are considered lackeys of the status quo at best and conniving neocolonialists at worst. In the end, how apolitical can and should a group of socially conscious young Americans be expected to remain under the conditions of ferment prevalent in countries like these? That is not a rhetorical question.

The Stratagem of Specialization

It is not easy to find definite answers to the over-all question put here, yet something may be encompassed in a setting of specialization and limitation. The basic issue is what supplementary talents Americans have to offer in a situation already quite thoroughly covered by great numbers of competent Western technicians. If some of the fields in which the Corps is working seem somewhat unnecessary, there are others in which it can undoubtedly go on making useful contributions. Certainly the teaching of a third language, such as English, is utterly superfluous in an area where the elite is already entirely bilingual, and where the educational system is moving toward a mass bilingualism which, though functionally useful, already imposes an enormous learning strain on students. Remembering that the preferred national sports in these countries are, first, soccer, and, second, bicycle racing, one wonders whether some of the Corps' athletic activities might not be subordinated to an intensification of the effort in fields where American skills are admittedly potent: farm extension services, public health, and medicine come to mind at once. Tunisia's request for PCVs with these specialities suggests that it has found those areas where American skills can be most fruitful.

A useful precedent in specialization, but in a completely different environment, has been set by the American University of Beirut. In the face of growing competition from national universities in Arab countries (and with something of the same problem of rivalry with French institutions in a Lebanon that has a strong emotional tie to France), it has placed its emphasis on subjects in which American competence is unquestioned: its medical facilities, business administration and economic research departments, and experimental farm are universally considered outstanding.

The Arab Cultural Substratum

Another form of specialization could be the admittedly difficult one of "Arabizing" the program as much as possible. If even a small number of Volunteers could work at grass-root levels directly in Arabic, their impact would be much greater, as has been shown in the few cases where Americans of Arab descent have been able to do this to some degree. A more direct approach could be made, and the need to compete on purely French terms reduced. Within a few years the pool of young trained Arabists in America should grow, particularly with the development of the NUPOSA (National Undergraduate Program for Overseas Study of Arabic) scheme, a junior-year-in-Lebanon program administered by Princeton on behalf of several American universities. If this or a similar program were extended to North Africa, as the State Department Arabic Language Program has been, eventual encouragement could be given to combine programs and persuade universities to grant fixed credit for Volunteer work.

PROSPECTS

An emphasis on specialized concentration automatically implies a kind of limitation and brings the ultimate question: Does the Peace Corps have a vital role to play in areas where, as here, direct American political contact has either been reduced in recent years (Morocco) or is limited to economic assistance without pacts or bases (Tunisia and possibly Algeria) and where its cultural influence is distinctly secondary? I suggest that it does, and in so doing, it is without any thought of great-power rivalry or retaliation. America need not stoop to maintain a toehold in a region intellectually dominated by France merely because the latter is pursuing a more active diplomatic policy with regard to Canada or Latin America. Nor, if abandonment were ever to be considered, should it be on the grounds of accepting cultural and technical spheres of influence. The United States is, of course, competing with France, more than it probably realizes itself, but much less than the French suspect and for reasons not entirely so selfish as those ascribed to it. In the larger sphere of this still friendly rivalry, the principle of limitation may be useful in reflecting what is happening to the general political world in the mid-1960's: the Maghrib is a good vantage point for seeing that America is not omnipotent and that its skills, which seemed overwhelming in the decade or so after World War II, are only one part of the ensemble of Western civilization.

The most valid criterion for final decision is what will provide the quickest, most efficient, and most rational means for an effective developmental transformation of a given society, and for stimulating and catalyzing those forces that will cause it to grow internally. Looked at in this way, a sound rule is that standardization of technical learning processes in underdeveloped lands is a useful shortcut *up to a certain point.* It is as unreasonable to expect Algeria to graft onto its already staggering burden of French-inspired behavior everything implied in the Protestant, postmercantile American way of doing things as it has been to try to quickly substitute neo-Marxist patterns for French-learned techniques there. Beyond that certain point, however, a supplementary amount of diversity can be a leaven that increases the chances for growth in various ways. Mexico, Lebanon, and Iran, chosen at random, are examples of societies where plural sources of cultural influence have stimulated usefully. In North Africa today, Tunisia shows a few embryonic signs of following in such paths, and this may be one reason for the relatively greater acceptance-cum-understanding for the Peace Corps there than in Morocco. Tunisia may be arriving at the certain point where it can assimilate more diversity. It is, however, a sensitive operation to decide how far the United States should push such deep, national movements—as delicate as following those recipes that call for "seasoning to taste." It seems clear that what the Peace Corps is contributing cannot be the principal ingredient, or even an important ingredient perhaps, for forming the new society being shaped in North Africa; but if a limited number of future objectives are chosen with care and the quality of performance is steadily maintained and polished, it can be one of the subtle spices which will help give that society a fuller flavor. *Caveat emptor et venditor.*

NOTE

[1] Most of the material in this chapter appeared originally in "The Peace Corps in the Maghrib," an AUFS Report published by American Universities Field Staff, Inc. (Copyright 1964).

BIBLIOGRAPHY

ASHFORD, DOUGLAS A.
    1961 *Political Change in Morocco.* Princeton, N.J.: Princeton University Press.

BARBOUR, NEVILLE, Editor
    1962   *A Survey of Northwest Africa: The Maghrib.* Second Revised
           Edition. London and New York: Oxford University Press.
GALLAGHER, CHARLES F.
    1963a *The United States and North Africa.* Cambridge, Mass.:
           Harvard University Press.
    1963b "Tunisia," in Gwendolen M. Carter, ed., *African One-Party
           States.* Second edition, revised. Ithaca, N.Y.: Cornell University
           Press.
    1963c "Language, Culture, and Ideology," in American Universities
           Field Staff under the editorship of K. H. Silvert, *Expectant
           Peoples: Nationalism and Development.* New York: Random
           House, pp. 199-231.
GORDON, DAVID C.
    1962   *North Africa's French Legacy.* Cambridge, Mass.: Harvard
           University Press.
HALPERN, MANFRED
    1963   *Social Change in the Middle East and North Africa.* Princeton,
           N.J.: Princeton University Press.
JULIEN, CH.-A.
    1956   *L'Histoire de l'Afrique du Nord.* Two volumes. Second edition,
           revised. Paris: Payot.
MICAUD, CHARLES A., with LEON CARL BROWN and CLEMENT H. MOORE
    1963   *Tunisia: The Politics of Modernization.* New York: Frederick
           A. Praeger.

12

Lessons from Jamaica

LAMBROS COMITAS *is Associate Professor of Anthropology and Education at Teachers College, Columbia University, and Associate Director of the Research Institute for the Study of Man. In addition to his teaching duties at Columbia, he serves as Executive Secretary of the Columbia-Cornell-Harvard-Illinois undergraduate program of supervised field work in Latin America. Dr. Comitas has specialized in the Caribbean for ten years and made numerous field trips to the area. His research interests include interethnic relations, social change, economic development, and education. In 1961 and 1962, Dr. Comitas did program consulting and field exploration for the Peace Corps in connection with a number of actual and potential programs in the Caribbean. He served as Director of the training program for Jamaica One at the Research Institute for the Study of Man, and Area Studies Coordinator for St. Lucia One at Iowa State University; and later he was able to visit both groups in the field. Professor Comitas' latest major publication is the forthcoming* Caribbeana 1900–1965, University of Washington Press, *the first comprehensive bibliography of the West Indies.*

WHILE much has been written about the general accomplishments of the Peace Corps during its first four years, comparatively little of any analytic value has been presented about the various structural problems faced by working units overseas. In the formative stages of Peace Corps development, there were ample reasons for this imbalance. For one, with so little time in the field, there was insufficient information about routine operations. Second, the actual difficulties encountered overseas appeared to be of a considerably lower order of intensity than had been feared. Finally, prolonged public discussion of difficulties or failures at that time would have adversely affected the organization's image and diminished its chances for public acceptance and support.

These conditions, however, no longer hold. The Peace Corps, as government agency and national institution, is now firmly established; masses of data concerning overseas work situations are being

201

rapidly accumulated; and perhaps most importantly, fundamentally similar field problems occurring in different parts of the world are now being conceptually linked together. For these reasons, it is of positive value for the Peace Corps, at this point in its development, to expand and coordinate its facilities for the scientific analysis of operational problems. Accordingly, investigation by social scientists of apparently not-too-successful Peace Corps field units would, by comprehending the structural nature of problem situations continuously encountered, limit errors in planning and implementation before a group is sent overseas, thereby considerably increasing the Corps' potential impact in the field.

In this spirit, I shall discuss some of the difficulties and problems of Jamaica One, a group of Volunteers with which I was personally acquainted. As trainees, the members of this group completed what was probably one of the most comprehensive and highly rated training programs provided by the Peace Corps up to that time. And yet, during their first year as a working unit in Jamaica, they gained the widespread reputation of being one of the most troublesome contingents in the entire Peace Corps. Even *The New York Times* singled them out as an exception to the generally laudatory performance of the Peace Corps, in an editorial on the second anniversary of that organization:

> The Peace Corps has not butted in where it wasn't wanted, nor has it wasted time or funds. It has had its problems—on the island of Jamaica, for example—but taken as a whole it has been a genuine success. It has done solid work—the sort of work that can be done by well-trained and enthusiastic teachers, nurse's aides, nutritionists, and sanitation experts— in forty-one different countries.[1]

This general opinion of the Peace Corps in Jamaica was undoubtedly unfair, for although the difficulties that beset Jamaica One were real enough, they were not unique to that contingent. In part or in whole, similar structural problems have been faced by many other Peace Corps contingents as well, although generally with less public attention. It is this *recurrence of structurally similar problems* in different settings that makes an examination of the Jamaica case of general interest.

THE JAMAICAN BACKGROUND

In the spring of 1962, twenty-nine men and twelve women were put into training for Peace Corps service in Jamaica. The stated objectives of this unit were "to help the Government of Jamaica's existing vocational and adult education program, and to assist in the island's Agriculture Development Program. . . ."[2] To achieve these goals, Volunteers were to be provided as industrial arts instructors, vocational teachers with various skills, librarians, nurse-health educators, commercial practices instructors, agricultural teachers, rural cooperative assistants, basic science instructors, and audiovisual specialists.

The island to which this vocationally heterogeneous unit was assigned is one of the newest and smallest countries receiving Peace Corps assistance. Although it is the largest of the British West Indian islands, Jamaica is only 146 miles at its longest point and 51 miles at its widest, with the total land area measuring some 4,400 square miles. The island is ecologically diversified: out of a population over 1,600,000, about 25 per cent live in expanding urban areas such as Kingston; another 25 per cent dwell in the low-lying sugar belt parishes or depend economically on these areas; the remaining 50 per cent manage to eke out an existence in the mountainous expanses of the interior or in restricted pockets along the coastline. Full independence within the framework of the British Commonwealth of Nations was granted on August 6, 1962, several weeks after Jamaica One had arrived to take up its duties.

With its beautiful climate, tropical foliage, beaches, and towering mountain ranges, Jamaica has long been a tourist attraction. This natural beauty, however, tends to conceal from the casual eye many deep-rooted problems—problems often endemic to developing societies—such as high population density, a large percentage of unemployed or underemployed, and an illiteracy rate that poses a serious obstacle to economic and social development. Agriculture, the primary economic activity, has two incompletely integrated components: a well-developed plantation system geared to the production of sugarcane, and small-plot agriculture devoted to food crops for local consumption. Large-scale agricultural development is hindered by traditional practices of the small farmers, who, moreover, lack the capital and incentive necessary for modernization. A complex system of land tenure, including legal as well as extralegal forms, further complicates the implementation of agricultural development programs.

The gross domestic product has increased three and a half times during the last decade, resulting largely from the development of bauxite mining and a vigorous industrialization program. Yet a rapidly increasing population has prevented this growth from raising per capita income as much as might be hoped. Not only this, but an estimated two thirds to four fifths of the population exist on a minimal subsistence level in rural areas or urban slums and are essentially excluded from, and unprepared for, participation in the nascent industrial life of the island. Emigration of Jamaicans to the United States in the past, and to the United Kingdom up to a year or two ago, has provided some temporary alleviation of the immediate problems of the island. But this outward flow has also had the debilitating effect of depleting Jamaica's short supply of skilled and semiskilled workers.[3]

Other factors that have tended to restrict rapid national advances and that affect the functioning of Volunteers on this island revolve around the nature of the Jamaican social system. Contemporary Jamaican society is a product of a long heritage of slavery, monocrop cultivation of sugar, and metropolitan exploitation. The present racial and ethnic composition reflects quite clearly the economic history of the island: almost 75 per cent of the population are classified as Negro, descendants of Africans brought to the Caribbean in the seventeenth and eighteenth centuries to work on the sugar plantations; 15 per cent are a mixture of Negro and white; less than 1 per cent are white. The remainder includes small but economically significant clusters of Chinese, "East Indians" from the Indian subcontinent, Syrians, and a variety of mixtures. Present-day control of economic and social power, however, bears no relationship to the numerical strength of the various racial and ethnic elements. Whites rank highest on the socioeconomic scale, browns are intermediate but important in political matters, and the blacks, though in great majority, are a poor third.

Although many Jamaicans would disagree, racial origin and its most visible symbol, skin color, is a critical determinant of social and economic position. As put by the noted Jamaican social anthropologist, M. G. Smith, ". . . local 'nationalism' has developed a convenient mythology of 'progress' according to which race differences are held to be irrelevant in personal relations" (Smith 1961:249). In very general terms, this anthropologist's conception of Jamaican society consists of three hierarchically arranged social sections, each of which correlates roughly with one of the three most significant racial groups. Each social section is characterized by a distinctive set of institutions so that there is considerable difference between the sections in modal forms of kinship, family, mating, magico-religious behavior, education, occupational patterns, and the like. The white section, for example, which ranks highest, carries to a considerable degree the culture of modern Western European society and is composed of individuals born in Jamaica but often reared abroad from early childhood. The black, or most subordinate section, is characterized by a culture that includes many elements similar to those found during the period of Caribbean slavery and in West African societies. The brown intermediate section, a cultural and biological amalgam of the first two, practices a mixture of patterns that stem from both the white and black sections. The integration of these three social sections has been and still is weak. According to Smith's analysis, social cohesion is only maintained through controls that are derived partly from the economic system and partly from the fact that the ranking social sections possess an effective monopoly over such regulative institutions as the courts and the police.[4]

An observer of Jamaican life need not accept this theory as completely proved in order to appreciate many of its accuracies in description. For example, it is evident that interpersonal relations among members of different social strata are minimal and that the significant values held by each stratum may differ substantially from those held by the others. Under such conditions, what one group considers of value and of import may not necessarily have similar meaning for the others. In any case, there appears to be a general consensus among most social scientists who have studied Jamaican life that they are dealing with a rigidly stratified society characterized by substantial social and cultural differences between the principal social segments. Some of the difficulties inherent in this complex of value systems and social arrangements with regard to the implementation of action programs are readily obvious.

THE TRAINING OF JAMAICA ONE

During a two-month period from April through May 1962, training for Jamaica One was the responsibility of the Research Institute for the Study of Man (RISM), an anthropological foundation in New York City specializing in Caribbean affairs. With its strong area concentration, RISM was in a position to develop an over-all curriculum in which all the study units required by Peace Corps/ Washington were *specifically* related to Jamaica and the West Indies. This meant that the entire program was given a strong area focus, so that technical refresher courses, American studies, world affairs, health training, and the like were taught, whenever possible, by specialized personnel with relevant field experience in Jamaica or in other parts of the British Caribbean.

The training institution enjoyed one unusual and valuable advantage: since it did not have commitments to a permanent faculty, it was free to pick and choose specific lecturers for specific purposes and to obtain the *best* available lecturer in each case. For example, over twenty area specialists—West Indian, American, and British— constituting a majority of the social scientists specializing in this part of the Caribbean, presented descriptions and analyses of the culture and society of the region and dealt as well with particular and idiosyncratic problems that some of the Volunteers would face. Agricultural economists from Jamaica taught the fundamentals of agriculture as they pertain specifically to Jamaica. Nurse-health education work in the West Indies was taught by the Principal Nursing Officer of Jamaica; health training for the entire group was given by a lecturer in Social and Preventive Medicine from the University of the West Indies. In every case, lecturers were informed of the material that had already been presented by other staff members. Quite frequently, several members of this temporary faculty would attend the classes given for the Volunteers, forming a kind of ad hoc panel discussion group. Outside of the classroom, ample opportunity was provided for frequent contact and communication with the West Indian community in New York.

There was no disagreement as to the merits of the training program. The Volunteers were enthusiastic. Almost a year later, one of them wrote from the field, "I feel that I knew almost as much about Jamaica when I left RISM as it is possible to teach a person in two months." The core training staff was also satisfied. The diversity of technical skills required for Jamaica One meant the recruitment of trainees with wide disparities in schooling and orientation; nonetheless, the staff felt that the general program, and especially the coordinated area approach, tended to bridge these substantial differences in the academic backgrounds of their charges. Peace Corps/ Washington gave repeated indication that it considered the program highly successful and suggested it as a model for training programs then being prepared by other institutions for other areas of the world.

Anxiety over Selection

Only two hints of possible future difficulty emerged during this two-month period. The first of these was extreme nervousness concerning final selection for the project, which became almost the psychological leitmotif of the trainees. Although selection anxiety seems to be usual for all Peace Corps groups, in this case it was abnormally high, induced and aggravated perhaps by the initial handling of selection warnings by officials from the Peace Corps itself. The group's antipathy toward anyone from Peace Corps/ Washington grew as the date for selection drew near. All Peace Corps officials were considered potential screeners who had influence in the selection process. These antipathetic leanings were further reinforced when delays in the civil service clearance procedures threatened to keep five Volunteers from departing with the group.

Anxiety over Field Leadership

The second hint of possible future difficulty concerned field leadership. There was open apprehensiveness among the trainees about the fact that no Country Representative had been selected to direct them in Jamaica. When at last an appointment was made in the final stages of the training program, this general apprehension turned to sharp criticism of the appointee's lack of previous experience in, or knowledge of, the area. Notwithstanding these concerns, the group departed for Jamaica with assurances of continuing support from the training staff, with friends already on the island, and, as far as can be judged, with an optimistic outlook on its coming tour of service.

EARLY PROBLEMS IN THE FIELD

Upon the Volunteers' arrival in Jamaica, a very rapid deterioration of their sanguine expectations was evident. During the group's first six months on the island, over half of the original work assignments were changed; the Country Representative was replaced; six PCVs of the thirty-eight finally selected were returned to the United States for a variety of reasons; and morale was extremely low. Critical attention was focused on the project by several vitriolic letters to various authorities from the Volunteers themselves, by a series of special investigators sent by Washington to stabilize the project, and by the ensuing publicity it had received in both the Jamaican and American press. From the perspective of the PCVs, who were obviously the persons most immediately concerned, the general situation was a by-product of two interlocked issues: problems revolving around the work situation and problems involving Peace Corps direction and administration.

Unfortunate Timing

Initial confusion surrounding work assignments resulted in part from unfortunate timing. The Volunteers arrived in Jamaica as the school year ended for the summer holiday. Consequently, some fifteen of them destined for the public schools required temporary assignments for the first three months. These arrangements were far from satisfactory: a commercial course teacher became a secretary for a Jamaican educator; a number of PCVs were sent to government youth camps where they did a minimum of instruction and a maximum of manual labor; a few became part-time instructors in an in-service training course in the industrial arts, while others were assigned to the same course as students! Few, if any, thought they were doing the kind of work that a Volunteer should be doing.

Problems of Status and Structure

Volunteers who immediately assumed their permanent assignments also encountered difficulties. Job content and relevance was one issue. Peace Corps librarians assigned to one organization discovered that they were superfluous and, on their own, negotiated a transfer to a reference library that was in desperate need of professional assistance. Other Volunteers ran into structural conflicts with their local supevisors. One such example of status incompatibility led to the removal from Jamaica of two of the most capable and dedicated Volunteers in the unit. These two mildly described their overseas experience as follows:

> We then began working as . . . Volunteers in the . . . system whose . . . processes we were assigned to bring up to date. Most unfortunately, the director of the system is a sort of madperson who cannot bear to have persons with much . . . knowledge near. The result was that our actions were intentionally misinterpreted, and threats were made which were so drastic that we were literally forced out of the country. The Peace Corps was anxious to assign us elsewhere, but none of the current possibilities seemed to call for our qualifications, so we reluctantly gave up our status as Volunteers.

The reaction of the unit to the outcome of this incident was that Volunteers were being punished for doing their job well under trying circumstances, and that they were not being protected by the Peace Corps staff in Kingston or Washington.

On another and more general level, this incident involving Volunteers and their local counterparts or superiors is reminiscent of similar occurrences in other countries where differences in experience and training threaten already established status and prestige positions. Fortunately, few of these incidents have engendered the drastic solution of this Jamaica case. The important point here is that in order to systematically confront such situations, the causes and solutions must first be sought in the nature of the local social system, rather than in assuming that there must be idiosyncratic psychological pressures at work.

Logistical Frustrations

One group of Volunteers was assigned to government youth camps in the mountainous interior, where they found themselves immediately harassed by logistical problems. Contrary to assurances received, neither their living quarters nor the special workshops in which they were to teach had been constructed by the time they arrived. Various Volunteers spent periods of from three to twelve months doing unskilled pick and shovel work, constructing school buildings. Only rudimentary hand tools were available to them for this purpose, and members of the Representative staff were often of little help in providing tools—even cheap ones that were relatively easily available. Even when they received the full cooperation of their Jamaican superiors, the teaching and work opportunities of these Volunteers were circumscribed. The nurses had few medical supplies and were underutilized; the commercial course teacher had no typewriters or other teaching aids; and the vocational teachers had no shops, no equipment, and in some cases, no students. During the first few months of residence, discontent and frustration grew and grew among most of these Volunteers. Soon some began making invidious comparisons between their mismanaged work situations, cramped physical and social setting, and bare subsistence fare—and that of their peers assigned to the Kingston area not far away, who might or might not be deriving satisfaction from their job assignments, but at least enjoyed comfortable apartments and the full amenities of city life. Such invidious comparisons could hardly be avoided in circumstances such as these, where the project is vocationally heterogeneous, and where the host country is very small so that news and gossip get around readily. The result was a growing alienation by the PCVs in the mountain area, both from the Peace Corps staff and from their fellow Volunteers. In retrospect, it seems clear that much of this problem of invidiousness and envy could have been avoided if Jamaica One and perhaps Two had been assigned only to upcountry stations, and then, perhaps, Jamaica Three exclusively to Kingston.

Lack of Administrative Communication

Job anxieties within the entire contingent continued, and dissatisfaction mounted. The tendency was for the Volunteers to ascribe responsibility for all problems to the local Peace Corps administration, alleging that the Representatives spent too little time in the field with the Volunteers; that they knew little about the Volunteers' problems; that they were of little help in bureaucratic procedures; that they were ineffective in resolving work impasses and anomalies with the Jamaican governmental hierarchy; and that they created intragroup tensions by capitulating to the demands for equipment or requests for job transfer made by the more aggressive Volunteers. Disciplinary problems increased, and the whole effectiveness of the Peace Corps seemed threatened amid a series of petty squabbles. Even after personnel changes in the administration were made, the relationship between the PCVs and their leadership remained somewhat distant. One Volunteer described the gap separating the Volunteer and administrative subcultures as follows:

> The Country Representatives have been so far removed from the Volunteers that there has been no common meeting ground. . . . They are so different that we seldom have common attitudes and breakdown of communication is fairly common.

ANALYSIS

Through systematic investigation, social science can be of fundamental value in the analysis of action programs operating in different sociocultural milieux. In the past, such scientific investigation has generally revealed that the operation of "problem" programs has been considerably affected by a *number* of complexly linked factors. Repeated findings of this order should serve as a constructive check on many non-social-scientists—especially those personally and emotionally involved—who tend to assess programs in black and white terms, often after identifying only partial causes or symptoms to explain involuted issues. Unfortunately, many laymen still attempt to analyze and to explain problems in purely vocational, or administrative, or psychological terms—to the almost complete neglect of social structure and cultural value systems. Three newspaper accounts of Jamaica One will illustrate such tendencies toward oversimplification.

In November 1962, *The Jamaican Weekly Gleaner* carried a story on a public lecture devoted to Jamaica's foreign affairs which was held at the local campus of the University of the West Indies. The article was captioned "Peace Corps Activities Here Called Fiasco."

The Chairman of the meeting, a Jamaican, made the following observations:

> It is well known that the Peace Corps in Jamaica is a fiasco. But the U.S. Government is not all to blame for this. In this business of requesting and receiving technical aid it is very necessary that the country requesting aid should first of all find out where its need is greatest, and ask for assistance in filling those needs. And in this particular case of the Peace Corps, I think that the Jamaica Government is to blame for not having ascertained in the first instance, the fields in which it really needed the assistance of the Peace Corps.[5]

A month later, a two-column story appeared in *The New York Times* under the heading "Peace Corps Men in Jamaica Feel Their Skills Are Wasted." It developed in some detail the point that Volunteers were "struggling with what many of them regard as a badly planned program," that morale was generally low, and that "there is a prevalent feeling that they are being wasted in their assignments."[6] In this account Volunteers in the field ascribed responsibility for their troubles to the Peace Corps staff, especially to those departments responsible for overseas operations. This assumption is much more fully and graphically documented from Volunteers' correspondence. One such letter states emphatically, "Peace Corps/Washington would seem to be one of the biggest reasons for low morale in this project."

A third position emerges clearly in February 1963, in another story in *The New York Times*. This article was captioned "Snags in Jamaica Vex Peace Corps—Shriver and High Aides Will Review Project on Scene." The Jamaica Project was conceded to be the "main headache" in the Latin American program, but

> Peace Corps officials have been unable to pin their Jamaican difficulties on any single problem, and they dispute the contention that the project was poorly planned. Many of the assignments didn't work out, said [a high Programing official]. It's hard to generalize on why. It could have been failure to adjust on the part of some Volunteers, failure to get along well with their Jamaican supervisors for others, lack of equipment, lack of strong leadership from the Peace Corps Representative, and a major error on our part was the failure to have an assistant for him.[7]

While eschewing any single cause, this particular analysis strongly suggests a psychological dimension. Its main point is that, with more flexible and resilient Volunteers and more dynamic leadership, essentially minor problems could have been transcended. This position, it would seem, implies failure in the selection and/or training process and errors in the selection of field administrators, but no fault is found with the basic structure of the project.

Among the Volunteers, the tendency was to ascribe their difficulties to personality deficiencies in the field staff. In their opinion, such deficiencies clearly led to inadequate administrative backstopping and faulty interpersonal relations. Here again psychological factors are offered as an explanation.

There is merit in this position as there is in each of the three newspaper stories, although none, by itself, accounts fully for the problems that dogged the Jamaica One operation. Factors involving the structure of the program and the social and cultural matrix in which the Peace Corps operated in Jamaica are, in my judgment, much more basic than are, for instance, the personality configurations of particular individuals.

Factors Affecting Intraorganizational Relations

The initial plan for Volunteer activity in Jamaica, the first series of administrative decisions implementing this plan, and the ensuing development of the Jamaican program, are all elements of great importance in identifying the causes of early trouble. Many of the problems and inadequacies of Jamaica One were inherent in the structure of the program well before a single Volunteer had set foot on the island. For example, long after the trainees had begun their training in New York, no Peace Corps Representative had been appointed for Jamaica. Whether or not this delay was unavoidable, it was certainly unfortunate. When a Representative was finally appointed, he turned out to be a person who, despite professional qualifications, was totally unfamiliar with the island. This lack of knowledge about Jamaica and the West Indies also characterized his immediate successors. As a consequence, these administrators knew much less about the sociocultural realities of Jamaica than did the Volunteers to whom they expected to give transcultural leadership and guidance. Little wonder, then, that the Volunteers whose subculture, as the editor has pointed out, places a high value on intimate knowledge of the host country, had difficulty in completely relating to the latecomers suddenly and tardily placed in charge of them. Furthermore, by the time of the first appointment, the Volunteers had already formed strong in-group links and loyalties. It would not have been easy for any outsider to gain their acceptance, but certainly it was doubly difficult for persons unfamiliar with Jamaica. Also, the simultaneous arrival in Jamaica of Representative and Volunteers allowed the Representative little opportunity to familiarize himself either with the complexities of Jamaica or with the Volunteers before the very real problems began of settling down to work.

Additional difficulties grew out of the fact that the first Representatives were called upon to administer an intricate program for which they had no original programing responsibility. Not only did they lack detailed knowledge of the arrangements and understandings already made by Peace Corps/Washington and the Jamaican government, but they arrived on the island, each in turn, lacking any acquaintance or rapport with the Jamaican officials most closely involved.

In short, my belief is that faulty organizational arrangements, such as those outlined, strongly predisposed Jamaica One in the direction of trouble and that given the nature of the structural end-product, trouble would still have ensued even if both Representatives and Volunteers had been veritable paragons.

Superficial Cultural Similarity

None of the three newspaper stories considered cultural factors as a possible cause of difficulty; nor, to my knowledge, did any of the responsible officials involved with the program. Perhaps the reason for this neglect of cultural factors was that Jamaica bears a *superficial* cultural similarity to the United States, in somewhat the same fashion that Szanton has already described for the Philippines (page 49). Jamaica is nearby, utilizes English and an English Creole, has a familiar political orientation and organization, and is well represented by its citizens on our shores. Geographical proximity and some surface similarities in language and dress, however, do *not* make Jamaica and the United States culturally homologous, as has already been explained at some length. Nevertheless, it is unfortunately true that such external appearances of sameness, if taken at face value, might well have operational consequences for Peace Corps programs. In most of Africa and Asia (except the Philippines) the stranger *expects,* and is psychologically prepared for, gross cultural differences in almost every aspect of life. In Jamaica and the British Caribbean, apparent similarities in specific behavior very often obscure from the stranger's view numerous basic differences in the reasons for, and implications of, such behavior. The dangers of misunderstanding in such a situation can very well be *greater* when the cultural cues are close but do not fit one's own. Yet, Peace Corps/Washington has often given the impression that the Jamaica situation should possess inherently fewer difficulties than those of supposedly more exotic lands. Precisely because of this, additional pressure was placed on the Volunteers. While they were struggling to function effectively in a truly complex sociocultural system, outside observers considered them fortunate in being where they were and, not infrequently, ascribed their problems to personal shortcomings.

Jamaica's Atypical Cultural Position

In its operations, the Peace Corps usually seeks to make two contributions to the host country: one is technical, to help the people of the host country meet their needs for trained manpower; the other is ideological, to promote a better local understanding of the American people. There is little question of the need in Jamaica for the kind of technical services that the Peace Corps can provide. Pursuit of the ideological objective, however, runs into an almost unique situation in Jamaica, a small island with a population that includes many other North Americans, both permanent residents and transients. In addition, there are many native Jamaicans who are highly sophisticated about Americans and the United States. Together, these two facts can severely strain the original enthusiasm and motivation of a Volunteer, such as the one who wrote

> If our purpose in Jamaica is to let Jamaica get to know Americans it is ridiculous. This is a big tourist area. Many Americans, Canadians and English live and work on the island, but more important, thousands of Jamaicans go to the United States to work and study. Many of them have seen more of the United States than some members of this project. What is our purpose in being here?

Other factors also render Jamaica somewhat atypical. Jamaicans, until recently colonial wards of Great Britain, have had considerable experience with innovative programs of various sorts. They possess a modern civil service of proved ability and critical acumen, at least at the higher levels. Through excellent communication media, they are keenly aware of conditions and events in the outside world.

Clearly, there was a need to take into account the above sociocultural characteristics of the host country if Jamaica One was to register immediate and important ideological gains. In order to be publicly successful, Jamaica One would need to produce an unusually visible and clearly demarcated output. This, however, did not happen. Instead, the program assigned Volunteers to a number of different governmental and quasi-governmental units, a dispersal that was geographical as well as organizational. As a result, the total effort and accomplishment of the first contingent was never clearly identified as that of the Peace Corps. Structured as it was, even a trouble-free operation would not have guaranteed an early Peace Corps impact on Jamaican public opinion. It should be added, however, that the *person-to-person* impact on Jamaican opinion (as distinct from the on-the-job impact) was often valuable. The PCVs often effectively projected an image of a different kind of American on the minds of Jamaicans who had theretofore seen only American tourists.

Inadequate Planning of Job Goals and Assignments

Given the unusual position of Jamaica in terms of the Peace Corps' ideological mission, it would seem all the more important, from the standpoint of Volunteer morale, that the technical mission in that country be clearly conceptualized and carefully planned and executed. The primary purpose for voluntary service in a place like Jamaica must be sought in the nature of, and satisfaction in, the work itself. Personal observation in Jamaica (and also in the British Caribbean island of St. Lucia) has convinced me that if a Volunteer were satisfied that he was contributing to the material development of his host country or territory, then other difficulties tended to take care of themselves. If, for example, the Jamaica One Volunteers stationed in the mountains had enjoyed reasonably high job satisfaction, they probably would not have felt any great envy of the PCVs stationed in Kingston.

In Jamaica, as we have seen, many work assignments proved ephemeral. Others were unclear as to their particular objectives. Without clear aims, there are few firm guidelines for the Volunteer. Is he there to promote change or simply to replace someone going on long leave? To what extent can he experiment or innovate while at his job? Are there any end-products expected as the result of his particular service? Where these finite work objectives are not or cannot be supplied, arbitrary action and communication break-down between Volunteers and Peace Corps staff may very well occur. For example, in several cases of marked difference of opinion over work between a Volunteer and a host country supervisor, where the objectives of the job were not spelled out, it was almost impossible for the local Peace Corps administrators to judge systematically and objectively whether a Volunteer should be reprimanded, defended, exonerated, or privately praised. Without these work goals, the principles for deciding each actual case may vary, resulting—among other things—in sentiments such as the following:

> Peace Corps treatment of withdrawn Volunteers has contributed to a feeling of distrust of the intentions of Peace Corps/Washington as well as to the feeling that we have no support or protection from our organization. . . . On this same subject the very flexibility of some aspects of policy breeds a lack of security and a feeling of confusion.

In my opinion, the relative rigidity and compartmentalization of the program made for lowered technical efficiency and morale. The officials from Peace Corps/Washington's Division of Program Development and Operations (PDO) who made the original arrangements set up a design calling for very few specialists in each of a relatively large number of specialties. Such arrangements might have worked quite well in a larger, economically more diversified nation. But for Jamaica's less complex socioeconomic system, the design was incapable of absorbing unexpected exigencies. A highly skilled factory-trained machinist, for example, proved to be difficult to place satisfactorily when his original teaching assignment did not materialize; he ended up teaching English. The same held true for Volunteers in a number of other relatively specialized skills or trades.

SUBSEQUENT IMPROVEMENT

Keeping to the purpose of this chapter, I have presented the negative aspects of the field situation rather than the positive accomplishments of individual Volunteers and of the group. Most emphatically, however, there was a brighter side. As 1963 wore on, there was increasing evidence that the worst was over. Most Volunteers were working in situations in which they felt they were making positive contributions, and dissension and discontent were no longer the dominant themes. Even a note of optimism had returned to the public utterances of the group. In an editorial in their local Peace Corps newsletter, the editors had this to say:

> Ironically, April Fool's Day [1963] represented our first anniversary in the Peace Corps. Except in the company of punsters, this is hardly relevant. There was nothing foolish in our joining, nor is there anything foolish in our situation. There is not one among us who is not accomplishing something worthwhile, and despite the loud noises which occasionally erupt on our little island, there is much of value in what we have done and we have all gained immensely by our personal experiences.

This must also have been the opinion of the Jamaican government, for at about that time, additional Peace Corps Volunteers were requested, this time to play an integral part in a massive new program aimed at the development of local Jamaican communities. For their part, a high proportion of the Jamaica One Volunteers extended their service in Jamaica beyond the two-year tour in order to finish teaching the school year, or to complete a particular project. Perhaps it can be said with some comfort that all's well that ends well—provided only that we learn from mistakes and attempt to avoid their repetition.

CONCLUSIONS AND RECOMMENDATIONS

This chapter should serve to make clear that responsible Peace Corps authorities, before accepting the specifics of a particular program, should be knowledgeable about the country, its people and its needs, as informed as possible about the motivations of the host government in extending an invitation to the Peace Corps, and realistic about the abilities of the Volunteers available for service. To ensure maximum effectiveness, a program should fit, as closely as possible, the realities of the host country in relation to the services the Peace Corps can offer. In the hectic days of 1961, such exploratory care and effort were virtually impossible. At the present time, with the considerable experience gained and with additional personnel available, this initial effort should be axiomatic.

The Crucial Importance of PDO

It would be difficult, without careful field study, to go beyond this discussion and establish the exact priorities and relationships of the factors already considered. Given the present purpose, however, I do not think this necessary, for even at this level of discourse, the Jamaica case provides lessons to be learned and insights to be exploited by the Peace Corps. Among the most important of these, in my judgment, are the lessons that deal with organization: the Jamaican experience suggests quite conclusively the apportionment of responsibility that must be made by the various line divisions of the Peace Corps. It is clear that Recruitment, Selection, and Training, as indispensable as they are, depend upon the particular projects designed by Program Development and Operations. This latter division is responsible for the context, tone, and administration of every unit overseas. If it functions well—comprehending and adjusting for the sociocultural realities of each host country—then inadequacies in other divisions tend to be minimized and overcome. On the other hand, badly conceived or badly executed projects may mean that even superlative efforts on the part of Selection or Training will be wasted. PDO is first among peers and should be instrumental in integrating and directing the professional efforts of all the other divisions.

The Need for Social Science and Area Competence

To carry out these responsibilities, PDO needs assistance. Officers of the division have many assignments: program exploration overseas, project administration from Washington, project implementation abroad, and middle-level policymaking. From the beginning, they have been overworked and overextended. Often, they are initially unfamiliar with the areas of the world in which they will do their work. Few of them, if any, are social scientists. From the point of view of minimizing field problems and providing expert knowledge on project development and direction, it is desirable that cultural anthropologists, comparative sociologists, and political scientists be more closely integrated with PDO. (Their efforts up to the present time have almost invariably been confined to the training programs.)

In this connection, I recommend the establishment of a small advisory committee to serve each of the four regional offices within PDO: Latin America, Africa, North Africa-Near East-South Asia, and the Far East. These small committees of three or more members would be selected on the basis of proved area competence and interest in the problems of change in underdeveloped territories. As returned Volunteers enter graduate school and finish their advanced degrees, the most competent should be integrated into these committees at the earliest moment.

In collaboration with PDO officials, these committees would advise on location, type, and size of projects within their respective regions. Having no administrative burden, each committee would serve as a board of objective advisors to the regional directors on cultural and structural problems. At relatively small cost and minimal organizational disruption, PDO could thus assure itself of a regular professional service which, until now, has only been approximated in the sporadic and rudimentary use of individual consultants.

NOTES

[1] This is from an editorial entitled "Second Birthday" in the March 4, 1963 issue of *The New York Times*.

[2] The original description and rationale for Jamaica One can be found in the Peace Corps Project Description, Form PC-104, Unclassified.

[3] The gist of these introductory remarks on Jamaican conditions was presented by the author in an unsigned section of Syllabus for the Peace Corps Training Program for Jamaica, 1962, pp. 5-6. More detailed references on economic, occupational, and demographic issues in Jamaica can be found in Comitas 1964; Edwards 1961; Eisner 1961; International Bank for Reconstruction and Development 1952; Roberts 1956; Roberts and Mills 1958; Smith 1956.

[4] M. G. Smith's most detailed statements to date on plural society theory in general, and on Jamaica, can be found in Smith 1960 and 1961.

[5] This article is in the *The Jamaican Weekly Gleaner*, November 23, 1962, the overseas edition of a prominent West Indian newspaper, *The Daily Gleaner*, published in Kingston, Jamaica.

[6] This article, by Richard Eder, appeared in the West Coast Pacific Edition of *The New York Times*, December 27, 1962.

[7] This article, by Hedrick Smith, appeared in *The New York Times*, February 28, 1963.

BIBLIOGRAPHY

COMITAS, LAMBROS
    1964   "Occupational Multiplicity in Rural Jamaica," in *Proceedings of the American Ethnological Society*. Seattle, Wash.: University of Washington Press, pp. 41-50.
EDWARDS, DAVID
    1961   *An Economic Study of Small Farming in Jamaica*. Kingston: University College of the West Indies.
EISNER, GISELA
    1961   *Jamaica 1830–1930: A Study in Economic Growth*. Manchester, Eng.: Manchester University Press.
INTERNATIONAL BANK FOR RECONSTRUCTION AND DEVELOPMENT
    1952   *The Economic Development of Jamaica*. Baltimore, Md.: The Johns Hopkins Press.
ROBERTS, G. W.
    1956   *The Population of Jamaica*. London: Cambridge University Press.
ROBERTS, G. W., and D. O. MILLS
    1958   *Study of External Migration Affecting Jamaica 1953–1955*. Supplement to *Social and Economic Studies*, Vol. 7, No. 2.
SMITH, M. G.
    1956   *A Report on Labour Supply in Rural Jamaica*. Kingston: Government Printer.
    1960   "Social and Cultural Pluralism," in Vera Rubin, ed., *Social and Cultural Pluralism in the Caribbean*. Annals of the New York Academy of Sciences, Vol. 83, Art. 5, pp. 763-785.
    1961   "The Plural Framework of Jamaican Society." *The British Journal of Sociology*, Vol. 12, No. 3, pp. 249-262.

13

Pitfalls and Progress in the Peruvian Sierra

PAUL L. DOUGHTY[1] *is Assistant Professor of Anthropology at Indiana University, where he also serves on the executive committee of the Latin American Studies Program. During the mid-1950's he spent two and a half years with the American Friends Service Committee's rural community development programs in Mexico and El Salvador, first as a village-level worker and later as a service unit director. He then became a doctoral candidate at Cornell University; his field work for the dissertation entailed living for eighteen months in the district of Huaylas, Ancash, in the Peruvian highlands. In the summer of 1962, Professor Doughty was Director of Area Studies, and also a lecturer, in the Peru Three training program at Cornell (where one of his trainees was Scott Palmer, author of the chapter following this). In December of that year, he became Field Director (and Contractor's Overseas Representative) for a Peace Corps-sponsored study of the impact of the Volunteers on rural development programs in the Peruvian sierra. He spent almost two years in this capacity, and the present chapter is an outgrowth of that experience. Dr. Doughty has published numerous articles in English and Spanish, and is currently completing work on* Huaylas: An Andean District in Search of Progress, *for the Cornell University Press.*

THE PERUVIAN SITUATION

L IKE many countries in the underdeveloped world, Peru is geographically and culturally fragmented. The massive ranges of the Andes have splintered the country into hundreds of valleys and basins. In these isolated areas local cultural differences have developed and persisted. Until recently, millions of Peruvians have lived and died in virtual ignorance of events beyond the walls of their native valley. Indeed, many of them did not even know that they were citizens of Peru. The nation's major cities are far away, both physically and culturally. All but three of them are located along the coastal desert. On the central coast is Lima, the capital,

221

with a population of two million—roughly one fifth the entire population of the country.

Conspiring with these geographic factors are perniciously divisive ethnic ones. The nation is politically and economically controlled by "Caucasian" Peruvians of largely Spanish background who rarely are able to speak any of Peru's indigenous Indian languages, such as Quechua or Aymará. Next in prestige and power come the racially mixed "mestizos," who speak Spanish and often an Indian language. At the bottom of the pyramid are the Indians, largely illiterate, who usually speak only an Indian language. The mestizos identify with the ruling class and often despise the Indians. Bilingual mestizos serve as political, economic, administrative, and cultural mediators between the ruling class and the Indians. Many mestizos exploit the Indians in a variety of ways.[2]

But things are changing in Peru. In the rural areas the number of schools, teachers, and pupils is continually on the increase. The inexpensive transistor radio has leapt over the mountain barriers and given the isolated mountaineers at least the sounds of the outside world: the cha-cha, the roar of the stadium crowds, Radio Havana, and the Voice of America. New roads stimulate geographic mobility, and the rate of internal migration in Peru has grown to enormous proportions in the past ten years. This migration has served to integrate the country socially and culturally to a greater degree than ever before. (Dobyns and Vásquez 1963, Doughty 1963, Mangin 1959 and 1964). There has been a rapid and spontaneous growth of ideas and an anticipation of things to come. The Andean peasants, in becoming aware of the privileges and conditions of life that others enjoy, now feel that they have too long been deprived of many good things which should rightfully be theirs—schools, roads, land, health.

Thus when the first Peace Corps Volunteers arrived in Peru in 1962, they arrived in a situation that was ripe for change. It was a situation characterized by what Homer G. Barnett has called a "conjunction of differences." The new and the old were in confrontation, and people were making choices as to new courses of action. "Innovation," as Barnett has pointed out convincingly, "flourishes in an atmosphere of anticipation of it." And the withholding or withdrawal of something that people believe they have a right to expect, or the denial of something which they have enjoyed in anticipation but not yet realized, can create strong impulses toward social and cultural change (Barnett 1953: 40, 56, 80).

Since the arrival of the Peace Corps there have been two marked phases in Peruvian politics. Prior to July 1963, political power was held by a military junta. This was followed by the popularly elected Belaunde administration which has attempted to launch numerous reforms and development programs. Prominent among the changes being introduced are serious attempts to resolve land tenure problems, to establish effective rural development programs, to institute tax reforms, and to re-establish popular municipal governments—local elections were held in December 1963 for the first time since 1919! To keep in touch with the long-neglected hinterland, the President holds regular meetings with the leaders from various levels within the departments.* As a result, for the first time, national politics and consciousness are penetrating into virtually every Andean valley and hamlet.

THE PEACE CORPS PROGRAM

The first contingent of PCVs arrived under inauspicious circumstances. A military junta had just overthrown the constitutional government and annulled a recently held presidential election. The United States government, not wishing to seem to approve such a departure from constitutionalism, halted much of its foreign aid program in Peru. It also kept the PCVs—who had just finished training—in uncertain limbo for an entire month. Finally, after deliberation, it was decided to initiate the Peace Corps program despite misgivings about working under a military regime.

The Volunteers were received cordially but with restraint. A "wait and see" attitude was adopted by the interested Peruvian agencies as the PCVs were dispersed over the country to begin their assignments. The initial 130 Volunteers were supplemented by the arrival of almost 300 more during the next year. By early 1964 there were PCVs working in towns in virtually every province, and also large groups of them working in the "barriadas," or squatter settlements, in Lima, Arequipa, and Chimbote. The Peace Corps was working with people of all social classes—ex-

---

* A department is roughly equivalent to a state in the United States, but without the political attributes of a legislature or other elected officials. Peruvian departments are further subdivided into provinces and districts.—P.L.D.

cept the national upper class—and at altitudes from sea level to 13,500 feet or more. The programs in which the PCVs participate are varied and include such activities as health and nutrition projects, self-help housing, city planning, social work, university teaching, agriculture, cooperatives, savings and loan associations, land reform, and community development projects.

Volunteer activities in Peru were coordinated and guided by a full-time staff composed of eight members: four in the Lima office and one in each of four regional offices located in Cuzco, Chimbote, Arequipa, and Puno. In addition, the United States Public Health Service assigned three medical doctors to attend to the varied needs of the Volunteers.

Generally, the Volunteers work in collaboration with ongoing programs and agencies, usually under Peruvian government auspices. Yet there are a number of Volunteers working with private agencies such as church groups, clubs, and cooperatives, and still others who work without formal sponsorship by any organization.

The success of the Volunteers on the whole has been most gratifying. Many of them have become respected figures in the communities where they live and work. The impact of the Peace Corps has inspired requests from communities and government agencies for well over five hundred more Volunteers. This demand is difficult to meet.

The successful impact achieved by the Volunteers' programs has not been attained with the ease originally envisioned by many people. In this chapter we will be concerned with an examination of some of the major adversities the PCVs have confronted in the cultural setting of the Andean highlands, or "sierra."

THE VOLUNTEER AS AGENT OF CHANGE

The Volunteers in Peru come from widely differing backgrounds. In age they range from nineteen to seventy. Some have yet to choose their lifetime professions, while others have retired from long careers. Such diversity of background makes generalization difficult. Nonetheless, it is possible to discern a number of important attributes possessed by the vast majority of the PCVs, attributes that spring from shared values and from similar motives for joining in the first place.

One of the most obvious characteristics of the PCVs in Peru— and doubtless everywhere—is their motivation to promote change in the host society. They are dissatisfied with the status quo as they perceive it, particularly in a technological and material sense.

They see in the Peace Corps a movement that has something new and dynamic to offer toward the solution of some of the developing world's pressing problems. Not only this, but the Peace Corps makes it possible for the individual to make a *personal* contribution, to "do something," to "add his little grain of sand," as the Peruvians would put it. And most PCVs would like to leave behind some concrete evidence of their twenty-one months of service in Peru.

The PCVs bring to Peru a variety of valuable skills. For example, in one group of thirty working in the sierra, there were five with extensive agricultural experience and training; three with bachelor's degrees in sociology or anthropology, one of whom was a Ph.D. candidate in the latter; four with backgrounds in cooperatives; six with building trade skills; three teachers; and three with nursing experience. Considered as a group, their fund of knowledge and education surpasses that of their Peruvian counterparts. The PCVs are thus able to make available to Peruvians who solicit their aid a large and varied assortment of new ideas, of new dimensions to the solution of old problems. Among the Volunteers we find a certain "concentration of ideas," to use the words of Barnett (1953: 3, 7, 42), which in combination with their motivation provides a tremendous stimulus for innovative behavior.

Therefore, it is not surprising upon visiting Volunteers that one encounters an amazing variety of exotic contraptions and inventions designed to cope with the rustic conditions in which they live. Notable efforts are expended in the construction of privies (one with a plastic-covered picture window overlooking Lake Titicaca), cavernous fireplaces, dubious running-water systems, and the like. But energies are also expended on devices intended for introduction into the material culture of the host society. In Puno, the great need for a regular supply of irrigation water prompted four Volunteers to begin construction of three different types of windmills for use on the windy Andean plain. Other PCVs attempted to design a potato sorter, low-cost greenhouses, and spinning wheels. Mazelike rabbit hutches made their appearance in the patio or corral of many a Volunteer residence. Another PCV designed a road grader made of railroad rails with a special suspension system to avoid large rocks. And so on.

Another favorable factor is that the PCVs can call upon large and diverse sources of support to backstop their efforts in the field. The Peace Corps staff provides each Volunteer with the field tools of his trade or specialty, and is available for advice and counsel. The PCV may call upon the appropriate member of other United States overseas missions such as AID and its many contract representatives, or the Geodetic Survey team. He also discovers that his access to other experts in the host country is greatly facilitated because of his nationality, connections, and aggressiveness. Finally, aside from these resources within Peru, the Volunteer may write to several United States or international organizations for technical advice.

THE BARRIER OF BUREAUCRACY

Despite all of the above-mentioned favorable factors, innovative progress often moves at a distressingly slow pace. A primary obstacle is the Peruvian bureaucracy (Whyte and Holmberg 1956). For example, a recent study revealed that the employees in the municipality of Lima were working at only *one* per cent of capacity! This incredibly low output was attributed to low pay, bad morale, and poor methods of work and organization. It was noted that this was not the exception but rather the rule in all public offices.[3] In Peruvian bureaucracy, every penny must be counted and recounted. Endless reports are required—in triplicate. Documents and vouchers must be signed by four or five "executives" before a single shovel can be released from the warehouse for a community development project. Authority is rarely delegated on a rational basis. Top executives—even cabinet ministers—must personally sign employees' pay checks, approve vouchers for small purchases, and attend to other minor details of day-to-day administration.

The bureaucracy grows and grows. The government is swamped with applications for government positions from hordes of socially mobile Peruvians eager to gain social classification as "employees" rather than manual laborers.[4] This constant addition of new employees means, of course, that whatever little real responsibility is held by low-level bureaucrats becomes diluted even further.

Since competition for government employment is so keen, fear of losing one's position, once attained, is ever-present. The employee must therefore devote himself to "keeping up his contacts" —the network of relatives, "compadres," and friends who support him in his job. Thus, the Peruvian field director of one development program with which the Peace Corps works, felt it necessary to spend at least five months of the year in Lima defending his position and cultivating friends.

Another result of the intense competition for jobs is that the ministerial employee is likely to shy away from even minor innovations in his work if he sees the slightest chance of failure. As we shall see later, when a group of PCVs tried to start a tourist industry in the Vicos area, the Peruvian personnel of the development program carefully stood to one side, placing all the responsibility on the Volunteers and offering only very limited support. Their specific reason for doing this was a fear of "what the minister would say" if the project failed. In another notable case, the Peruvian administrator of a land reform program initiated an experimental project with the assistance of a PCV. Despite the fact that the program was developing smoothly, the man's superior grew apprehensive and, fearing scandalous publicity if anything misfired, dismissed him from his post. Through the persistence of the Volunteer, the program continued successfully—but it cost the originator of the project his job.

This work situation contrasts markedly with that of the Volunteer, whose motivation, organizational goals, training and resources impel him to be an innovator. The Volunteer has nothing to lose. He can take large risks. Short of causing a major catastrophe, a mistake will not cost him his job. It is therefore not surprising that the great majority of Volunteers identify "red tape" and bureaucratic inefficiency as major obstacles to their work, and a major source of frustration. For the many young Volunteers whose own experience with bureaucratic organizations in the United States is limited, these problems can assume unwarranted proportions. To deal effectively with the local bureaucracy, noted a successful Volunteer, one needs lots of "patience, tact, and persistence." Through the use of his three-point "formula" this Volunteer managed to arrange a project in which three rival government and international agencies collaborated, albeit reluctantly, on the same project.

FACTORS OF STATUS AND PRESTIGE

Of all the attributes possessed by the Volunteer, none is quite as important, at least at the outset of his service, as his United States citizenship, by virtue of which he is automatically ascribed the status of "gringo." Peruvians use this term to refer, nonpejoratively, to fair-skinned* persons from Europe or "North Amer-

* Negro Volunteers were often referred to as "gringos negros," thus providing the sophisticate with a bit of humor.—P.L.D.

ica," that is, the United States or Canada. The Peruvian expectation, quite naturally, is that these new gringos will conform to roles traditionally played by other gringos. The Volunteer, however, often comes to regard the Peruvian expectation with considerable ambivalence. His predecessors in the role of gringo have usually been high-salaried, high-status businessmen, diplomats, or professionals, whose Peruvian associates were of similar backgrounds and thus were members of the technical and governing elites. Since gringos are either admired or despised, the PCVs tend to inherit a stereotype: a pattern of relationship, of status and prestige—as well as potential contacts, both friends and enemies.

Because of the high status accorded to the traditional gringo, the Volunteer is treated with considerable deference—at least initially. He is often ascribed a status that does not correspond to his training or experience, a status that no one in the United States would attribute to him without prior demonstration of his qualifications. When Peruvian counterparts come to recognize that a Volunteer does *not* actually possess the qualifications they had assumed he possessed, they tend to withdraw much of the esteem originally expressed.[5]

This situation is further explained by certain cultural and social phenomena. Peruvian culture, with its hierarchical social system, impels people to seek formal recognition of their socioeconomic position in the form of titles affixed to one's name as a permanent reminder of his status in the society—much like the use of noble titles such as "Sir" or "Lord." Thus, doctors are always called by title; architects and engineers are addressed as such; school teachers are called "normalista," "maestro," "professor," and so forth. In this manner, one's status and title become intimately a part of one's personal identity—as Palmer's evidence in the next chapter will further confirm.

When the Volunteer arrives in a town or rural hamlet, there is much concern over his title. Sometimes the local people will ask him what his title is. On other occasions, people simply assume that he is "Doctor" Roberto or "Engineer" José, and address him accordingly. Because of his artificial prestige, the PCV often finds himself dealing with Peruvians who, under other circumstances and free of the assumed status of their gringo visitor, would have nothing to do with him.

Being placed on an artificial pedestal can be of advantage to the Volunteer as innovator. Because the capabilities, resources, and power of North Americans in Peru are almost legendary, people tend to trust and believe the gringo's advice if it is adequately explained. There are often high expectations, however, that the PCV will perform wonders. The problem of the Volunteer is to strike a balance. He must make intelligent use of his prestige as a gringo. At the same time, he must avoid overbuilding the people's expectations and, above all, avoid letting his prestige separate him from the people he is trying to help. This is not an easy task.

Since the Volunteer is expected to live in the locality where he works, and since much, if not all, Volunteer activity is in close association with members of Peru's lower classes, the "deprestiging" process is initiated, willy-nilly. It is up to the individual Volunteer to decide at what point he wishes to stop. Most PCVs choose to "go native" to a limited degree. In fact, few would be able to lose their identity completely as Americans (even if they so desired) because of language or personal habits. A survey conducted among the first 150 Volunteers in Peru indicated that those judged as most successful by the Peace Corps/Peru staff were those who had retained their cultural identity and perspective, while at the same time making suitable adjustments in their habits. Those who seemed to have made great efforts to "go native" appeared on the whole to be less efficacious in their work *and* were more inclined to be dissatisfied. On the other hand, Volunteers who played the role of the "traditional gringo" proved to be even less satisfactory in their performance.

The extent to which the factor of prestige constitutes an asset or liability depends to a large degree upon the way in which the Volunteer perceives and interprets his role in the community. The subtleties of behavior necessary to deal effectively with Peruvians of different social classes requires considerable sophistication in both thought and action. A brief review of the structure of sierra society will illustrate this point.

CLASS CONFLICT AND THE VOLUNTEER

The people of the Peruvian highland regions are divided into two basic groups, the town-dwelling mestizos and the rural Indians who comprise approximately one third to one half of the total national population (Beals 1953; Vázquez 1961). The mestizo speaks Spanish as his first language (but also often speaks Quechua or some other Indian language), and controls the social, political, and economic life of the region where he lives. In general, he takes advantage of the services offered by the government—education, health, social security, and so on. The Indian, by contrast, is principally Quechua-speaking and does not usually participate in national life. As an illiterate, he does not have the privilege of voting. Although sometimes active as a petty merchant, the Indian is most frequently a low-paid (thirty-five cents daily) farm laborer, often living as a serf on a large estate. He is, in short, excluded from positions of power, be they political, economic, or social.[6]

The pattern of relationships among members of these two groups obliges the Indian to show deference to the mestizo who, reciprocating, demonstrates his superiority (Doughty 1965). Thus, in the presence of Indians, the mestizo will expect to occupy the best facilities. He sits while the Indian stands (or vice versa, whichever is more prestigious in the particular situation) and rides in the front of the truck while the Indian accommodates himself in the back. When meeting his mestizo boss, the Indian doffs his hat, bows, or in some places even kisses the hand of his superior. The Indian is addressed (no matter what his age) as a child by the use of his first name or by the familiar form of address, "tu." The Indian responds by calling the mestizo, "patron" (boss), "taita" (father), "papacito lindo" (beautiful father) or "wiracocha" (white god). This social dichotomy is strengthened by the fact that the Indian is "visible"—not so much because of racial features as because of his general comportment and clothing. His traditional homespun garb is derived from models of Spanish lackey uniforms introduced during colonial times, and as such constitutes an unsavory though quaint reminder of past servitude, overlapping into the present. The mestizo on the other hand attires himself as dictated by current style trends of the modern Western world.

Between these polar extremes in highland society is a large and growing transitional population—the "cholos"—who combine the above-mentioned characteristics in various ways. This group is highly mobile, both socially and geographically. While on one hand they may adopt mestizo attitudes toward the Indians, on the other they are aggressive and hard working.

The PCVs working in the department of Ancash found themselves naturally attracted to persons who had equivalent educational backgrounds and interests. As a result, they tended to develop excellent rapport and relationships with the middle and upper-class mestizos in the provincial and departmental capitals. Some of these Volunteers began to adopt, to a limited degree, the same types of negative attitudes toward Indians and Indian culture that were held by their mestizo friends. As a case study will soon make clear, the Indian population of the community of Vicos, Ancash, with whom the Volunteers were attempting to work, viewed these relationships with suspicion and eventually came to feel that some of the Volunteers were working with the mestizos against their interests.

Quite the opposite was the case in the department of Puno where Volunteers were also working in a similar social situation. Here, as in the department of Ancash, mestizos tended to suspect anybody who worked exclusively with Indians, often accusing them of being "Communists"—that is, people who promote the alteration of the social order. One PCV who was organizing consumer cooperatives among the Indians to help them escape the high prices charged them by mestizo storekeepers, soon found himself the object of anonymous attacks. Adverse rumors were circulated about him in the town, and the mestizos tried to convince the Indians that he was really going to abscond with their money. On fourteen different occasions the Volunteer found the tires of his jeep either deflated or punctured. Far from losing faith in this Volunteer, the Indians, seeing that he was subject to such abuse on their behalf, tended to confide and trust in him even more.

THE LANGUAGE BARRIER: SPANISH IS NOT ENOUGH

A major premise of all Peace Corps work is that the Volunteer will learn the official language of the host country, in this case Spanish. Following intensive language study during their training period, the Volunteers are cast abroad with varying degrees of proficiency. Once in Peru they "pick up the language" through that wonderful osmotic process called "living with the people." Few PCVs have arrived in Peru with a bilingual level of fluency, and few attain it even by the end of their tour. Nevertheless, the great majority do acquire an adequate working knowledge of Spanish and in particular of Peruvian slang and accents. One United States Foreign Service language examiner who administered tests to terminating Volunteers was amazed at their comparatively high level of fluency. Referring to one examination he had given, he remarked that, "If I had closed my eyes while listening to [John] speak, I might have taken him for an Indian from Cuzco." There can be no doubt that an effective control of the language is the major asset of the Volunteer.

In the sierra regions, the Volunteers are confronted with a more complex situation, linguistically as well as socially. There are approximately three million persons residing in the sierra who speak only Quechua or Aymará. Because the typical PCV must spend great effort learning Spanish, he simply cannot find the time necessary to study an autochthonous language, much less master it.[7] Of the hundred or so Volunteers working in the sierra, there were only four or five who could manage even short conversations in Quechua. There is little question, however, but that the vast majority of them would greatly increase their effectiveness if they acquired even a rudimentary speaking knowledge of this language. The success of the Volunteer teacher in Vicos, and of another Volunteer literacy instructor in Ayacucho, was achieved in large part by the ability of these girls to speak some Quechua. Barring this, Volunteers have a difficult time in building intimate contacts and rapport with the Indian community. As we will soon see, the inability to make oneself understood properly was at the root of the crisis in Vicos.

The communication problem can be overcome in part through the use of interpreters. But this technique becomes impersonal; and who can tell how faithfully the interpreter may be translating one's sentiments? While most sierra Volunteers have used this device from time to time, only two acquired the services of a full-time interpreter.

THE MAJOR ENEMY: IMPATIENCE

If I may offer a general opinion, I would say that the greatest single enemy of the PCV in Peru, the greatest obstacle to his effectiveness and personal happiness, is impatience. Most Volunteers fervently desire to launch themselves into their work and are determined to leave behind a measurable contribution. Many arrive in Peru with high expectations and a sense of urgency to accomplish all that they can during their twenty-one months in the country. For these people, encounters with bureaucratic limitations, linguistic barriers, and personality conflicts are demoralizing at best. Continued inability to resolve such problems not only heightens the anguish of frustration but may also radically lower the level of motivation and interest. Naturally, the more mature individuals survive the effects of these irksome stumbling blocks better than the others. These are the people who have, in moments of introspection, thought through their own position, as members of the Peace Corps and as Volunteers in Peru. They are the ones who have acquired a realistic perspective on their potential contributions, both short-run and long-run.

The avid desire to "get down to work" may often eliminate the possibility of developing successful long-term projects. Many Volunteers thus found themselves led into a series of minuscule activities which kept them busy but which formed no part of an over-all plan of action leading to any specific goals.[8] The consequence of this has at times resulted in a series of completed or semicompleted privies, rabbit hutches, and inventions which may or may not be used when the Volunteer departs. Such activities also tend to steer the Volunteer away from organizational types of projects because he comes to rely so heavily upon his personal contribution in order to "finish" the project. This was particularly true in the case of construction projects.[9] Regardless of the nature of the project, however, eager Volunteers often showed little desire to collaborate with, or train, Peruvians in job assignments. This point emerged clearly in interviews with departing PCVs. A substantial percentage of them declared that they would rather work alone or with other Volunteers than with Peruvians—because they either "found it easier," or wished to finish their projects "on time." Here, then, is an attitude contrary to two of the main Peace Corps objectives: meeting the people and helping them to help themselves.

Working with organizations, or working to help people get organizations started, requires infinite time and patience. One must be willing to spend considerable time in rapport-building activities such as fiestas, or in just passing the time of day with one's neighbors. Far from being a "waste of time," however, participation in this type of activity is necessary if the social and educational aspects of Peace Corps goals are to be attained. The many Volunteers who saw this as part of their job and who took the time to do it well, found their efforts amply rewarded and their Peace Corps experience generally more satisfactory.

CRISIS AND EXPULSION AT VICOS

To illustrate a number of the generalizations thus far put forward, let us take the concrete case of the community of Vicos in the department of Ancash. Vicos, a former manor with a population of 2,100, has only a rudimentary "urban" center, most of the population living in homesteads dispersed over its 30,000 or so acres. The first Volunteers arrived in Vicos in October 1962. Their jobs involved close collaboration with the development and research program initiated there in 1952 by the Cornell-Peru Project (Holmberg 1960). Since 1957, the development aspects of this program had been under the direction of the Peruvian Ministry of Labor and Indian Affairs and its agency, the National Plan for Integrating the Aboriginal Population (hereafter, PNIPA). The initial contingent of eleven PCVs moved into quarters provided for them in the community center. Here the Volunteers lived at close quarters with their Peruvian program counterparts: nine school teachers, six members of the PNIPA project, and the Cornell Field Research Director and his wife. As might be expected, relationships among the Peruvian personnel had not always been harmonious over the years, and some disagreements between the PNIPA director and individual members of the staff existed.

It was not long before the Volunteers not only discovered this difficulty, but also developed their own disagreements within the community of outsiders assigned to work at Vicos. Eager to work and leave their mark, the Volunteers seethed at the phlegmatic nature of the program. Soon several of them began to develop their own activities, independent of PNIPA direction. Within their first three months, the Volunteers had formed a clique, living and eating together with minimal contact with their counterparts. The Peruvian personnel for their part perceived the gringos and their proposed assignments with mixed feelings: Are they here to do *our* job? Take over our program? The initial high prestige accorded the Volunteers as gringos was gradually withdrawn by the Peruvian staff as well as by elements in the community as Volunteer projects failed to materialize with the success anticipated and as personal hostilities developed. While the PCVs recognized some of these problems, they were either insensitive to their importance or failed to take adequate steps to eliminate them.

Partly because of their cohesiveness as a group, the Volunteers developed only limited contacts in the broader Vicos community. These relationships were further limited by the lack of effective communication because the majority of Vicosinos speak only rudimentary Spanish, or else none at all. In this situation, several Volunteers found it much easier to develop contacts in the Spanish-speaking mestizo community outside of Vicos.

An Entrepreneurial Adventure

It was through these relationships in the capital that the PCVs were instrumental in securing the purchase by Vicos of a small, adjacent farm that the Vicosinos had long wished to acquire. This property, called Chancos, had formed a part of Vicos until 1933, when it had been sectioned off by its owner (the Public Charity Society of Huaraz) to be rented separately. Remaining attached to the Chancos land as serfs were thirteen families of Vicosinos who since the outset of the Cornell project had wished to rejoin the Vicos community. The Vicosinos were of like mind and thus supported the project to purchase the land and liberate these families from serfdom.

The Volunteers, however, saw another opportunity. (See also Patch 1964.) Chancos was also a popular local resort because of the thermal springs found there, and a small, decrepit hotel catering to visitors. By improving the bathing facilities and rebuilding the hotel and restaurant, a new and potentially substantial source of income could be secured for Vicos. The venture could also provide productive, nonfarm employment for enterprising Vicosinos who might otherwise migrate out of the community.

With this in mind, the Volunteers engineered the purchase of the land, and with it the rental of the hotel and baths.[10] To the Volunteers, this capitalistic venture presented marvelous possibilities for development. They mistakenly assumed, however, that the community would see it in the same way. After much effort at persuasion, the project was reluctantly accepted by the community, many of whose members, it later turned out, had not understood that the profits from the hotel business would go into community coffers. Through Volunteer efforts, two low-interest loans from private sources in the United States were obtained to cover the costs of purchasing the land and improving the hotel. While the key community leaders understood the conditions of the loans, the community-at-large came to believe that they were falling into a great debt[11] and feared that the United States bank which had granted the loan for the hotel might be able to take over their hard-earned right to the lands.

By this time, some ten months after the Chancos project had been conceived and begun, relations between Volunteers and Peruvian staff had, with some notable exceptions, reached a particularly low ebb. Moreover, the nature of the construction work at Chancos had thrust the Volunteers directing the work there into the hated position of "patron" in Vicosino eyes. PCVs found themselves ordering the Indian laborers about, hiring and dismissing personnel, facing labor-management disputes over wages (paid by the Vicos community from the bank loan), and trying to impose a more rigid work day—such as one finds in professional construction projects—on Indians who were not accustomed to it. As fate would have it, the Vicosino selected by the Volunteers as foreman was a man who was *not* in good standing in the community. Moreover, some of the workers who had been dismissed (for being drunk on the job) turned out to be influential men in the community. A difficult and unsatisfactory situation became more complex by the day.

Events then unfolded rapidly. The Cornell Field Director, a Peruvian, had been in the United States for several months. His absence as mediator between the PNIPA personnel, the Volunteers, and the Community gave opportunity for the spread of unfounded rumors and suspicions. The wife of the Field Director, who shared with the Vicosinos many of the misconceptions and misgivings about the hotel project, also nursed a deep personal dislike for some of the Volunteers. Finding support among some members of the PNIPA staff, she abetted the negative rumors about the PCVs and urged the community to withdraw from the project, dismissing the Volunteers at the same time.

The Volunteers Are Expelled

With relatively weak community relations and unable to communicate effectively in Quechua, the Volunteers were at a loss to stem the rising wave of mistrust and fear that spread in the community. The community council met and decided to ask for the suspension of the Chancos Hotel project and withdrawal of the Volunteers at a community assembly the following day. After considerable confused debate, the assembly accepted the recommendation of the council and the Volunteers were withdrawn by the Peace Corps Representative until such time as they might be requested to return.

In this unfortunate series of events we find many of the classic problems which have afflicted economic and community development projects throughout the world. Motivated by the best of intentions, the Volunteers had become enmeshed in the cultural and social conflict between Indians and mestizos so common in the sierra. To a certain degree, this was inevitable. The Volunteers' failure to define successfully their position vis-à-vis the community, and the resulting ambiguities, led the Vicosinos to identify them with the mestizo element who were both feared and mistrusted. Moreover, having to work as "boss" on the construction project reinforced the Indians' view of the Volunteers as "patron."

The hotel development project itself raises a question when

considered in the light of community development procedures. One of the basic assumptions of organizational work is that successful community development projects *must* have the general support and interest of the people in order to succeed. The need for the project must be felt by the majority of community members, and not just by the development worker.[12] The Vicosinos, although supporting the purchase of the Chancos lands and the incorporation of the Chancos serfs into their community, were far from convinced of the necessity of entering the hotel business, incurring additional debts, and entering into contractual arrangements that they did not fully understand. The fact that the money obtained in the loan was handled by the Volunteers created additional misunderstandings and even outright suspicion that the gringos were misappropriating the money. To the Volunteers, such was simply unthinkable, and they had automatically assumed that the people thought likewise. In Peru, however, it is commonplace to suspect the integrity of persons who handle public funds—particularly when the accounting procedures are unclear to the public. For these reasons, the community not only withheld its active support of the project, but eventually came to oppose it upon the urging of disgruntled opponents of the Volunteers. The potential importance of the project—as envisioned by the Volunteers—went unappreciated by the people.

Return to Vicos

In contrast to the grave problems arising over the hotel, the popular program carried out by another Volunteer at Vicos eventually proved to be the key factor which prompted the community to request the return of the Peace Corps. At the request of the community, she had opened a small experimental primary school in an isolated zone of Vicos far from the community's central elementary school. Her program brought an immediate and positive response from the community, which greatly appreciated the school and the affection which she showed toward their children. They also valued her ability to converse with them in Quechua, albeit in limited fashion. Her interest in them *as people* was quickly perceived and reciprocated.

When the Cornell Field Director returned from the United States in an attempt to resolve the problems described in preceding paragraphs, he soon discovered that the people wanted the Volunteer-teacher to return. They had been in complete accord with her work. Further inquiry revealed that the community wanted a second

Volunteer teacher to open another branch school. The community was even ready to support the hotel project—once their questions were answered and they had assured themselves of more direct control over it. These things were done and three weeks after the withdrawal of the Volunteers, the Peace Corps found itself invited back to work—this time directly sponsored by the community.

A BY-PRODUCT: THE PERUVIAN "PEACE CORPS"

One major innovation instituted by the Belaunde regime has been the establishment of an eight-week summer volunteer work program for Peruvian university students. As Palmer will make amply clear in the next chapter, these students often have few constructive outlets for their energies. The Peruvian "Peace Corps" hoped to provide the students with a positive orientation, and to acquaint them with the realities of the country outside of Lima. In its structure and methods, the program bears a strong and not accidental resemblance to the United States Peace Corps. In fact, Peace Corps/Peru staff (including myself) consulted with Peruvian officials in the planning stages and assisted in the training program for the Volunteers, who numbered more than four hundred. In the field, six United States PCVs worked with their Peruvian Volunteer colleagues. The United States Embassy assisted by providing surplus army overcoats and sleeping bags.

The Peruvian Volunteers were assigned according to their academic specialties, which they were supposed to implement in the field. Students lacking technical skills were set to work on minor construction projects, the government providing the tools and materials where necessary. Considering the haste with which the program was arranged (about four months) it was a remarkable and gratifying success—especially in the face of the criticism that it drew from the public. Interestingly enough, this criticism was similar to that heard in the United States during the early Kennedy days when the Peace Corps was just getting started. However, there was one additional element of criticism. As Palmer will point out, Peruvian university students tend to be highly political, and many early critics expressed apprehension that politically minded Peruvian Volunteers would seize every opportunity to "talk politics" to the villagers. Fortunately, this did not occur, except in isolated cases.

It was fascinating to observe the close parallels between the United States and Peruvian Volunteers' experiences in the field. The Peruvian Volunteers, much like their North American counterparts, suffered great trauma—indeed, culture shock—in adjusting to life in isolated communities. Diarrhea, altitude sickness (soroche), fleas, and monotonous diets were common complaints. Like their North American counterparts, they also soon learned a vital lesson, namely that sheer enthusiasm alone was not enough to bring about the successful conclusion of their projects.

CONCLUSIONS

The Peace Corps has met with a gratifying degree of success in Peru. Nonetheless, there is ample room for improvement. The skills and advantages possessed by the typical Volunteer could be put to much more effective social use. While most PCVs have made reasonably good progress in the Spanish language, true effectiveness in the sierra demands that they also command the local Indian language. While the technical preparation and background of the Volunteer is often quite impressive, there remains the important need to program his activities more carefully, and to train him more adequately in the techniques and sensitivity necessary for him to find his proper, effective role in the local sociocultural context. For although the primary problems are not technological but human, the Volunteer is more often more deficient in cultural than in technological knowledge. And it is only the Volunteer who possesses cultural sophistication who is likely to appreciate and put into effect the essential elements of "patience, tact, and persistence."

NOTES

1 Cornell University has carried on anthropological research in Peru for the past 13 years, with financial support from the Carnegie Corporation of New York (Holmberg 1960). Peace Corps/Washington contracted with Cornell to conduct a series of studies on the impact of Peace Corps programs in representative regions of the sierra in 1962–1964. I served as the senior contract representative in Peru and as Research Coordinator of the Cornell-Peru Project, and under this aegis prepared the present chapter. I wish to thank the following people for reading one or more drafts of this chapter: Drs. David H. Andrews and Eileen Maynard, my colleagues in the field; Drs. Allan R. Holmberg and Henry F. Dobyns at Cornell; Dr. Mario C. Vázquez of the Cornell-Peru Project; and Dr. William Mangin, Frank Mankiewicz, and Dr. Samuel Guarnaccia of the Peace Corps staff in Peru and Washington. Needless to add, the opinions and analysis presented are my own, and I accept sole responsibility for them.

2 For a more complete description and analysis of modern Peru, the reader may wish to consult Holmberg 1960, Owens 1963, or Ford 1955.

3 *La Prensa*, Lima. May 8, 1964, p. 10.

4 This is an important consideration. The status difference between the classification of *empleado* (white-collar employee) and *obrero* (laborer) is considerable. The social security system, including hospitals and medical care, pensions, and so forth, is also geared to this classification.

5 I am indebted to Frank Mankiewicz for calling this point to my attention.

6 For a detailed description of the hacienda system and the Indian problem see Vázquez 1961, and Holmberg, et al., 1965.

7 In training the Peru Three contingent in 1962, Cornell University offered instruction in Quechua to some twenty trainees who were already fluent in Spanish. (In training Bolivia Thirteen in 1965, the University of Washington followed a similar policy with respect to Quechua.) For the Peru Volunteers, the learning of Quechua is complicated by the fact that there are at least four dialects of the language spoken in that country.

8 This was much less apt to occur in places where Volunteers had the benefit of effective direction by Peruvian or Peace Corps officials. The Peace Corps staff, however, often found itself shorthanded in administering the large numbers of Volunteers spread over such an extensive and difficult geographic area. Shortwave radios helped to relieve many communication difficulties. The use of a light plane, piloted by licensed staff members, is also proving to be a most efficient administrative tool.

9 Recognizing this problem, the Peace Corps staff in Peru has directed Volunteers away from such projects. Great emphasis is now placed on the social and organizational aspects of development. The number of Volunteers now directly engaged in construction work is probably less than fifteen.

10 While the farm land could be purchased outright, the thermal baths could not, because of a law prohibiting the sale of mineral-bearing lands.

11 The Vicosinos were already purchasing the former hacienda on which they reside. Still remaining to be paid was a loan of approximately one million Peruvian soles (roughly $45,000 US) over a twenty-year period. See Holmberg et al., 1965.

12 For a recent discussion of these points, see Goodenough 1963.

BIBLIOGRAPHY

BARNETT, HOMER G.
1953 *Innovation: The Basis of Cultural Change.* New York: Mc-Graw-Hill.

BEALS, RALPH
1953 "Social Stratification in Latin America." *American Journal of Sociology,* Vol. 58, No. 4, pp. 327-339.

DOBYNS, HENRY F., and MARIO C. VÁSQUEZ, Editors
1963 *Migración e Integración en el Perú.* Lima: Editorial Estudios Andinos, Monografia 2.

DOUGHTY, PAUL L.
1964 "La Migración Provinciana, Regionalismo y el Desarrollo

Local." Lima, *Economia y Agricultura*, Vol. 1, No. 3, pp. 203-212.

1965 "The Interrelationship of Power, Respect, Affection and Rectitude in Vicos, Peru." *American Behavioral Scientist*, Vol. 8, No. 7 (March), pp. 13-17.

FORD, THOMAS
1955 *Man and Land in Peru*. Gainesville, Fla.: University of Florida Press.

GOODENOUGH, WARD HUNT
1963 *Cooperation in Change*. New York: Russell Sage Foundation.

HOLMBERG, ALLAN R.
1960 "Changing Community Attitudes and Values in Peru: A Case Study in Guided Change," in Council on Foreign Relations, *Social Change in Latin America Today*. New York: Vintage Books.

HOLMBERG, ALLAN R., et al.
1965 "The Vicos Case: Peasant Society in Transition." *American Behavioral Scientist*, Vol. 8, No. 7 (March), pp. 3-33.

La Prensa (Lima)
1964 May 8, p. 10.

MANGIN, WILLIAM
1959 "The Role of Regional Associations in the Adaptation of Rural Populations in Peru." *Sociologus*, Vol. 9, pp. 21-36.

1964 *Sociological, Cultural and Political Characteristics of Some Rural Indians and Urban Migrants in Peru*. Paper presented at the symposium on "Cross-Cultural Similarities in the Urbanization Process," sponsored by the Wenner-Gren Foundation for Anthropological Research, Burg Wartenstein, Austria, in September 1964. Dr. Mangin is a former Deputy Peace Corps Representative in Peru.

OWENS, R. J.
1963 *Peru*. London: Oxford University Press.

PATCH, RICHARD W.
1964 "Vicos and the Peace Corps: A Failure in Intercultural Communication." New York: *American Universities Field Staff Reports*. Vol. 11, No. 2.

VÁZQUEZ, MARIO C.
1961 *Hacienda, Peonaje y Servidumbre en los Andes Peruanos*. Lima: Editorial Estudios Andinos, Monografia 1.

WHYTE, WILLIAM FOOTE, and ALLAN R. HOLMBERG
1956 "Human Problems of U.S. Enterprise in Latin America." *Human Organization*, Fall 1956.

14

Expulsion from a Peruvian University

DAVID SCOTT PALMER *received his bachelor's degree in international relations* cum laude, *from Dartmouth College in 1959. During two of the next three years he pursued his academic interest in Latin America, supported by Leadership Grants from the Edward John Noble Foundation. The first year was spent at the University of Chile's Escuela de Ciencias Políticas, during which time Mr. Palmer acquired fluency in Spanish. Then, after an interlude of a year in the international division of a Boston bank, he enrolled in the Hispanic American Studies Program at Stanford University, earning a master's degree in 1962. From there he entered the Peace Corps, serving as Volunteer and later as Volunteer Leader at the University of Huamanga in Ayacucho, Peru; the present chapter is based on that experience. He has since drawn on that experience in serving as visiting lecturer in a Peace Corps training program for Peru at Cornell University. Since 1964 Mr. Palmer has been Assistant Dean of Freshmen at Dartmouth College, where he also serves as Assistant to the Director of Admissions in charge of foreign student applications.*

D URING three short weeks in 1963, a series of events took place at the University of Huamanga in Ayacucho, Peru, which terminated the teaching services of four Peace Corps Volunteers, three of whom had been serving there for more than a year. The four Volunteers had been handpicked for their facility in the Spanish language and their knowledge of Latin American culture and history. And yet, ironically, they were expelled—not for professional incompetence, not primarily for errors in human relations, but basically because they were inadvertently caught up in capricious political currents of great complexity. Their expulsion epitomizes the sort of "unintended consequence" that can befall even the most carefully planned and manned project.

I was one of those four Volunteers. I was intimately involved in the events to be described. This chapter is based on my own observations, and on innumerable talks with students, professors, and administrators at Huamanga, with local officials and townspeople in

243

Ayacucho, and with Peace Corps Volunteers and staff concerned. I have made full use of my collection of most of the relevant documents and published materials that bear on the case. In order to achieve perspective and objectivity, however, I purposely waited several months before doing the actual writing. After my term as a Volunteer was finished, I spent several weeks in Peru assembling the facts and writing the first draft of this chapter.

For one who has specialized in Latin American Studies in graduate school, it was not, of course, a pleasant experience to be expelled from a teaching position in a Latin American university. If this chapter succeeds in imparting to the reader some of the insights that, I hope, the experience has given to me, I shall feel rewarded.

THE UNIVERSITY

The University of Huamanga is located in the isolated town of Ayacucho, which nestles in a dry Andean valley at an elevation of more than 9,000 feet. Ayacucho is the capital of a department of the same name, with a population of somewhat over 500,000, a large proportion of whom speak only Quechua and are little touched by the outside influences of the Spanish tradition. So isolated is this state, and so economically stagnant, that in recent times the name Ayacucho—which incidentally means "corner of the dead" in Quechua—has become practically synonymous with backwardness.

The University of Huamanga first opened its doors in 1704, under the auspices of the Catholic Church. In 1886, because of the economic stagnation of the region and the prostration of Peru that resulted from losing the War of the Pacific to Chile, the doors were closed, and remained closed for two generations. Then, after some fifteen years of negotiations by high school students, townspeople, and National Congress representatives, the university was legally reconstituted by the central government. The doors swung open again at the beginning of the academic year in March 1959, with a staff of some 20 professors and 150 students. The student body now numbers some 500, of which about seventy per cent come from the department of Ayacucho.

Heroic Attempts at Innovation

The first Rector (or President) of the re-established university was Dr. Fernando Romero, a well-known and respected leader in Peruvian education. He was a man of creative vision, determined to introduce innovations of a truly heroic nature. He was dedicated to the creation of a new Huamanga which would become a landmark,

towering high above the level of dreary mediocrity that unfortunately characterizes the majority of Latin American universities.
Surrounding himself with capable men, he worked prodigiously to
implement his dream. The importance that he, his contemporaries,
and his successors attached to the need for an institution that could
resist the strongest winds of adversity is one of the fundamental
themes underlying this case study.

Under Dr. Romero's leadership, the University of Huamanga set
out to implement several specific goals, each designed to remedy a
problem typical of Peruvian universities. Among these were the
following:

1. Programs of study closely related to the needs of the local area,
and geared to its socioeconomic modernization.

2. Full-time, responsible professors.

3. A student body whose principal role would be educational, not
political.

4. Student responsibility in university government.

5. Rejection of the student strike as a means of satisfying
demands.

6. The meticulous investment of government funds.[1]

7. University autonomy.[2]

8. The elimination of "influence" to obtain admission or position.

9. The absolute priority of the "university spirit" over the interests of individuals or groups within the university.

It is extremely difficult for the North American reader with a
United States university education to appreciate just how heroic a
departure the new University of Huamanga represents. One brief
quotation will begin to suggest its magnitude. A North American
ex-professor from the University of Cuzco contrasts Huamanga with
his own university in the following fashion:

> At Cuzco no professors are full-time, a student may cut as many classes
> as he desires, and this applies to professors as well. Politics is the central
> theme; jobs are provided through favoritism; there are no office
> hours; . . .

Evidence is abundant to show that the new Huamanga has indeed
been able to build a scholastic and administrative structure well
above the Latin American norm in several important ways. For
example, a liberal-arts type course of instruction, appropriately
called the "Basic Cycle," is taken by all first-year students. Its
primary purpose is to provide all aspiring professionals with a broad

base before they begin to specialize. Furthermore, the eight institutes of special study making up the three faculties of the university were carefully designed to meet the pressing needs of Ayacucho: Anthropology, Social Service, and Education in the Faculty of Social Sciences; Biology, and Nursing and Obstetrics in the Faculty of Natural Sciences; Mining, Chemical, and Agricultural Engineering in the Faculty of Engineering. There is NO school of law—and thus the university has avoided providing what has traditionally been a base for politicking.

The university engages as many professors as possible on a full-time basis. In 1963 this was 90 per cent of some sixty-odd professors. As full-time professors, they are not allowed to hold another remunerative position at the same time, and they are required to be in their offices a certain number of hours each week for consultations with students. If a professor fails to meet his classes without a justifiable reason, his salary is accordingly reduced.

A number of major innovations have been attempted with regard to the student body. University law states that a strike is not a legal means of achieving student objectives. All lost days are supposed to be made up over weekends and holidays. Students absent from more than 30 per cent of their classes fail that course for the semester. Failure of a student to maintain a minimum average for two consecutive semesters results in his separation from the university. During at least one year, letters requesting special consideration in the admission of students by virtue of friendship or influence were posted in a conspicuous place for the express purpose of embarrassing their authors. To give the students a maximum of opportunity to study without having to worry about material needs, there is a full-time director of student welfare who is in charge of a student dining hall and residence where students pay a total of fourteen dollars a month for room and board. Professors and employees alike contribute to a special fund to provide the best and most needy students with scholarships for room, board, and books. Tuition, formerly twenty dollars a year, is now free—thanks to Congressional reform of the national university law.

University funds are determined yearly by Congress; unfortunately, their allocation often depends upon political factors. Huamanga, which had rejected all political influence, had few partisans in Congress and thereby found itself in grave danger. However, because of the prestige which Huamanga almost immediately achieved (and because of the efforts of the senators from Ayacucho), Congress has allocated to Huamanga more funds per student than to any other university in the country. In order to gain some degree of economic independence, Huamanga has obtained several income-producing properties, as well as important contributions from international organizations. Huamanga has been among the few institutions which have invited government inspectors to check their accounts each year.

Obstacles and Inertia

Despite all the assets just outlined, the rejuvenated university has had to face serious obstacles. Many of these were inherent in what might be called a general social inertia. The 70 per cent of the students who come from the department of Ayacucho suffer from an endemic inadequacy of preparation at the elementary and secondary levels. These students are unable to advance at the same rate as the 30 per cent of the students who come from other, more advanced areas of Peru.

Attempts to rebuild the curriculum so as more nearly to meet the socioeconomic needs of the region are beset with cultural obstacles. The most needed fields, social service and nursing, have attracted pitifully few students. Here, as throughout Peru, hospitals are few and generally poorly maintained. Social workers are even fewer. Youth has few models on which to base career aspirations in the social services.

In addition, politics has reared its ugly head, all institutional efforts notwithstanding. Ambitious professors have not been unknown to take advantage of uninformed, naive students to advance their own careers. Students have gone on strike and then failed to make up the days lost. As will soon become clear, the greatest single obstacle to progress at Huamanga is the intense, irrational, and often irrelevant type of politics that goes on there.

STUDENTS, POLITICS, AND POWER

In order to understand the case study presented in this chapter, it is first necessary to look at the peculiar political role of the students. At Huamanga, as generally in Latin American universities, the students possess two weapons not commonly found at a North American university: co-government and the strike.

Under the terms of co-government as practiced at Huamanga since July 1962, students comprise one third of the voting membership of every policy body in the university.[3] This is a far cry from the relatively feeble forms of "student government" often found on North American university campuses. It means that the students actually possess a powerful weapon to use in bringing their influence directly to bear upon the most basic of policy questions, such as the university budget and the appointment of top administrative authorities.

When they feel frustrated in exercising their influence through co-government, Latin American students not infrequently resort to the strike. The strike is the most extreme measure by which the students can peacefully protest their dissatisfactions. And it is important to realize that Latin American culture actually *encourages* the student to engage in social protest—for there is a tradition tracing back to medieval Spain that defines the university student not only as someone who studies but also as someone who protests against social evils. The culture designates the university as a haven where critics may flourish—and make themselves heard. Moreover, the students are culturally expected to criticize not only the university itself but the entire society. This tradition also explains the sacred principle of the inviolability of the Latin American university by the police or military.

To be a student in a Latin American university, therefore, it is necessary in effect to play three different, and often conflicting, roles. First, one must study. One is expected to become, at state expense, a trained professional dedicated to elevating himself and his community. Second, the student has a role of administrative responsibility; within the administration, he helps make decisions that determine the future course of the university. Third, the student plays a role of dissent. In the best Latin American tradition, the university is the fortress from which his protest is launched. The sources of role conflict are obvious. As legislator, the student helps make policy that affects the content of the subjects he is going to study. As dissident, he might find himself striking against an organization he is helping to run.

Role conflict is especially likely to occur at Huamanga. The students who come from Ayacucho are coping commendably with their problems; nonetheless, honesty requires adding the observation that they are generally ignorant of sophisticated intellectual matters. They have a limited point of view regarding themselves and the world. Moreover, they suffer from a scarcity of books, and from pedagogical methods that rely on the memorization of class lectures. They are thus conditioned to respond to immediate oral stimuli, rather than encouraged to dig patiently for the truth in books, periodicals, and other written materials. These influences combine to produce a type of student who falls easy prey to sophisticated, articulate student leaders and faculty members, who usually come from outside Ayacucho.

Role conflict is further exacerbated by the appeals of communism. These are several: (1) communism is a total, though simplistic, view of the world; (2) it portrays a decadent capitalist society which in many ways resembles that of Ayacucho; (3) it advances a convincing theory of a type of imperialism not too dissimilar from that which the students believe is active in their country; (4) it includes a strong emotional element and a record of protest and persecution.

Communism's grip on the interest and idealism of Ayacucho students is, ironically enough, in a sense abetted by Catholicism. For Ayacucho's students grew up under Catholicism but are now largely rejecting it, or rejecting at least the local clergy, many of whom tend to be quite tied to outdated traditions. As Huamanga's students assume their role of protest, they tend to fall away from the Church even more, and to search for another, equally all-encompassing explanation of life. It is thus the very all-encompassing nature of communism that makes it so attractive to many Huamanga students, who adopt its framework and then attempt to fit—or stuff—all facts into that framework.

ARRIVAL OF THE PEACE CORPS

In early 1962, Rector Romero, in the name of the University Council, requested several Volunteers from the Peace Corps, including three teachers of English. While these Volunteers were in training at Cornell University and in Puerto Rico in the summer of 1962, events were taking place at Huamanga and in Peru that were to affect them seriously.

In May, a new statute to govern the university was approved by the University Assembly.[4] For the first time, it provided for co-government, as described earlier. Students would now comprise one third of the voting members of the University Council and of each Institute and Faculty Council. A majority of these student delegates would almost inevitably be hostile to the presence of the Peace Corps, since the "Revolutionary Students' Front," a diverse union of Communist and far-Left groups,[5] had always dominated student affairs.

In June, another portentious event occurred. Rector Romero resigned. Thus one of the principal supporters of the request for Peace Corps teachers was gone before the PCVs arrived. He was also one of the men most dedicated to the ideals of the reborn university.

In July, another blow fell. A military junta overthrew constitutional government in Peru shortly after national elections. The United States demonstrated its displeasure by temporarily suspending diplomatic relations. As a result, there was a considerable delay before the Volunteers entered Peru. The three PCVs assigned to teach English at Huamanga, who had originally been scheduled to arrive at the beginning of the second semester, arrived seven weeks late.

The three Volunteers assigned to Huamanga had been carefully chosen by the Peace Corps staff. One was a recent Princeton graduate in political science, who had spent summers in Mexico. The second had a bachelor's degree from Dartmouth in international relations, a year of graduate study at the University of Chile, and a master's degree from Stanford in Hispanic American Studies. The third had a B.A. in Education from Seattle University, a master's degree in Central American History from San Carlos in Guatemala, and had taught English in a Guatemalan labor-union school. All three spoke fluent Spanish. On the basis of qualifications alone, prospects looked good.

OFF TO A GOOD START

Personal relations between the Volunteer teachers and the rest of the university community appeared to get off to a good start. The Volunteers ate at a faculty restaurant, played basketball with students and their fellow professors, had periodic folk music gatherings with students, and spent long hours with their new acquaintances over coffee.

Professionally, too, things moved swiftly and well. As it happened, one of the two expatriate English teachers had to go to Lima for medical reasons, and turned her classes over to the Peace Corps teachers within a week after their arrival. The other expatriate divided up his largest English class soon thereafter.

The major problems involved in teaching English at the university were immediately apparent. To handle 400 students, there were just the two expatriate professors. (Neither of them, incidentally, was from the United States.) English, although required of all students, was taught only two hours a week. Some sections were altogether too large, with up to seventy students. Furthermore, classes were formed on the basis of the student's academic year and specialty of study—not on the basis of his level of proficiency in English. And the standard method of teaching was sheer translation. Thus, during an academic year, the chemistry students simply translated a chemistry text from the English, the anthropology students an anthropology text, and so forth. At best it was a tedious, boring exercise of little profit to the students. Indeed, the method tended to discourage, rather than stimulate, serious interest in learning the language.

The principal task of the newcomers was to collaborate with the two regular expatriate language professors in the establishment of an effective English teaching system. The Volunteers' first three months on the job coincided with the last three months of the 1962 academic year. During this period, lengthy discussions were held within the English Department, aimed at working out a feasible program to be introduced at the outset of the next academic year in March 1963.

INTERNATIONAL POLITICS INTRUDES

The subject of international politics was almost never broached until the confrontation in October between Kennedy and Khrushchev over Soviet missile bases in Cuba. For the duration of this crisis, the Peace Corps teachers found themselves in continual discussion with students and faculty—but always outside the classroom. On several occasions they were surrounded in the central plaza of Ayacucho by students who had been listening to the latest developments over Radio Havana, and who asked many pointed, but usually intelligent, questions. On the streets appeared a flyer, issued by the Students' Revolutionary Front, that was highly critical of United States foreign policy and included a reference to "the ill-named 'Peace Corps'." When a Peace Corps staff member visited Ayacucho at the height of the crisis, about one hundred students marched past his hotel shouting, "Peace Corps, War Corps," and, "Cuba, Yes! Yankees, No!" A group of them discussed with a professor their plans to request that the Peace Corps leave Huamanga. However, the professor was able to convince them to desist by arguing that they lacked sufficient grounds for their demand.

For the first time, the Volunteers in Ayacucho were made keenly aware of the widespread though latent hostility toward the United States and its foreign policy about which the new Rector, lawyer-anthropologist Dr. Ephrain Morote, had earlier warned them. They now understood why he had meticulously insisted on treating the Peace Corps instructors no differently from any other regular faculty member.

FURTHER PROFESSIONAL PROGRESS

During the Peruvian summer of January and February, 1963, a summer school at the university gave the English Department its first chance to experiment with a new teaching program. More than one hundred students and townspeople enrolled in English classes. With regular professors unavailable, the Director of the Summer Program authorized a request for two additional Peace Corps teachers for the duration of the course.

For the first time an oral method[6] was employed in the teaching of English. Classes were divided into levels on the basis of the actual proficiency of the student, with a maximum of twenty in each class. As the six-week intensive course drew to a close, both the students and the Volunteer teachers agreed that the new system was a good one, and that it should become a permanent part of language teaching program in the university.

Sixty-seven students received certificates of completion of the intensive course at a ceremony officiated by Rector Morote and several members of the University Council. In a short program, students played and sang North American folk songs and danced a few squares that the Volunteers had taught them. While congratulating the PCVs the next day, one of the University Council members remarked, "You have given us much food for thought—especially concerning the degree to which the Peace Corps has penetrated our community . . . ."

The new academic year opened in March 1963, and the semester and a half which followed were marked by important professional successes. All three faculties accepted the basic changes in the teaching of English that had been employed during the summer school. The University Council established a semiautonomous Department of Native and Foreign Languages, whose chairman, a North American professional linguist, gave the pedagogical innovations his strong political and professional support. This new department coordinated the introduction of the new system, in which the Volunteer teachers were assigned the role of "Aggregate Professors." This was a special classification, established in order to fit the Volunteers into the university framework. The question of status had been a sensitive one almost since the PCVs' arrival. The previous December, a member of the Representative staff had made a personal appearance before the University Council and, somewhat tactlessly and impatiently, requested that the status of the Peace Corps teachers be worked out. Unfortunately, this did not create a good impression.

The proper introduction and implementation of the new English teaching program required considerable extra work by the members of the new department. Special examinations had to be given to all students to place them in classes geared to their level of proficiency. A teaching schedule had to be arranged to accommodate them at hours when all members of a given level were free. As a result, classes ran at intermittent hours from 7:00 A.M. to 8:00 P.M. Many students had trouble adjusting to the new methods. About one third of the final grades at the end of the first semester were failing ones— an abnormally high rate. From their comments, however, there was no doubt that the majority of the students approved of the new system.

During the second semester of 1963, far fewer organizational and teaching problems were encountered. It was a time, rather, of trimming up and insuring the permanence of the innovations. Special classes for the faculty were offered. Upon the recommendation of the Dean of the Faculty of Social Sciences, an accelerated English course was offered to outstanding students who were thought to have a chance to obtain graduate scholarships for study abroad.

ACADEMIC JEALOUSY AND POLITICS

The greatest frustrations for the PCVs during this period were of a purely nonprofessional nature. One of these was the growth of a serious rift in the new Department of Native and Foreign Languages. In the course of the 1963 academic year, the regular professors of the department came to resent what they considered to be a Peace Corps "takeover." They perceived the new English teaching program as too much in the nature of a *fait accompli* for their taste. In all probability they felt a deep ambivalence: on the one hand, they agreed that the new system was more effective than the old; on the other hand, they resented the outsiders who so quickly took the leadership in making these necessary changes. On one occasion, they expressed this ambivalence clearly: they elected Volunteers to positions within the department, but then criticized them for their role of responsibility. On another occasion, they succeeded in annulling the election of a PCV as delegate from the department to the Directive Council of Freshmen. They argued that the Volunteer did not have official university status and was not qualified to represent those who did—and the University Council agreed. Under circumstances such as these, it became very difficult to work smoothly together.

One social event occurred that illustrates nicely how a PCV's very success in relating to people can have adverse political ramifications. The event was a birthday celebration for one of the Volunteers, at which a large number of student and faculty friends played guitars and danced until the small hours of the morning. As a result of the "good" relationships evidenced, some professors became disturbed by what they felt to be excessive faculty-student fraternization. The proper "social distance" had not been maintained. To make matters worse, some students later claimed that the presence at the party of certain professors known for their leftist sentiments was proof that they had deserted their principles and become "gringo lovers."

On another occasion, there was a formal reception offered by the university at the Rector's home. Two of the Volunteers attended, even though they had not received the customary formal invitations. They simply assumed that the Rector had wanted them to attend, but that through an oversight no invitations had been delivered to them. They believed that the oversight was either purely accidental, or else that it was deliberate on the part of the new Secretary-General of the university, a Marxist who had been going far out of his way to cause difficulty for the PCVs.[7] One of the ways in which the Secretary-General had been harrassing the PCVs was by failing to send them official university communications, and forbidding them to pick up their mail at the university. It therefore seemed somewhat logical to suspect that this man had deliberately prevented the PCVs from receiving their formal invitations. Unfortunately, however, the Volunteers were in error. The Rector had *not* intended to invite them, and was therefore highly perturbed by what he rightfully considered to be an intrusion.

INTERNATIONAL POLITICS INTRUDES AGAIN

In September 1963, the Faculty Director of Freshmen invited a Volunteer to give three lectures to 150 freshmen on the subject of United States-Latin American relations as part of a regular social science course. The Volunteer supplemented his lecture by handing out several mimeographed pages of basic information, such as important quotations and economic data about United States investments and trade relations in Latin America. All of the data came from such basic sources as the Organization of American States, the United Nations, and the United States Department of Commerce.

Unfortunately, questions and commentary by the students indicated that they interpreted lectures by a North American on a subject such as this as an overt attempt to present a defense of United States foreign policy in the classroom. A group of them even invited one of the prominent leftist student spokesmen to attend the lectures and help direct the questioning. It seemed that, for many of the students, academic considerations were secondary. To them, the important factor was not, apparently, that the lecturer held an advanced degree in Hispanic-American Studies and was hence presumably qualified but rather that he was a North American and a member of an official United States government organization. Therefore, they reasoned, he *had* to be biased.

A few days later, a faculty member[8] presented to the University Council the data sheets that the lecturer had handed out, as evidence that the Peace Corps was introducing "political propaganda" into the classroom. A commission set up to investigate the matter cleared the PCV of the charge. In retrospect, however, it seems evident that these lectures served as the catalyst that hardened opinion against the Volunteers among extremist students and faculty, leading them actively to seek the Volunteers' ouster.

A most disagreeable event during this period clearly showed the difficulties involved when an individual opposed to the Peace Corps occupies an important post. The three Volunteer English instructors received copies of a University Council resolution (taken several months previously) concerning their status. It contained a very disparaging clause prohibiting their engagement in "political" activities. Upon investigating the matter with other university authorities, it became clear that this was a personal interpretation inserted by the Secretary-General while in the process of transmitting the resolution. Although the Rector reprimanded the Secretary-General and immediately ordered that the correct version be distributed, this event confirmed the Volunteers' suspicions that this official had been responsible for many of the difficulties they had been experiencing.

THE CRISIS

Although the Peace Corps instructors were aware of the incidents and pressures building up in apparently isolated fashion, they failed to attach enough significance to these foreboding signs. Thus, they encouraged efforts to bring two new Volunteer instructors to the university. In one case, a highly qualified chemist was actually requested by the University Council and began to teach early in October. Another Volunteer, a biologist, started to work as an informal research assistant, but did not enter the classroom. The inappropriate timing of these efforts to increase the number of PCVs at Huamanga certainly contributed to an increase in tensions.

Thus the stage was set for a complex series of events which began to unfold on October 14, 1963, and which led, three weeks later, to the expulsion of all the PCVs from the university.

The Fuse Is Lit

The incident which touched off the crisis was a relatively minor one, involving a PCV who will be known here as [Jane Wilson], the sole woman Volunteer at Huamanga. Miss Wilson, like her Peace Corps colleagues, was feeling the stress of the situation. On October 14, she was teaching one of her freshman classes, the one she usually found most difficult to handle, and on this day it was unusually difficult. Incredibly enough, she found herself ushering a recalcitrant girl freshman out of the classroom by the arm and administering two light pats on the student's bottom in the process. (The accepted procedure in such a situation would have been to leave the class and report the disobedience immediately.) Next day there appeared on the Student Federation bulletin board a letter signed by the aggrieved student, protesting this insult to her "physical and moral integrity," and requesting just satisfaction. Miss Wilson sent a note of apology to the student and a brief report of the incident to the Faculty Director of Freshmen. She assumed that this would resolve the situation. But the student leaders had other ideas. And although the girl said she was satisfied with the apology, she indicated that the situation was now "out of her hands."

The Rector grasped the implications immediately, and requested Miss Wilson's resignation in order to keep the crisis from spreading. He feared that "certain groups" were maneuvering for the removal of all PCVs from the university by establishing a case to present to the National Student Congress. (This Congress, scheduled to meet in Ayacucho at the end of the month, would be attended by student delegates from all universities in Peru.) The Rector felt he could cut student demands short if he had in hand the resignation of the PCV directly involved. Miss Wilson, realizing that she had made a serious mistake, accepted the Rector's judgment and reluctantly submitted her resignation on October 17.

The Chain Reaction Gathers Momentum

Student meetings were held to discuss the incident, and they took on unexpected dimensions. A freshmen assembly merely requested that Miss Wilson no longer teach English to first-year students. An assembly of all student delegates voted that Miss Wilson be removed. This assembly was dominated by members of the Students' Revolutionary Front, who resorted to the extreme stratagem of refusing to make available a copy of Miss Wilson's statement of her own interpretation of the incident—even when independent student delegates demanded to hear the statement. Although this procedure was not equitable, it was certainly understandable, and even predictable, in the light of the Revolutionary Front's radical ideological tendencies.

What was not predictable, however, was the extreme stand taken by delegates from the University Reform Front. This minority group, though vociferous, is ideologically moderate. It is allied with the reformist Aprista movement.[9] Yet, oddly enough, the Reform Front placed themselves in the vanguard of the attack on the Peace Corps. The Communists in the Revolutionary Front apparently came to the conclusion that the Reform Front was attempting to achieve several tactical objectives: to drive a wedge between the Student Federation and the University Council;[10] to gather support in upcoming student-body elections; and to create a chaotic situation in Ayacucho in order to force cancellation or postponement of the National Student Congress, at which they would be greatly outnumbered. Thus, the extremist majority found itself in the unaccustomed position of having to shout at least as loudly as its moderate opposition!

On October 18, the day after Miss Wilson resigned, the Revolutionary Front circulated a flyer accusing her of having violated the United Nations Universal Declaration of Human Rights. She was alleged to have violated Article 5, which provides that "no person shall be subject to torture nor to cruel, inhuman, or degrading treatment or punishment." The flyer went on to request the immediate separation of *all* Peace Corps Volunteers at Huamanga! It should be emphasized that there was *no* criticism of the other Volunteers, either as individuals or as teachers. It was simply a matter of guilt by association.

On October 21, the General Student Assembly held a meeting. Several hundred students attended. A few students publicly attempted to defend the PCVs, among them the freshman girl responsible for the original protest. But these speakers were shouted down. Spokesmen for the majority took the line that the Volunteer instructors were representatives of a political arm of United States foreign policy, and hence were dedicated to a campaign of slowing down the inevitable revolutionary process incubating in all Latin American universities, including Huamanga. A final vote was taken by show of hands. All but twenty of the several hundred students present voted to declare a student strike unless all of the PCVs withdrew from Huamanga within forty-eight hours.

Radicalism Despite Ambivalence

The overwhelming vote favoring expulsion of the PCVs would seem to indicate that almost all the students agreed with the analysis presented by the student leaders. However, the next day so many students approached the PCVs expressing their opposition to the decision that the Volunteers came to other conclusions.

It seems clear that many of the students were torn by ambivalence. Ideologically, they viewed North American institutions—public or private, State Department or International Petroleum Company—with deep suspicion. Personally, they looked upon North American "people"—including those they knew best, the Volunteers at Huamanga—as warm friends. Psychologically, it must have been extremely difficult for these students to equate suspect institutions with personable people. The crisis situation forced them to define the situation primarily in terms of one or the other, institutions or people—and they opted for institutions. Professionally, there was no criticism of the Volunteers; even some of the leaders of the ouster movement admitted that the PCVs were among the best teachers at Huamanga. Finally, it seems probable that many students were acting out of fear—fear of expressing their true sentiments when confronted with an emotionally charged situation, with leaders who presented a "popular" view, and with a visible vote by show of hands. "They're our leaders; let *them* take the responsibility," was an often expressed viewpoint. They preferred to be sheep than shown up.

The University Council met the following evening, October 22, to consider the resignation of Miss Wilson and requests by the other Volunteers for clarification of their status in view of the student resolution. The Council did not accept Miss Wilson's resignation. Instead, it fired her outright, hoping thereby to placate the students and thus bring the whole matter to a close. The Council did not consider the other PCVs' requests for clarification of their status, but it did form a Committee of Conciliation to deal directly with the student representatives.

The Extremes Are Reached

The Committee on Conciliation labored assiduously to work out a compromise, but to no avail. The next day, October 23, the General Student Assembly again met and this time voted to begin an indefinite strike—"to the last consequences."

Hearing this, the University Council that same evening resigned en masse. They resigned NOT in support of the Peace Corps, but in defense of the principle of university authority and in opposition to the student body's having "generalized an individual act."[11] As if matters were not already quixotic enough, the Faculty Councils and the University Assembly—who are empowered to consider such actions—refused to accept the resignations. Instead, they gave the University Council a vote of confidence on the eve of the National Student Congress. (The only members who indicated lack of confidence were the Apristas.)

The Huamanga students, faced with these decisions and with the impossibility of convening the National Student Congress in Ayacucho if they were on strike, voted to go back to class until after the termination of the Congress. If no action had been taken by that time, they affirmed, they would go on indefinite strike once again, "for the offense committed by the 'Peace Corps' against the moral and material integrity of the University of Huamanga student body."[12] The transition from individual to institutional guilt was now complete. Leaders, both faculty[13] and student, had successfully polarized student opinion behind their factional objectives: the Apristas, for tactical reasons; the Communists, for ideological ones. The Communists believed it especially important to present the Peace Corps issue before the National Student Congress in order to get the University Council out of a difficult situation. By elevating the problem to the national plane, they reasoned, the Huamanga University Council would cease to view it as an internal problem that it felt responsible to resolve.

This was, in effect, exactly what happened. Although the four days of the Congress[14] were filled with discussion of such problems as peasant invasions, the nuclear agreement, the conflict between Moscow and Peking, and disputes between the Communist majority and the Aprista minority,[15] a stand on the issue of the Peace Corps was taken only on the final evening, Wednesday, October 30. The Congress resolved unanimously[16] to declare a *national* student strike if the Peace Corps instructors were not removed from the University of Huamanga within seventy-two hours. The student bodies of the other institutions were to decide for themselves what positions to take with regard to PCVs teaching in their respective universities.

Early the following morning, the University Council summoned the Peace Corps instructors to urge that they present their resignations: an about face from the Council's stand a week earlier. They argued that, since the National Student Congress had taken a stand against the Peace Corps and NOT the university, the University Council could no longer be obligated to defend the individual members of the faculty who were also members of the Peace Corps. The Council members also expressed their fear that the Apristas were attempting to force them into a position of resistance to the Student Congress resolution, which would provoke a national student strike and, most probably, their own "irrevocable" resignations. They believed that the Apristas, as a minority among the students and the executive branch of the national government, were attempting to foment dissension that they could subsequently turn to their own advantage.

NEGOTIATION, SACRIFICE, AND SETTLEMENT

The Volunteer instructors refused to consider resigning. They believed the student demands to be unjust. To resign under such pressure would appear to be an admission of guilt, would adversely affect the university's hard-fought battle in defense of the principle of authority, and would jeopardize the position of the twenty-odd Peace Corps Volunteers then teaching in other Peruvian universities. Nevertheless, they accepted a compromise suggested by Rector Morote, under which the University Council would send a representative, with full powers, to Lima to negotiate with the Peace Corps Representative. This person and two of the PCVs then proceeded to Lima to meet the Peace Corps Representative.

Unfortunately, while one settlement was being worked out in Lima, the University Council was reaching another in Ayacucho. Communications difficulties contributed greatly to a complete lack of coordination of efforts.[17]

In Lima, the Peace Corps Representative wanted the PCVs to remain at Huamanga at least until the end of the academic year to avoid placing the Peace Corps in an unfavorable light. At the same time, he and the other participants in the negotiations wanted to adhere to the basic principle that Volunteers be withdrawn whenever the requesting organization no longer needs or wants their services; but all believed that the semester was too far advanced to find adequate replacements. The Lima group reached an agreement to this effect, and a concise letter was sent to Ayacucho.

In Ayacucho, however, the University Council considered only that part of the letter which stated that the PCVs would be removed when the University could find replacements for them. They proceeded to ask a newly arrived faculty member—a ceramicist—if he would teach English! The Lima group sent back a very explicit statement that the Peace Corps Representative was not prepared to accept the immediate removal of the Volunteers, as well as an agreement with the new President of the Peruvian Student Federation tacitly accepting the PCVs' continuance at Huamanga. These efforts, however, came to nought. On November 4, the University Council met and formally decided to terminate the services of the PCVs and to request their class lists and grades within a week.

Although the university justified its decision by stating that replacement professors had been found, this was actually not the case. The class of the Volunteer chemistry instructor was suspended. The classes of the PCV English teachers were simply parceled out among the regular members of the department; needless to add, the ceramicist assumed no English teaching duties. The University Council's justification was, therefore, a euphemism which pointed up the fact that, in this case, high principle was secondary to intra-university realities of student intransigence and fear of a minority plot.

THE AFTERMATH

With the decision taken, there was an attempt by all parties concerned to adjust to the new reality. On the one hand, the Peace Corps wished to avoid similar incidents in other universities and the appearance of a major setback. On the other hand, the university wanted to avoid tarnishing its newly acquired national and international prestige, important for obtaining an adequate budget from the Peruvian Congress and significant financial assistance from abroad. In order to refute the adverse publicity in Lima newspapers, the Rector inserted in leading dailies a statement of his interpretation of the events.

Within ten days of the University Council's decision, the Rector asked the Volunteer ex-instructors to assist in translating some university documents, with full access to university facilities. After the tragic assassination of President Kennedy on November 22, he made the university auditorium available to the Volunteers and other American residents of Ayacucho for a memorial service.

The Peace Corps staff, still smarting from the injustices of the incident and what they considered to be inaccuracies in the Rector's declarations, had two main choices of action open. Either they could argue publicly or privately with the university for the Volunteers' readmittance on the basis of "legalities," or they could refrain from any comment and avoid further troubles. They decided on the latter course. Peace Corps officials made no comment to the press. They were pleased that the Volunteers had sufficient work in other fields to justify remaining in Ayacucho, since their return to that city had the effect of minimizing the importance of the incident in the eyes of students and townspeople. The Volunteers themselves accepted the Rector's offer of translation work for the same reason, in spite of strong personal reservations.

The PCVs found little evidence of any personal animosity toward them on the part of either students or faculty. Indeed, they worked closely with students and professors alike in such projects as forestation, literacy, and basketball. They came to the conclusion that student willingness to cooperate in such programs was due in part to friendships built up during their months as instructors. It was also apparent that the students saw a closer relation between these new activities and Peruvian welfare than had previously been the case when they taught English. For the first time, many students seemed to appreciate the contribution the Peace Corps could make to the development of Ayacucho. Indeed, this new Volunteer role complemented that of the students as protesters against the ills of their society.

In the annual student-body election subsequent to the crisis, the dominant Students' Revolutionary Front was unable to get a majority of the votes on the first ballot and eked out only a bare margin of victory on the second. In addition, they won only one of the three elections in the faculties for student delegates to the University Council. The Revolutionary Front's difficulties may be attributed in part to student resentment at their questionable dealings on an electoral commission that annulled a second slate of candidates, and in part to the union of political opposition groups for the first time. It appears, however, that an important third factor was that many students had felt opposed to their leaders' stand on the Peace Corps but had not spoken up in the assemblies. The secret ballot gave these students their first free opportunity to express opposition.

It was soon painfully evident that the fears of the University Council regarding a minority plot to unseat them were justified. Two strikes occurred, and two deans were forced to resign within the Faculty of Engineering. An abortive attempt was made by Aprista newspapers to prove that the university had misappropriated public funds. An Aprista-sympathizing faculty member of the University Council challenged the Rector to a duel after allegedly suffering a personal affront. The objective of this professor and a small group of his faculty supporters (most of them within the Faculty of Engineering) was to force the Rector to resign—for legally he could not fight a duel while holding the post of Rector. Instead, the

Rector preferred to hold up the incident for public ridicule. Finally, a public protest organized by Aprista faculty members gathered several hundred backers among the townspeople, and resulted in the sending of an open letter signed by all to the President of the Republic. It requested the reorganization of the University of Huamanga, including the resignation of the principal authorities. But by this time the entire issue had acquired too strong a tint of partisan politics, and no action was taken.

A final incident, consummated during the first semester of academic year 1964, reveals some of the consequences of the precedent set by the removal of the Peace Corps instructors. A strike by the Institute of Education students was effective in securing the termination of the services of a professor as director of a university teacher-training school. The students had apparently concluded that they could achieve their objective the same way they had with the Peace Corps members—through a strike. Instead of moving toward the set of ideals originally outlined for their university, the students were forcing their institution in the opposite direction.

CONCLUSIONS

In pushing for the ouster of the PCVs from Huamanga, some of the students were motivated by ideological considerations, others by tactical ones. Many were protesting an abstraction which their new quasi-religious ideology told them just had to be true: the evil of Yankee "imperialist" efforts to slow down an incubating revolution at the very nerve center of its activity—the university. Many were swayed by the words of clever students and professors to take a stand that was in absolute contradiction to the students' responsibilities under co-government. This would be tragic anywhere in Latin America, but was all the more so at Huamanga, where the University Council was struggling desperately to maintain the infant traditions of educational stability and student responsibility.

The Volunteers resisted submitting their resignations in the face of student demands because they believed that to give in would contribute to the destruction of these infant traditions. They also felt that the university authorities, and not the Volunteers, were the ones who properly should assume responsibility for determining the course of the university. The authorities were in a much better position to see the total picture and the implications of their decision. As it turned out, factors that had *nothing* to do with the Volunteers were instrumental in convincing the University Council that the PCVs should be sacrificed. In so doing, the Council corroded the principle of university authority, but avoided what the members considered to be an even greater danger: an indefinite strike and the possibility of their own replacement, which might have toppled the whole university.

Quite naturally, the Volunteers involved in the incident were chagrined at the outcome, which at first glance appeared to be a resounding defeat for them and for the Peace Corps effort. After some reflection, however, they came to the conclusion that the success of the move to get them out was, oddly enough, in many ways a result of the very success they had achieved within the university.

From the point of view of the university, the Volunteers had indeed been successful. They had accomplished what the university wanted them to accomplish. In cooperation with the regular members of the English Department, a new and vastly more effective system of language teaching had been established. The sequel, however, is a sad one. By mid-1965, according to reports, the teaching of English at Huamanga had reverted all the way back to the previous antiquated, inefficient methods—because the pedagogical reforms had been so closely identified with the Peace Corps that political support for their continuation was simply not forthcoming.

From the point of view of the Peace Corps, the Volunteers were in Ayacucho not only to carry out their assigned job, the teaching of English, but also to work toward the broader objective of mutual understanding through personal contact. The PCVs made a special effort, therefore, to develop close personal relationships with faculty and students.

Unfortunately, many of their acquaintances in the university showed considerable sensitivity to this latter mission of the Volunteers. As has been brought out, some interpreted this personal contact as an attempt by the Volunteers and the Peace Corps to "penetrate" the university: to achieve status and elective posts through which they could influence university policy and make propaganda for the United States. Among other factors, the Volunteers' amiability, the positions they came to hold in their department, and finally, the "propaganda" lectures tended to confirm the suspicions of sensitive Peruvians.

It would be a mistake, however, to ascribe this sensitivity purely to the propaganda and machinations of the Communists. As has been pointed out, historical and cultural factors are also important and, indeed, help to explain why communism has made any headway at all. Many at Huamanga were keenly conscious of the special role of the Latin American university in its society, and keenly sensitive to any act that could be interpreted as an intrusion by the representatives of a country which had a record of supporting dictatorships, and of favoring what they perceived as "exploitation" through unregulated overseas private investment, through restrictive trade policies on Latin American raw materials and minerals, and through a general failure to understand the psychology of Latin Americans. As a result, they tended to believe that the Volunteers must have had ulterior motives for their presence and friendship—such as "stopping their revolution" or "spying for the C.I.A."

Cultural factors were also important. Much of the Peruvian sensitivity stemmed from a finely developed sense of formality, which meant that everything must be done in the proper fashion and through proper channels. Formalism expresses itself in a strong emphasis on legal fine points, as the inevitable "legalistic" flavor of this chapter doubtless suggests. As the Volunteers tended by nature to be informal, it was very difficult for them to adjust to this cultural difference. Part of the difficulty might also have been caused by the Peruvians' sensitivity to status and position. This was evident in the ill feeling caused by the election of Volunteers to minor posts. Because the Volunteers failed to appreciate the depth of this sensitivity to their presence and to their every action, they created a rather disappointing closing scene to their university experience.

There was considerable discussion within the Peace Corps staff before a decision was made. One staff member favored taking a hard and somewhat legalistic line which would have insisted that the PCVs be reinstated in their jobs. Another member—an anthropologist with long experience in Peru—favored a softer and more subtle line. In the end, the latter line was followed. This decision to back off was a wise one, for several reasons. It had the effect of avoiding future crises at Huamanga for which the Volunteers could be blamed, however unfairly. By arranging to keep the Volunteers in Ayacucho, the staff succeeded in further de-emphasizing the entire affair. This, plus the avoidance of publicity, meant that similar and simultaneous moves to oust Volunteers from other Peruvian universities gained little headway. In Ayacucho itself, the ouster of the PCVs provoked a reaction among students, professors, and townspeople which cast the Volunteers in the role of martyrs. Above all, the staff successfully avoided creating the impression that the Peace Corps is part of a "big stick" foreign policy, and instead eloquently reaffirmed the Good Neighbor Policy, as well as the basic Peace Corps principle that Volunteers will serve only where Volunteers are wanted.

NOTES

[1] All national universities in Peru depend on government funds for their operation. University authorities are very sensitive to any "strings" attached to this economic support that might attempt to mold the educational program or the political orientation of the university. A common means of avoiding such strings is to develop outside sources of income which are independent of central government control.

[2] The University Council is the highest regularly constituted governing body of the university. At Huamanga, it is made up of the Rector, the Vice-Rector, the Deans of the three faculties, an elected faculty representative from each faculty, a student delegate from each faculty, and the President of the Student Federation. These members have voice and vote on most matters relating to university administration. Participating with voice but without vote are the Secretary-General (the administrative chief responsible for communicating all decisions), and the Faculty Director of Freshmen.

The other principal organs of the university are the Faculty Council, the Institute Councils, and the Directive Council of Freshmen. The Faculty Councils, headed by the Deans, are made up of all the full-time professors in the faculty with at least three years of university teaching experience, and enough students from the institutes of the faculty to comprise one third of the total members. They deal with intrafaculty academic, economic, and administrative matters, and make proposals on these matters to the University Council. The Institute Councils are made up of all the professors in that specialty, also with one third students; they elect coordinators (department heads) and pass institute problems to the Faculty Council. The Directive Council of Freshmen is comprised of representatives of all those professors who teach freshmen students. Their main function is to work out the Basic Cycle teaching program for each year.

Source: *Estatuto,* Universidad Nacional de San Cristobal de Huamanga (Ayacucho, Peru), 1963.

[3] This principle is called *co-gobierno.* It was originally demanded, together with other reforms, by Argentine students at the University of Cordoba in 1918. Since then, it has gradually been extended to most Latin American institutions of higher education. "Co-government" has been denounced by many of Peru's most reputable educators, including former Rector Romero, because of its tendency to divide the universities into ideological cliques of students and professors. Nonetheless, co-government is included in the 1960 basic law that sets the norms for all national universities in the country. During the first years after its reopening in 1959, the University of Huamanga was governed by special legislation which did not include co-government. Provisions were made, however, to introduce students gradually into the governing organs of the university during the transition period. After the first year, the students held elec-

tions for student-body leaders who acted as spokesmen before university authorities.

4 The University Assembly is made up of the faculty and student members of the University Council and the Faculty Councils. It meets at the instance of the University Council to consider modifications in university law and elections for Rector and Vice-Rector.

Source: *Estatuto*.

5 The Revolutionary Students' Front (Frente de Estudiantes Revolucionarios) is a catchall for most of the splinter parties of the far Left. Included in the FER are student members or sympathizers of several national political parties, among them the following:

a. The Partido Comunista Peruano (PCP), made up of both Moscow and Peking partisans until late 1963, when the factions split. There are now two PCPs with separate leadership hierarchies. The student elements belong to Juventud Comunista, of which 90 per cent of the regional cells are dominated by the Peking faction.

b. The Frente Izquierdista Revolucionario (FIR), aggressive radicals whose standard bearer is the peasant leader Hugo Blanco.

c. Partido Obrero Revolucionario-Trotskista (POR-T), one of the most active groups in the peasant leagues and land invasions in Ayacucho.

d. Frente de Liberacion Nacional (FLN), an overlapping group made up mostly of Communist Party members attempting to form a popular front and headed by an ex-priest, "Padre" Salomon Bolo Hidalgo. This group has special influence at Huamanga because the faculty "advisor" to the FER is also the Secretary of FLN for the department of Ayacucho.

As can be imagined, these factions have had many conflicts within the FER. Nonetheless, they have been able to stay under the same roof. In 1963 about 200 Huamanga students, or 40 per cent of the student body, belonged to the FER.

Opposition groups at Huamanga are considerably smaller. The University Reform Front (Frente Universitario Reformista—FUR) is the student counterpart of the APRA (Alianza Popular Revolucionaria Americana) party, and probably had about seventy local members in 1963. (See footnote 9.) The Catholic youth group, Democrata Christiana (DC), had just over fifty members. There are a small number of "Belaundistas," who support President Belaunde's Acción Popular party (AP). Most of the remaining 180 students are not affiliated with any party.

Huamanga students are free to form their own political groups, but they are not allowed to hold their meetings within the university grounds.

6 The essential parts of the oral approach to teaching a language are the following: (1) teaching *in* that language to the greatest extent possible; (2) maximum student participation—including choral repetition, question and answer, dialogues; (3) oral examinations.

7 The post of Secretary-General is one of the most important in the university, and does not have a precise counterpart in a United States

institution. As director of the university secretariat, he is responsible for the details of admissions, teaching norms, pay scales, legal advice, correspondence, and archives. All papers, memoranda, protests, replies, and the like, pass across his desk en route up to the university authorities or down to professors or students.

The Marxist in question assumed the post of Secretary-General at the beginning of the academic year in March 1963.

[8] Surprisingly enough, this faculty member was a former devout Catholic turned Communist, who soon after this incident accepted an Aprista offer to make him the new Rector of the university should their plan to oust the university authorities succeed!

[9] The Apristas view the United States as having abandoned the exploitative "dollar diplomacy" stage of imperialism and entered upon a more enlightened phase of international relations. They view the Soviet Union and China as the dangerous imperialist powers of the present generation.

The Alianza Popular Revolucionaria Americana (APRA) was founded in 1924 by Victor Raul Haya de la Torre, who was then in exile. The party originally attempted to align all peoples of "Indo-America" behind a basic platform of anti-imperialism and integration of the Indian population into the national life. Only in Peru, however, did the Apristas develop a wide base of followers. APRA was illegal for most of the years from its founding until 1956. It is a good example of a national party whose ideology springs directly from the objective conditions of a country. Its strong base in the lower class resulted in slowing the growth of the Communist parties. In 1955–1956, however, APRA entered into a compact to support a center-right presidential aspirant in return for legal status and cabinet posts. Since then, the Apristas have been accused of turning their backs on their original lower-class support. The founding of Acción Popular (AP), the moderate Left party of current President Fernando Belaunde Terry; and of Apra Rebelde, now known as Movemento Izquerdista Revolucionario (MIR), both came about largely due to the great dissatisfaction stemming from APRA's apparent shift to the right. (See footnote 5.) After the 1963 elections APRA, in order to secure a majority in Congress, made a compact with the rightist, and formerly anti-Aprista, Union Nacional Odriista (UNO). At this point, many observers believed that the Apristas had irrevocably aligned themselves with the Right.

[10] Several points are important to bear in mind. First is the fact that the vast majority of members of the University Council are anti-Aprista and leftist—though their leftism does not necessarily involve either extremism or party affiliation. Second, the majority of the Student Federation representatives are members of the FER and hence also leftists. In general, the leftist student leaders have attempted in good conscience to respect the wishes of the leftist University Council members that there be no student strikes. In doing so, however, they have drawn charges from Aprista and other non-Communist students of having sold out, of having

deliberately attempted to keep down student opposition to administration policies, of having emasculated student freedom. As a result, the FER student leaders of the Student Federation find themselves forced to go to the extreme measure of declaring a strike in order to maintain their own position of leadership over the student movement.

11 This was stated in a five-page mimeographed document written by the Rector and signed by the University Council, which was distributed to explain their reasons for resigning.

12 Statement in the Student Federation strike committee bulletin mimeographed and distributed on October 24, 1963.

13 Certain members of the faculty played a direct role in helping the student leaders plan and carry out the crisis. Two professors were overheard bragging about the speeches they were writing to give to the students for presentation in the student assemblies.

14 The official ninth annual meeting of the Peruvian Student Federation was attended by some three hundred delegates from twenty-one institutions of higher education. Of the twenty-one delegations, only two had an Aprista majority; two more were dominated by the Christian Democrats; the rest by Communists.

15 These topics exemplify quite well the sort of national and international sociopolitical issues to which Peruvian students attach importance. The vast majority of the Congress participants favored the "Peking line," which for them meant (1) opposition to North American "imperialism"; (2) opposition to the Moscow line of "peaceful coexistence"; (3) a violent national revolution as soon as possible. This revolution, they believe, should not wait for historical conditions to become more propitious or for the proletariat to become more class conscious; it should be a revolution of peasants rather than urban factory workers.

16 This is perhaps another example of not voicing opposition when the tide is obviously against you. Once again the voting was done by a show of hands. Even the Christian Democrat delegates from the nonpolitical private Catholic University of Lima went along, presumably in order to gain strength for their party in the other universities.

17 The 360-mile overland trip to Lima is, for more than half the way, by one-lane dirt highway. The trip takes at least sixteen hours. There is a plane three times a week. Ayacucho has no public telephone service. A telegram takes from one to three days. Urgent communications are transmitted via one of the three "ham" radio operators in Ayacucho.

BIBLIOGRAPHY

NOTE: See also the Bibliography for the Doughty chapter, page 240.

ATCON, RUDOLPH P.
    1962 "The Latin American University: A Key for an Integrated Approach to the Coordinated Social, Economic, and Educational Development of Latin America." *Die Deutsche Universitätszei-*

tung, February, pp. 9-49. This article, written in English, is an outstanding analysis of its subject.

CARDOZO, MANOEL, Editor

1961   *Higher Education in Latin America: A Symposium.* Washington, D. C.: Catholic University of America Press, for Catholic University of America's Institute of Ibero-American Studies. See especially Carlos Cueto Fernandini, "Problems and Issues of the Peruvian University," pp. 22-35.

GUARDIA MAYORGA, CESAR

1958   *El Problema de la Reforma Universitaria.* Lima. A leftist's views.

NUNEZ, CARLOS

1958   *Mariategui y la Cuestión Universitaria.* Lima. The author is a Peruvian anthropologist for whom many Volunteers have worked on community development projects.

ORTEGA Y GASSET, JOSÉ

1944   *Mission of the University.* Translated, and with an introduction, by Howard Lee Nostrand, Princeton, N.J.: Princeton University Press.

ROMERO, FERNANDO

1961   "New Design for an Old University: San Cristobal de Huamanga," *Americas.* Washington, D.C., Pan American Union, December, pp. 9-16. This article was written while the author was Rector of the University of Huamanga.

SANCHEZ, LUIS ALBERTO

1961   *La Universidad no es una isla. . .Un estudio, un plan, tres discursos.* Lima: Ediciones Peru. Reflects the views of an Aprista educator who is a former Rector of the University of San Marcos.

WHYTE, WILLIAM FOOTE

1965   "High-Level Manpower in Peru," in Frederick Harbison and Charles A. Myers, eds., *Manpower and Education: Country Studies in Economic Development.* New York: McGraw-Hill Book Co., pp. 37-72.

15

The Emerging Volunteer
Subculture in Bolivia

DWIGHT B. HEATH *is Associate Professor of Anthropology at Brown University and a Research Associate in the Research Institute for the Study of Man. He has carried out a number of anthropological and historical field research projects in various regions of Bolivia since 1956, and has published widely on economic and political problems at the national level as well as on local cultures. Since the early days of the Peace Corps, Dr. Heath has served as program consultant, training officer, and visiting lecturer in connection with Peace Corps activities in Bolivia. Currently he is engaged in a research project sponsored by the Peace Corps, on culture and health in that country. Professor Heath's numerous publications in English and Spanish include* Contemporary Cultures and Societies of Latin America, *in which he shares editorship with Richard N. Adams (New York: Random House, 1965). He has also directed a film (with Fritz Albert) on the socioeconomic development of eastern Bolivia, which won first prize as a documentary at the 1964 Berlin Film Festival.*

THE purpose of this chapter is to describe and analyze the emerging Volunteer subculture as I have observed it in Bolivia. Since the Peace Corps is still young, my formulations are necessarily tentative. Nonetheless, it does not seem too early to begin attempts at specifying and analyzing that amalgam of esprit de corps, style, and shared concepts and values which comprises the Volunteer subculture in Bolivia and which sets the Corpsmen off quite distinctly from their fellow Americans in Bolivia—businessmen, diplomats, AIDmen, missionaries—and indeed from most members of the salaried Peace Corps staff in Washington and elsewhere.

My field observations are limited to the Bolivia Volunteers, many of whom I have helped to train. In 1962 I accompanied Bolivia One on their trip to La Paz. In the summer of 1963 I returned to Bolivia and was able to observe Bolivia One, Two, and Three in action.

271

From September 1964 until August 1965 I was again in Bolivia, as associate director of a Peace Corps-sponsored research project on culture and health. I am not able to say how closely my summary of the emerging Volunteer subculture in Bolivia would apply to PCVs serving in other countries. I have, however, been careful to analyze the emerging subculture in Bolivia in terms of what I consider to be its basic, or core, value patterns, so as to facilitate subsequent comparison between the subculture in Bolivia and the subcultures found among Volunteers in other countries. My guess is that these basic value patterns will be found to be fairly similar more or less regardless of host country. And if the notion of a worldwide Volunteer subculture proves to be a valid one, then it is certainly something worth studying, for an understanding of it will lead to an understanding of the processes of transcultural learning, and of value change, which the Volunteer experience tends to produce. An understanding of the Volunteer subculture will also help to explain and predict the long-run impact of the returned PCVs on our own greater American culture—especially since the returnees seem to seek out each other's company once back in the States, and hence seem likely, to a degree, to carry on their subculture long after the Volunteer experience itself has ended.

The next four sections will provide preliminary information about Bolivia, about what the Peace Corps has been trying to do there, and about what some of the positive and negative results have been to date. After this background, I will present eight elements, or patterns, that seem to be important in the emerging Volunteer subculture in Bolivia.

THE BOLIVIAN SITUATION

Whatever else may be said of Bolivia, it is certainly a land of contrasts. It has been called "the planet in microcosm," because it includes virtually the entire range of ecological and climatic variation, within an area the size of Spain and France combined. The Andes dominate the western one third of the nation, with majestic snow-capped peaks soaring to more than 20,000 feet. Between two parallel chains of mountains lies a high plateau, the Altiplano, at about 12,000 feet. This cold, barren plateau is rich in minerals, which have long constituted almost the only products that Bolivia exports. And yet the Altiplano offers only a meager living to the majority of the Aymará Indian farmers who live there. Farther to the east is a more temperate and fertile range of mountains, whose well-watered valleys support a dense population of Quechua Indians. The Quechua are descendants of the Inca, who formerly dominated the entire Andes region. They follow an agricultural way of life which is in many respects quite similar to that of their ancestors four centuries ago. East of the mountains is the Oriente, a vast tropical plain of savannah and dense jungle. Although the Oriente comprises 70 per cent of Bolivia's area, only 20 per cent of the nation's four million people live there. Indeed, large sections of the Oriente are still unexplored.

Bolivia has also been likened to a "beggar sitting on a throne of gold," an allusion to the very real poverty of the Bolivians, a poverty that persists in spite of their country's abundant and varied resources of natural wealth. Tin, silver, tungsten, and other valuable minerals are found in the highlands. The lowlands produce some rubber and petroleum, and could be made to produce much more, as well as to develop herding and tropical agriculture. The country remains economically underdeveloped, however, as the result of a complex of factors. Sheer distance and natural barriers combine to make transportation difficult. Cultural heterogeneity is a major barrier to economic development. The situation is in many respects similar to that in Peru, as already described by Doughty. More than half of Bolivia's population speak indigenous languages rather than Spanish, and retain much of their traditional native social organization, value system, religion, and other beliefs and practices. Cultural variation is almost as great as geographical, although the Quechua and Aymará peoples predominate. The Spanish-speaking townspeople live in a vastly different world of their own, as do the relatively few Indians still maintaining a tribal form of social organization, who live scattered throughout the far-flung lowland jungles of the Oriente.

Only since the 1950's has there been any systematic effort to bring the majority of the people into political and economic relation with the nation and the world. In 1952 Bolivia experienced a revolution—a genuine social revolution for which there is, as yet, no parallel in Peruvian history. The Nationalist Revolutionary Movement which came into power in that year overthrew a rigidly stratified society in which a wealthy few enjoyed a virtual monopoly of power and of profits from mining enterprises. The Movement effected sweeping changes in the entire social system. Major industries were nationalized. Effective land reform was carried out.

Universal suffrage was instituted. Education and industrialization were promoted. This social revolution is still in process.*

Bolivia's social revolutionaries have benefited from technical assistance from the United States, from other nations, and from international agencies. This aid has been generous and varied. Its impact, however, has too rarely been felt by Bolivians outside of government. It was in such a context that the Peace Corps was invited to work in Bolivia late in 1961.

THE PEACE CORPS PROGRAM IN BOLIVIA

Bolivia One arrived in La Paz in July 1962. The contingent included thirty-six registered and practical nurses, sanitarians, health educators, well-drillers, and others, to work in jobs throughout the republic, as assigned by the Inter-American Cooperative Public Health Service. Although the initial job assignments for this group were uniformly inappropriate, each PCV eventually found a useful job for which he was suited, and much was accomplished by the time the two-year term expired in April 1964. Two Volunteers terminated prematurely for health reasons, and one to enter the Catholic priesthood. Three others, however, chose to extend their service beyond the normal two years.

Bolivia Two, numbering thirty-four Volunteers, arrived in November 1962 for work in agriculture, animal husbandry, and community development. The group included agronomists, farm machinery repairmen, dairy specialists, visiting nurses, and others. Assignments were concentrated in the Cochabamba Valley and the northern Santa Cruz area. Before their term of service expired in June 1964, four of these PCVs had left for reasons of health. On the other hand, four remained beyond their term, and one reenlisted and has again been sent to Bolivia.

The third group, consisting of forty-two Corpsmen, arrived in January 1963 to expand work in public health and community development. The health specialists were stationed throughout the northern half of the country, in various ecological and cultural regions, while the community developers were focused in the Alto Beni region where people from the overpopulated highlands were

* On November 4, 1964, a "Revolution of Restoration" occurred which brought a military junta to power and unseated the Nationalist Revolutionary Movement. Nonetheless, my field observations in Bolivia from September 1964 to August 1965 give me no reason to doubt that most of the social and economic reforms enacted by the previous regime will be continued.—D.B.H.

being encouraged to resettle in virgin lands on the eastern edge of the Andes.

The fifteen university teachers of Bolivia Four arrived in September 1963, and have been offering courses in mathematics, physics, embryology, electrical engineering, architecture, humanities, and several other subjects in universities throughout the republic.

During 1964 and 1965 the buildup continued. Plans called for about 380 PCVs to be working in a variety of specialties by early 1966, and for further expansion thereafter.[1]

EARLY PROGRAMING PROBLEMS

It is, unfortunately, a historical fact that official programs of the Peace Corps—at least in the early days—have often been drafted by administrative personnel largely or totally lacking in any first-hand acquaintance with the areas, peoples, cultures, social and administrative structures, or problems that had to be faced. I refer here not only to American officials but also to host country officials, who are often naïve, uninformed, and even unconcerned about the way the majority of common folk in their country actually live. In their eagerness to obtain PCVs to give luster to their organizations, some host country officials have planned programs that bore little relation to the realities of physically and culturally remote situations. In other instances, sheer political expediency has weighed more heavily than the actual and felt needs of local people—and again the result has been unrealistic or inappropriate programing.

Misassignments

In the early days of the Bolivia program, misassignments were the rule rather than the exception. Volunteers were sent to Tarija, for example, for the purpose of starting a new program of health education. On arrival, they discovered that Tarija already had what local people considered the most advanced, intensive, and effective health education program in the republic, and that this program was already two years old. Not only were the PCVs not needed there, but it soon became abundantly clear that their presence was not wanted by the local Bolivian health educators.

In similar fashion, seven PCV nurses were assigned to a health center in Cochabamba, which turned out to have, in full operation, one of the best curative programs in the country. Their arrival served to convince the local Bolivian nurses that the North Americans had come to usurp their jobs.

Another nurse found that the "clinic" to which she had been assigned did not exist, and would not be built and in operation for at least another year.

Still another nurse was assigned solely to assist a brain surgeon in the General Hospital in La Paz. He rarely performed more than one operation a month.

In other, less flamboyant ways, misassignment has proved to be a general problem. Some PCVs have been underqualified, others overqualified. Misunderstandings have arisen because of differing cultural definitions of jobs. For example, what the Bolivians call a "social worker" is more nearly what North Americans would call a "visiting nurse." Other difficulties have arisen because some Peace Corps/Washington official incorrectly assumed that a "rice agriculturalist" was to work in an irrigated rather than a dry-rice area, or neglected to ascertain what kind of machinery a "farm machinery repairman" was expected to repair.

I hasten to add, in fairness, that in addition to many misassignments, there have also been many quite appropriate assignments. With growing experience, programing problems have become less serious. The greatest credit, in my opinion, should go to the PCVs, who have generally shown initiative in seeking new or more appropriate assignments where the initial assignment was faulty, or else have enlarged an existing assignment in such a way as to perform more active and appropriate service.

Problems of Strategy

Early programs did not always take careful advantage of past experience in similar programs. It was sometimes necessary for Peace Corps staff administrators to learn from trial and error what ideally they should have known prior to their participation in the program. An example is the strategy of the Bolivia health program. In the early days, this program emphasized curative approaches. More recently, the emphasis has been abruptly and completely reversed, and now focuses on preventive programs. This reversal reflected in part the simple fact that highly qualified therapeutic personnel are difficult to find and recruit as Peace Corps Volunteers. Further, however, the decision reflected the growing sophistication of officials in Peace Corps/Washington with respect to intercultural problems in health work. Peace Corps administrators have learned through experience what has been known professionally for a long time, namely, that in a country like Bolivia there is so much suffering that even the maximum possible program of therapy would hardly scratch the surface. Therefore, as numerous social scientists have learned in a variety of cultures around the world, it seemed logical to shift the emphasis from cure to prevention. By helping the Bolivians to help themselves toward better sanitation and better preventive personal and public health care, the Peace Corps Volunteers may eventually register a much more powerful long range impact than could be expected if the program had continued to place primary emphasis on therapy.

OTHER PLUSES AND MINUSES

As part of general background, there are a number of other brief observations that should be made at this point.

First, I should clearly state my opinion that, in spite of early mistakes—most of which were unnecessary and preventable—the program in Bolivia has been an over-all success. In both programed activity and unprogramed, spontaneous activity, the great majority of PCVs have shown dedication and effectiveness to an unusual degree.

One of the most effective "multiplier effects" that a Peace Corps program in any country can produce, is to stimulate the formation of a *local* Peace Corps. I am happy to report that this has already occurred—though how permanently remains to be seen—in the city of Sucre. Early in the Corps' history there, several Volunteers working in the field of public health began to devote much of their time to the improvement of physical conditions in several public institutions, such as an orphanage, a prison, and a mental hospital. Teaming together with local people, they managed to get walls painted, roofs repaired, and sanitary facilities installed. As a result of this, an unprecedented event occurred. A group of citizens of Sucre joined together to form the Bolivian "National Peace Corps," a social service group which mounts occasional work camps to do such jobs voluntarily. Supplies have been contributed by local businessmen. Funds have been raised through city-wide promotional campaigns. PCVs have sometimes helped by soliciting contributions from people in the United States through letters and hometown newspaper articles. If the Bolivian "National Peace Corps" survives, grows, and becomes institutionalized—and already similar programs have emerged in one or two other cities—this alone could serve to justify the United States Peace Corps effort in that country.

Training has generally been excellent. Much of the relatively greater effectiveness of the PCVs—as compared with other American and foreign assistance personnel—can be ascribed to superior language and area training.

Geographic distribution, on the other hand, leaves much to be desired. Large areas of Bolivia have few or no PCVs—and the reasons for this seem essentially political and hardly relevant to local people's actual felt needs. Incidentally, the PCV in Bolivia, as elsewhere, is generally happier and more effective in rural than in urban settings.

Logistical support has generally been inadequate, and often grossly so. Since the PCVs are working at "middle manpower" jobs, they cannot function effectively without supplies and equipment. One entomologist, for example, waited several months to receive a microscope. Well-driller Volunteers, though prepared for any hardship, simply could not do their jobs in the complete absence of rigs or piping. Logistical frustrations have sometimes driven Corpsmen to find other jobs for themselves, or to affiliate themselves informally with another organization where better equipment was available.

A serious morale problem results from the fact that—with notable exceptions—local Peace Corps staff have frequently been lacking in knowledge of Bolivia, as well as in knowledge of the requirements of a particular job. It is difficult for the PCVs to respect and have confidence in administrators who seem to know less about these important things than does the PCV himself. Relations are further exacerbated by the fact that some of the staff require the Volunteers to submit periodic written reports, which the latter resent, feeling that this is unnecessary paper work and an unreasonable diversion of their energies away from doing the job they came to do.

MAJOR PATTERNS IN THE VOLUNTEER SUBCULTURE

Anyone who has ever spent much time with Peace Corps Volunteers knows that they are a decidedly individualistic lot and that generalizations about them are difficult. Nevertheless I will attempt to generalize here, for it is only through progressive generalization (with qualifications) that a social-science type of understanding of the Peace Corps experience can move ahead. If some of my generalizations seem too hasty or too locally based, I hope that other observers, including returned PCVs, will improve upon them.

Even after spending only a short period of time with the Volunteers, it becomes clear that their subculture is something real indeed. They have a distinctive set of understandings, of values, and even of jargon, which is peculiar to them alone. These understandings and values and modes of expression are in part the product of the peculiar nature of the Volunteer experience and of the host culture. In part they are also the product of the PCVs' subjective reactions to their environment, communicated and shared with other PCVs. Some of this sharing is "intergenerational" in the sense that older Volunteers help to orient, and shape the attitudes of, newer Volunteers who arrive in a later contingent. On the other hand, one serious complaint that I would register is that the "Rep" staff does not permit and encourage as much as I would wish to see of this orientation of new Volunteers by older ones. The result is much loss in continuity, and, if you will, a less tightly and clearly patterned Volunteer subculture than would otherwise be the case.

My trial formulation of the Volunteer subculture in Bolivia takes the form of the following eight elements, components, or "patterns": Energetic Activity, Egoistic Altruism, Proud Humility, Local Identification, Realistic Idealism, Planned Expediency, Situational Austerity, and Organizational Loyalty. Another observer might, of course, describe and summarize the PCV subculture in Bolivia differently, and might distinguish a different number of patterns as being worthy of prominent mention. The nature of anthropological method is such that precise agreement between two observers as to the content of a particular culture is seldom achieved. About the most that can usually be expected is essential agreement on all points that both observers consider to be important.

Energetic Activity

Whatever else might be said of the Volunteers in Bolivia, no one would dispute the statement that many of them are engaged in energetic, almost frenetic, activity—motivated in part by a genuine desire to be helpful, and in many cases doubtless in part by a psychological need to keep busy, to fight boredom, and to preserve mental stability. Where energetic activity is a response to the boredom that characterizes many Peace Corps assignments, it might develop quickly or it might emerge only after some monotonous weeks or months of aimless idleness. Sooner or later, however, most Volunteers find themselves discontent with just putting in the hours called for by their formal job assignments, especially when these assignments turn out to be more apparent than real. A significant number of PCVs look for extra work to do in their "spare" time. And when a PCV finds himself misassigned or underutilized, he will often, sooner or later, take personal initiative to seek out new or additional ways in which to make himself useful to the local people.

Many Volunteers thus find themselves working almost incessantly, allowing themselves virtually no "free time" except when they temporarily leave their work to get completely "away from it all" in a town, city, or other situation some distance removed.

Regardless of formal job assignment, almost all of the Volunteers find themselves, willy-nilly, becoming part-time instructors of English. So widespread is the Bolivians' interest in learning this language—a major key to intellectual and professional advancement—that engineers, nurses, pharmacists, sociologists, and all manner of PCVs find themselves more or less formally teaching their native language to the local people. Many PCV nurses have undertaken large-scale immunization projects against such diseases as smallpox, tuberculosis, and whooping cough—and have had little trouble finding other Volunteers willing to spend hours helping them with the "leg work." Some PCVs have gathered the first accurate census data ever compiled for the communities in which they were stationed. Others have taken part in sports and a variety of other young peoples' activities that had never before been organized. Agriculturalists have often initiated 4-S clubs, which have become foci of enthusiastic activity in the manner of 4-H clubs in the United States.

Other forms of energetic activity take on a more unusual, almost heroic, complexion. One nurse wrote and illustrated a booklet on sanitation which became popular among children in the tropical lowlands, taught English not only in the university but also in a kindergarten and by radio, and designed and made sandals for lepers whose feet were deformed—all in her "spare" time. One architect Volunteer was not content merely to design buildings, but went further and achieved remarkable success in mustering material and labor from local people, so that members of several rural communities have now collectively built schools where none before existed. One community developer Volunteer not only oversaw the building of a schoolhouse by a community of Mosetene Indians but also served for several months as the school's sole teacher. Not content with this, he introduced a cottage industry that has become the first source of cash income these Indians have ever enjoyed: miniature bow-and-arrow sets which are accurate representations of the immense weapons the Mosetenes use in hunting; these are easy to make and have become popular souvenir items in the capital city.

At this point honesty requires that we not neglect the other side of the coin, the small minority of Volunteers in Bolivia who do little more than enjoy themselves. Unfortunately, it is precisely these

PCVs who are most visible in the major cities, where their behavior has come to be generalized in a popular play on words: the *Cuerpo de Paz* (Peace Corps) is often called the *Cuerpo de Paseo* (Vacation Corps)—even by Bolivians who are strongly pro-United States in their political and emotional sentiments.

Egoistic Altruism

The energetic activity of the typical Volunteer in Bolivia is unquestionably motivated by a genuine altruism—and yet it is an altruism that is accompanied by a considerable amount of consciously recognized egoism. There is little in the PCVs' altruism that could be called either compulsive or self-abnegating. In this respect the Volunteers stand in contrast to some North American Protestant missionaries one meets in Bolivia who, to hear them speak, seem to feel that by increasing their own suffering they could somehow automatically relieve that of the Bolivians. Few Volunteers are hobbled by any such self-defeating notions. Their altruism usually takes the form simply of wanting to share with others some of the advantages that they themselves have enjoyed.

When I say that the Volunteers' altruism is egoistic, I am not expressing criticism. On the contrary, I take the position that a certain element of egoism, especially conscious egoism, is often a healthy thing to mix in with one's altruism. For purposes of objective analysis (as distinct from mere moralizing), I believe it is proper, and indeed necessary, to regard almost all human behavior as in some sense self-enhancing. When one takes this position, the crucial question then becomes whether helping another to enhance himself contributes positively to one's own enhancement. (Guthrie and Szanton have already discussed the "helping relationship" in terms of the Philippines on pages 30 and 59.) By and large, I believe that the egoism engendered in the Volunteer subculture in Bolivia is indeed constructive. Three forms which this egoism-within-altruism assumes, and which are worthy of mention here, are career advantages, personal growth, and sense of accomplishment.

There is no doubt that service in the Peace Corps carries with it definite career advantages for many PCVs, and that many of them are consciously aware of this fact. As the Peace Corps has become more and more of an institution in American life, becoming a PCV has taken on more and more of a potential "calling card" advantage —especially to those young people who contemplate careers in international work. Beyond this, the Peace Corps offers unusual opportunities in specific occupations—opportunities of a breadth and scope that the typical Volunteer could not hope to find, at the same age, back home. One architect PCV had the opportunity in Bolivia to design several schools, a hospital, and a low-cost housing development—despite the fact that back home he had not even received his license to practice. Many nurses hope—realistically or not—that the variety of experience and level of responsibility which go along with an assignment as the only medically trained person in a whole community or other sizable area, will be recognized when they return to work in the United States. And Volunteers teaching in Bolivian universities sometimes seize waiting opportunities to conduct small-scale research projects that will yield data likely to be valuable to them later in their graduate careers.

The fact that the Volunteers are consciously motivated by a desire for personal growth needs little elaboration here. Suffice it to say that almost all of them will readily acknowledge their desire to grow personally through learning another culture and through directly confronting the challenge of a work assignment in that culture. And no doubt some PCVs would decide among several ways to spend their spare time with some view to the alternative that would lead to greatest personal growth. This, however, is not likely to be their strongest consideration; more weight will usually be given to the relative needs of the local population.

The third form of egoism-within-altruism involves the Volunteer's personal desire for a sense of accomplishment—and it is here that egoism is somewhat less likely to produce a constructive result. Many Volunteers, particularly those assigned to community development, spend as much as one third of their period of service in Bolivia just looking for an especially congenial community or social milieu. Moreover, it often happens that a PCV is willing and even eager to help a community do what interests *him*, but has little patience with activities that may be of more interest to the Bolivians. It is, for example, not uncommon for a Volunteer to spend great amounts of time and effort in trying to stimulate local interest in building latrines or improving the village road, while ignoring the people's repeated suggestions that they would gladly contribute their labor to build, say, a local soccer field. Lest I seem too critical at this point, however, let me add that the degree of egoism involved here is generally far less than would probably be the case with other types of North American overseas workers. Not only this, but from what we know about the relationship between morale and efficiency, it is altogether likely that such egoism often improves the ability of the Volunteer to be effective in his altruism.

Proud Humility

Handmaiden to the Volunteer's altruism is his humility. It is a humility in which he takes intense pride, although his very humility often inhibits him from expressing this and other pride. The PCV's humility leads him to expect to work with humble Bolivians in disadvantaged social circumstances. He expects to be inconvenienced by a shortage of supplies and equipment—and in this expectation he is often readily obliged by improper logistical planning on the part of his Peace Corps staff and Bolivian superiors. At the same time, he takes quiet pride in his ability to "make do," to "scrounge" supplies from somewhere, anywhere, in order to get on with the job. Nurses, for example, will dispense to the local people the contents of Peace Corps medical kits which were issued for their own personal safety—and then perhaps team up with a missionary organization that does have adequate supplies.

Another facet of proud humility is the modesty that the PCVs show toward their own activities. In private conversation, each PCV evinces obvious, and often justified, pride in what he or she has accomplished—whether in terms of number of children vaccinated against smallpox, percentage of families in a community who have built latrines, rise in average crop yield per hectare, or whatever. The format of the monthly reports that Volunteers working in public health are supposed to submit to La Paz lends itself to quantification, and many of the Peace Corps' public pronouncements are couched in such terms. However, when writing in expository style as they often do, whether for a hometown newspaper or for an organ of the Peace Corps, Volunteers almost uniformly use the first-person *plural,* referring to themselves and the local people, or else take pains to mention specifically the generous cooperation of local Bolivians. Or, the Volunteer will speak of his own work in the context of the entire national Peace Corps effort, and this will be true even in those instances where his own individual accomplishments are readily identifiable.

Local Identification

Anthropologists, after many months of intensive fieldwork among people of a different culture, usually identify mightily with the local people. When they return home, they constantly find themselves referring to "my" people, "our" community, "our" language, and so forth. Strikingly but not surprisingly, Peace Corps Volunteers develop a similar form of local identification. When referring to his duty station, the PCV will more often than not refer to "my" town.

And he will often identify himself with Bolivians in general, to the point of making statements like, "Well, I see we finally broke off diplomatic relations with Cuba." On the other hand, it ought to be emphasized that the Volunteer is usually also acutely aware of his sensitive role as a representative of the United States and often is an eloquent spokesman in expressing his own views (while carefully explaining that they are not official views) on difficult and sensitive questions such as civil rights in the States, presidential campaigns, and so forth.

At the heart of the Volunteer's local identification is, of course, his concern for the masses of less privileged Bolivians among whom he lives. He sees how these people suffer, and how little the government or the upper class seems to care or do about this suffering. He develops a "we-they" attitude—sometimes a black-and-white dichotomy with few if any gray halftones. Subtly, he develops a distrust and a disdain for urban Bolivians, especially those of the upper class who seem so remote from what he considers to be the real problems of the country. And by the same gradual processes, he comes to disdain other members of the "American colony," those North Americans working for various oil companies, for the United States Embassy and its attached agencies, and in some cases, for various missionary organizations. Volunteers often feel self-righteously superior to the inhabitants of the "golden ghetto" of modern houses built especially for the American colony in a new suburban area of La Paz. The PCV in the field often thinks that his fellow North Americans are almost hopelessly out of touch with the social realities in Bolivia—and sometimes he says so. (And, it should be added, some members of the Peace Corps/Bolivia Representative staff also seem to be more similar to members of the golden ghetto than PCVs think they ought to be.) It is understandable that United States Civil Service personnel do not appreciate this inverse snobbery, nor, for that matter, are they enthusiastic about having Volunteers coming to Bolivia to perform tasks that in many instances are somewhat similar to the kind of work they themselves had supposedly been doing.

Within limits, this local identification can be constructive. Some PCVs are indeed qualified to "speak for" the masses of Bolivians in the community to which they are assigned. Emotional identification does in some cases lead to genuine sociocultural understanding —both intuitive and intellectual. Some PCVs do indeed achieve considerable insight into the informal forces that shape political, economic, and other social relations. Unfortunately, however, understanding is *not* an inevitable consequence of identification. There are many PCVs who remain relatively innocent of any deep understanding of local social phenomena—while being at the same time blissfully confident that they have achieved expertise as if by osmosis. There are, sad to report, a good many PCVs who could well stand to be admonished on this score.

Realistic Idealism

Every American who applies for membership in the Peace Corps has, of course, his own peculiar complex of reasons and motivations for doing so. In the case of the Bolivia trainees and Volunteers, these reasons commonly included a considerable component of idealism, usually phrased in terms of the relief of human suffering, the provision of a fuller life for the people of Bolivia, and the improvement of international relations as a requisite for peace. This early idealism is often of a "gung ho" quality, and is characterized by wild fantasies as to how quickly a single PCV can help Bolivian peasants to reorient their values and reorganize their lives. The training programs, with some exceptions, have been quite effective in introducing realism into the attitudes of such trainees, without unduly dampening the idealism that is at the very core of their motivation to serve as Volunteers.

And then they reach Bolivia and start to work. At last, the PCVs are confronting the Bolivian social reality directly. They experience for themselves, in unforgettable terms, just what poverty means, and how poverty breeds ignorance, and ignorance disease, and disease poverty, and so on around the vicious circle. They see that it takes *time* for people to change themselves. In many cases the new Corpsman will find himself stationed near a more experienced Volunteer from an earlier group, with whom he can discuss problems and develop some detachment and perspective on his situation. From all this emerges, in quite short order, the adoption—or confirmation— of a decidedly healthy attitude that combines an idealistic view of what is desirable with a realistic view of what is possible.

In the fields of nutrition and sanitation, for example, the PCV soon learns to take a gradualistic stance. He learns to appreciate that half a loaf is often better than none. He learns to accept the ideological and material limitations of the situation in which he works, and to gear his aspirations accordingly. In managing his aspirations in such a realistic fashion, the Volunteer quite effectively protects his own morale and mental health, which in turn, of course, makes him more effective on the job. The nutrition situation, for example, is a bleak one by North American standards. The Bolivian adult male farmer is almost perpetually hungry on a diet of about 1,000 calories a day. The U.S. National Research Council recommends a daily intake of about 3,000 calories for a workingman of 150 pounds. Most PCVs, faced with this sort of knowledge, would be inclined to accept 3,000 calories as a rough ideal, while immediately asking the question of whether there is realistic hope—given Bolivia's soil and climate, level of education and innovation-readiness, quality and quantity of agricultural extension facilities, and the like—of achieving that ideal. After pondering the realities of the situation, most PCVs would probably arrive at the conclusion that a realistic nutrition improvement program ought to aim at a target of, say, 1,500 calories a day. In similar fashion, the PCV would come to favor a simple and inexpensive slit-trench latrine as a worthwhile improvement over random waste disposal—even though it would be obvious to him that a covered latrine, far removed from the water source, would undoubtedly be much more sanitary.

Planned Expediency

By "planned expediency" I mean a kind of "hook-baiting" in which the PCV makes compromises in his short-term tactics with a view toward facilitating the accomplishment of long-range strategic objectives. Volunteers often refer to such compromises as "playing politics" or "using psychology." Planned expediency can be of immense value in intercultural development programs anywhere, and perhaps more in Bolivia than in some countries. For in Bolivia, as elsewhere in Latin America, the predominant local ethos includes a strong emphasis on *personalismo,* that is, the use of close personal relations as a means of getting tasks accomplished. It is this aspect of the Bolivian value system which disallows "coming to the point," and makes "constructive criticism" a contradiction in terms, while underscoring the value of reciprocity.

Of the eight patterns within the Volunteer subculture that are covered in this chapter, "planned expediency" probably represents the greatest deviation from the personal value system of the typical Volunteer prior to his entering the Peace Corps. The new PCV is usually not a very political animal, and tends to regard his two years in the Corps as a period during which he will hold in abeyance whatever political interests or proclivities he might have. It is therefore particularly noteworthy, and in individual cases even a little amusing, to observe the Volunteers becoming past masters at planned expediency after having earlier made frequent and vehement statements to the effect that they intended at all costs to "be straight-forward and open," and to avoid any "beating around the bush."*

Planned expediency can be an excellent antidote to the form of egoistic altruism exemplified by the PCV who wanted to build roads and latrines while the people in the community wanted a soccer field. In such a case, the expedient move would perhaps have been to collaborate enthusiastically in the construction of the soccer field in the hope that the citizenry would in the process gain sufficient confidence in themselves and in the PCV that, after adequate discussion and consideration, they would cooperate actively and enthusiastically on a road or latrine project.

Examples of planned expediency range from the episodic to the serious. In a sense, I suppose, one could call it "planned expediency" every time a community developer drops in to visit a family in the community and pass the time of day. The conversation may not even touch on a single community development project. The principal purpose of the visit, as far as community development is concerned, is simply to build rapport—that indispensable precondition to effective community development in any culture. Or, an agricultural extensionist PCV might give seed or fertilizer to an influential "opinion leader" farmer in the community, with the expectation that he will later receive a convincing testimonial from that villager. Or, a community developer might cultivate acquaintances in a variety of local organizations because he wants the contributed labor of members of those organizations six months later when, he hopes, the community will be ready to join hands and build a new, sanitary public well.

The danger inherent in "planned expediency" is, as in all matters of expedient behavior, that in some cases the expedient *means* tend to displace, distort, or actually become, the *ends* themselves. This has sometimes happened in Bolivia in the field of health. As we have seen, the supply of trained medical personnel in Bolivia is so hopelessly inadequate to the needs of the population that surely the end goal of almost any Volunteer health worker in that country could profitably be to emphasize prevention rather than cure of disease. And, as earlier noted, the official approach of the Peace Corps in Bolivia now favors total abandonment of clinical work and full concentration by the Volunteers on health education. This makes it especially difficult for newer Volunteers, who are constantly being

* This recalls the early situation in the Philippines, where some of the Representatives were advising the Volunteers to "be perfectly frank." See pages 28 and 43.—Ed.

compared with their predecessors who treated patients. The new preventive health worker will be asked by Bolivians—after, say, a three-month intensive campaign in sanitation and public health—"When are you going to start working?" (On the surface at least, the solution would appear to be simple: preventive health workers should be assigned to communities where no Volunteers have previously served in a therapeutic capacity.) A major difficulty, of course, is that the average Bolivian (like the average citizen in any developing nation) is emotionally unconcerned as well as ignorant about prevention, while immediately concerned and upset about, say, the raging fever of his miserable, wailing infant daughter whom he holds in his arms.

Here, then, is a "natural" opportunity to employ the tactic of planned expediency. (Indeed, the health field is usually the one where this tactic is most expedient—in any culture.) The obvious thing to do is to treat the little girl's fever, thus gaining rapport with her father. It is then possible to give a few words of health education to the father—though not more, usually, because a long line of other patients is waiting. And later, when the health education team comes to the village, it can presumably avail itself of the goodwill the nurse has gained with the father.

The difficulty is, however, that things seldom work as simply as that. Just because the father is grateful for the cure of his daughter's fever, it does not necessarily follow that he will be willing, or able, to absorb the health education he receives, immediately or later. Or, it may happen that so much time and energy go into the rapport-building curative program that too little is left over for the essential job of education. Most importantly, however, the pattern of egoistic altruism will often intervene. PCVs in nursing and other health work have come primarily from curative rather than preventive fields back in North America. Their humanitarian values practically require them to do what they can to relieve immediate suffering of people right around them, before turning to other tasks. Emotionally, they are more attuned to receiving gratification from curative than from preventive work. The deep, warm, immediate gratitude of the father whose daughter has been relieved or cured is much more rewarding to a PCV—or to anyone—than is the uncomprehending, slow, slipshod reception that a community gives to a health education campaign emphasizing prevention—a campaign involving much longer, less dramatic, and often more patient and difficult work on the part of the PCV.

In summary, then, it can be said that most Volunteers learn to make considerable use of planned expediency; on the other hand, there are definite limitations on the effectiveness of this stratagem, limitations both of a psychological and a programing nature.

Situational Austerity

Another pattern in the Volunteer subculture that develops gradually over the course of the PCV's term in Bolivia—often to his surprise—is that of "situational austerity." The Volunteer practices austerity, and with real pride and persistence as long as the situation calls for it. But when he gets away from his village or other field situation, to a place where austerity is not called for, he generally "lives it up."

As numerous other chapters have already pointed out, an integral part of the popular image of the Peace Corps, and one on which many Volunteers pride themselves, is physical austerity. The idea of living in a thatched hut, bathing in a river, "doing without" electricity and commercial entertainment, being "isolated" among an alien people, and generally "roughing it"—has fired the imagination of a large sector of the North American public, including many of the applicants for Peace Corps service. Some of the trainees in Bolivia One and Three even complained about the comfort and modernity of the facilities at the University of Oklahoma. And in Bolivia itself, PCVs stationed in cities sometimes admit to feeling guilty about the comfortable apartments and modern conveniences they enjoy.

The majority, however, live and work in situations considerably less attractive than those they enjoyed back in the United States. Food is often in short supply and monotonous in quality; few North Americans have ever been known to wax poetic over a steady diet of rice, manioc, and black coffee. Housing in small towns and rural areas—even when it is the best available locally—is often cramped and dark. PCVs living on the Altiplano complain that they simply cannot get warm at night, while those stationed in the tropical lowlands find that even the local people complain about the oppressive heat, ubiquitous dust, and unceasingly annoying insects. Female Volunteers suffer particularly, as they grow wary from having their informal cordiality misinterpreted by Bolivian men accustomed to greater reserve in female behavior. But for either sex, the isolation from North American companionship, the lack of sociability, or the alien forms that local sociability sometimes takes—can be monstrously trying.

Despite all these privations and frustrations, a majority of the

Volunteers manage nonetheless to make a good adjustment. Griping serves as an essential safety valve for those who get "fed up"—and almost every PCV reaches this stage at one time or another. At the same time, however, the Volunteers take fierce pride in their ability to bear up under such adversity.

But even the proudest, most perseverant PCV does not wear a hairshirt jauntily for too long. It is a rare individual who does not go into a city or sizable town at least every other month, and some feel that they must visit an urban area almost weekly. Newer Volunteers feel some guilt over these excursions and resort to various rationalizations to explain the necessity for them—such as the need to "get out of the altitude." As time goes on, however, the PCV feels more and more comfortable about his escapes from the local situation, which he comes to see as necessary recreation, as a form of recharging his psychological and cultural batteries.

Once in town and away from the particular Bolivians at whose level he is supposed to live, the Volunteer forgets about austerity. Although he certainly does not go lavishly out "on the town" like a sailor in port, neither does he economize on the little luxuries he has missed. He tends to stay at a comfortable hotel, where he might pay twice the minimum price of a room just to be assured of a hot bath. He will patronize a variety of good restaurants in quest of leisurely dinners, which he values as much for their symbolic associations as for the taste of the food. Or perhaps he will launch forth on a "movie binge," taking in several shows in rapid order.

It is, incidentally, a bitter irony to Bolivians to learn that a PCV's monthly "living allowance" is nearly three times as generous as the monthly salary of a Bolivian middle-level white-collar worker, and is nearly equal to the estimated average per capita *annual* income for that country. This living allowance is intended to cover little more than room, board, and a few personal expenses—in addition to which the Peace Corps provides clothing, transportation, medical care, furniture, and other necessities. Under these circumstances, perhaps it is just as well that Volunteers rarely complain to Bolivians about the deprivations they are enduring.

By contrast, it came as a bitter irony to Volunteers in Trinidad, Beni, to be accused by the local biweekly Communist newspaper of sabotage. The charge was that the PCVs were using large quantities of electricity for a washing machine, hot water heater, and other appliances—but were cheating the municipal electricity department by rigging their electric meter so that this excessive use of electricity did not register. The Volunteers felt confident that most towns-people knew that they did not even have electricity in their house.

Organizational Loyalty

There are few Volunteers who do not have a profound emotional commitment to the Peace Corps, and a sense of gratitude to the organization for having provided them with an appropriate and almost unique opportunity for service. Although few PCVs are the breast-beating type, almost all of them quietly but sincerely endorse the ideals of the organization as these have repeatedly been stated by the late President Kennedy and by Sargent Shriver—though they personally might express matters with markedly different emphasis. Indeed, the phrase "Ask not . . ." has developed as a half-humorous, half-serious byword among Bolivia Volunteers—a means of soothing frustration in difficult moments, and of gently reminding the Volunteer that he did indeed volunteer himself into his present predicament. The phrase stems, of course, from President Kennedy's memorable challenge in his inaugural address: "Ask not what your country can do for you; ask what you can do for your country!"

One form that organizational loyalty takes is the continual and energetic efforts which individual Volunteers devote to public relations. Many send articles to hometown newspapers telling more about the virtues of the Peace Corps than about their own particular activities. Many of these reports express a quiet pride in the organization, in its spirit of "can do," in its relatively low operating budget and relatively simple and direct administrative structure. Other Volunteers send open letters to groups at the training sites, describing relevant aspects of the local situation and making practical recommendations about how the trainees should prepare themselves, what they should bring with them, and so forth. These public relations efforts, it should be emphasized, are almost entirely spontaneous; seldom are they inspired by the local "Reps."

Organizational loyalty does not, however, preclude criticism by Volunteers of particular Peace Corps policies and of particular staff personnel. Such criticism does exist, and it is often strong and even caustic. But this is not to be interpreted as evidence of disloyalty. On the contrary, it betokens the very intensity of the PCVs' loyalty to the organization and its ideals. Often, those Volunteers who are loudest in their expression of criticism in closed meetings of PCVs and staff are the very same ones who most adamantly defend the Corps against criticism from the outside. Feeling as strongly as they do about the Peace Corps ideal, the Volunteers experience particular frustration and disappointment when they observe events or policies or personnel which seem to stand in the way of actually realizing the organization's ideals. In particular, members of the staff sub-culture come in for a sizable share of the criticism.

The very structure of the Peace Corps helps to promote in-group loyalty. Being a member of "Bolivia One" or "Bolivia Two" from the inception of training right on through the field experience is somewhat like belonging to the Class of 1961 or 1962 at a small college—except that it is much more intense. People live in close quarters at the training site. Everybody gets to know everybody else. The training and selection experience is an emotionally intense one and fosters a powerful "we-they" feeling—the "they" being, of course, the selection officials, visitors from Peace Corps/Washington, and, to a lesser extent, members of the training faculty. Following the emotion-laden farewell at the airport and the long flight to Bolivia—which for many Volunteers is their first time away from the United States—come the trials and anxieties of learning how to function effectively in a distinctly alien culture, which further force the PCVs to rely on each other for emotional support. Then there is the separation as Volunteers are parceled out to a variety of field assignments, many of them to one- and two-man posts, and the pattern of "situational austerity" emerges. Hereafter, PCVs get together for fairly frequent weekends in towns and cities—to "talk shop" and compare experiences by the hour—or assemble at periodic in-service training seminars in their occupational specialty, conducted by the Peace Corps staff. Finally, either on long vacations or at the end of their service in Bolivia, the Volunteers usually visit other Latin American countries—and they will generally stay with a locally stationed Volunteer wherever this is practicable. Partly, of course, this is done for reasons of economy. But an equally strong reason is that PCVs from whatever country seem to "talk the same language" and quickly discover how much they have in common.

THE VOLUNTEERS' ANTHROPOLOGICAL PERSPECTIVE

As a cultural anthropologist, I have been gratified by the anthropological point of view readily adopted by a number of PCVs I have observed in action in Bolivia. While they might not express their ideas in anthropological terms, nonetheless their point of view is unmistakably anthropological.

Like the field anthropologist, the PCV is more or less constantly seeking to learn and understand the local social and cultural realities. He is more or less constantly asking himself, his colleagues, and the Bolivians what it is that Bolivians really want and value in life. And, as we have earlier seen, the PCV attempts to keep his own innovative aspirations within the limits imposed by these realities.

The longer the Volunteer remains in Bolivia, the more keenly aware he becomes of the relativity of values. Cultural relativism, which started out by being simply an intellectual term used by his lecturers during training, now becomes fully accepted, emotionally as well as intellectually. In Szanton's terminology (page 54), he becomes "acceptant" of the local culture. He is on guard against his own possible ethnocentrism. Quite characteristically, the Volunteer becomes self-conscious about his own behavior, asking himself whether he is imposing his own North American concepts and values upon the Bolivians—and whether he has a right to do so. (He cannot always expect the same tolerance on the part of the Bolivians, however, so that, for example, what some Volunteers consider casual dress is sometimes resented or ridiculed by their hosts as sloppy and inappropriate in an urban setting.)

On the other hand, the more thoughtful Volunteers are at least vaguely aware of a nearly universal consensus among cultures on a few fundamental principles. The survival of most infants to adulthood is everywhere valued, as is the absence of debilitating disease, even though many Bolivians accept the endemicity of certain infections or infestations that practitioners of Western medicine consider unhealthy. In some cultures physical suffering may be accepted, or even actively sought, as a means to an end—but never as an end in itself. In some cultures, certainly including some of those found in Bolivia, excessive wealth is deprecated—but all cultures have some conception of minimal material standards requisite for adequate living. Thus the Volunteer sees himself, and accurately so, as helping the Bolivians to help themselves toward the realization of ideals that are nearly universal among the peoples of the earth. The ideals they strive for are "pan-human"; it is the specific *means* of achieving these ends that vary, that are specific to a particular culture or nation.

We can summarize this section by saying that most Volunteers in Bolivia are anthropologically sophisticated enough to avoid taking the position that they are "just there to help and not to change the local culture." Their very activities, if continued over a considerable period of time, will certainly have the effect of promoting change in some aspects of the local culture. The Volunteers *are* intervening, are aware of the fact, and are concerned over it in a healthy way. Most of them experience healthy self-doubts and second thoughts, and I hope this will always be so. At the same time, it is clear to the PCVs that if the Bolivians are to satisfy certain of their wants, then they will need to change certain related behavior patterns: higher agricultural productivity, for instance, will require more emphasis on planning, on saving, on seed selection, and so forth. In summary, then, we can characterize the anthropological sophistication of many of the PCVs by saying that they experience ample self-doubt but relatively little self-deception.

CONCLUSIONS

This summary of the patterns within the emerging Volunteer subculture is highly tentative. I hope other observers will soon improve upon it, and generalize the analysis beyond Bolivia.

I think the Peace Corps operation in Bolivia has been, relatively speaking, a success. In my opinion, the primary explanation for this success has been the quality and dedication of the Volunteer, mediated through a peculiar value system and set of shared understandings and ways of doing things that go to make up the Volunteer subculture. I think this subculture, in its over-all shape and design, is reasonably appropriate to its task. There are, though, two noticeable weaknesses in the subculture as it now stands, which I think should be corrected. First, I would like to see a higher value placed upon learning to speak the indigenous language— Quechua or Aymará—rather than stopping short at Spanish. And second, it would be helpful if the subculture could somehow discourage the sort of "secondary ignorance"—not knowing that one does not know—of which a sizable minority of PCVs are as yet still guilty. Perhaps a greater and more systematic use of social science in the in-service training seminars would be helpful.

The success of the Peace Corps in Bolivia has taken many forms. Several of the immunization programs will have long-lasting effects, if only because some of the serums remain potent for many years. A few members of the Corps made modest contributions to the expansion of agricultural production. Bolivian university students have received much knowledge which will be retained and used. More important, however, there is some basis for optimism that the essential "human relations" spirit and method introduced by the Peace Corps will become incorporated into local cultures, structures, and organizations. By this I mean getting across to the Bolivian people such elemental ideas as that health (or whatever) is a *problem* and that it is a problem about which they themselves can *do* something. This is an important first step, and hence a real gain. Similarly, just getting across the idea that community cooperation is possible—that it is effective in solving problems—is a major gain that far outshadows in its potential importance any particular technological or medical innovation. Of course, in many cases these ideas did *not* get across (even though the PCV might have thought they did); in other cases, however, they apparently did get across, and with some prospect of eventually becoming institutionalized.

Quite apart from specific innovations and their prospects for permanent adoption into Bolivian cultures, there is the added and undeniable fact that the PCVs have indeed, by and large, succeeded in projecting a new image of North Americans. Many Bolivians have learned, for the *first* time, that there are North Americans who are not wealthy, bigoted, or afraid to work with their hands— and who are not only willing to speak their language, but also to take an interest in them as human beings. Many stereotypes have gone crashing. Many genuine friendships have been made. Things will never be quite the same again.

The Volunteer subculture stands in considerable contrast to the *staff* subculture. Many staff members administering the program in Bolivia have left much to be desired in the way of understanding people in general and Bolivians in particular. Rarely has there been a staff member assigned to Bolivia who has been distinctively *better* qualified—intellectually, experientially, and empathically—than the average PCV over whom he had control.*

Finally, let me say that the value system and general esprit that one finds in the Volunteer subculture is of enormous potential importance back in the United States. The reasonedly egoistic altruism and the energetic activism which characterize the Volunteer in Bolivia can serve greatly to brighten the dark spots in our own society—the blighted areas of economic deprivation and racial discrimination. The PCV's local identification—provided it is not carried to excess and is tempered with intellectual honesty and curiosity—can lead to transcultural understanding of real depth and validity. As the Volunteers return and make their influence felt at home, the result will be a much better informed American public

* It would be an unfortunate mistake to assume that this problem has been solved and is now a thing of the past. As this book was going to press in August 1965, a returned Volunteer from Bolivia complained that a new Representative had just been chosen for that country who had never been there before and did not speak Spanish.—Ed.

opinion, electorate, and foreign policy. I consider it highly likely that historians in the year 2000 will regard the Peace Corps as one of the great accomplishments of Twentieth Century America. And their reasons for doing so might be cast more in terms of what the Peace Corps did for *us* than what it did for countries like Bolivia.

NOTES

[1] Twenty-seven public health Volunteers and five university teachers arrived in January 1964, and twenty-four more public health workers in April. In September, forty-two community development workers arrived, together with twenty-one university teachers. October brought twenty-one agricultural specialists and another twenty-three in public health. In December, a dozen more university teachers and thirty-six more public health Volunteers began work in Bolivia.

In late 1965, a large-scale community development project, administered in collaboration with AID, was due to bring about 120 Volunteers, and about forty more Volunteers were expected then for work in agriculture and public health.

BIBLIOGRAPHY

ARNADE, CHARLES W.
>A detailed study of Bolivian history, now in press, to be published by the Oxford University Press, London and New York.

HANKE, LEWIS
>1962   *Latin America: Continent in Ferment.* New York: Anvil Books. Two volumes. Includes a summary discussion of Bolivian history which places major events and processes in perspective.

HEATH, DWIGHT B., CHARLES J. ERASMUS, and HANS C. BUECHLER
>*Land Reform and Social Revolution in Bolivia.* Forthcoming. A description and analysis of recent changes in various regions of the country.

OSBORNE, HAROLD
>1964   *Bolivia: A Land Divided.* London: Royal Institute of International Affairs. Third revised edition. While it is difficult to encompass the immense and rich diversity of Bolivia in a single book, this exceptionally comprehensive and yet readable little volume comes close.

PATCH, RICHARD W.
>1960   "Bolivia: U.S. Assistance in a Revolutionary Setting," in Richard N. Adams and others, *Social Change in Latin America Today.* New York: Harper and Brothers. A generally sound description of political and economic trends.

SPECIAL OPERATIONS RESEARCH OFFICE
>1963   *U.S. Army Area Handbook for Bolivia.* Washington, D. C.: Special Operations Research Office. This handbook complements the Osborne book by providing more detail on social and political institutions.

UNITED NATIONS
   1951 *Report of the United Nations Mission of Technical Assistance
         to Bolivia.* New York: United Nations. Many of the basic
         economic and social problems of Bolivia remain little changed
         since they were critically analyzed in this volume, which is
         sometimes referred to as the "Keenleyside Report."
ZONDAG, C. H.
   1956 *Problems in the Economic Development of Bolivia.* La Paz:
         U.S. Operations Mission (AID). A realistic evaluation of the
         subject.

16

Conclusions, Problems, and Prospects

Robert B. Textor*

POLITICAL SURVIVAL AND INSTITUTIONALIZATION

SARGENT Shriver's "political gamble" has been won, and won
handily. The Peace Corps has survived. It has become more or
less firmly institutionalized—as any unwary politician would soon
find out if he were now to attack it frontally.

That the political gamble has now been largely won is a fact of
far-reaching significance. It means that the officials of Peace Corps/
Washington now enjoy sufficient trust and support from Congress
so that they can get on with the job of coping with the "cultural
gamble," that of more adequately realizing in forty-odd host countries the three basic objectives set forth in the Peace Corps Act (page
5). As the sections that follow will make clear, success in achieving these objectives has to date been far from uniform.

AN IMPROVED AMERICAN IMAGE OVERSEAS

As far as the thirteen countries described in this book are concerned, there seems to be little question that the Peace Corps

* This chapter represents my views only. Most of the contributors have not
seen it in manuscript, and none of them is in any way responsible for its content. It is based on seven months service with Peace Corps/Washington in
1961–1962; on twenty-two visiting lectureships at various training sites during
which I have met some 1,600 Volunteer trainees bound for Southeast Asia; on
numerous conversations with returned Volunteers; and on talks with past and
present Peace Corps/Washington officials and with my fellow contributors to
this book. Unfortunately, I have not had a chance to observe Volunteers in the
field.

This chapter applies specifically to the thirteen host countries covered in this
book, and not necessarily to any of the other thirty-three countries where the
Peace Corps is at work.

Volunteers have succeeded to a remarkable degree in projecting a new and better image of Americans. Mahony, Gallagher, and Heath bring this out with particular clarity, and none of our authors seem to disagree. The altruism, sincerity, and humility of most Volunteers seem clearly to have registered a favorable impression. Few Volunteers have been guilty of the ethnocentrism, arrogance, or opportunism that have at times characterized personnel sent overseas by other American governmental or private organizations. Unlike many other Americans working in the developing countries, the PCVs are "doers," and often provide direct, person-to-person service of a type that is immediately and deeply appreciated. The extreme example is the nurse or other medical Volunteer who personally relieves immediate and acute suffering.

The Volunteer has, of course, typically lived and worked at a considerably lower socioeconomic level than that enjoyed by most other Americans in the same host country. At many posts, the PCV has been the first American ever personally known to the local people, whose previous impressions of Americans might have been based on hearsay, on stories of varying reliability appearing in their local press, on Hollywood movies, or on radio broadcasts originating in Washington, Moscow, Peking, or Havana. In other localities, the PCV has been the first American ever known to have spoken the local language and to have shown a willingness—even a desire— to live modestly and to mix with the local people on their own terms as friendly equals. In still other localities, the PCV has not been the first American known to be conversant with the local culture and language, but he *has* been the first such American to have come in a service role devoid of such customary motives as financial profit, political propaganda, or the conversion of local souls to a strange religion. This is not to say, of course, that the Volunteer has no "angle" of his own. Often he does, seeing himself as a "change agent." But in such cases, his motive is still generically different from those of his predecessors, in that he is usually attempting, with considerable determination and varying degrees of skill, to promote change of a kind that will help satisfy the local people's wants and needs more or less as *they* perceive them—as distinct from the wants and needs *he* thinks they ought to perceive.

The PCVs have also made favorable impressions on members of the governing elites of the thirteen host countries discussed in this volume. Indeed, throughout the world, it is significant that virtually every host government has requested more Volunteers after observing the first contingent of Volunteers in action. Even when one grants that the need for manpower is ordinarily the prime reason behind such requests, the record remains an impressive one.

The temptation should be firmly resisted, however, to regard the Volunteers as paragons of perfection. Among returnees whom I know, many a ripe anecdote circulates, indicating beyond doubt that the PCVs have been guilty of numerous cultural gaffes, and are susceptible to the usual human foibles and peccadilloes. The fact that few of these stories have appeared in the press is a tribute to the PCVs' own discretion, and to the alertness of the Representatives, one of whose principal unwritten tasks is that of avoiding unfavorable publicity. Perhaps it is also true that American journalists have avoided unfavorable stories because of a high regard for the Corps as an embodiment of their own personal ideals. Nor does it seem likely that any very large proportion of the American public would want to read such unfavorable stories—for similar reasons. In the host countries, too, one suspects that many journalists and governmental officials have suppressed the impulse publicly to criticize particular incidents because of a generalized feeling of gratitude and respect toward the PCVs, and an appreciation of their humility, service orientation, and cultural empathy. Incidentally, nothing is more likely to gall Volunteers and ex-Volunteers than glib publicity exalting their purported superhuman qualities.*

This section may be summarized by quoting briefly from one of the most interesting testimonials to the PCVs yet to appear. This testimonial comes, oddly enough, from the Communists. The Peace Corps has frequently been attacked and slandered in both the Moscow and Peking presses. The first Red Chinese diplomat to defect to the West has paraphrased the position taken by officials in the African Affairs Division of the Foreign Ministry in Peking as fol-

---

* At this point it is worthwhile to make clear, in passing, that the performance of some Representative staff members still leaves much to be desired. At this writing, Peace Corps/Washington is still appointing "Reps" who in many cases know considerably less about the host country than do the Volunteers whose activities they are charged with supervising. And it is still true that the Representatives are seldom given as much language and area training as the Volunteers. Admittedly, some duties of some members of the Representative teams do not call for as much cultural and linguistic proficiency as do most assignments of the Volunteers. Nonetheless, the cultural naiveté of some "Reps" remains a problem affecting the "image" and the success of the Peace Corps in particular countries. For example, one of the "Reps" in an Asian country in 1965 was a man who had never previously served in the non-Western or developing world. Among his practices was that of visiting local schools while dressed in Bermuda shorts—in a culture where the only persons who wear shorts are children and manual laborers.

lows: "A political vacuum exists in Africa, and we intend to fill it. Our enemy in Africa is not Russia, but the United States. American agents under the name of the Peace Corps are the most dangerous opposition we have." The defected diplomat then speculates: "Perhaps the effect of this dedicated organization has been vastly underrated by the American press and public." (Tung 1964: 25). It need hardly be added that the PCVs are not "agents" in any political sense; they do not proselytize in any overt, systematic, or explicit manner (Heath, page 284). Indeed, the very fact that the Volunteer engages in *no* such activities helps to explain why he has become, among other things, an important political asset to the United States. By treating local people according to their own local wants and needs, without undue reference to their political importance, the Volunteer builds the kind of goodwill that does, in the end, have considerable political significance.

THE ACHIEVEMENT OF CULTURAL SENSITIVITY AND PROFICIENCY

A second objective stated in the Peace Corps Act is to promote understanding on the part of the Volunteers of another way of life. The process of achieving such understanding can be analyzed under three rubrics: humility, sensitivity, and proficiency. Humility refers to a person's ability to keep his egocentric tendencies under control. Sensitivity grows out of humility, and refers to his abilities to keep his *ethno*centric tendencies under control and to maintain a lively awareness that any host culture might prove to be quite basically different from his own in a variety of important respects. In Szanton's terms, sensitivity implies a predisposition to be "acceptant" (page 54). Proficiency grows out of humility and sensitivity, plus appropriate training and guidance, and refers to the specific linguistic and cultural competence needed to cope efficiently and effectively with a variety of problems of living and working in a particular host culture.

As far as humility is concerned, I would give the Peace Corps Volunteers high marks. Even raw trainees at the training site, of whom I have met many hundreds, seem appropriately humble in their attitudes toward other cultures.

Sensitivity, too, seems to characterize the great majority of Volunteers. My impressions are based on conversations with trainees before they leave for the host country and with returnees back in the United States; they are therefore superficial observations, lacking the essential ingredient of field observation. Nonetheless, these conversations yield a very favorable impression. I have only rarely met a returned Volunteer who seemed clearly lacking in cultural sensitivity. On lecture visits to trainees destined for Thailand, I have been struck by the sensitivity revealed in the nature of their questions, and all the more so in view of the fact that these people were yet to experience Thailand at firsthand. On the basis of such admittedly sketchy evidence, I would characterize most of these trainees as being considerably more sensitive than most American officials I knew in Thailand during the 1950's. Much of the explanation for this apparent difference would seem to lie in the fact that the emphasis on sensitivity in the Volunteer subculture of the sixties is pronounced, while this was not the case in the subculture of American officials stationed in Thailand during the fifties.

Cultural sensitivity is, of course, a generalizable ability. The Volunteer working in the Hausa culture area of Nigeria will find himself considerably sensitized to differences between Hausa value standards and those he meets in other culture areas of Africa. Most of all, he will be sensitized to the differences between Hausa culture and his own American culture. For deep immersion in any alien culture provides the opportunity for contrast with one's own culture, for detachment and perspective. Time and again, one hears ex-Volunteers making remarks like this: "It was only after I got to Africa that it began to be possible for me to question many American values and assumptions which I'd previously just taken for granted." Herein lies a fact of vast potential significance to future intellectual developments in the United States.

FACTORS AFFECTING THE ACHIEVEMENT OF CULTURAL PROFICIENCY

Humility and sensitivity are necessary but by no means sufficient preconditions to the achievement of cultural proficiency. Among the returned Volunteers one meets some who seem remarkably humble and sensitive, and yet who patently have learned little of the host country's language, and appear to have learned less about the rest of its culture than might have been expected.* It should be immediately added, however, that such observations are subject to considerable error. For example, a PCV might be culturally quite proficient even though his language knowledge is limited, and

---

* I speak here only of PCVs returned from Thailand and Malaysia, since the Thai and Malay languages and cultures are those with which I have some familiarity.

even though he is not able to verbalize his knowledge of the host culture very convincingly. Nonetheless, there is considerable variation among returned Volunteers in this respect.

At this point the analysis becomes complicated by the fact that the particular subculture in which the Volunteer works might be quite different from the general host culture. A teacher working in Bangkok might find himself surrounded by acculturated Thai colleagues who speak much better English than he can speak Thai (Guskin, page 100). An engineer stationed in Penang, Malaysia, might confront a similar situation, but with the added complication that his closest colleagues are English-speaking Malaysian Chinese who are not particularly happy at his attempts to address them in Malay. A further complicating factor is that large numbers of Volunteers—especially English teachers, but others as well—are besieged on all sides by local people who want to practice their English.

Undoubtedly, Volunteers of the types just described often become quite proficient in their on-the-job contacts with members of the particular English-speaking subcultures in which they find themselves. Similar proficiency is also achieved by some PCVs in French-speaking Africa or Spanish-speaking Latin America (Doughty, page 231; Heath, page 294). Nonetheless, in countries where English, French, or Spanish is not the language that the great majority of local people prefer to speak in the home or wherever opportunity permits them choice, there seems little doubt that the Volunteer would be more effective if he knew the "home" language of the people. While knowing this "home" language may admittedly be much less useful in some situations than in others, it is difficult to think of a situation where it would not be useful at all. I have yet to meet anyone who *has* learned the "home" language under such circumstances, who would appear to disagree with this statement.*

---

* Some who did *not* learn the "home" language might, however, disagree. An appropriate response to such disagreement has been made by F. Kingston Berlew, Acting Associate Director for Peace Corps Volunteers. Berlew modestly concedes that, as Peace Corps Representative in Pakistan, he was so preoccupied with administrative work that he "did not become fluent enough in either Urdu or Bengali to participate fully in the life of Pakistan." He nonetheless argues that

". . . the greatest value and strength of the Peace Corps does not lie in the accomplishment of physical construction or in the simple transfer of knowledge. It is rather in the effect of the individual Volunteer on the minds and attitudes of those with whom he lives and works. . . . Language is of primary

Speaking of cultural proficiency in the sense that involves a local "home" culture and language, the wide variation among returnees can doubtless be explained, in good part, in terms of personal characteristics such as intelligence, motivation, and temperament. Beyond these, however, are a number of other factors that also seem important; these are outlined in the subsections that follow.

Quality of Training

The quality of training has ranged from very good to very poor. Not infrequently, lecturers have been chosen more because they happen to be regular faculty members of the training university than because they are experts on a relevant subject (see Comitas, page 205). Technical training, especially, has often lacked a realistic relationship to host country conditions and limitations. In language training, too, there have been serious problems. For example, early training programs for one Asian country offered far too little training in the local language, in part because responsible officials in Washington had themselves never been through the experience of learning an exotic tongue and assumed that the PCVs would simply "pick up" the language once in the country. This assumption turned out to be largely erroneous. Other things equal, Volunteers who arrive in the host country with a well-aroused cultural sensitivity, with a sound basic command of the local language, and with good training in such areas as the local culture's value system, administrative tradition, and social and economic structure are likely to continue to learn efficiently day by day in the manner called for by Guthrie (page 32). Poorly trained PCVs, by contrast, start from such a low base of sophistication that their total learning accomplishment is likely to be much more modest.

---

importance to this kind of contribution. Those few persons who by example, warmth of personality, and dedication are able to transcend this communications barrier to a degree are truly exceptional. Even in those countries where English is the second language, inability to speak and understand the first language is a major handicap to full effectiveness as a Volunteer. . . . Even where English comprehension is good, cultural barriers persist without the ability to approach students and co-workers through their own language. It is not enough that the student hear the word and understand its meaning. Lessons must be related to some relevant part of the student's experience, and built on that."

Berlew recommends that the Peace Corps "should seriously consider limiting membership in the organization to those Volunteers and staff members committed to learning (and using) the primary language of their communities" (Berlew 1965: 2).

Difficulty of the Local Language

An important factor influencing the degree of achievement of cultural proficiency is the relative ease of learning the host country's language. The easiest such languages are those most closely related to English, such as Spanish and French. Results of language proficiency examinations indicate that PCVs in Hispanic America have progressed well in Spanish. Where the local language is not related to English, results are generally much less encouraging. Even among such languages however, there are important distinctions. It is much easier for an American to learn Malay, for example, than Somali.

Cultural Distance

Related to the language factor is the matter of cultural distance. It seems generally true that a PCV's cultural proficiency will be greatest where the host culture is not too vastly different from his own. The culture of Costa Rica, for example, is essentially Hispanic and Catholic, and considerably closer to American culture than is the non-Western, Buddhist culture of Thailand. Thai civilization, in turn, is much closer to American civilization than are those smaller tribally organized cultures of sub-Saharan Africa which lack writing, cities, and an international religion. As far as proficiency in the "home" language and culture is concerned, I would expect PCVs in Costa Rica to do better than those in Thailand, who in turn would do better than those working with members of a tribal culture in Africa. There are no available data to permit this hypothesis to be checked systematically, but all three of our chapters on sub-Saharan Africa point to the difficulty experienced by the PCVs in developing proficiency for dealing with unacculturated Africans on their own traditional African terms (Friedland, page 150; Cowan, page 162; Dorjahn, page 182). In a similar vein, Doughty has shown how Volunteers in Peru developed much more proficiency in dealing with the Hispanicized portions of the Peruvian population than they did in dealing with unacculturated Quechua Indians (page 231). While language difficulties are doubtless also involved in the foregoing examples, it seems plausible that cultural distance would be an important factor even if language difficulties were held constant. A final point worth noting is that the PCV can sometimes underestimate cultural distance, with the result that the development of cultural proficiency is hampered. This problem of superficial cultural similarity has been discussed for the Philippines and Jamaica (Szanton, page 49; Comitas, page 213).

The "Third Culture" Problem

As many of our authors have pointed out, the PCV's task of gaining cultural proficiency is further complicated when a "third" culture must also be learned. This is the culture borrowed, with adaptations, from the former European colonial ruler. Among our thirteen countries, there are only three where this is not a problem: the Philippines, Thailand, and Afghanistan. Generally speaking, the PCV must concentrate his energies on this third culture first, rather than on the indigenous culture, in good part because the third culture is used to a significant extent by the political, governmental, and administrative elite. In four of the ten ex-colonial cases, learning the third culture entails knowing a European language that is often new to the PCV. Thus Spanish is necessary for Volunteers in Peru and Bolivia, and French for Tunisia and Morocco; and in the former Italian portion of Somalia PCVs find very useful any facility they might develop in Italian. This extra learning burden adds heavily to the difficulty of gaining proficiency in the "home" language and culture of the local people. The problem is compounded even further where members of the elite— such as the Spanish speakers in Peru—tend to look down on their compatriots who are able to speak only the indigenous tongue. Considering the brevity of the Volunteer's tour, it is little wonder that he has usually come back from Peru without knowing much Quechua or Aymará, or back from Morocco without knowing much Arabic (Doughty, page 231; Gallagher, page 197).

Openness of the Host Society

The relative openness of the host society is another important factor. Of our thirteen countries, Afghanistan is probably the least open. Its inward-looking society presents great obstacles to outsiders attempting to cross the cultural frontier (Dupree, page 111). Even a "transitional" country like Tunisia, however, feels the definite isolating effects of Islam, particularly upon its womenfolk. Similar situations are found in the more conservative Catholic areas of such countries as Bolivia (Heath, page 289). Countries where considerable local political power is still in the hands of tribes or other fractional groups, such as Sierra Leone, are also likely to be relatively closed to the Volunteers (Dorjahn, page 172).

Rural Versus Urban Assignments

In the developing countries, even including the minority of them that are linguistically homogeneous, there is typically a vast cultural gap separating the urban elite from the rural masses. Urban life, even when lived away from members of the elite, normally contains many more elements borrowed from Western culture: imported motion pictures, efficient transportation, relatively convenient commercial and financial facilities, Western-style athletics, food, and dancing—and many others. Such elements of Western culture often become tempting "props" on which a Volunteer may lean, or formidable barriers that discourage him from reaching out for contact with less acculturated, more traditional people. Indeed, PCVs stationed in large cities like Kuala Lumpur, Bangkok, Dar es Salaam, or Kingston sometimes must actually *struggle* in order to achieve meaningful contact with people of traditional outlook and values.* The typical rural PCV is under little such temptation or pressure. Willy-nilly, he instead finds himself under another kind of pressure—that pushing him to develop an acceptant attitude toward the traditional culture (Szanton, page 54). Incidentally, in part because the "Peace Corps image" portrays the PCV in rural conditions interacting with traditional people, it is perhaps generally true that PCVs stationed in smaller towns and villages are more satisfied with their lot than those assigned to cities (Maryanov, page 77; Guskin, page 99).

---

* Some readers might question the emphasis here being placed on achieving an understanding of the traditional culture, and object that this is really not necessary for the PCV assigned to a modern urban area. Such objections may well be valid in some cases. However, the argument that most PCVs—including those assigned to urban areas—would do well to develop considerable understanding of the traditional culture remains a reasonably convincing one, and one that parallels the argument for learning the "home" language. An example is seen in Thailand, where Westerners typically confine their learning efforts to the modern subculture of Bangkok. These efforts seldom succeed in achieving deep understanding of the behavior of Bangkok people. On the other hand, Westerners who start by attempting to understand the traditional rural Thai subculture usually have little difficulty later in making sense out of the urban, modern, somewhat Westernized Bangkok subculture. By first developing an understanding of the cultural "baseline" from which Westernization departs, they are able to perceive the varying degrees of acculturation among urban Thais whom they meet, and to act accordingly. They are able, in short, to cope with the problem of "superficial cultural similarity" mentioned by Szanton and Comitas (pages 49 and 213).

Political Factors

As Palmer clearly demonstrates for Peru, the local population's political loyalties, aspirations, animosities, prejudices, and whims can constitute a formidable barrier to the PCV's attempts to achieve meaningful people-to-people relationships. These political barriers can loom important not only in "transitional" countries like Peru but also in largely "traditional" countries like Somalia and Tanzania (Mahony, page 132; Friedland, page 153).

Job Structure

The opportunity to develop cultural proficiency seems also to depend heavily on how "structured" the PCV's job is, as well as on the nature of that structure. The community developer's job, for example, is usually relatively "unstructured." Indeed, he is frequently forced to help *create* a new structure in order to get a job done. The amount of cultural proficiency required in order successfully to create a structure—even a simple one—in a host society is usually far greater than that required simply to fit into an existing structure. It seems a plausible hypothesis that the more "structured" the job, the easier it is for one to withdraw from deep transcultural involvement. The PCV who retreats more and more into his well-structured job can avoid feelings of guilt and shame to a considerable degree because he is, after all, doing his job. A PCV with an unstructured job enjoys no such luxury. It should be added, though, that some community developers try to create a local structure and fail—doubtless with the result, in some cases, that they withdraw from the local culture (Szanton, page 53).

Some jobs are structured in a highly "people-oriented" manner, and demand that the PCV relate frequently and intensively to large numbers of local people. Other jobs are much less oriented toward people, and more toward technology and material things. A Volunteer nurse in an outpatient clinic, for example, can hardly avoid intensive contact with a wide variety of local people. A Volunteer draftsman, by contrast, might spend every working day at his drawing board in an office where there are just two or three local people present.

CONTRIBUTIONS TO THE HOST COUNTRY'S DEVELOPMENT

The final Congressionally set objective of the Peace Corps is to help the peoples of the host countries "in meeting their needs for trained manpower." The Peace Corps Act tactfully avoids any reference to the host countries as "underdeveloped." It also avoids any specification as to whether the "trained manpower" provided by the Corps will be used for the promotion of self-expanding "development," or whether it will simply be used to meet immediate needs, without any particular reference to contribution to "development." Apparently Peace Corps/Washington has avoided taking any final decision as to whether "developmentally significant" projects will receive priority over projects lacking such significance. Such ambiguity of policy can be defended. Nonetheless, this section is concerned with the PCVs' contribution to development, because it seems fairly clear that this is what the great majority of host governments are eager to achieve. And the various host countries will probably not consider themselves "developed" until the day is reached when they no longer need to rely on outside sources for manpower of the type provided by the Peace Corps.

"Developmentally Significant" Versus Simple Service Programs

Judging whether a particular program is "developmentally significant" is an extremely complex matter, involving theoretical issues and assumptions far beyond the scope of this book. Nonetheless, it might be helpful at this point to illustrate the distinction between a developmentally oriented program, and one that simply contributes a service. An example is seen in the nurses of Tanganyika Two described by Friedland (page 141). These nurses were evidently rendering excellent service in the relief of human suffering—service that probably would not have been performed, or performed as effectively, if they had not been present on the scene. The relief of suffering is a worthy ethical end in itself. It is deeply appreciated by the local people and profoundly satisfying to the Volunteer. It is also, incidentally, an effective means of projecting a positive American image. But whether it is developmentally significant is a totally separate question. The answer depends on chains of events that occur, or seem likely to occur, as a consequence of these nurses' activities. It depends on whether the cured Tanganyika patient uses his new strength and health toward some end that he (or someone) considers "developmental"; on whether he learns from the Volunteer nurse how to take care of his health more effectively in the future; on whether the nurse, in treating the patient, imparted by her example to a Tanganyikan nurse some more effective technique of nursing (page 151); or perhaps on whether the PCV nurse replaces the Tanganyikan nurse while the latter attends an advanced training course to upgrade her skills. Considerations such as these were apparently behind the decision of Peace Corps/Bolivia to deemphasize service nursing and increase the emphasis on health education designed to teach people how to stay well (Heath, page 276).

The Difficulty of Contributing to Development

Making a lasting contribution to the host country's development is by far the most difficult of the three objectives outlined or suggested in the Peace Corps Act, principally because it involves many social, cultural, political, and administrative factors far beyond the control of the individual Volunteer. By contrast, a PCV can project a positive image by such comparatively simple devices as being a "nice guy," taking a sincere interest in the local culture, working with his hands where appropriate, and meeting local people as equals. He can also achieve considerable cultural sensitivity and proficiency, even where his training and assignment have not been too conducive, by dint of individual initiative. While it is true that culture fatigue, illness, frustration, psychological isolation, or boredom might make it difficult to muster the needed motivation, the point remains that in both these efforts the initiative is essentially individual, and so is the accomplishment. Contributing to the host country's development, by contrast, is much more of a team operation. And the product of the operation is essentially cultural[1] rather than individual. Making a lasting contribution means that the PCVs' efforts will serve effectively to strengthen existing tendencies toward kinds of change that are, ultimately at any rate, cultural in nature. And cultural change usually occurs slowly, as the result of complex need-gratifying and adjustive processes permeating far beyond the immediate problem area in which the innovator is attempting to induce change. There is a considerable professional literature on the subject of cultural change, a small portion of which is cited in the bibliography at the end of this chapter.

Unrealistic Initial Aspirations

Whatever our data permit or do not permit us to say about the Peace Corps' contribution to the development of various host countries, one conclusion seems warranted, namely that this contribution has in most respects been smaller than originally envisaged by many early senior staff members of Peace Corps/ Washington. Many of these individuals—particularly those recruited from political circles—brought with them highly unrealistic notions as to how much the PCVs could contribute, and how fast. Many members of Congress, of both parties, were similarly afflicted with this "gung-ho" syndrome (Guthrie, page 28). They were impatient and angry at investing taxpayers' money in foreign aid projects that apparently yielded too few tangible results. They thus responded eagerly to the idea and the hope that perhaps the PCVs would be different. Quite understandably, the press releases of Peace Corps/Washington in the early days seized upon such sentiments and attempted, with considerable success, to turn them into political assets for the Peace Corps cause. The exploits of the Volunteers in the field—especially concrete, visible, quantifiable technological exploits of individual PCVs—were highlighted in news releases and in the monthly *Peace Corps Volunteer*. In due course, there developed a new "Peace Corps mystique." An integral part of this mystique, incidentally, was the strong early emphasis on athletics and physical conditioning, and the selection of well-known athletes for important staff positions, suggesting an underlying assumption that physical energy and athletic prowess were somehow going to make a vital difference. Useful as this mystique may have been in winning crucial Congressional and public support in the early days, it was hardly a realistic basis for the laying of plans or the setting of goals.

Many Volunteers, too, have started out with unrealistic aspirations (Maryanov, page 84). Before long, however, they usually learn just how unreasonable their initial ambitions were. More important, they learn a good deal about what *can* be done, about how to gear their aspirations down to a realistic level and proceed to realize some of them (Heath, page 285). Unfortunately, by the time the PCV has thoroughly learned all these vital lessons, he or she is in most cases ready to return to the United States. Even so, the learning of these lessons is perhaps the single greatest benefit derived by the PCVs from their experiences overseas. It will prove immensely valuable when they later return to intercultural work, as some of them already have, and many others hopefully will (Cowan, page 166).

Paucity of Evaluative Data

The remainder of this section will be much briefer than would be desirable, for two reasons. First, at this writing it is still far too early to make many confident statements on the lasting, cultural impact of the PCVs overseas. Second, even if it were not too early, there are simply not sufficient data available on which to base conclusions. It is doubtful if even Peace Corps/Washington has sufficient data. The measurement and prediction of cultural impact is an immensely complex problem involving careful observation of many variables. An enormous—and expensive—amount of research is usually required, of the general type carried out in the Philippines by Lynch and Maretzki (page 32). The sections that follow outline some of the types of developmental contributions which it seems reasonable to suppose the PCVs are making, even in the absence of systematic field data.

Relatively Noninnovative Contributions

The simplest way of contributing to the host country's development is the relatively noninnovative approach of stepping into a well-organized, highly structured job and carrying it out more or less in the manner that a host country citizen would, if one were available. The purposes of such an assignment are well accepted in the host culture—for example, the teaching of science. No effort is necessary to "sell" the local people on science as being a good thing. Nor is any effort needed to "sell" them on having a school: the school is already there. The essential contribution of the Volunteers is a quantitative one: they are bringing important services to a larger number of local people than would otherwise be reached by such services. Jobs such as this can contribute greatly to development. It is a fact, for example, that in six African countries in 1965 at least half of the college-graduate secondary teachers were PCVs. This type of contribution should have an enormous influence in unifying these culturally and linguistically fragmented countries into viable national units—especially if the Peace Corps is willing and able to keep replacing PCVs with other PCVs until such time as African teachers are available. It need hardly be added that programing should include some feature that will hasten the day when the supply of qualified African teachers will be adequate. One such feature might be the assignment of especially well qualified PCVs to teach in African institutions for teacher education. Another approach would be to utilize Volunteers to replace local teachers in the classroom while the latter receive additional training to upgrade their skills. Reports indicate, unfortunately, that this approach, when attempted in Liberia, attained only limited success because of administrative and other problems.

On the negative side, one wonders with Gallagher about the wisdom of sending American PCVs to teach English to Moroccan students already saddled with the need to be proficient in both Arabic and French (page 196).

Intentional Innovative Contributions

In a sense, the foregoing term "relatively noninnovative contribution" is contrived and artificial, for most PCVs seem bent on improving things. It is safe to assume that the Volunteer teacher who willingly accepts the existing text, syllabus, and mode of pedagogy is in the minority. The majority of Volunteer teachers would probably attempt to innovate by using inductive techniques, visual aids, and other approaches and materials from their own experience. Doubtless many of their innovations have proven, or will prove, to be inappropriate and ineffective—especially if the PCV lacks training in techniques of education appropriate to the particular cultural context of the host country—as has often been the case (Szanton, page 39). On other occasions, however, these innovations are undoubtedly rational and effective, and may eventually become part of the "culture" of the local school, or even of the entire school system. The Volunteer teachers at the University of Huamanga, for example, introduced a new English-teaching system that was widely appreciated for its effectiveness. But for political difficulties, this innovation might well have survived. (Palmer, page 252).

Since American culture places emphasis on gadgets and tinkering, it comes as no surprise to learn from Doughty that PCVs in Peru have devised, or attempted to devise, items ranging from windmills to potato sorters to spinning wheels (page 225). It is too early to say which of such new technological items will be widely adopted and hence contribute to the development of Peru or some other host country—but it seems likely that this will occur in a fair number of cases. The fact that the Volunteer tour is so short does, however, militate against highly elaborate, time-consuming technological innovation. It also makes difficult the PCV's acquisition of the kind of intimate cultural knowledge sometimes needed to fit a technological innovation to the local people's traditional motor habits, workways, economic attitudes, and the like. Other limiting factors are that the PCV is often technically underqualified, and that he usually works in a situation where supplies and equipment are far from abundant.

Unintentional Innovative Contributions

It is a fair guess that many of the contributions that the Volunteers leave behind will turn out not to have been consciously intended at all. Such contributions will often take the form of simply causing local people to think differently about a subject. As teachers particularly, it is likely that the PCVs have had—or will have—considerable impact merely by getting their students to think critically and inductively, rather than remaining content with rote learning. The developmental impact of some of the toolmaking, tinkering community developers described by Doughty might prove to be similar. They might register greater developmental results through demonstrating a new way of thinking about technological innovation than by the innovations that they themselves introduce while in the host country. New ways of perceiving problems, of worrying through available alternatives, of "trying it out," are sometimes contagious. The pay-off of such new modes of thinking might not be immediate; conceivably, it might in some cases occur many years later, in connection with problems not yet foreseen.

Unintentional innovation also occurs importantly in the realm of social relations. Quite possibly, for example, Guskin's students at Krungthep University had never before seriously entertained the notion that a professor can teach his class outdoors, seated on the lawn (page 103). As Guskin points out, Thai students who enjoy this kind of easy informality with Volunteer teachers might begin to ask themselves and each other why they cannot have something of the same kind of relationship with their own Thai professors. "Rocking the boat" in this fashion can have a significant impact on a university community over a period of time. Much of this impact might be considered, from some points of view, to be constructive and "developmental."

Another form of usually unintended impact would seem to stem from the fact that many PCVs are "job-oriented" and place emphasis on carrying out their duties fully and perhaps even a bit compulsively. Most of the non-Western developing countries where the Peace Corps serves are characterized by systems of administration and social service that have been borrowed from the West and that are ostensibly intended to carry out such Western-style functions as modern education, health services, and the like. Quite often, however, as Dorjahn suggests (page 179), the officials who man these services are hardly zealous about their duties, and are at least equally concerned about the comforts of their status and the perquisites of their office. When the Volunteer is assigned to this kind of organization, he brings with him the simple value standard that the organization ought, indeed, to carry out conscientiously the modern, specific function that it was ostensibly created to carry out. And, in significant contrast to many AID advisors and U.N. consultants, he brings this value standard right into the middle of the administrative situation, by virtue of his status as a "doer" and as a subordinate to a local supervisor. As the PCV acts out this value standard on the job, he perhaps causes some unpleasantness, but he also becomes a "role model" for the more or less conscientious carrying out of both the letter and especially the spirit of duty—on time and in the manner called for. I suspect that in the long run the simple fact that the PCVs usually do what they are supposed to do on the job, will constitute one of their more important indirect contributions in some host countries.*

Unintentional impact is particularly likely to be registered during the Volunteer's off-duty hours, especially where he is deeply involved in the total local community. (Indeed, for the community developer it is difficult to make a distinction between "on-duty" and "off-duty" hours.) Whether this unintentional impact will prove to be "developmentally" significant or not depends on many factors. But some impact is virtually inescapable, for the PCV is inevitably presenting to the local people a vast variety of value standards that spring from his own American culture: "standards for deciding what is, standards for deciding what can be, standards for deciding how one feels about it, standards for deciding what to do about it, and standards for deciding how to go about doing it" (Goodenough 1961: 522).

Intentionally Indirect Contributions

Many of the examples so far presented have involved more or less "direct" contributions. Other types of contribution are more "indirect." One of the best examples of the Volunteer who quite intentionally sets out to achieve an indirect result is the community developer. Doubtless he often confronts the temptation— and sometimes succumbs to it—of simply going out and building a sanitary public well "for" the people with his own hands. The better community developer, however, resists such temptation.

---

* I am indebted to Professor David A. Wilson for first suggesting this point to me in the summer of 1961 as we discussed the Peace Corps' possible long-range impact on various host countries.

Instead, he adopts the role of "social catalyst," and works patiently with local leaders until they in turn can convince their people that it is time for *them* to build "their" sanitary well, with their own labor and perhaps materials. Such patience may never receive the plaudits of the press back home, or of Congress, but it can produce at least two results of vital significance to members of the local community. First, the people are much more likely to use the well because they feel it is theirs. And second, the people are now more likely to adopt and carry through another community self-help project because of a new-found confidence in themselves.

Such indirect, action-catalyzing contributions also occur in a variety of situations other than those formally referred to as "community development." An example is the case of one Volunteer university English teacher in Venezuela. Realizing how little he himself could contribute directly to the solution of local problems, given the shortness of his tour, he hit upon an indirect approach. He decided to stimulate open-minded thinking which could catalyze Venezuelan efforts toward coming to grips with long-range Venezuelan problems. He therefore worked with his students and with Venezuelan faculty colleagues to establish both a newspaper and a discussion club where English would be the medium of communication. Far from being mere exercises in English forensics, however, these two enterprises became free forums for the discussion of a wide range of problems and issues. Such forums had previously been unavailable to many of the students, especially in situations where faculty members also participated. Among the issues and problems discussed were those of urban community development, and of Venezuelan national development. These in turn led to joint student-faculty projects in the local urban slums. Modest literacy and health projects were carried out—providing an experience that was totally new to many of the participants. When this Volunteer revisited Venezuela more than a year after his termination, he found that these projects were still being continued under Venezuelan auspices and leadership.

Political Contributions—and Dangers

Basic to the various types of contribution that have been discussed is the notion that members of the host country will perceive a goal as desirable, then perceive it as reachable, then equip themselves to reach it, and finally, sooner or later, actually reach it. It seems clear that the PCV will often be influential in getting local people to perceive goals as desirable and reachable, which previously they had not perceived in this light. This will be particularly common among less-privileged members of the host society, to whom most Volunteers seem naturally attracted because of an egalitarian interest in the underdog (Szanton, page 36; Heath, page 284; but see also Doughty, page 234).

But a danger looms. The Volunteers, intentionally or unintentionally, are contributing to a "revolution of rising expectations." By bringing modern education to more young people in a large number of host countries, for example, they are reinforcing a process in which many of their students will develop vastly higher expectations than before. The crucial difficulty is, however, that expectations have a way of expanding much more rapidly than a society's ability to fulfill them. Often the host society simply does not have sufficient jobs available for all these new graduates, at a level appropriate to their new expectations. For many of them, the gap between expectation and achievement will grow broader and broader. Such gaps, exacerbated by runaway population growth rates, can lead to political instability and explosion. When and if this happens, it might be difficult to say whether the presence of the Peace Corps has been conducive to "development" or not. For a further discussion of these problems, see Staley (1961).

To some degree, it is evident that Peace Corps planning has taken these political implications into account. In politically "transitional" Latin America, for example, about half of the Volunteers are working in community development—rural or urban. Community developers are also at work in a number of other, more "traditional" host countries. The great positive contribution that these PCVs might make—assuming wise programing and good training—is that they will equip local people with the necessary social and technical skills to satisfy enough of their aspirations in time. Sufficient political and administrative stability may thus be achieved to permit numerous other developmental processes to move forward. The difficulty, however, is that as these aspirations grow and proliferate, fewer and fewer of them will be satisfiable through local village or barriada action. More and more of them will require responsible, competent, timely action by a higher echelon of government. The complex political processes that might then ensue are beyond the scope and competence of this chapter. Suffice it to say here that in many host countries the Peace Corps must in this sense be regarded as a calculated risk.

FACTORS LIMITING CONTRIBUTIONS TO DEVELOPMENT

While it is difficult to predict whether particular projects are likely to contribute to "development," however defined, it is relatively easy to specify factors in the Peace Corps situation that will almost certainly militate *against* developmental objectives. All of the factors limiting the PCV's gaining of cultural proficiency (page 305) can in particular cases be regarded as limiting also his contribution to the host country's development. In addition, however, there are a number of other factors, seven of which are worthy of attention.

Inflexibility of the Host Society

The most stubborn factor of all—one that is beyond the control of the Peace Corps—is that most of the host societies and cultures are far less flexible than they need to be to utilize optimally and absorb the contributions of the Volunteers. Social and economic development require that the necessary factors be reasonably mobile —that men, money, materials, energy, talent, and facilities can be moved around and combined in various ways so as to maximize gain and minimize costs. In the United States, Germany, the Soviet Union, and other relatively "developed" societies, there is an enormous amount of geographical and social mobility. Not only this, but the American, German, and Soviet national cultures place great value upon progress. In the underdeveloped world, by contrast, relatively few societies have this kind of mobility and relatively few cultures (as distinct from the subcultures of the modernizing elites) have this kind of value system. Most of the underdeveloped countries have some kind of entrenched privileged elite, jealous of its perogatives and wary of rapid change. Transportation and communication are inadequate. People tend to be rooted to their villages. Great emphasis is placed upon kinship and other kinds of ascribed statuses. Loyalties are diffuse, and "get in the way" of technological and managerial innovations aimed at functional specificity. These and a host of other factors making for inflexibility, immobility, and "irrational" rather than "rational" allocation of human and material resources all conspire to make the task of promoting economic and social change a difficult one. Obstacles such as the foregoing are found the world over, but especially in the so-called "traditional" societies of Africa and Asia. The "transitional" societies, found particularly in Latin America, are often more amenable to modernizing change, while at the same time feeling greater popular pressure to hasten such change (Doughty, page 222; Palmer, page 249).

Political Instability

This factor is often one of the least predictable and most crippling. Among the thirteen countries covered in this book, it had serious effects on events described for both Somalia and Peru (Mahony, page 132; Palmer, page 255). The 1965 India-Pakistan crisis disrupted some Peace Corps activities in those countries. Political instability was also behind the withdrawal of Peace Corps programs from Cyprus and Indonesia. The ability of PCVs to weather political storms is also, however, notable. In the 1965 civil war in the Dominican Republic, for example, PCVs moved unmolested across lines separating government and rebel forces, looking after Dominican wounded regardless of their political affiliation.

Administrative Inefficiency

Glimpses have been given of administrative inefficiency in Afghanistan and Somalia (Dupree, page 120; Mahony, page 130). These are, of course, extreme cases. In most countries characterized by general "underdevelopment," however, one can expect to find also an "underdeveloped" governmental mechanism, often hampered by irrational organization, professional incompetence, favoritism, nepotism, and corruption. A major factor limiting the Volunteers' contribution to development in numerous host countries would thus appear to be sheer administrative inefficiency in local assignment, support, and follow-up (Doughty, page 226). Among our thirteen countries, the one least plagued by administrative inefficiency would appear to be Malaysia (Maryanov, page 72).

Brevity of the Volunteer Tour

The typical PCV spends less than two years in the host country. This is far too short a period of time in which to produce or catalyze lasting, constructive change. When rapid cultural change occurs, it usually entails considerable suffering on the part of all or many members of the culture. Such suffering may be confined within tolerable limits if attempts to change a culture proceed gradually and allow sufficient time for adjustment in all aspects of the culture which are to be importantly affected, directly or indirectly. For example, change in the technology of a village will often require beforehand, and/or produce as a consequence, change in such additional areas as world view, attitudes toward causation, respect and prestige patterns, consumption patterns, and the distribution of political and economic power. With complexities of this order, it is little wonder that PCVs often despair at the difficulty of "leaving something behind" following a mere twenty-odd months in the host country.

Underqualification of Some Volunteers

Another major factor holding back the developmental contributions of many PCVs is the simple fact that they are not adequately qualified to carry out the job to which they were assigned. This problem has been discussed by a number of our authors, especially Szanton, Maryanov, and Guskin (pages 39, 73, and 104). Butts (1963: 74–92) has searchingly examined the question of Volunteer teacher qualifications in Africa, found many PCVs wanting, and offered a number of suggestions for improvement.

Inappropriate Assignments

In a sense the Volunteer is more or less a prisoner of a situation not of his own making. His job assignment has already been arranged for him by the host government, in consultation with his country Representative (or, in the earlier days, with an official from Peace Corps/Washington). The Representative, in most situations, is thus in a crucial position. He ordinarily has considerable bargaining latitude, and the opportunity to select those job "slots," out of a wide range of actual and potential alternatives usually available, that will permit a particular Volunteer to make a maximal contribution to the host country's development, as well as to derive maximal personal satisfaction and growth. This is a demanding and subtle task, requiring that the "Rep" know the host country and its needs well, and that he also know his Volunteers well (Maryanov, page 74). Such has not always been the case. The slotting of early Philippines Volunteers in the ambiguous role of "educational aide" brought in its wake not only untold personal frustration but also a considerable wastage of talent that might otherwise have contributed more effectively to Philippine development. This error, incidentally, was made by Peace Corps/Washington, not by the "Reps" (Guthrie, page 27; Szanton, page 39). Jamaica One was an almost classic case study in how not to design a program (Comitas, page 208). While individual PCVs have often shown resourcefulness in getting out of inappropriate assignments and into new, appropriate ones, it should be borne in mind that this is not always possible or desirable (Maryanov, page 76). Moreover, it is frequently a slow and wasteful process (Heath, page 282).

The examples cited are, of course, from the earlier days of the Peace Corps. Unquestionably, program planning has improved with experience. For example, a recent report gives reason to believe that the programing of Volunteer "co-teachers" in the Philippines has markedly improved (House Hearings 1965: 167). However, the continued practice of sending out senior Representative staffers who lack previous Volunteer-type experience, previous host country experience, and previous experience in the field of development is not likely to improve matters.

Inadequate Continuity

Because cultural change is complex and must usually proceed very gradually, it is essential that continuity be tightly built into Peace Corps programs and administration. Dupree has convincingly illustrated how a Volunteer's effectiveness can be largely dissipated because he was never replaced by another to carry on (pages 114, 118). Even in cultures less resistant to change than those in Afghanistan, it is essential that new Volunteers replace old ones. This will often be necessary not just once or twice, but many, many times.

This section has attempted to show how various host countries are only partially capable of absorbing the Volunteer's potential contribution because of their sociocultural inflexibility, political instability, and administrative inefficiency. It has also pointed out how the PCV's individual contribution is limited by the shortness of his tour, and often also by his professional underqualification. It has weighed the further exacerbating factors of misassignment and lack of continuity. Despite this somewhat discouraging report, there is considerable hope for improvement through better policies and greater skill and sensitivity in executing them. As long as the Peace Corps continues to produce "transcultural men" in large numbers, it will be contributing importantly toward the ultimate solution of many of the problems of its own partial ineffectiveness— provided only that it finds wise and adequate ways to make use of this new resource that it has brought into being.

THE "IN-UP-OUT" PRINCIPLE

Threaded through many of the country chapters has been the implication that it would be well if officials of the Peace Corps staff, both at home and overseas, knew more about field conditions and partook more of the value standards of the PCV subculture. There is only one effective way to accomplish this end, and that is to employ carefully selected ex-PCVs in staff positions. As a corollary to this approach, it is important to ensure that staff members do not retain their positions too long, so that there will always be room for more recent returnees to move into the organization and up within its ranks. Fortunately, this rare and desirable state of affairs has been achieved by the Peace Corps organization.

October 10, 1965, marked a turning point in the history of the Peace Corps. Effective on that day, an amendment to the Peace Corps Act required that no Peace Corps staff member above the grade of GS-9 would be permitted to remain in the organization's employ longer than five years. Congress took this unprecedented action at the request of Mr. Shriver himself. As far as is known, this is the first time in the history of the American republic that a federal agency has deliberately moved to limit drastically the tenure of its own personnel for the specific purpose of avoiding bureaucratic arteriosclerosis. In taking this action, Congress provided legal sanction for the "In-Up-Out" principle, under which returned Volunteers and other qualified persons move into the staff structure, move up rapidly if they merit promotion, and then mandatorily move out to permit room for newer persons in their turn to move in and up. Some light is shed on the history of this idea within Peace Corps/Washington in Appendix 3, which reprints the original "In-Up-Out" memo (page 350).

It would be difficult to find a more emphatic symbol of the "non-bureaucratic" nature of the Peace Corps than the simple fact that it was Mr. Shriver himself who asked Congress to enact the "In-Up-Out" amendment. Far from being just a symbol, however, this principle goes a long way toward guaranteeing that the organization will remain permanently responsive to new ideas and to fresh reports and recommendations from the field—that it will, in short, be a permanently creative agency.

Mr. Shriver began informally applying the "In-Up-Out" principle well before it became law. As soon as the first Volunteers began arriving back in the United States in the summer of 1963, he began hiring them. With characteristic vigor and determination, he pressed his senior staff to bring more and more of them "on board." By the spring of 1965, returnees numbered 183 out of a total of approximately 1,000 Peace Corps staff employees. Of about 700 employees in Washington, 101 were returnees. Of about 300 employees overseas, 82 were returnees (Senate Hearing 1965: 68). Thus ex-Volunteers comprised about 14 per cent of the Washington staff and 27 per cent of the overseas staff.

Ex-Volunteers who have accepted employment in Peace Corps/Washington have discovered for themselves, in intensely personal terms, the validity of the distinction between the "Volunteer subculture" and the "Peace Corps/Washington subculture." Reports indicate without exception that most of them are genuinely frustrated. Many have left in disillusionment. Partly, this frustration stems from the fact that the purposes and goals of Peace Corps/Washington are in some respects basically different from those of the Volunteer in the field. Headquarters must cope with Congressional opinion, with public relations, with the demands of numerous other federal agencies, and with complex budgetary and management problems. Such matters seem remote indeed from problems of human resources development overseas, which are at the heart of most returned Volunteers' concern. An equally important cause of difficulty is the fact that the returnee soon discovers that there are important differences in value standards, and in humility and sensitivity, that separate him from many of his superiors who have not had a Volunteer-type experience or its equivalent. The ex-Volunteer is likely to feel that his supervisor suffers from excessive "secondary ignorance"—or not knowing the importance of the things he does not know. Secondary ignorance frequently gives rise to "gung-ho" attitudes, which the returnee is likely to find particularly galling. Under such circumstances, true communication is difficult, and frustration mounts.

For their part, senior staff members are far from uniformly satisfied with the returned Volunteers serving under them. Among their complaints are that some ex-PCVs are impractical, are administratively inexperienced and inept, and are innocent of the ways and wiles of bureaucratic maneuver. Unquestionably there is considerable legitimacy to such complaints. Apart from this, it is also probably true, at some psychological level, that some senior staffers feel threatened by the field-experienced returnees in their midst.

Ironically, there is a certain parallel between the PCV working in the host country's bureaucracy, and the ex-PCV working in the bureaucracy of Peace Corps/Washington. In each case, the Volunteer must learn to communicate and cooperate with persons adhering to a culture, or subculture, different from his own. In each case, he must develop the technical skills and cultural proficiency necessary to personal effectiveness. All of this requires enormous patience and tact—possibly even more so in the case of the Peace Corps/Washington subculture than in the case of the host country's culture. In this sense, there is a parallel to the problem of "superficial cultural similarity" mentioned by Szanton and Comitas (pages 49 and 213). The returnees, that is, are likely to feel that they have more of a "right" to criticize, and less of a need to be patient and tactful, in the Peace Corps/Washington subculture because the latter is, after all, a part of their own American culture. While one might concede this "right," the fact still remains that unless and until they are willing and able to work within the Peace Corps/ Washington system, the effectiveness of their efforts to change that system will be limited.

Scattered evidence suggests that the ex-PCVs serving on Representative staffs overseas are much less frustrated than their fellows serving in Washington, apparently for three principal reasons. First, the job of Associate Representative is usually much freer of the constraints of American bureaucracy than is true of jobs in Washington. Second, the Associate "Rep" is close to the Volunteers and can provide direct assistance to them as they cope with their problems. And third is the fact that, particularly where the Associate "Rep" is serving in the same culture where he earlier served as a PCV, his cultural proficiency will usually be so visible to all concerned that he will ordinarily have little difficulty in getting a hearing for his ideas and suggestions.

Fortunately the problems of returnees in staff positions, however severe they might appear at the moment, are likely to prove temporary. These problems usually spring from the youth and inexperience of the returnees. The passage of time and the proper application of the "In-Up-Out" principle will soon produce constructive change. By 1970, the Peace Corps will have some 50,000 returnees to choose from—a genuine luxury of choice. Not only this, but the median age of the ex-PCVs will have risen by some years; there will be many more "mature," seasoned returnees than was true in the 1963–1965 period. By then, it will even be possible, as a general policy, to require as a prerequisite to staff employment that a returnee first make a successful readjustment to his own American culture, perhaps winning in the process an advanced degree in some relevant field, or gaining valuable experience in a relevant job. By 1970, there is no reason why most of the senior staff positions in Peace Corps/Washington, and most of the Representative, Deputy Representative, and Associate Representative positions overseas, should not be occupied by qualified, rigorously selected returned Volunteers.* An added favorable factor is that the Peace Corps staff has often placed young men in positions of high responsibility; Bill D. Moyers, for example, was Deputy Director before the age of thirty.

Even during their first two years of service on the Peace Corps staff, the returnees have made important contributions. Despite all of the pain—or perhaps often because of it—the returnees have quite evidently had their impact on the Peace Corps/Washington subculture. So, one may add, have many of the returned "Reps" who have been working to remold this subculture since about 1964. There is little question that, on the whole, training programs are now more relevant and effective than they were in the early days, that program planning is more sophisticated, that goals selected are more realistic. These changes doubtless seem unbearably slow to individual returnees working at low echelons of administration. Relative to the pace of any ordinary bureaucracy, however, the improvements have occurred at an encouragingly rapid rate. An excellent way of assessing these changes is to read a collection of issues of the monthly *Peace Corps Volunteer*, starting in 1961 and proceeding to the present. Some of these changes, and the further challenges they embody, will be outlined in the section that follows.

PROBLEMS AND CHALLENGES

The problems facing the Peace Corps during its second five years are more challenging, if less dramatic, than those to which it gave primary attention during its first five years. Now that the organization is a domestic political success, and now that a favorable Peace Corps image has been firmly established overseas, it is possible for a number of long-needed developments to occur. Of these, four are worth specifying here. First, it is now possible to appoint more members of the senior staff on the basis of proven merit and transcultural experience, and less necessary to take purely political considerations into account. Second, it is now possible to concentrate more on continuity of administration and on careful follow-up of policy decisions. Third, there is now less need to emphasize sheer quantity of Volunteers—the "numbers game"—and more freedom to concentrate on the *quality* of the Volunteers selected and the

* According to an informal report as of the fall of 1965, returnees in Peace Corps/Washington tended to hold positions graded at GS-7, -9, and -11. A few even held GS-13 positions. Overseas, they were almost invariably Associate Representatives. As of mid-1965, reportedly only one returnee had been appointed a Deputy Representative, and none had become a full Representative.

quality of the training and field supervision they receive. Fourth, it is now possible for some of the organization's officials to free themselves somewhat from the incessant administrative hurly-burly, to sit back and reflect, to develop perspective, to ask hard questions and seek new answers.

The Peace Corps/Washington of 1965 was an organization caught in intellectual ferment. More and more "think pieces" appeared that year in the monthly *Peace Corps Volunteer*. Contributing richly to this ferment have been substantial numbers of returned PCVs, who have brought to bear their fresh insights derived from field experience. Taking the lead in this intellectual process have been such officials as Deputy Director Warren W. Wiggins and Associate Directors Harris Wofford and F. Kingston Berlew, former "Reps" in Ethiopia and Pakistan, respectively. Under such creative leadership, a variety of new, even "far out," ideas and approaches were being discussed and tried out. The most important of these seemed to concern the facilitation of the PCV's achievement of cultural sensitivity and proficiency, and of his more effective contribution to development in the host country. In the subsections that follow are listed some of the more important problems and more exciting challenges that will face the agency during its second five years. Since most of my recent contact with the Corps has been in training programs, my suggestions naturally center on that domain of activity.

Improving Language Training

One of the most inspiring aspects of the entire story of the Peace Corps has been the growth of its sophistication in linguistic matters, and the development of its language training capacity. In 1961–1962 relatively few Peace Corps/Washington policymakers were familiar with modern linguistics or with what is involved in learning an exotic tongue. Partly for this reason, many early contingents of PCVs were sent to the field with woefully inadequate language training, or with none at all (Guthrie, page 20; Preface, page xiii). It was, of course, the Volunteers who suffered most from these inadequate training projects, and they were often far from shy in expressing their dissatisfaction. In the Philippines, a number of them plunged into the task of analyzing local languages as best they could, taking advantage of whatever professional linguistic assistance was locally available. In this process, not a few of the PCVs have developed keen sophistication in the strategy of language learning (Foley 1965).

Feedback from the Volunteers and Representatives in the field has been increasingly effective in convincing Peace Corps/Washington officials of the basic importance of language proficiency, with the result that "Peace Corps training programs now devote more than half the instructional time to intensive language instruction. During the 12-week training program, about 300 hours are spent on this training" (House Hearings 1965: 58). Results are far from uniform, but are definitely encouraging. An extreme example of what proper language training can accomplish is the case of Nepal Two, twelve of whose members scored "S-4" in Nepali, in State Department Foreign Service Institute examinations administered at the end of their tours of duty. An "S-4" rating indicates "full professional fluency" and is an extremely difficult level to attain (House Hearings 1965: 60, 64–66).

Since its beginning, the Peace Corps has offered training in forty-nine languages, including such exotic tongues as Amharic, Baoule, Ewe, Hiligaynon, Kannada, Nyanja, Pashto, Quechua, Twi, and Yoruba. The Corps has also inaugurated two-language programs designed to cope with the "third culture" problem (page 307). Thus, for example, trainees bound for Senegal have received instruction in both French and Wolof (House Hearings 1965: 61). By the same token, trainees who entered Peru Three and Bolivia Thirteen already capable of speaking Spanish were placed immediately in a Quechua class. Since most of the Peace Corps' host countries are multilingual, a serious problem remains of devising means to ensure that the Volunteer is trained in the language or dialect of the particular area to which he will be assigned (Guthrie, page 21; Cowan, page 162).

In a number of instances, Peace Corps/Washington officials discovered that it was impossible to teach a particular language effectively because no instructional materials were available that would meet modern standards of training efficiency. Accordingly, headquarters has contracted with professional linguists to analyze some of these languages and prepare training materials that will not only be linguistically sound but also pedagogically effective and appropriate. Drill materials, for example, will be set in the context of the local culture as the PCV will experience it. To date these linguists have turned their talents to such languages as Afghanistan Farsi, Chinyanja, Djerma, Nepali, Somali, Susa, Tumbuka, and Tunisian Arabic (House Hearings 1965, 62). Since such materials will doubtless be made available to users outside the Peace Corps as well, the entire country, and indeed the entire international community, will benefit from these linguistic projects.

Making Training Culturally More Relevant

A serious problem in almost all training programs is that cultural training lacks realism because it is conducted in the United States rather than in the host country. From this standpoint, the entire training program should ideally be conducted overseas. Until now, however, there have been numerous administrative and some political considerations requiring that all or most of the training must occur before the Volunteers leave the United States. Only one training project, an experimental one, has been conducted entirely within the host country. If this experiment succeeds, and if administrative and political considerations permit, then hopefully in the future more and more training programs will be carried out, largely or completely, in the host nation. In such cases, a large part of the training should probably be postponed until *after* the PCVs have spent a month or two in the host country attempting to perform duties similar to those of their ultimate assignment. Experience indicates that it is only *after* a Volunteer's "moment of truth" on the job that he discovers how little he knows and how much he needs to learn. Only after this humility is developed is he fully ready for the training program.

Short of conducting the training in the host country, there are a number of devices that some of the training sites have employed in order to infuse at least a certain measure of realism into training. In conducting the Jamaica One training program, for example, Comitas facilitated contact between trainees and Jamaicans residing in the New York area (page 206). Many training programs have made effective use of nationals of the host country who reside in or near the training site (Preface, page xiii). Most training programs in which I have participated have employed host country nationals to serve as members of the training staff; often, however, these persons are inappropriately selected (Szanton, page 36). The University of New Mexico, among others, has sent community development trainees into nearby Mexican-American villages for trial periods of field work, as preparation for service in Latin America. The University of Hawaii at Hilo has done similar things in Filipino-American communities, as part of training for the Philippines. To simulate the cultural atmosphere of Nepal, some training sites have constructed "Nepali Houses," replete with cow dung on the floor (House Hearings 1965: 60). Many of these devices have evidently produced salutary results. More are needed.

Beyond the need to simulate host country conditions is another need that would be important even if the entire training program were carried out in the host country. This is the intellectual need to achieve organic integration of cultural studies with other elements of the training curriculum. Thus "Philippine Studies" can be organically integrated with "American Studies"—but *only* if the syllabus is written by scholars whose expertise covers both these areas (Guthrie, page 22). By the same token, "Nursing in a Tanganyikan context" can be properly offered only where the instructional staff know something about nursing and something about Tanganyikan hospitals, nurses, and patients (Friedland, page 146). Similarly, a lecture on the Somali cultural value system will be considerably more effective if the lecturer is sufficiently familiar with the Somali language so that he can present key "untranslatable" concepts in Somali rather than just in English terminology. Jamaica One exemplifies many of the principles by which various elements of a training program can be placed in cultural context (Comitas, page 205). Many other training programs have also registered progress on this front. But much remains to be done.

Fostering Continued Learning in the Field

The ideal training program is the one that never stops. The entirety of a Volunteer's tour should be a learning experience. Volunteers who feel that they need guidance or in-service training ought to receive such help. In not a few instances, they have asked their Representatives to set up in-service training seminars (Szanton, page 54). Such seminars will often be of limited value, however, unless they include well-qualified "resource persons" who can help the PCVs make sense out of their field experiences. Such resource persons can ensure a professional atmosphere in what might otherwise degenerate into a "bull session." If the Representative is an expert on the local culture, he could serve in such a capacity—but not too many of them are. Returned Volunteers— many of them now serving as Associate Representatives in the same culture where they served as Volunteers—can often contribute richly. This would be especially true in cases where the returnee, before joining the "Rep" team, first did graduate work in a relevant social science or other field. Host country nationals with advanced disciplinary training and appropriate personal qualities are another invaluable resource—though in some host countries there are very few such persons. Another possible source is social scientists from the United States who are experts on the host country, and who have helped to train the PCVs earlier, so that some kind of personal bond has already been established. Such social scientists should preferably be regular members of the faculty of the training institution, so that they can return with "feedback" which will be of value in constantly improving the quality and relevance of training course content for subsequent programs.

Improving Feedback from the Field

One of the most inspiring examples of good feedback I have seen occurred in 1965, when I lectured a group of trainees at the University of Missouri who were preparing for rural community development work in Thailand. Serving as regular members of the training faculty were two returned Volunteers who had recently served in Thailand in community development or other rural work. Both spoke good Thai and were deeply familiar with the problems of rural Thai villagers. Also present at the training site, and due to remain for several weeks, was one of the Associate Representatives from Thailand. This official was a community developer with long experience in Asia, and with considerable experience as the staff member in charge of previous Peace Corps community development efforts in Thailand. He had been principally responsible for designing the present project, and his design was carefully shaped in such a way as to avoid repetition of numerous earlier programing errors. Also present was a Thai official who would assume charge of the PCVs' further training after arrival in Thailand. All four of these men were constantly besieged with questions from the trainees about all manner of problems. The instant, reliable feedback they were able to provide—both about rural Thai culture and about matters of administrative policy—was of great importance in keeping the morale and motivation of the trainees high. Not only this, but the Associate Representative was getting to know his Volunteers well, and was developing the kind of intimate awareness of their individual strengths and weaknesses that is utterly essential to good "slotting" (Maryanov, page 72). He planned to return to Thailand some weeks in advance of his Volunteers, so as to pave the way for their arrival by making detailed arrangements with the local Thai officials at each site where the PCVs were scheduled to work. Despite the fact that community development in Thailand is inherently more difficult and risky than it is in many other countries, the evidence suggests that this particular project will be relatively successful.

Unfortunately, examples of this type of effective feedback and administrative continuity are as yet altogether too rare. Too often, members of the training staff are innocent of any deep awareness of what is actually involved and implied in the project. This is not ordinarily a fault of their own but results from the fact that relevant policymakers do not place sufficient emphasis on this type of intimate relationship with the field. And too often, there are too few qualified returned Volunteers on the training faculty in positions where their views can be adequately heard.

A post deliberately created in order to ensure feedback and continuity is that of "Contractor's Overseas Representative." A number of training universities, as part of their contracts with Peace Corps/Washington, maintain Contractor's Overseas Representatives in the various host countries. These "CORs" can be of enormous value in providing professional guidance, as well as feedback and continuity. Unfortunately, however, it not infrequently occurs that the COR is technically qualified but knows less about the host culture than the Volunteers do. In other cases, he lacks both professional and cultural qualifications, being simply a university official or faculty member who was thrown into the breach in order that the university would not go unrepresented. In still other cases, the COR is not even from the training university; his feedback and recommendations are hence not too likely to be taken seriously by policymakers at the training site who have no structural relationship or obligation to him. The COR role is one which increasingly should be occupied by returned PCVs as they acquire additional academic, professional, and administrative qualifications. Even at present, despite deficiencies in professional preparation in some cases, it would seem that more use could be made of the returnees in this role.

Stabilizing Relationships with Training Institutions

In the early days, political considerations seem to have materially influenced Peace Corps/Washington's decisions in awarding training contracts. It was presumably important to distribute these contracts with an eye to the constituencies of important members of Congress. Another kind of political consideration was also relevant: broad distribution of these contracts meant that more Americans "got into the act." These Americans included not only university and college administrators, faculty, and students but numerous nearby townspeople as well. Volunteer teacher trainees at Northern Illinois University, for example, do practice teaching in a number of local schools in and around the city of DeKalb, thus inevitably bringing a Peace Corps "exposure" to the students and teachers of those schools, and even to some of the students' parents. Volunteer community development trainees bring a similar exposure to personnel of local social service agencies. Unquestionably, this proliferated exposure has made it possible for many more Americans to identify with the Peace Corps than might otherwise have been the case. The magnitude of this proliferation is suggested by the fact that by 1965 some 120 different institutions had conducted at least one training program.

Now that the Peace Corps is politically accepted, however, it is time to take a hard look at these training contracts. The primary object of a training program is, after all, to prepare the Volunteer for maximally effective service and for maximal personal growth during his overseas tour. All other considerations should be distinctly secondary to this. Good training demands a certain amount of specialization. It demands that the training institution develop genuine competence in the host country's culture and problems, as well as in many other relevant areas. Such specialized competence cannot develop unless there is reasonable stability in the training university's relationship with the host country and with the Peace Corps organization. It is only in the context of stability that the university's Campus Overseas Representative and other specialist personnel can make their feedback count effectively toward constant improvement of curriculum design and course content (Maryanov, page 79).

Unfortunately, however, this stability has often been lacking. All too often, training contracts shift frequently and almost capriciously from one institution to another. While some shifting is necessary for administrative reasons, and some is desirable in order to preserve healthy competition and deter undue complacency, it is difficult to understand why training relationships remain as unstable as they do. The price that must be paid is a high one, and it is the Volunteers who must pay it in the end. Each time a training contract is transferred to a new university, many of the same mistakes must be made all over again, and many of the same lessons relearned. This is particularly true where, as frequently occurs, the training contract is awarded at the last minute, after the university's teaching and administrative personnel and facilities have already been otherwise committed. Typically, an enormous scurry results. Miraculously, administrators somehow materialize from nowhere. By dint of long overtime hours, they somehow learn Peace Corps policies and procedures. Often, however, there is little time or opportunity for them to consult officials of universities that conducted previous training programs for the same country. Thus an enormous amount of know-how is lost. Exacerbating all of this, the administrators at the new university are often unfamiliar with the host country, and sometimes need to deal with training officials in Peace Corps/Washington who are equally unfamiliar with host country conditions.

These observations are hardly original. They have long been shared by many Peace Corps/Washington officials. By the time of this writing, relatively stable "year-round" contracts had been signed with four universities: the University of New Mexico at Albuquerque, the University of Hawaii at Hilo, the University of Wisconsin at Milwaukee, and the University of Washington at Seattle. These stable contracts permit more efficient, year-round use of faculty and facilities, and presumably permit more effective feedback from the field. It is to be hoped that this tendency toward stability will continue.

When a university enjoys stability as a training site, there are a number of side-benefits that might result. An inspiring example is the case of Northern Illinois University at DeKalb. Not long ago, this was a teacher training institution. Then suddenly it became a university, and began experiencing the usual growing pains. As a university, it was eager to build up its resources for graduate study, and to increase its international involvements. Through a series of improbable events it was awarded the training contract for Malaya One. Since then it has trained virtually every Peace Corps project for peninsular Malaya, plus a number of other contingents bound for Southeast Asia. Coupled with this Peace Corps involvement, the university has also established an interdisciplinary Southeast Asia area studies program, and has already commenced to award graduate degrees in various disciplines, where the student's area focus is on Southeast Asia. Quite possibly, if it had not been for the Peace Corps, this area program would never have been started. In any case, the Peace Corps has helped this program materially. A number of Volunteers trained at Northern, for example, have returned there at the end of their overseas service to pursue graduate work connected with Southeast Asia, often on fellowships from the university. Thus has the Peace Corps engaged in unintended but valuable "institution building," and helped to bring an awareness of the problems of the developing world to a small prairie city that until a generation ago was quite isolated from international concerns.

Integrating Training with the Undergraduate Curriculum

Peace Corps/Washington has been turning more and more of its attention toward plans and experiments in a new and exciting direction, that of integrating the Peace Corps experience into the individual's total educational experience. Since the vast majority of PCVs have had at least some college work, in effect this usually means integration with the individual's preservice and postservice college experience. Such integration, if successful, promises great benefits both for the individual and for the Peace Corps.

There is a need to identify potential Volunteers in our colleges well before their senior year, which is apparently when most of them now make the final decision to enter Peace Corps training. Potential Volunteers who are reached and counseled early in their undergraduate careers will have time to make well-considered, mature decisions as to whether they wish to enter the Corps. Such gradually growing conviction is an infinitely sounder motivational base on which to build, than is the snap decision, the impetuous choice, which has sometimes steered a person into the Peace Corps. Among the counselors whose advice would be most meaningful would be returned Volunteers studying on the same campus or living in the local community. Undergraduates who find their interest in Peace Corps service growing will be in a position to choose some of their courses accordingly: a course on Africa for those who wish to serve there; or an extra seminar on resources utilization for the engineering major who knows that the host country where he hopes to serve will suffer from certain kinds of materials shortages; and so on. At least one university has already established a special undergraduate colloquium on the Peace Corps, in which the Volunteer's experience is examined from an anthropological perspective; various returned Volunteers give slide presentations focusing on field problems, as a means of stimulating discussion. Courses such as the three mentioned are valuable in any case, and doubly so in the event that the student does finally decide to enter the Peace Corps or some similar program.

Beginning in 1964, a series of "advanced training projects" was inaugurated. These projects receive potential Volunteers at the end of their junior year and provide a summer of intensive language, area, and technical training. The individual then returns to his college and completes his senior year. The following summer he rejoins his group for further training, and is then sent overseas. Ideally, during his senior year he receives counseling and other assistance, as he gears his reading and course work more closely to his future role as a Volunteer. Results to date are somewhat inconclusive, in good part because of the high rate of attrition on the part of potential Volunteers who drop out to get married, accept a graduate fellowship, or the like. It should be added, however, that even a dropout of this sort is by no means a total loss from the standpoint of the nation as a whole, for he constitutes one more citizen with basic language training and some area knowledge relevant to a developing country.

A variety of moves are being made by colleges and universities to give recognition to the enormous "experiential" educational value of Peace Corps service. Numerous institutions now award at least some academic credit for Peace Corps experience. Western Michigan University has established a "five-year 'Peace Corps B.A.' A student would complete two years in college, serve two years in the Peace Corps, then come back for a final year. Franconia College in New Hampshire adopted a similar plan, and a number of other institutions are considering the idea" (Fox, Nicolau, and Wofford 1965: 17).

Integrating the Peace Corps and Later Educational Experiences

About half of the ex-Volunteers have returned to colleges and universities, mostly to graduate work. The university seems to be a natural "decompression chamber" in which to readjust to American life; to sort out intellectually the emotional and intuitive results of intense "experiential" learning overseas; and to acquire further professional qualifications prior to continuing on a career path that in many cases will involve further intercultural work (Cowan, page 166).

Volunteers returning to the university, despite generally high motivation, often meet with disappointment. Most of them have clear ideas of what they want—but frequently have difficulty finding it because, understandably, many university courses have not been devised for persons with either the experience or the interests of the returnee. Many ex-PCVs want interdisciplinary programs oriented toward problems of social and economic development (Guthrie, page 32). Instead, they sometimes find course offerings rigidly discipline-oriented and often unduly confined within the ambit of our own Western culture. By their participation in classes and seminars, the ex-Volunteers often make clear their quest for a different kind of educational orientation. As time goes on, their cumulative influence on American higher education is likely to be considerable.

Already at a number of universities the response to the returnees is becoming evident. Perhaps the readiest response will occur in professional schools, such as those of education, public health, and agriculture. Other rapid accommodations can be expected in special interdisciplinary centers oriented toward "development." One example, with which I am personally familiar, is illustrative. This is the Stanford International Development Education Center (SIDEC), which was established in 1954 by Professor Paul R. Hanna of Stanford's School of Education. Thus long before 1963, when the first PCVs came back, Professor Hanna and his center had developed a flexible interdisciplinary post-Master's doctoral program oriented toward promoting the use of education for general socioeconomic development overseas. By 1965, about one quarter of SIDEC's student body were returned Volunteers. The other three quarters, both non-American and American, had likewise had transcultural experience in the field of education. Professor Hanna and his faculty (including several professional educators, three anthropologists, two economists, and a political scientist) discuss in detail all curricular and many other matters with an elected student advisory committee, and by this means ensure that the perspective of the students is brought to bear on all major decisions. By this device, new interdisciplinary and problem-oriented approaches are constantly being tested and evaluated, in an attempt to come to intellectual grips with the problems of the developing areas. Graduates of SIDEC contemplate careers involving considerable service in the developing countries as educational administrators, consultants, analysts, and the like. Some will do this from a "base" in AID or a U.N. agency, while others will be serving on faculties of American or foreign universities.

Increasing Evaluative Research

During its first five years, the Peace Corps has been a highly pragmatic organization, little given to research of a deliberate or deeply probing nature. Its Division of Evaluation has focused primarily on troubleshooting inspection trips which have been valuable as a means of detecting and obviating immediate operational problems, but of little value in developing deeper or more systematic understanding of persisting intercultural problems. Senior officials of the Division of Evaluation have tended to be lawyers and journalists rather than social scientists. Often, these officials have lacked previous experience in the host country in which they are evaluating Peace Corps operations, and sometimes they have lacked

previous transcultural experience of any kind. During the Corps'
second five years, it is to be hoped that this nonprofessional, pragmatic emphasis will gradually be supplanted by a more professional,
searching approach aimed at discovering the deeper origins of
operational problems. More ex-Volunteers with relevant social
science credentials are needed in the Division of Evaluation.

Peace Corps/Washington's Division of Research has been modestly staffed and financed. It has relied primarily on outside organizations to conduct evaluative research on a contract basis, and
properly so. A number of these contracts give promise of yielding
results that will greatly improve the quality of policy decisions.
Most promising, perhaps, are those projects involving teams of
investigators with complementary skills and qualifications, including at least one member who is fully conversant with the local culture. An example is that of the Lynch and Maretzki project investigating the impact of Volunteer teachers on Philippine communities
(page 32). Another exciting project is that led by Professor Allan
R. Holmberg on the impact of Peace Corps community development
projects in Peru, with which Professor Doughty has been associated
(page 239). Professors Comitas and Heath are conducting highly
promising research on Bolivian villagers' behavior and attitudes in
the area of public health, as a guide to future assignments of PCVs
in health work there.

If this book succeeds in nothing else, it will hopefully succeed in
convincing even the most skeptical reader that much more research
on the Peace Corps is needed. In particular, we need to know more
about processes of transcultural adjustment, about ways and means
of more effectively preparing and assisting the Volunteer to achieve
cultural proficiency, and about the Corps' developmental impact
in various host countries. If even 1 per cent of the total Peace
Corps budget were devoted to research—a much smaller percentage
than a forward-looking industrial firm would spend—the quality
of administrative and policy decisions could be greatly improved.
And the need for systematic research, incidentally, is considerably
increased in an organization whose "In-Up-Out" principle forces
personnel turnover at a much more rapid rate than that which
characterizes the typical industrial firm. Considering these facts,
it is difficult to believe that Congress would not be enthusiastic
about Peace Corps/Washington's desire to increase its research budget. Disappointingly, however, Mr. Shriver's 1965 attempt substantially to increase the research budget failed (Senate Hearing
1965: 51–55).

PROSPECTS

The most exciting aspect of the Peace Corps is not what it has already become, but what it has the potential of becoming. The precise dimensions of this potential are as yet far from clear. What is clear, however, is that this potential is indeed enormous. Whether the full possibilities of this great incipient social movement will be realized depends on creative leadership—within the Peace Corps itself, elsewhere in the federal government, within our national "establishment," and indeed throughout our national social and political structure.

Educational Prospects

The most exciting potential contribution of the Peace Corps lies in the area of education in its broadest sense. Greatly transcending in importance the immediate, tangible contributions by the PCVs to the host country, is their intangible educational contribution. Often this contribution has simply taken the form of showing local people that there are different ways of looking at the world, and that some of these ways might be better, or more appropriate, or more useful. For their part, most of the Volunteers have received an invaluable "experiential" education. They have had their perspectives enormously broadened, their concern for their fellow man rendered more knowing and more sophisticated. If and as the Peace Corps' language, area, and technical training programs improve, there will be a concomitant improvement in the education that the PCVs impart to local people, and also in the education they receive in return. Imparting and receiving education are indeed mutually reinforcing parts of the same process.

The returned Volunteer is a national educational resource of untold potential value. Ex-Volunteers returning to ten thousand American communities, to business and government and labor and education, to our voluntary agencies, bring with them their new-found international, intercultural sophistication. And they bring much more: they bring an attitude toward service, a posture of "can-do" confidence largely devoid of disguised egocentrism of the "gung-ho" variety, a concern for their fellow man wherever he may be, an attitude toward mutual and cooperative education that is democratic in the best sense of that word.

It is up to our colleges and universities to welcome these specially sensitized Americans, not with special favors which they do not seek or expect, but with a dignity borne of a genuine respect for what most of them have indeed accomplished in their transcultural learning abroad. Specifically, our institutions of higher learning must offer them flexibility without loss of rigor, interdisciplinary and problem-oriented approaches without sacrifice of resort to the great thinkers of the past. And the rewards will be bilateral. Many an engineering professor will learn in this manner that much of what he teaches is irrelevant to the underdeveloped situation. Many an economist will grow by learning once again that man is more than just an economically self-maximizing animal. Psychologists and social psychologists will be reinforced in their earlier knowledge that theory based on Western individualistic and democratic assumptions is not necessarily valid across the entire spectrum of mankind. Similarly, political scientists will be freshly stimulated to an awareness that theories of comparative politics must comprehend more than just the political phenomena of the North Atlantic nations. And not a few anthropologists will come to a renewed realization that in some respects their preference for the study of relatively isolated and static social groups could well afford to be supplemented by study of human groups caught in the middle of demographic explosions and "nation-building" efforts. In short, the ex-Volunteer, humble gadfly that he is, has much to offer his teachers.

"Overseasmanship" Prospects

The Peace Corps can and should bring about revolutionary change in American "overseasmanship" (Preface, page xiv). For the first time in our national history, we will soon have on hand an adequate supply of Americans eager for further overseas service who are *both* technically and culturally qualified to do a particular job in any of a large number of countries around the world. The day is not long off when it will no longer be possible for a personnel officer in AID, for example, to throw up his hands in despair and complain, "Of course we'd like a sanitary engineer who can also speak Aymará, but there just aren't any!" Indeed, before too long the supply will be, if anything, more than adequate. In many specialties, there will be more ex-PCVs than desirable jobs immediately available. The resulting competition will force standards even higher. And hopefully, among these new technical-and-cultural specialists will be many thousands who are willing to dedicate *long* periods of time to particular tasks in particular host countries—for in many cases this is the only proper and promising way to ensure constructive, lasting change.

The first American agency that can and should be "revolution-ized" is the Peace Corps organization itself—and indeed that pro-cess is under way, though perhaps a bit more slowly than necessary. Within the Peace Corps, the "In-Up-Out" principle stands as an important guarantor of the opportunity to promote corrective and constructive change.

Unfortunately, however, the rest of the world has no "In-Up-Out" principle. Returnees will accordingly find it much more diffi-cult to penetrate many of the other "establishments" that deal with problems of overseas development. While the policies of both Presi-dents Kennedy and Johnson have pointedly favored the hiring of returnees by the State Department, AID, and similar agencies, progress in this respect has been uneven. As of the spring of 1965, for example, a Peace Corps staff member reported that 865 former Volunteers had applied for the Foreign Service, 579 had actually taken the examination, 110 had passed the written examination, 14 had passed the oral examination, and of those, only 3 had yet been appointed (Fox, Nicolau, and Wofford 1965: 29). Perhaps a little additional Presidential "arm-twisting" would not be amiss.

With or without Presidential support, however, numerous diffi-culties inevitably lie ahead. The first is that many returnees simply do not have the professional qualifications necessary for important, creative, meaningful jobs in the overseasmanship field. This is espe-cially true of the many PCVs whose overseas learning has motivated them to enter a wholly new profession upon their return. Even assuming the best of professional training, however, it does not necessarily follow that the returnee can step into just the kind of job he wants, and into just the kind of situation in which he can be effective. In some cases, the right job and situation simply do not exist and will need to be created—a task that will not always be easy. In other cases, the job does exist, but someone else already holds it, and the seniority that goes with it. For many returnees, the waiting period will prove sadly long. The solution, if there is one, lies in their own patience, persistence, and political skill.

Political Prospects

It is difficult for a Volunteer to return to the United States and *not* be interested in politics in the broad sense. There are simply too many things about America that seem in need of changing— and the only way to change them, ultimately, is through political action. Whether the returnees will "get political" enough to realize their immense educational and leadership potential remains to be seen—but one can hope. One can hope that the ex-PCVs will become proficient enough in the politics of bureaucracy to achieve a commanding influence in their own Peace Corps staff organization, and increasing influence in our State Department, AID, and other governmental and nongovernmental agencies in the "overseasmanship" field. Numerous returnees ought to find active roles in such politically significant programs as the War Against Poverty, where their skills in intercultural communication and cooperation should prove visibly useful in dealing with members of America's own "forgotten subcultures"—the Negroes, the American Indians, the Mexican-Americans, and similar depressed groups. For other returnees, there is the politics of local community action. For still others, there is elective politics at the local, state, and national level. One may hope for the day when it will be as politically appropriate for a candidate to say, "I am a returned Peace Corps Volunteer," as it now is for him to say, "I am a veteran of World War II." Each returnee, obviously, must seek out those ways of making himself effective that he personally finds most appealing—or least repelling. But politics there must be, if policy is to be influenced.

THE PEACE CORPS AND HISTORY

Two or three generations hence, when historians look back upon our century, they will find much to praise and to blame. Among those features of American life in the sixties that will stand the test of time most adequately, the Peace Corps will, I think, rank high. The establishment of this great organization both symbolized and facilitated an important change in American life, a new dedication to service on the part of America's young people, a new interest in crossing cultural frontiers in order to deal directly with the developing world's problems, and a new readiness to shed old ethnocentrism in favor of enlightened sensitivity. The great potential of the Peace Corps has only begun to be realized. Our returned Volunteers, as their numbers grow, will take increasing leadership of movements designed to offer a better life to all men everywhere—"better" in terms of *their* value standards as well as ours. In such manner, they will truly be serving the cause of peace. And their dedication will reach out into the blighted and neglected areas of American society as well, as we give life and energy to our own domestic wars against poverty, disease, ignorance, inequality, and ugliness. I wish them well.

NOTE

1 A few comments are required at this point to supplement those made in the Note at the end of Chapter 1, page 11. In the present chapter, the

meaning of the term "culture" will necessarily shift from time to time. In some cases, it will refer to culture in the sense implying intergenerational transmission. In other cases, it will refer to culture in the sense that does not carry this implication, such as the culture or subculture of a government bureau in a host country. Hopefully, the nature of these shifts in reference will be clear from context.

It is, of course, usually much easier to change the culture of a particular bureau in the government of, say, Somalia, than to change the general Somali culture in the sense that implies intergenerational transmission. For purposes of this chapter, "development" can mean certain kinds of change in either type of culture. Indeed, "development" often occurs in a two-step fashion, in which the culture of a bureau or other power-holding organization is first altered, and then the bureau proceeds to bring about, usually very slowly, certain changes in the general culture.

BIBLIOGRAPHY

ALMOND, GABRIEL A., AND JAMES S. COLEMAN, Editors
    1960   *The Politics of the Developing Areas.* Princeton, N.J.: Princeton University Press.
ARENSBERG, CONRAD M., AND ARTHUR H. NIEHOFF
    1964   *Introducing Social Change: A Manual for Americans Overseas.* Chicago: Aldine Publishing Co.
BARNETT, H. G.
    1953   *Innovation: The Basis of Cultural Change.* New York: McGraw-Hill.
BERLEW, F. KINGSTON
    1965   "The Volunteer Must Use the Language." *Peace Corps Volunteer,* June–July, p. 2 ff.
BUTTS, R. FREEMAN
    1963   *American Education in International Development.* New York: Harper & Row.
COLEMAN, JAMES S., Editor
    1965   *Education and Political Development.* Princeton, N.J.: Princeton University Press.
CLEVELAND, HARLAN, GERARD J. MANGONE, AND JOHN CLARKE ADAMS
    1960   *The Overseas Americans.* New York: McGraw-Hill.
DIXON, JAMES
    1965   *The Peace Corps in an Educating Society.* Excerpts from a discussion at the Brookings Institution. July 22. Multilithed. Washington, D. C.: Peace Corps.
ERASMUS, CHARLES J.
    1961   *Man Takes Control: Cultural Development and American Aid.* Minneapolis, Minn.: University of Minnesota Press.
FAIRFIELD, ROY P.
    1964   "The Peace Corps and the University," *Journal of Higher Education.* Vol. 35, No. 4, pp. 189–201.
FOLEY, DOUGLAS E.
    1965   *A Rationale and Strategy for Learning a Philippine Language.* Multilithed. Stanford, Calif.: Stanford International Development Education Center.

FOSTER, GEORGE M.
    1962   *Traditional Cultures and the Impact of Technological Change.*
            New York: Harper & Row.
FOX, ERNEST, GEORGE NICOLAU, AND HARRIS WOFFORD
    1965   *Citizen in a Time of Change: The Returned Peace Corps
            Volunteer.* Report of a Conference, Washington, D. C., March
            5–7. Peace Corps.
GOODENOUGH, WARD H.
    1961   "Comments on Cultural Evolution," *Daedalus,* Vol. 90, pp.
            521–528.
    1963   *Cooperation in Change.* New York: Russell Sage Foundation.
HAGEN, EVERETT E.
    1962   *On the Theory of Social Change: How Economic Growth
            Begins.* Homewood, Ill.: Dorsey Press.
HART, DONN V., AND PAUL MEADOWS, Editors
    1962   *Selected Abstracts in Development Administration: Field Re-
            ports of Directed Social Change.* Syracuse, N.Y.: Maxwell Grad-
            uate School of Citizenship and Public Affairs, Syracuse
            University. Publication 3.
"HOUSE HEARINGS" (U.S. House of Representatives)
    1965   *Hearings Before the Committee on Foreign Affairs, House of
            Representatives, Eighty-Ninth Congress, First Session, on H. R.
            9026, A Bill to Amend Further the Peace Corps Act.* June 2,
            3, and 8. Washington, D. C.: Government Printing Office.
MEAD, MARGARET
    1956   *New Lives for Old.* New York: William Morrow.
MEAD, MARGARET, Editor
    1961   *Cultural Patterns and Technical Change.* New York: Mentor.
PAUL, BENJAMIN D., Editor
    1955   *Health, Culture, and Community: Case Studies of Public
            Reactions to Health Programs.* New York: Russell Sage
            Foundation.
"SENATE HEARING" (U.S. Senate)
    1965   *Hearing Before the Committee on Foreign Relations, United
            States Senate, Eighty-Ninth Congress, First Session, on S. 1368,
            A Bill to Amend Further the Peace Corps Act, As Amended.*
            April 26. Washington, D. C.: Government Printing Office.
SPICER, EDWARD H., Editor
    1952   *Human Problems in Technological Change.* New York: Russell
            Sage Foundation.
STALEY, EUGENE
    1961   *The Future of Underdeveloped Countries: Political Implica-
            tions of Development.* New York: Frederick A. Praeger, for the
            Council on Foreign Relations.
TUNG CHI-PING (As told to Quentin Reynolds)
    1964   "Red China," *Look.* December 1, p. 25.

Appendix 1

Professional and Editorial Considerations

The ideal way to prepare a book of this kind would have been to convene a meeting of all contributors and map out a common research strategy. Each author would then journey to the country of his specialty and carry out empirical field research in accordance with the common research design. Such an operation, however, would have been highly expensive, and vastly beyond the limits of our budget. Instead, it was necessary to depend, in most cases, on what our authors had already observed in the field.

Because of the wide latitude given each author, it has been necessary to edit the chapters quite closely, so as to secure greater coherence among chapters. In this process, I was in close touch with each author by correspondence and especially by long-distance telephone. The end result has been that each author completely approves the editing, in the sense that his essential message has not been distorted and yet additional material or ideas (with which he also agrees and which he often suggested) have been supplied for the purpose of reinforcing or qualifying a related point made by one of the other authors. The one author who is a partial exception is Mr. Gallagher, who was out of the country and not available by telephone.

Each contributor is responsible for his chapter only. Contributors did not have an opportunity to see each other's chapters in manuscript, except where two authors wrote about the same country (Guthrie and Szanton; Doughty and Palmer). Although it may well be that most of the contributors would agree with most of the points I make in the opening and closing chapters, it is important to emphasize that most of them have *not* seen my chapters prior to publication, and that responsibility is mine alone. By the same token, each contributor has been a free agent and under no pressure to express ideas that agree with mine. Although I agree essentially with the great majority of opinions expressed by our contributors, I must confess that now and then I disagree, especially on matters of emphasis.

In three respects, there is a certain imbalance among our authors. First, all fourteen of them are Americans. Serious efforts were made to enlist several non-American social scientists, but these efforts always failed, usually because of the difficulty of communicating at great distances. Second, only three of our authors are returned Volunteers; at the time of selection, it was not possible to find any more returnees who possessed the necessary credentials in social science or history. The problem of availability has also led to some imbalance in the disciplines represented by our contributors: seven of them are anthropologists; two each are psychologists, political scientists, and historians; and one is a sociologist. Serious efforts were made to find an economist or two who would meet our other requirements, but without success.

One saving grace, however, is that our authors generally have not felt it necessary to confine themselves to the subject matter of their respective disciplines; instead they have ranged quite widely, searching out problems that they felt deserved greatest attention.

Because this is a book about *ideas* rather than personalities, individuals are not usually identified by name. Where any individual comes in for criticism, or for what might be construed as criticism, we have made maximum efforts to conceal his identity. The protective masking of such individuals is planned in such a way, however, as never to distort the substantive accuracy of the presentation. Where such individuals are given names, the names are always fictitious, and the first use of such a name will always appear in square brackets.

Appendix 2

The Organization of Peace Corps/Washington

The salaried staff of Peace Corps/Washington has expanded rapidly. During 1961, it grew from zero to about 250. By 1965, the figure had reached about a thousand American employees, of whom some 700 were in Washington and 300 overseas (Senate Hearing 1965: 96). This amounted to one staff employee for every thirteen PCVs or trainees. By this time, Volunteers were working in 3,000 locations throughout the developing world (House Hearings 1965: 9).

The Table of Organization of Peace Corps/Washington appears in the diagram on the next page. Indicated in heavy lines are the offices and divisions that will be briefly discussed in this appendix because of their especially important bearing on the success of the Volunteers overseas.

THE OFFICE OF PROGRAM DEVELOPMENT AND OPERATIONS

This is the "line" unit within the entire Peace Corps to which all other units are "staff." "PDO" is responsible for conceiving and developing programs and for administering these programs in the various host countries. As Comitas makes clear (page 217), if PDO does its job well, the program in a particular host country is likely to succeed, even in the event that other units do not perform up to par. On the other hand, even in cases where selection and training are of the highest caliber, if PDO has not done its job well, or if the Representative is not sensitive, efficient, and effective, then the program is not likely to be highly successful—at least in terms of its contribution to the host country's development. In 1961–1962, the key positions within PDO in Washington were filled overwhelmingly with former officers from AID—often program officers. These officials were relatively strong in economic training. They also tended to be strong in administration; indeed,

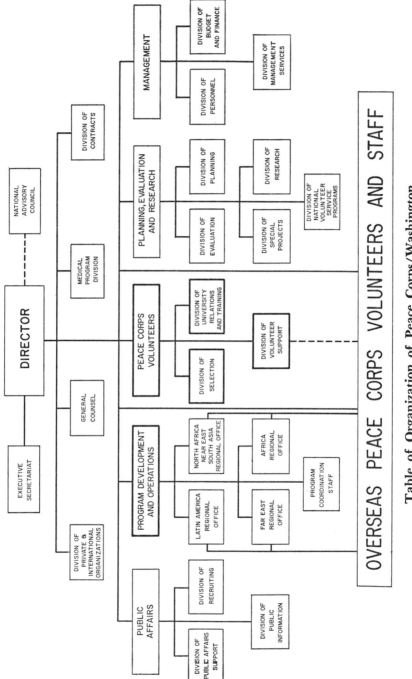

Table of Organization of Peace Corps/Washington

Source: U.S. Government Organization Manual, 1965–1966
(Washington, D. C.: Government Printing Office), p. 629.

their practical knowledge of how to move the levers of government was an indispensable contribution to the survival and success of the Peace Corps as an agency.

The Representative teams overseas, who report to PDO, normally consist of a Representative, perhaps a Deputy Representative, and as many Associate Representatives as are deemed necessary. The "Rep" is also assisted by one or more American medical doctors, and by one or more American secretaries. The "Rep" and his team are given wide leeway in conducting the country operation, and wisely so.

THE OFFICE OF PEACE CORPS VOLUNTEERS

This office consists of three divisions: Selection, University Relations and Training, and Volunteer Support.

The Division of Selection is responsible for receiving and processing applications from the tens of thousands of Americans who apply for service each year. It decides which applicants will be invited to join which training programs for which countries. It also decides (subject to ultimate review by the director) which trainees will be "selected in"—that is, given Volunteer status and sent overseas—and which will be "selected out." Top officers in the division have always been professional psychologists.*

The Division of University Relations and Training is responsible, among other things, for the training of the Volunteers. It sets general standards for the content of various training programs.† It negotiates with universities and other training institutions, and contracts for needed training services. Senior officers in this division have usually been professional educators.

The Division of Volunteer Support offers a wide variety of kinds of support to the individual Volunteer, starting before the beginning of his service and extending through to the completion of his tour and even beyond.

---

* By contrast, professional psychologists are only minimally involved in the selection of overseas Representatives, Deputy Representatives, and Associate Representatives. Such decisions are made almost exclusively by Mr. Shriver.

† The amount of language and area training given to the Volunteer trainees is normally considerably greater than that given to members of the Representative teams.

Appendix 3

The "In-Up-Out" Principle

In a sense the "In-Up-Out" principle is as old as the Peace Corps itself. From the earliest days of the Peace Corps/Washington organization, Mr. Shriver's opinions about bureaucratic tendencies toward sluggishness and complacency were widely known and discussed. The unclassified memo reprinted here did not, therefore, originate the idea; it simply gave the idea a name, formulated it in actionable terms, and provided it with a specific rationale.

December 11, 1961

TO: Franklin H. Williams, Chairman
           Talent Search Panel

FROM: Robert B. Textor, PDO/FE

SUBJECT: A Plan to Keep the Peace Corps Permanently Young, Creative, and Dynamic

1. *Recommendations for Immediate Implementation:*

   a. Recommend that each new appointee to an overseas Representative job be told that Peace Corps is *not* a life-long career; that he will have to move on after a few years, to make room for a deserving PCV alumnus.

   b. Recommend [members of the Planning and Evaluation staff] be asked to keep their eyes open on field trips for promising qualified PCVs who might be promoted to Associate, Deputy, or Representative jobs, where needed, even *before* they have completed their full two-year hitches.

2. *Recommendations for Implementation During 1962:*

   a. Recommend that PC seek amendment to the Peace Corps Law to provide that PC may set up its own autonomous personnel system. As justification, it could be pointed out that PC, like the State Department, has peculiar needs and functions, and therefore should be independent of the Civil Service Commission.

   b. Recommend that the new autonomous PC Personnel system provide that:

   (1) Almost all substantive jobs in PC should be filled, as soon as possible, by qualified PCV alumni. A "substantive" job is a job—high

350

or low—which influences the shape and gusto of PC programs, e.g., officers in Recruitment, Selection, Training, and PDO, including overseas Representatives.

(2) PCV alumni, and all other staff employees, should follow the principle of "in-up-out". The law should set a maximum number of years—perhaps eight years—after which all staffers are required to leave and find jobs elsewhere.

3. *Advantages of this Plan:*

   a. *Excellence:* Only the "cream-of-the-cream" of PCV alumni would be chosen for staff jobs.

   b. *Sound Programs:* Programs would be planned by ex-PCVs who have fresh valid field experience, who know field conditions intimately. Impetuous, impractical, and unsound projects would thereby be avoided.

   c. *Effective Field Operations:* Our PCRs would *really know* the language, customs, politics, family systems, economics, etc., of the host country, having learned all this as PCVs. PCRs' orders would be sound, because the men *giving* the orders would already have been through the experience of having *taken* orders.

   d. *High Morale:* A Volunteer would know that he has a chance for a later staff position *if* he performs well, shows leadership, and truly masters the language and customs of the host country.

   e. *Elimination of Inappropriate Applicants:* This plan would discourage applicants who might be looking for a cushy life-long berth where promotion depends on seniority rather than dynamic creativity.

   f. *Facilitation of Careers:* Because of the eight-year limitation, there would always be "room at the top" for deserving staffers. PCV alumni could therefore move up rapidly.

   g. *Impact on Foreign Policy:* The "in-up-out" principle would result in immense benefit to American foreign policy. Young ex-staffers would move rapidly into jobs in State and AID, in foundations and universities, etc. And they would move in at *high* levels of responsibility, because they would already have worked at high levels of responsibility in PC. Thus we would reduce by *many* years the time it would otherwise take to make our impact felt at policy levels within key organizations connected with U.S. foreign policy.

   h. *Youthfulness:* Above all, this plan would make PC the first organization in U.S. administrative history that was not only *born* young, but *stayed young!*

Franklin H. Williams immediately forwarded the memo to Mr. Shriver. Some while later, Williams further pressed for the "In-Up-Out" principle by circulating the memo verbatim, together with suggestions for implementation, throughout headquarters. Doubtless numerous persons helped in getting this principle written into law. Besides members of both houses of Congress, credit should go to Mr. Shriver, Peace Corps General Counsel William Josephson, and Ambassador Franklin H. Williams.

Congress' decision to apply the "In-Up-Out" principle to all employees above the rank of GS-9 is perhaps somewhat more stringent than the memo's recommendation that the principle apply only to "substantive" employees. Congress' decision to fix the maximum tenure at five years may well prove wiser than the memo's tentatively suggested period of eight years. The fact that Congress made no provision requiring or encouraging Peace Corps/Washington to recruit new staff members specifically from the ranks of the returned Volunteers may not prove serious, because headquarters is already under great and mounting pressure to employ returnees for available openings. Indeed, present policy reportedly provides that if two otherwise equally qualified candidates are applying for the same staff job and one is a returnee and the other not, the returnee will be employed.

Recommendation 1-*b* sheds some light on the situation in late 1961. At that time there were, of course, no ex-Volunteers available for recruitment to staff positions—and would not be for at least another eighteen months. As a member of the Talent Search Panel, I was aware of the difficulties headquarters faced in recruiting appropriate personnel for these overseas posts. Those personnel who had thus far been hired ranged from those who were very appropriate to those who were quite inappropriate. Meanwhile, I had met a few members of Thailand One and Malaya One whom I considered at least as well qualified as some of the personnel already hired. A few such Volunteers, I thought, might well be appointed to "Rep" teams after an initial period of seasoning in the field. Only the most mature, professionally qualified, culturally sensitive and proficient ones need have been selected, and it could have been arranged that they would not be giving orders to their former "buddies." Although this suggestion was not adopted at the time, it later developed that in at least one host country, the Philippines, selected Volunteers were appointed "Acting Associate Representatives," and carried out administrative tasks of very considerable difficulty and responsibility, often with great credit.

Index